CLAiT Plus 2006

for Office XP

ALAN CLARKE

Hodder Arnold

A MEMBER OF THE HODDER HEADLINE GROUP

Orders: please contact Bookpoint Ltd, 130 Milton Park, Abingdon, Oxon OX14 4SB. Telephone: (44) 01235 827720, Fax: (44) 01235 400454. Lines are open from 9.00 to 5.00, Monday to Saturday, with a 24-hour message answering service. You can also order through our website at www.hoddereducation.co.uk

British Library Cataloguing in Publication Data
A catalogue record for this title is available from The British Library

ISBN-10 0 340 915331
ISBN-13 978 0 340 915332

First published 2006
Impression number   10 9 8 7 6 5 4 3 2
Year   2009 2008 2007 2006
Copyright © 2006 Alan Clarke

Printed in Italy for Hodder Arnold, an imprint of Hodder Education, a member of the Hodder Headline Group, 338 Euston Road, London NW1 3BH.

Acknowledgements

To my wife and sons for their help and support, and particularly to Peter for his practical assistance and suggestions.

The author and publisher wish to acknowledge CorelDRAW® and the Microsoft® Corporation for the use of captured screen images.

Screen shots reprinted by permission from Microsoft® Corporation.

Screen shots reprinted by permission from CorelDRAW®.

OCR does not endorse the use of one software package over another, and all CLAiT qualifications are written in generic form. This book is written using the Microsoft Office® suite as examples, simply to provide clear support to the majority of candidates who will be using that package. The use of any other form of software is equally appropriate and acceptable to OCR.

Contents

Introduction

In a modern society it is essential to have information and communication technology (ICT) skills and knowledge. OCR has developed a suite of ICT user qualifications at levels 1, 2 and 3. This book covers the content required for the CLAiT Plus qualification. CLAiT Plus is a level 2 qualification for information and communication technology (ICT) users. In August 2005 CLAiT Plus was revised to produce a new structure based on eight units. This book has been written to meet the needs of learners studying for the CLAiT Plus diploma, certificate or individual units.

The book contains many exercises to help you develop your skills and knowledge. However, you should consult your tutor about the standard required to satisfy the CLAiT Plus 2006 assessment.

CLAiT Plus forms part of a set of ICT qualifications, with New CLAiT (level 1) and CLAiT Advanced (level 3). To achieve the full CLAiT Plus Diploma you must achieve five units, comprising one mandatory (unit 1) and four optional units. To obtain the CLAiT Plus Certificate you have to achieve three units, comprising one mandatory (unit 1) and two optional units. You have a choice of seven optional units (i.e units 2 to 8) with the mandatory unit (i.e. Integrated e-Document Production). The optional units cover subjects such as spreadsheets, electronic communication, desktop publishing, databases and computer art. You also have the option of studying individual units.

There are no formal entry requirements for CLAiT Plus. However, the course assumes that you have the skills and knowledge of ICT provided by New CLAiT. This book is based on Microsoft Office XP®. However, a large part of the material should be suitable for other versions of Microsoft® Office. Only chapter 6 (e-Image Manipulation) employs another application; CorelDRAW® 10 is the basis of this chapter. The mandatory unit and seven optional units are all covered within the book.

Chapter 1

Unit 1

Integrated e-Document Production

This chapter will help you to:

- use a computer's system hardware and software safely and securely to create a variety of business documents
- use an input device to enter and manipulate data accurately from a variety of sources
- work with data files, using database and/or spreadsheet facilities to select and import data
- use mail merge facilities
- create, format and print a mail merge master document and mail merge documents
- create and print an integrated document, combining text, numeric and tabular data, an image and a chart
- format page layout and manipulate text according to a house style.

This chapter covers the content of unit 1 of the CLAiT Plus course, which is mandatory. There are no preconditions for studying this unit. However, its content does assume that you have the skills and understanding which are provided by the OCR Level 1 ICT course New CLAiT (e.g. Unit 1: File Management and e-Document Production).

Assessment

After studying unit 1, your skills and understanding are assessed during a three-hour practical assignment. This is set by OCR and marked locally. However, the marking will be externally moderated by OCR. This ensures that the standard is being applied correctly across the many different providers of OCR CLAiT Plus. If you are unsuccessful, you can be reassessed using a different assignment.

An alternative approach is for you to be assessed by either an OCR set scenario or a locally designed assignment.

Files and folders

All information stored on a computer is held in a file. Each file has an individual name and they are stored within folders. Folders are also sometimes called directories. Folders serve essentially the same function as paper folders do in filing cabinets, that is, they allow records to be stored in an organised and systematic way. Computer files need to be organised for similar reasons that paper files and records do. You need to be able to locate them so you can read, update (change), copy, remove, rename or move a file.

The Microsoft Windows® operating system provides a range of functions that allow you to:

- create and name folders (directories)
- open, close and save files
- delete files and folders
- move files and folders
- copy files and folders
- rename files and folders
- protect files
- print the file structure.

The file management application provided within Microsoft Windows® is called Windows® Explorer, shown in figure 1.1. This is opened by clicking on the Start button, then highlighting the All Programs option to open another menu. Highlight the Accessories item

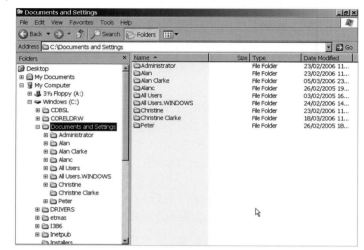

Figure 1.1 Windows® Explorer

to open a menu with the Windows® Explorer option. The Explorer's application window is divided into a number of areas. These are:

- title bar (e.g. Documents and Settings)
- menu bar
- toolbar
- address (i.e. the highlighted folder)
- folders (on the left-hand side of the display) – showing the structure of folders stored on the hard disk, floppy disk, CD-ROM or other storage media. The plus sign indicates that a folder has more folders stored within it. If you click on the plus sign, the structure will be opened up to show these folders. The revealed folders may also be shown with a plus sign, indicating further folders stored within the revealed ones
- contents of the folder (on the right-hand side of the display). This shows the files and folders stored within the highlighted folder.

The folders and files can be opened by double-clicking on them with the mouse pointer. The files will only open if an application which is able to read the file is present on the computer system. If no suitable application is identified by the system, a message will appear asking you to identify the correct application. When Microsoft Windows® is unable to locate a suitable application, it offers you the opportunity to select one in which to open the file.

Windows® Explorer functions

Windows® Explorer provides the tools to create new folders and to delete, rename, move, copy and save files and folders. These functions are available on the File (figure 1.2) and Edit menus. The Edit menu provides the Move, Cut, Copy and Paste options.

- **New** – create a new folder in the folder currently being viewed in Windows® Explorer
- **Delete** – deletes the file or folder highlighted in Windows® Explorer
- **Rename** – allows you to change the name of the highlighted file or folder
- **Cut** – allows you to cut a file or folder with the intention of moving it to a new location using the **Paste** option
- **Copy** – allows you to copy a file or folder to a new location using the **Paste** option, but leaving the original file or folder unaffected.
- **Paste** – allows you to place a copied or cut file or folder in a new location
- **Properties** – this allows you to control who has access to specific files and folders and to archive files.

These functions enable you to control your files and folders. They allow you to administer them in a similar way to moving paper files and folders in a conventional filing cabinet. When you have hundreds of folders and thousands of files it is essential that you are able to control them. When you initially start a task it is natural to create a folder to store the files you create. Later you may need to move it so that it relates to folders and files that hold similar information.

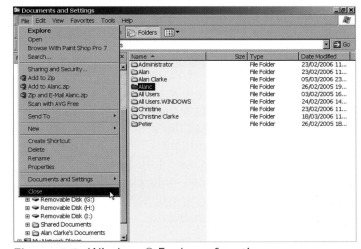

Figure 1.2 Windows® Explorer functions

Protect and secure files

All organisations and many individual activities rely on information technology (IT) to achieve their purposes. The main outcome of any IT activity is the file. It is therefore important to be able to protect files from unauthorised use, damage and loss. Microsoft Windows® XP provides several functions to control access and protect files. This includes controlling the operations that individual users can perform. Users are broadly divided into two groups:

- administrators
- limited.

Administrators are able to make changes to the computer system configuration. They are often senior or technical staff who have the skills to support other users. Limited users are only allowed to undertake their own activities. They are not authorised to carry out more extensive tasks.

Passwords are allocated so that when you log on to the system it knows

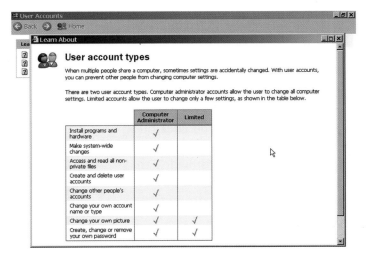

Figure 1.3 Types of user

what activities you are allowed to perform. Figure 1.3 shows what the two types of user are able to do.

Read-only

Some document files may need to be protected from unauthorised use, such as master documents which should not be changed. The Properties function allows you to designate a file as read-only, that is, computer users can read its contents but cannot alter it. A master file may contain the specification of a product, describe a standard business process or represent an agreement with a partner organisation. These types of document should only be changed as part of an agreed process, so it is useful to designate them read-only.

In order to make a file read-only, you need to highlight it within Windows® Explorer, select the File menu and the Properties option to open the Properties window. Click on the General tab and the Read-only option is displayed towards the bottom of the window (figure 1.4). To make the selected file Read-only, click in the radio button and you will see a tick appear to show it has been enabled.

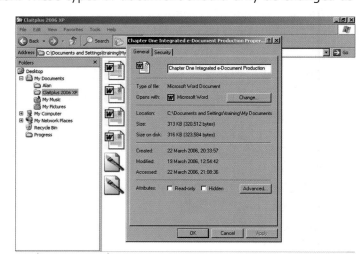

Figure 1.4 Properties

Archives

There are often files that come to the end of their lives but are important to keep. They may be records of projects, financial or other information that you may wish to refer to over a longer period. These files need to be archived, which is basically a process of long-term storage.

Another useful function available within the Properties window is to create archive files. Again, you need to highlight the file or folder within Windows® Explorer and then select the Properties option in the File menu. In the General tab is a button labelled Advanced . If you click on it, the Advanced Attributes window opens (figure 1.5). This provides an option to create archive files by clicking on the appropriate radio button.

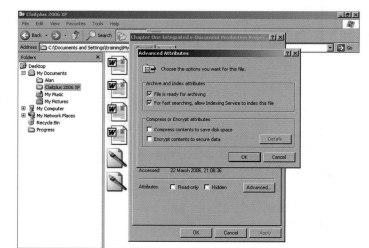

Figure 1.5 Archive files

Types of files

There are many different types of files; each is shown as a different icon (figure 1.6) or ending with a full stop and three letters that indicate the type of file and helps you to distinguish between them. Some examples are:

- .doc — Microsoft Word® document
- .bmp — bitmap image file
- .jpg/.jpeg — image file
- .txt — text document
- .htm — hypertext markup document (i.e. a web page)
- .exe — application file (i.e. an executable file)
- .ppt — Microsoft PowerPoint® presentation (i.e. presentation graphics)
- .mdb — Microsoft Access® database
- .xls — Microsoft Excel® spreadsheet

Figure 1.6 shows a range of file icons, such as:

- Acme Newsagent – Microsoft Excel® file
- CLAiT 2006 – Microsoft PowerPoint® file
- Customer Accounts – Microsoft Access® file
- East Wolds – bitmap
- Document – Microsoft Word® file

Most files can be opened by double-clicking on them if a compatible application is available on the computer. An executable file is one which launches an application.

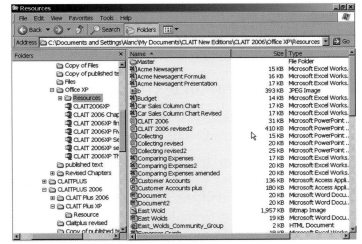

Figure 1.6 File icons

Printing a Window

If you wish to obtain a permanent record of a file structure or the contents of a window, Windows® provides a standard function to allow you to produce a printout of the contents. If you hold down the ALT key and then press the Print Screen (sometimes Print Scrn or PrtSc) key, a copy of the window contents is held on the Clipboard. This is a special area in the computer's memory used to store information. You can then paste the image into a document (e.g. in Microsoft Word®) and print it using the normal functions of the application. If you want to capture the contents of the whole display, you need only press the Print Screen key and then paste the image into a document.

You will be required to use the Print Screen option to capture images of your work as part of the assessment process. If you are asked to change a file into read-only, then the Print Screen function will allow you to show the Properties window as evidence that you have achieved the objective.

Entering data

When you apply for a bank account or credit card, or change insurance company, the forms you complete are often used to enter your information into the company's computer systems. Almost every organisation keeps records on its customers, clients, staff and suppliers. These all require people to enter data into the computer and many forms are now designed to assist the process.

Computer data can be used for a variety of purposes once entered into a system. It forms the basis for managers to make decisions which affect both the organisation and the individual or company the records refer to. If incorrect, a great deal of harm can potentially result. Many organisations check that both the input documents and the data entered are correct. Proofreading documents and screen displays is an important skill to master.

When inputting thousands of documents, even a small reduction in the quantity of data to be entered will make a substantial improvement to productivity. This is often achieved by encoding the data so that a single letter or code represents a chunk of information. For example:

- A means an overdraft limit up to £250
- B means an overdraft limit up to £500
- C means an overdraft limit up to £1000.

Spelling and grammar checkers

Applications can often assist you with checking the accuracy of your documents. Most modern word processors, spreadsheets and databases provide spelling and grammar checkers.

Microsoft Word® provides both. These are available in the Tools menu as the Spelling and Grammar option. This will check the document, starting from the position of the cursor, and work towards the end of the document before going back to the start. When the option is clicked, a dialog window (figure 1.7) appears and works through the document, stopping each time it locates what it considers an error. This can take several forms, such as:

- punctuation
- capital letter
- grammatical error
- spelling mistake.

You need to decide if you want to take the advice the checker is offering (i.e. use the Change button) or if you are going to ignore it (Ignore button). In some cases the checker will offer more than one answer and you need to choose which is correct or whether they are all wrong. When you make your decision the checker acts, then moves on, to stop when it finds another item that it considers to be incorrect. It will tell you when it has completed the whole document.

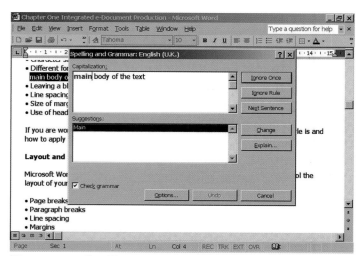

Figure 1.7 Spelling and grammar

Spelling and grammar checkers only suggest changes to you. You need to decide if you want to act on them. They may be wrong, so simply agreeing with the advice may add errors to the document. You must be sure that the change is correct. However, checkers are very good at locating typographical (data entry) errors.

You can set the spelling and grammar checker to work as you enter information. You select the Tools menu and the Options item to reveal the Options window. You need to choose the Spelling and Grammar tab, which allows you to configure both the checkers. When you enter information, the checkers underline items that they identify as a spelling mistake in red and grammar errors in green.

English date formats

The way dates are presented varies in different countries. For example, in Britain dates are shown as: day, month and year, while in the USA they are presented as month, day and year. Obviously there is room for confusion if they are mixed or used in an inappropriate way. In addition, there are several different formats for presenting English dates, such as:

- 13 February 1952
- 13/02/1952
- 13-02-52
- 13 Feb 52

Often, when you are entering dates, the format is specified and it is critical that you follow the specification. If you do not, it is likely that the application (e.g. the database) will not recognise the date format and thus will be unable to locate it. This will produce errors.

Font families

CLAiT Plus uses the term font families. There are two types, called Sans Serif and Serif. A serif type font has small projections on the ends of the characters, while a sans serif type font does not. You might say that serif fonts have more fancy characters or that sans serif fonts have plain characters.

The exercises sometimes use font names rather than families, so below are some examples of sans serif and serif.

Serif:
E Courier New
E Times New Roman

Sans serif:
E Arial
E Tahoma

Exercise 1

Data entry

1 Open Microsoft Word® by clicking on the Start button, highlighting All Programs and selecting Microsoft Word® or by double-clicking on the Word® icon on the Microsoft Windows® desktop.

2 Enter the data input sheet below:

Name: Janet Jenkins   Date: 12/01/02

Area: South-East

Visit – Order

Order taken during visit to Acme Engineering for period 1/04/02 to 30/06/02. Stock to be called off with delivery within 72 hours of request for stock.

Order

Part No. 123	64
Part No. 789	23
Part No. 901	74
Part No. 314	17

Discount 5% for volume purchase

Standards terms – payment of order within 30 days of delivery

3 Note the layout of the information, the standard format of the dates and the use of codes rather than describing the stock ordered (e.g. Part No. 123). There are several different ways of formatting dates and some applications will only accept particular ways, so it is important to get it right.

4 Systematically check your document against the input sheet to ensure that it is correct. If you find an error, move the cursor to the error by clicking once at the desired location. You can delete the mistake using either the backspace (deletes to the left) or delete (deletes to the right) key and entering the correction.

5 Check the spelling and grammar of the entry (select the Tools menu and the Spelling and Grammar option).

6 Insert a floppy disk into the drive and save your document by selecting the File menu and the Save option. This will reveal the Save As dialog window (figure 1.8). Change the Save in: box to Floppy (A:) by using the down arrow at

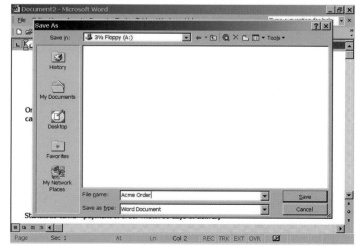

Figure 1.8 Save As

continued

end of box to show a list of options. Save the document as File name: Acme Order. When you are ready, click the Save button. You have now saved your document as a file called Acme Order.

7 Close Microsoft Word® by selecting the File menu and the Exit option (or continue with Exercise 2).

Amending documents

A key advantage of a computer application is that it allows you to amend your documents. Microsoft Office® applications let you delete, insert, copy and move information within a document. These functions operate in a similar way in all Microsoft Office® applications. They are available in the File and Edit menus. The functions operate in the following ways:

- Delete – insert the cursor before or after the word or phrase you need to remove and then use the delete or backspace key on the keyboard. The backspace key deletes to the left while the delete key works to the right. Alternatively, highlight the word or phrase and press the delete key to remove the selected items.

- Insert – place the cursor in the desired location and then enter the new information. This requires that you position the pointer at the new location and click the mouse button. In addition, on the keyboard is an insert key (labelled Ins). When this is pressed, any data entered from the keyboard will overwrite existing information. This occasionally happens by accident and can be confusing until you realise the key has been pressed. To cancel the key, press it again.

- Copy – highlight the word or phrase you want to copy and then select the Edit menu and click on the Copy option. Move the cursor to the location where you want to copy the information to and then select the Edit menu and the Paste option. The copied items will now appear at the new location and will also remain at their original place.

- Move – highlight the word or phrase you want to move and then select the Edit menu and click on the Cut option. The word or phrase will disappear. Move the cursor to the location where you want to move the information to and then select the Edit menu and the Paste option. The cut (moved) items will now appear at the new location.

Exercise 2

Amend a document

1 Insert your floppy disk into the drive.

2 Open Microsoft Word® by clicking on the Start button, highlighting All Programs and selecting Microsoft Word® or double-clicking on the Word® icon on the Microsoft Windows® desktop.

3 Open the file Acme Order by selecting the File menu and the Open option to reveal the Open dialog window. Change the Look in: box to Floppy (A:) using the arrow button at

the end of the box. This will reveal the files stored on the floppy in the central area of the window. Double-click on the file Acme Order or single-click to highlight it and then click on the Open button.

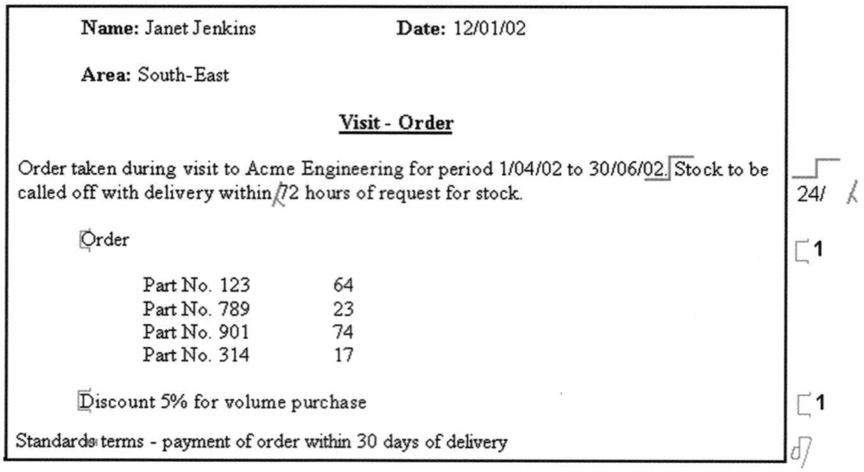

4 The document Acme Order will appear in the Microsoft Word® work area.

Figure 1.9 Proofreading

5 Figure 1.9 shows a printout of the input sheet after it has been proofread.

6 Make the changes indicated by the proofreading:

a) Insert a new paragraph between the sentence ending 'to 30/06/02' and sentence beginning 'Stock to be'.

b) Insert 24/ so that it reads 24/72 hours of request for stock.

c) Insert letters (2 tabs from numbers), as below:

```
Order
Part No. 123    64    A
Part No. 789    23    B
Part No. 901    74    C
Part No. 314    17    C
```

d) Indent the line starting with Order one tab.

e) Indent the line starting with Discount one tab.

f) Delete the letter 's' so that Standards now reads Standard.

7 Revised document should now look like this:

Name: Janet Jenkins   Date: 12/01/02

Area: South-East

Visit – Order

Order taken during visit to Acme Engineering for period 1/04/02 to 30/06/02.

Stock to be called off with delivery within 24/72 hours of request for stock.

Name: Janet Jenkins   Date: 12/01/02

Area: South-East

Visit - Order

Order taken during visit to Acme Engineering for period 1/04/02 to 30/06/02. Stock to be called off with delivery within 72 hours of request for stock.

Order

Part No. 123   64
Part No. 789   23
Part No. 901   74
Part No. 314   17

Discount 5% for volume purchase

Standards terms - payment of order within 30 days of delivery

```
Order
Part No. 123    64    A
Part No. 789    23    B
Part No. 901    74    C
Part No. 314    17    C
```

Discount 5% for volume purchase

Standard terms – payment of order within 30 days of delivery

8   Save your revised document as file Acme Order Amended by selecting the File menu and the Save As option.

9   You have now amended the document in relation to the proofreading corrections. This has allowed you to practise deleting and inserting information. You now have the opportunity to practise copying and moving text around the document. Try:

   a) Reordering the list of parts so that they are presented in numerical order

```
e.g.   Part No. 123    64    A
       Part No. 314    17    C
       Part No. 789    23    B
       Part No. 901    74    C
```

Use the Copy, Cut and Paste functions to achieve this result.

   b) Using these functions to move and copy text until you are confident that you understand their use.

10   Close Microsoft Word® by selecting the File menu and the Exit option.

Proofreading symbols

Proofreaders employ a number of symbols to identify changes they are recommending. The symbols are written on the document and then other symbols are placed in the margin to explain the nature of the amendment. Figure 1.10 gives some examples of common symbols.

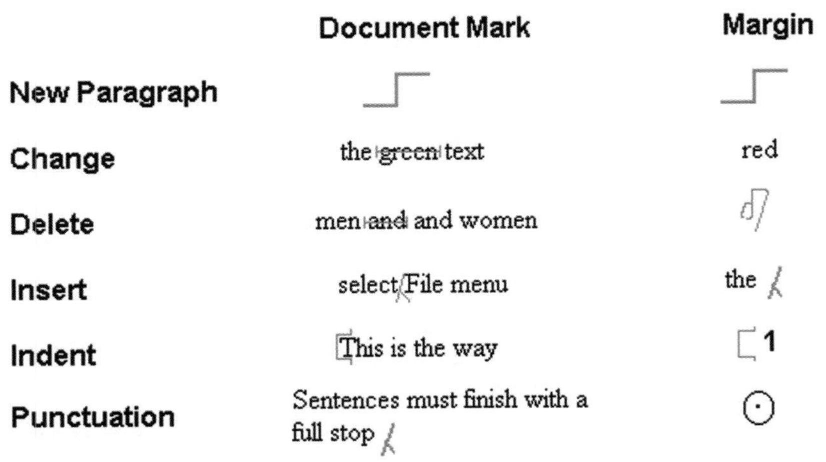

	Document Mark	Margin
New Paragraph		
Change	the green text	red
Delete	men and and women	
Insert	select File menu	the
Indent	This is the way	1
Punctuation	Sentences must finish with a full stop	⊙

Figure 1.10 Proofreading Symbols

Creating a new document

One of the most useful computer applications is word-processing. Modern word processors, such as Microsoft Word®, provide users with functions to lay out documents precisely, including:

- margins, line spacing, page and paragraph breaks
- headers and footers
- bullet point lists.

Many organisations want to present a standard appearance to their clients and therefore adopt a defined house style for all their documents. This normally includes:

- font (e.g. Times New Roman)
- character size (e.g. 12)
- different fonts and character sizes for headings and the main body of the text
- leaving a blank line between each paragraph
- line spacing (e.g. 1.5)
- size of margins
- use of headers and footers (e.g. page numbers and date inserted).

If you are working within an organisation you need to understand what the house style is and how to apply it.

Layout and formatting functions

Microsoft Word® and many other word processors offer a number of functions to control the layout of your documents. These include:

- page breaks
- paragraph breaks
- line spacing
- margins.

Microsoft Word® will automatically start a new page when the old one is full. Page break is the means of starting a new page when the last one is not full. You are thus controlling the layout of the document. Page break is available in the Insert menu under the Break option.

There are several ways of indicating a new paragraph and you select them in Microsoft Word® by using the Format menu and the Paragraph option. Within this option you can also change the line spacing of the text, that is, the space you want to leave between the lines of text. If you are creating a document which will be proofread, then often you will double-space the text so that the proofreader has space to write notes on the document.

Margins are the spaces at the left, right, top and bottom of the document in which you are entering information. Microsoft Word® allows you to change all four margins in any way that you want, by using the File menu and the Page Setup option.

Page setup

When creating a document it is often useful to start by setting up the layout of the pages. You are free to alter this later if you change your mind. Once you have opened a new document, the layout can be established using the File menu and the Page Setup option. This opens the Page Setup dialog window (Figure 1.11).

Page Setup has several tabs on the top of the window which, if clicked, reveal windows providing more options. The Margins tab in the Page Setup window allows you to change the right, left, top and bottom margins of your documents and to preview how the changes affect the appearance of the document. You can also change the orientation of the page – portrait or landscape.

By clicking on the Paper tab, the options shown in figure 1.12 can be seen.

By clicking on the Layout tab, the options shown in figure 1.13 can be seen. Among the options are the ability to change the size of the header and footer. These are special areas at the top (header) and bottom (footer) of the document in which you can place information which will be repeated on all pages of the publication. Headers are often the place to put the title of the document, while footers may contain details of the author. In both locations you can insert automatic fields which change, such as page numbers.

Headers and footers

You can insert a header or a footer (or both), depending on the type of document you are designing. The function is available on the View menu. Select the Header and Footer option, which opens a header area on your document and a toolbar providing extra options. If you scroll down the page you will find the footer area at the bottom of the page.

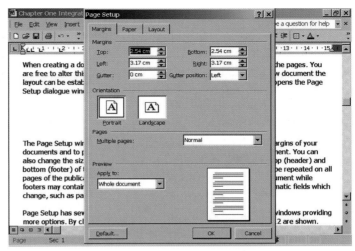

Figure 1.11 Page setup – Margins tab

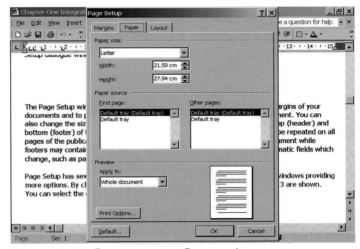

Figure 1.12 Page set up – Paper tab

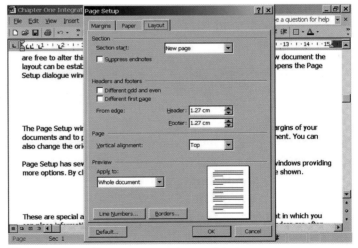

Figure 1.13 Page setup – Layout tab

Once the header or footer area is visible (i.e. the area enclosed by a dotted line) you can enter text. This will appear at the cursor which you will see flashing in the top left-hand corner of the area. To insert a field within the area, click on the menu option of your choice (e.g. Insert Page Number). If you place your pointer over each option, a small label will appear to name the function. The menu has wider functionality, including providing access to the Page Setup dialog window. At the start of the menu is a button, Insert AutoText, that allows you to insert a range of information, including the author's name, the last date the publication was printed, and so on. Figure 1.14 shows many of the options to add extra information and fields to either the header or footer area.

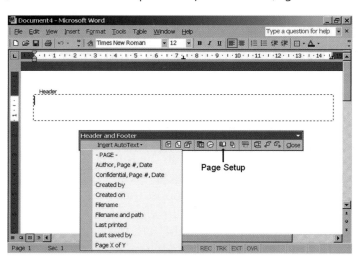

Figure 1.14 Header and footer options

Bullets and numbering

A useful way of presenting information is a list, which is easy to read and understand. Microsoft Word® provides you with the means of producing bullet point lists, which start with a symbol, letter or number so that the information is structured. They are accessed by selecting the Format menu and clicking on the Bullets and Numbering option. This opens the Bullets and Numbering window (figure 1.15).

Figure 1.15 shows some of the different bullet point options available. The window is divided into tabs. If you click on a tab (e.g. Numbered) you can see a range of other options, including numbered, aphabetical and indented lists. To select a bullet, you single-click to highlight it and then click on the OK button, or you double-click the selection.

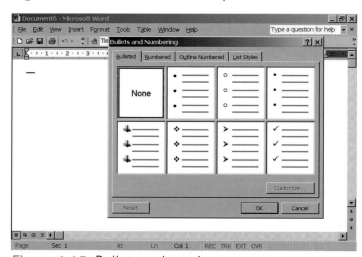

Figure 1.15 Bullets and numbers

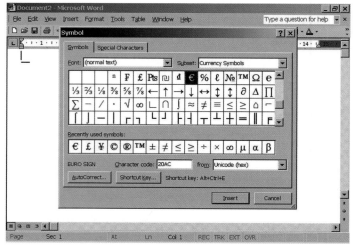

Figure 1.16 Special symbols

Special symbols

Microsoft Word® provides a wide range of special symbols which you can insert in your text. These are accessed by selecting the Insert menu and clicking on the Symbol option. This will open the Symbol window (figure 1.16), which provides access to a large number of symbols. These are selected by highlighting the symbol and then clicking the Insert button. The symbol is then inserted into the text at the cursor.

Search and replace

It is important in any word-processed document to be able to locate words or phrases in a document and replace them with an alternative. You could simply read through the passage and find each word or phrase and then replace it, by deleting the original words and entering the new ones from the keyboard. The problem with this type of approach is that it is easy to make errors (e.g. by incorrectly spelling the new word) or to miss one of the words you are seeking to change. Microsoft Word® provides you with a means to automate the process.

If you select the Edit menu and click on the Replace option, the Find and Replace window (figure 1.17) will appear. Enter the word or phrase you are seeking in the Find what: box, and then the words you are replacing them with in the Replace with: box. Start the process by clicking on the Find Next button. The function will search through the document until it locates a match. You then have the choice of replacing the words with your new selection. Clicking on the Find Next button will move the search through the document. This systematic approach will ensure no errors are made.

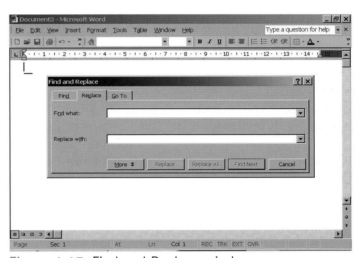

Figure 1.17 Find and Replace window

Widows and orphans

When creating a document there is always the risk that you will produce what are termed widows and orphans. These are isolated words or sentences. The page break may leave an isolated word or phrase on one page while the text it relates to is on another. This is poor presentation and Microsoft Word® provides you with a variety of ways to avoid it, including:

■ Insert a page break to avoid leaving text behind which relates to the new page.
■ Change the font or the character size so that the amount of text that can fit on a page is altered and may avoid widows and orphans.
■ Change the line spacing so, again, the volume of text that fits on a page changes.

Microsoft Word® also offers an automatic way of minimising orphans and widows. This is available in the Format menu within Paragraph option. If you select the Line and Page Breaks tab it will open a window with the Widow/Orphan control option. Click in the associated radio button, which will insert a tick in the box. This adjusts the line spacing and page breaks to avoid widows and orphans.

House style

Word-processing enables almost everyone to write letters and other documents. This provides considerable flexibility to organisations, but it does make it difficult to ensure the quality of documents. Organisations have addressed the problem of quality by setting standards which are often called house styles. This normally sets a standard for:

■ the layout for letters (e.g. position of address, date and size of margins)
■ fonts
■ character size.

This gives a standard look and feel to documents so that a minimum quality standard is established. Organisations often spend considerable effort developing a house style. They insist that all employees follow the standard.

Exercise 3 below is intended to help you practise laying out a document in accordance with a defined house style. The house style is:

Margins (left, right, top and bottom)	3 cm
Orientation	Portrait
Header	Text centred
Footer	Automatic date field and automatic page number – one line below date, both centred
Line spacing	Single
Body text	Times New Roman and size 12, left-justified
Bullet text	Times New Roman and size 12, left-justified
Tables	Times New Roman, size 12, left-justified Column headings, Times New Roman, size 12, bold and centred with gridlines

This house style should also be applied to Exercises 3, 4, 5 and 6.

Exercise 3

Layout

1 Open Microsoft Word® by clicking on the Start button, highlighting All Programs and selecting Microsoft Word® or double-clicking on the Word® icon on the Microsoft Windows® desktop.

2 Using the File menu and the Page Setup, set the four margins to 3 cm and both header and footer to 2 cm.

3 Enter the passage below, which includes using a bullet list, in accordance with the house style:

The Solar System consists of the Sun and nine planets which are in orbit around it. The Solar

System began life 4,500 million years ago when the planets condensed out of an immense cloud of gas. The nine planets are:

- Mercury
- Venus
- Earth
- Mars
- Jupiter
- Saturn
- Uranus
- Neptune
- Pluto

In addition to the planets there are approximately 63 moons and many thousands of asteroids. Moons orbit the planets while the asteroids orbit the Sun. Asteroids vary in size from several miles across to simple lumps of rock. They are often irregular in shape and have strange orbits.

The planets are divided into two groups. Those planets which orbit close to the Sun (e.g. Mercury, Venus, Earth and Mars) are called the inner planets. Planets that are further away from the Sun such as Jupiter, Saturn, Uranus, Neptune and Pluto are called the outer planets.

4 Systematically check your document to ensure that it is correct. If you find a mistake, move the cursor to the error by clicking once at the desired location. You can delete the mistake using the backspace (deletes to the left) or delete (deletes to the right) keys and enter the correction.

5 Check the spelling and grammar of the entry (select the Tools menu and the Spelling and Grammar option).

6 Insert your floppy disk into the drive and save your document by selecting the File menu and the Save option. This will reveal the Save As dialog window. Change the Save in: box to Floppy (A:) by using the down arrow at the end of the box to show the list of options. Save the document as File name: Solar System. Click the Save button. You have now saved your document as a file called Solar System.

7 Now add a header and footer to the document. The header should read Solar System, in Arial font with a character size of 16. The title should be centred. The footer should show the page number centred on the page and one line below the date.

8 Save your document again by selecting the File menu and the Save option.

9 Close Microsoft Word® by selecting the File menu and the Exit option.

Indenting text

In any document you may wish to indent your text. There are several ways of doing this. The most straightforward is to use the tab key on the keyboard, which will indent the text. You can set the size of the tab by selecting the Format menu and the Tabs option, which will open the Tabs window (figure 1.18). In this window you can change the size of the tab and the alignment.

An alternative approach is to select the Format menu and click on the Paragraph option. This will reveal the paragraph window (figure 1.19) that allows you to set the size of the indent from both margins (i.e. left and right) and see the effects in the Preview window. The Special box provides access to indents for the first line, hanging or none. First-line indent will indent only the first line of each paragraph, while a hanging indent sets the whole paragraph except the first line to be indented. For example:

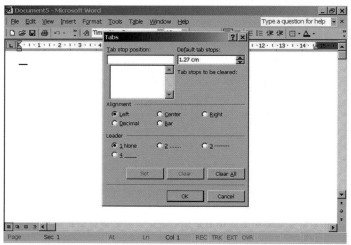

Figure 1.18 Tabs window

First line indent

     Aaaaaaaaaaaaaaaaaaaaaaaaaaaaaaaaaaaaaaaaaaaaaaaaaaaaaaaaaaaaaaaaaaaaaaaaaaaaaa
aaaaaaaaaaaaaaaaaaaaaaaaaaaaaaaaaaaaaaaaaaaaaaaaaaaaaaaaaaaaaaaaaaaaaaaaaaaaaaaaaa

Hanging indent

Aaaaaaaaaaaaaaaaaaaaaaaaaaaaaaaaaaaaaaaaaaaaaaaaaaaaaaaaaaaaaaaaa
    aaaaaaaaaaaaaaaaaaaaaaaaaaaaaaaaaaaaaaaaaaaaaaaaaaaaaaaaaaaaa
    aaaaaaaaaaaaaaaaaaaaaaaaaaaaaaaaaaaaaaaaaaaaaaaaaaaaaaaaaaaaa
    aaaaaaaaaaaaaaaaaaaaaaaaaaaaaaaaaaaaaaaaaaaaaaaaaaaaaaaaaaaaa

The Paragraph window also enables you to set line spacing and control pagination.

A third method is to use the ruler at the top of the Microsoft Word® work area. If it is not visible you can reveal it by selecting the View menu and clicking on Ruler. By dragging the stops at the end of the ruler you can create first-line and hanging indents. It is possible to change the right indent or tab by dragging the right ruler stop.

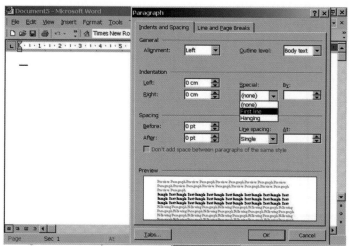

Figure 1.19 Paragraph window

Exercise 4

Indents

1 Insert your floppy disk into the drive.

2 Open Microsoft Word® by clicking on the Start button, highlighting All Programs and selecting Microsoft Word® or double-clicking on the Word® icon on the Microsoft Windows® desktop.

3 Open the file Solar System by selecting the File menu and the Open option to reveal the Open dialog window. Change the Look in: box to Floppy (A:) using the arrow button at the end of the box. This will reveal the files stored on the floppy in the central area of the window. Double-click on the file Solar System or single-click to highlight it and then click on the Open button.

4 The document Solar System will appear in the Microsoft Word® work area.

5 Experiment with the three alternative approaches to indenting your text. Try to indent the start of each paragraph and also to create hanging indents. Continue until you are confident you can use the alternative approaches.

6 There is no need to save your efforts.

7 Close Microsoft Word® by selecting the File menu and the Exit option. When you close without saving you will see a window appear asking you if you want to save. In this instance you do not, but on other occasions it may stop you making a mistake.

Tables

Microsoft Word® and many other word processors can present information in the form of a table. To insert a table into a document requires selecting the Table menu (figure 1.20), highlighting Insert and clicking on the Table option. This will open the Insert Table window (figure 1.21).

The Insert Table window allows you to set the number of rows and columns in the table and to set the size of each column. The features (e.g. size of columns, number of rows and columns) are altered using the up and down

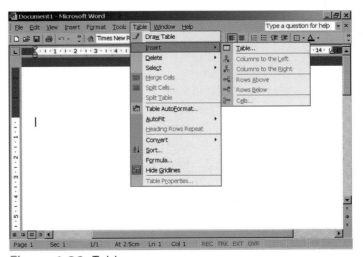

Figure 1.20 Table menu

arrows alongside the appropriate boxes. By clicking on the arrows, you can change the feature. Once you have set the parameters of the table you can insert the table by clicking on the OK button.

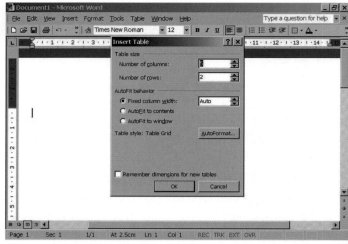

Figure 1.21 Insert Table window

Exercise 5

Tables

1 Insert your floppy disk into the drive.

2 Open Microsoft Word® by clicking on the Start button, highlighting All Programs and selecting Microsoft Word® or double-click on the Word® icon on the Microsoft Windows® desktop.

3 Open the file Solar System by selecting the File menu and the Open option to reveal the Open dialog window. Change Look in: box to Floppy (A:) using the arrow button at the end of the box. This will reveal the files stored on the floppy in the central area of the window. Double-click on the file Solar System or single-click to highlight it and then click on the Open button.

4 The document Solar System will appear in the Microsoft Word® work area.

5 You are now going to insert the table shown below into this document.

Planet	Year Length	Moons	Atmosphere
Mercury	88 days	None	None
Venus	225 days	None	Carbon dioxide
Earth	365 days	One	Nitrogen and oxygen
Mars	687 days	Two	Very thin
Jupiter	12 years	Sixteen	Gas planet
Saturn	29 years	Eighteen	Gas planet
Uranus	84 years	Seventeen	Gas planet
Neptune	165 years	Eight	Gas planet
Pluto	248 years	One	Thin

6 Insert this table at the end of your document by selecting the Table menu, highlighting Insert option and clicking on Table to reveal the Insert Table window. Set the table parameters to 10 rows and 4 columns. Text is added by clicking in the respective cells or by using the tab keys to move between the rows and columns.

7 Check the accuracy of your table and correct any errors by clicking in the appropriate cell.

8 Save your document by selecting the File menu and the Save As option. This will reveal the Save As dialog window. Change the Save in: box to Floppy (A:) by using the down arrow at end of the box to show the list of options. Save the document as File name: Solar System Table. When you are ready, click the Save button. You have now saved your document as a file called Solar System Table.

9 If you review the table you will see that the columns do not fit the information you have entered. To customise the widths of the columns you must highlight the columns you want to change. In this case, highlight them all by clicking in the Planets cell and holding down the mouse button, then drag the pointer down to the bottom right-hand corner of the table.

10 Select the Table menu and highlight the AutoFit option to reveal a range of options. Consider the different choices. Click on the AutoFit to Contents option. You will notice that your table changes. Figure 1.22 shows the table.

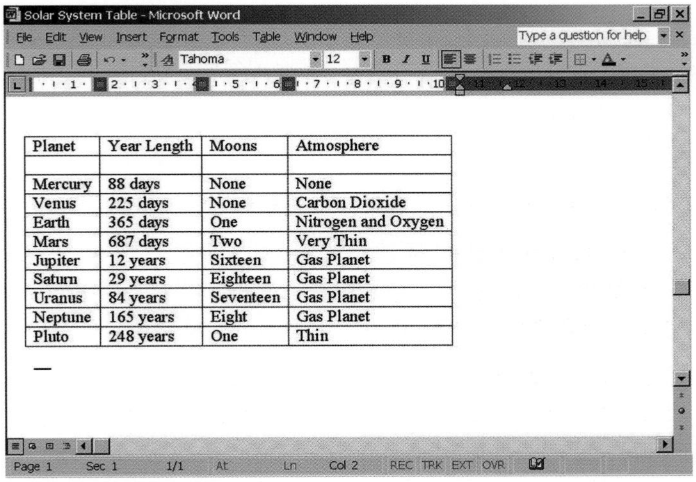

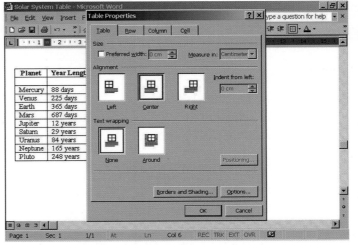

Figure 1.22 Table

11 You can change the appearance of the information within the table by highlighting the cells and selecting the option you desire, such as font, character size, bold, italics, change alignment (i.e. left, right and centre). Remember, your design is governed by the house style (see Exercise 3).

12 Centre and embolden the titles of the columns.

13 Change the font size of the whole table to 10.

14 You can align the table as well as the information it contains by using the Table menu and clicking on the Table Properties option. This will reveal the Table Properties window (figure 1.23). The window has a number of tabs, which will reveal tools to operate on rows, columns and cells.

Figure 1.23 Table Properties window

15 Table tab allows you to align the whole table. Use it to centre the whole table.

16 Save your document again by selecting the File menu and the Save option.

17 The other tabs allow you to change the height of rows, width of columns and alignment of text in each cell. Explore the options but do not make any permanent changes (i.e. use the Undo and Redo options in the Edit menu). Continue your experiments until you understand the different options.

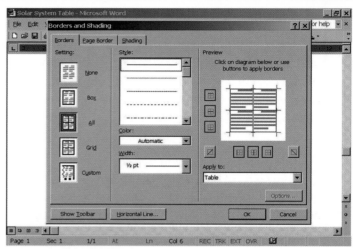

Figure 1.24 Borders and shading

18 You can also change the borders and shading of your table by using the Format menu and the Borders and Shading option to reveal the Borders and Shading window (figure 1.24).

19 The Borders and Shading window enables you to change the borders of your table by using the Setting, Style, Colour and Width of lines. You can explore the different options since the Preview window shows you what your choices look like.

20 Highlight your table and, using the Borders and Shading window, select an attractive border.

21 Highlight your table and, using the Borders and Shading window and the Shading tab, select an appropriate shading colour (e.g. yellow). Figure 1.25 shows our table.

22 Save your document again by selecting the File menu and the Save option.

23 Print your document by selecting the File menu and Print option.

24 You can now practise using the Find and Replace function available within the Edit menu. Searching from the start of the document, locate the words 'Gas planet' and replace them with the word 'Gas giant'. You should find the phrase four times.

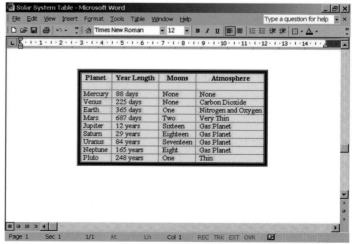

Figure 1.25 Revised table

25 There is no need to save the amended document since you are simply practising.

26 Close Microsoft Word® by selecting the File menu and the Exit option. When you exit without saving, you will see that a window appears to ask if you want to save. This is intended to prevent you losing data. In this case, you do not need to save, but sometimes you will, so always consider the question before making a decision.

Integrating documents

In the modern workplace you are often working with a variety of applications, such as word-processing, spreadsheets, charts and graphs and databases. It is useful to be able to import files from one application into another. Several integrated packages of applications, such as Microsoft Office®, provide tools to help you create an integrated document.

Microsoft Word® allows you to import files from other Microsoft Office® applications, to insert images from Clip Art collections and to add images you have created yourself. If you consider the options within the Insert menu you will see a variety of tools to import files into your document. In addition, you can simply use the Copy, Cut and Paste functions (i.e. Edit menu) to copy or move an image from one Microsoft Office® application and paste it into another.

The Picture option provides access to a range of functions to import images into your documents, including Clip Art, images stored as a file, WordArt, pictures scanned or photographed with a digital camera and charts produced in Microsoft Excel®.

Using the File option you can insert a file from another application to produce an integrated document. In many cases, Microsoft Word® will convert the file format into one with which it is compatible. However, some formats will not be accepted and you may see a warning message the first time you attempt to import a file, telling you that you need to install the file conversion software.

Warning Message
Microsoft Word® can't import the specified format.
This feature is not currently installed. Would you like to install it now?

To install the conversion program you need to insert the Microsoft Office® CD-ROM and click on the OK button, then follow the instructions on the screen.

Nevertheless, the Copy, Cut and Paste options are perhaps the most straightforward way of transferring resources between applications. You can copy a database table, spreadsheet or image and paste its contents into Microsoft Word® in the same way you can within an application.

The general process of importing images, charts, data or text using copy and paste is straightforward. In the original application (e.g. Microsoft Excel®, Access) highlight the sheet, table or data that you want to import and copy it using the Copy function, which is often available in the Edit menu. Now move to Microsoft Word®, or the application in which you are creating the integrated document, and use the paste function to insert the copied object. The copied image will appear at the cursor position in the document.

The different elements that you are integrating have probably been created without any intention of combining them. It is therefore important to be clear about how they need to be combined. If you have a specification then it is important to present the integrated document as it is specified. If you do not follow the specification, the required outcome will not be achieved.

The different components are likely to employ different fonts, character sizes and other layout features, and you may have to make changes so that the integrated document is effectively presented. In order to change the format of imported text or data, you need to highlight it and select the desired font and character size.

Images and charts will often need to be resized to fit into the combined document since they will have been produced for other purposes. In changing the size of an image or chart you need to ensure that its original proportions are maintained or the quality of the image will be reduced. When you import an image or chart it will appear in a rectangle, with small rectangles at each corner and at the midpoint of each side. If it does not, a single click on the image will enclose the image. This is the equivalent of highlighting it. If you place your mouse pointer on the enclosing small rectangles, the mouse pointer will change to become a double-headed arrow. If you hold down the mouse button you can reshape the image or chart by dragging the edge. In changing the shape you need to make sure that the proportions and quality of the image are maintained. You can also move the image or chart by placing the pointer in the centre of the image and holding down the mouse button, then dragging the whole image or chart to a new location. Figure 1.26 depicts inserting a Clip Art image into a Microsoft Word® document.

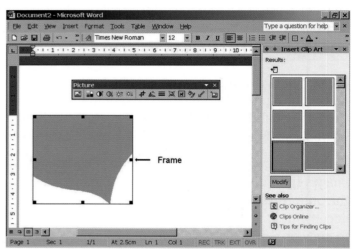

Figure 1.26 Clip Art

When you import a Microsoft Excel® spreadsheet into Microsoft Word® it will have a small rectangle with a star inside at the left-hand top corner. If you place your pointer on this square, it will change shape to a star, and by holding down the mouse button you can move the sheet to the location of your choice. At the bottom right-hand corner is a matching small square, which changes its shape to a double-headed arrow when you place your cursor on it. By holding down the mouse button you can resize the sheet.

Generic text and data files

Generic text and data files are ones which can be accessed by the majority of applications without their format needing to change. Earlier we discussed how to use the File option to import files into Microsoft Word®, which involves the conversion of the file format. Generic files do not normally need to have their files converted since they can be read by a large number of applications (e.g. word processors). A generic text file will often have the extension .txt.

A generic file can be imported using the File option within the Insert menu. When it appears, its format will often need to be amended (e.g. sentences broken up, extra spacings and gaps in the text). This is due to the limited formatting instructions contained in a generic file to make it compatible with many applications. Data files will sometimes be split across more than one page, owing to the position they are imported to. It is good practice to present data on a single page so that it is easier for the reader to understand.

When you are initially creating an integrated document you could begin by simply basing it on a generic text file. Microsoft Word® will open a generic text file in the same way it opens a Word® file. Select the File menu and the Open option. This will open the Open window. At the bottom of this window is a box called Files of type with a down arrow button, which, if clicked, provides a list of file formats. This should be All Files or Text Files so that the system can locate text files. When a text file is located, you can open it by either highlighting it and clicking on the Open button or by doubling-clicking the file. It will open within Microsoft Word®.

Printing an integrated document

The process of printing an integrated document is identical to printing any other. However, there is probably a greater need to check the appearance of the printed document since you are combining a number of resources into a single one. To preview prior to printing in Microsoft Word® you need to select the File menu and the Print Preview option. This will reveal the Print Preview window and show you how your integrated document will appear when printed. If you are satisfied, you can close the window, then select the File menu and the

Exercise 6

Integrated documents

1 Open Microsoft Word® by clicking on the Start button, highlighting All Programs and selecting Microsoft Word® or double-click on the Word® icon on the Microsoft Windows® desktop. A blank page will appear.

2 Enter the following text:

This is an example of a document combining different resources.

This should be in accordance with house style (see Exercise 3).

3 Leave three blank lines. Select the Insert menu and click on the File option to reveal the Insert File window. Using the down arrow button alongside the Look in: box change the folder to read your floppy disk. The files stored on the floppy disk will be shown in the central area.

4 Double-click on the Solar System Table.doc and it will be inserted into your new document.

5 Leave a blank line and again select the Insert menu, highlight the Picture item and click on the Clip Art option to reveal the Insert Clip Art pane on the right of the Microsoft Word® work area. You can search for a suitable image (e.g. astronomy) and a variety of thumbnail images will appear. If you place the mouse pointer over an image you want to insert, a button with a down arrow will appear. If you click on the button, a menu will be revealed (figure 1.27). If you select the Insert option, the chosen image will be inserted into the document. Select an image and insert it into your integrated document.

6 You may be presented with messages asking you to insert the Microsoft Office® installation disks if the Clip Art has not been installed on your computer.

7 Using the Insert menu and the File option, practise adding other resources to your document (e.g. Microsoft Excel® spreadsheet files). You may see messages that indicate you have to install extra facilities to convert the format of files. In order to do this, you will need the installation disks for Microsoft Office®. If you are not confident about carrying out this task, seek help before going on.

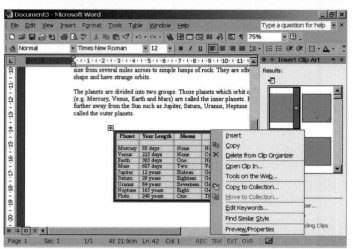

Figure 1.27 Insert Clip Art window

8 Save your document by selecting the File menu and the Save option. Name your file Integrated.

9 Preview your document in order to check its appearance when printed by selecting the File menu and the Print Preview option. Close the Print Preview window and either amend your document to correct any errors or print your document by selecting the File menu and the Print option.

10 Open a new blank document so that you can now practise importing text and data files, images and charts.

11 Select the Insert menu and the File option. This will open the Insert File window. In any order that you prefer, select text files, data files, charts and images and import them into your blank document. Continue to import until you are confident that you understand the process. Importing these files and images also provides an opportunity to format the integrated document. Practise your formatting skills again until you are confident. There is no need to save your changes.

12 Close Microsoft Word® by selecting the File menu and the Exit option. When you close without saving you will see that a window appears to ask if you want to save. This is intended to prevent you losing data. In this case, you do not need to save, but sometimes you will, so always consider the question before making a decision.

Print option to reveal the Print window. The document will be printed if you click on the OK button using the printer's default settings.

Mail merging

There are many occasions when you want to send the same document to a number of different people. Microsoft Word® provides a function called Mail Merge, with which you can automate the process. To carry out a mail merge you need to have a document and a source of information called a data source. The document is often a letter, while the data source contains the details about each person to whom it is going to be sent (e.g. names and addresses). The Mail Merge function lets you link the document and data source together to produce a series of customised documents (e.g. letters with each individual's address).

The Mail Merge function is accessed by selecting the Tools menu, highlighting the Letters and Mailings item to reveal a sub-menu with the option Mail Merge Wizard. Click on Mail Merge Wizard to open the Mail Merge task pane on the right of the work area (figure 1.28).

The Mail Merge task pane offers you a step-by-step method of undertaking a mail merge. The first step is to select the type of document you want to work with by clicking in the appropriate radio button. In figure 1.28 the letter has been chosen. At the bottom of the pane is the instruction Next: Starting Document. When you click on this instruction, the display changes to show figure 1.35. You select from the options and move on, clicking the instruction at the bottom. However, here you have an additional option of moving back one step. If you select Next, this changes the display to figure 1.29. The process is therefore to make selections from the options and to move on. Figures 1.30, 1.31, 1.32, 1.33 and 1.34 illustrate the method.

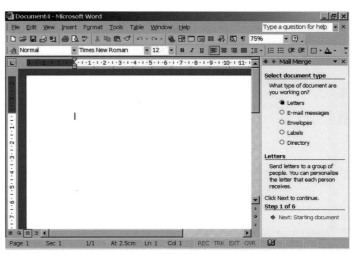

Figure 1.28 Mail Merge task pane

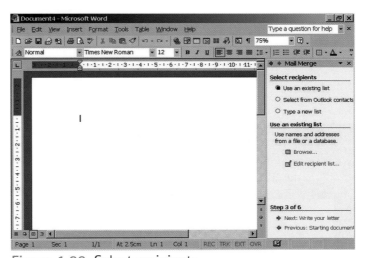

Figure 1.29 Select recipients

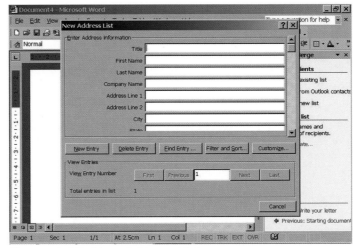

Figure 1.30 New Address List

Figure 1.31 Mail Merge Recipients

Figure 1.32 Write your letter

Figure 1.33 Preview your letter

Figure 1.34 Complete the merge

Mail merge

1 Open Microsoft Word® by clicking on the Start button, highlighting All Programs and selecting Microsoft Word® or double-click on the Word® icon on the Microsoft Windows® desktop. A blank page will appear.

2 In order to undertake a mail merge you need to have a standard letter or other document you want to customise for a variety of people. Enter the following text, which will form the basis of the merged document. Leave sufficient space at the start of the letter to enter the name and address of the recipient (six lines).

Dear

Invitation

I would like to invite you to the annual meeting of the Community Development Group. The meeting will consider the annual report of the organisation including the financial statement and agree the objectives for next year. It is important that members are able to attend in order to contribute to the group's plans.

Yours sincerely,

Gordon Donaldson
Chairman

3 Select the Tools menu and highlight the Letters and Mailings option to reveal a sub-menu. Click on the Mail Merge Wizard to open the Mail

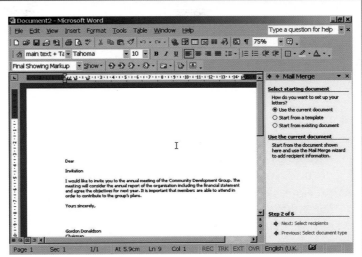

Figure 1.35 **Starting document**

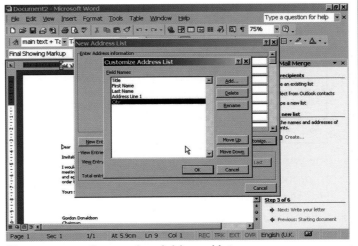

Figure 1.36 **Customize Address List**

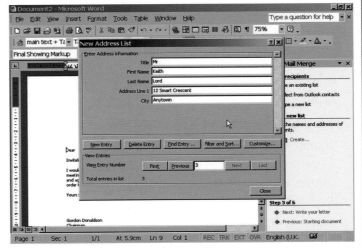

Figure 1.37 **Add Records**

Merge pane (figure 1.28). Choose the Letters option and click on Next: Starting document . The display will change (figure 1.35).

4 Select the option Use the current document and click on Next: Select recipients . If you need to, you can go back to the previous step by using the Previous: Select document type option. Select the Type a new list option and click on Create . The New Address List window will appear (figure 1.30).

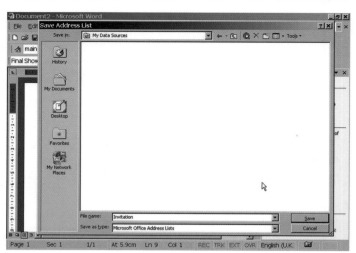

Figure 1.38 Save Address List

5 You are going to create three records, as shown in the table below:

Title	First Name	Last Name	Address1	City
Dr	James	Daniels	6 Long Street	Anytown
Ms	Karen	Brown	5 Short Road	Anytown
Mr	Keith	Lord	12 Smart Crescent	Anytown

The window asks you to enter details, but the first step is to customise the field headings to produce those you need. Click on the Customize button to open the Customize Address List. Use the Add , Delete , Rename , Move Up and Move Down buttons to produce a new data source. Figure 1.36 shows the Customize Address List window.

Once you have amended the address list, click on the OK button to open the New Address List window (figure 1.37) to enter the addresses of the recipients. When the three records have been added, click on the Close button. You will then be asked to save your new data. Figure 1.38 shows the Save Address List window. Save the list with the file name Invitation. Microsoft Word® XP saves the data in a folder called My Data Sources. When the list is saved (i.e. Save button selected), the Mail Merge Recipients window is opened (figure 1.45). When you are ready, select the OK button to close the window.

6 Now select the Next: Write your letter option. You need to insert into the letter the field names from the data source so that the application knows where to position the data. Click on the More items option to reveal the Insert Merge Field window (figure 1.40). This allows you to insert the fields by placing the cursor where you want the field in the letter, highlighting the field and clicking on the Insert button. Insert the fields in the letter.

Figure 1.41 shows the letter with the data fields added. You need to position the merged fields, allowing spaces between fields and adding any punctuation that is needed.

7 Now click on the option Next: Preview your letters to preview each merged letter (figure 1.42). It is important to check that the merged letters are correct.

You can use the arrow keys to move forward and backwards through the letters. The Exclude this recipient button lets you edit the merged letters.

8 Once you have checked the letters, you can click on the option Next: Complete the merge. Figure 1.43 shows the complete merge display. There are two options: Print, to send the letters to your printer and finish the task, or Edit individual letters. If you choose the second option then a new window (figure 1.44) will appear. This allows you to print all the letters, select a range or a single one. Explore the options and then select All.

9 Print the letters.

10 Word's Mail Merge facilities provide you with functions that allow you to query the information so that you can locate items. In this example we are going to find all the people receiving the letter who live in a particular location.

11 Query your data source to locate the recipients of the letter who live in Long Street. Select the Tools menu, highlight the Letters and Mailing option and click on Mail Merge Wizard. This opens the Mail Merge

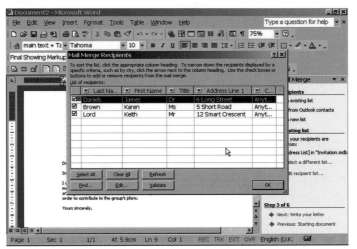

Figure 1.39 Mail Merge Recipients

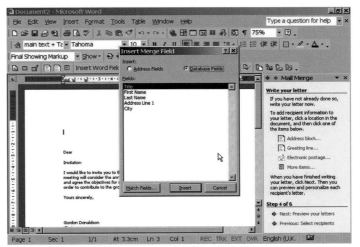

Figure 1.40 Insert Merge Field window

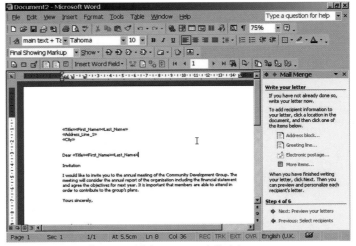

Figure 1.41 Letter with merged fields

Integrated e-Document Production

recipients – Office Address List. Select Edit recipients list to open the Mail Merge Recipients List window. Next click on the Edit button to edit the address details, then choose the Filter and Sort button which opens the Filter and Sort window. In the Files box use the down arrow to select the Address Line 1 option. In the Comparison box again use the down arrow button to select the Contains option, and finally in the Compare to: box enter Long Street. Click on OK and the query will locate all the recipients living in Long Street.

12 You will have noticed that there are many more options. You can base your query on any of the fields and use a range of comparison options (e.g. equal to). In our example we only had one condition for locating the information, but you may have noticed that in the second line of the Filter and Sort window is an AND which allows you to develop complex queries (e.g. recipients living in Long Street with first name James). Explore the different options until you are confident.

13 Close Word by selecting the File menu and the Exit option.

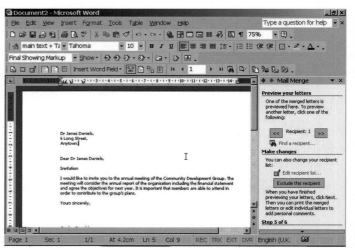

Figure 1.42 Preview merged letter

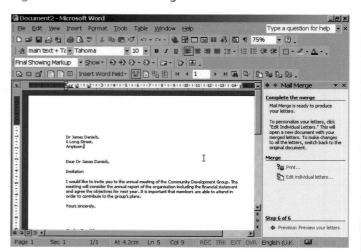

Figure 1.43 Complete the merge

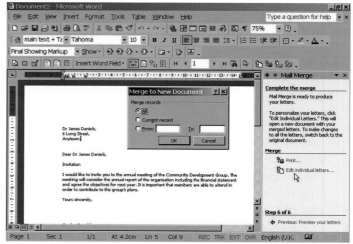

Figure 1.44 Edit individual letters

More practice

These exercises all refer to a set of related tasks that you might be asked to perform in a business or other form of organisation. They involve producing documents and related activities.

You are an admistrative assistant in the Countryside Timber Leisure Building Company. Your manager has asked you to prepare some sales literature. This consists of:

- a sales acknowledgement
- a direct sales letter
- an information leaflet.

This will involve you in producing a document that integrates text, graphics and data files.

You will need access to a set of resources, including:

- Timber Leisure Buildings (.doc file)
- Garden Shed product (.doc file)
- Contracts (Microsoft Word® data file)
- Specification (data file)
- CountryLogo (image file)

These are available on the Hodder Education website (www.hodderclait.co.uk).

Activity 1

The objective of this activity is to produce a sales acknowledgement, based on a mail merge document, sent to customers to acknowledge their order. You need to create a master mail merge document.

First Name	Last Name	Value	Contract
John	King	£1200	Garden Shed
Diana	Morris	£870	Broad Shed
Silvia	Francis	£657	Tool Bunker

1. Open Microsoft Word® and create a mail merge document
2. Enter the following text, leaving blank lines or paragraph space when they are shown. Insert the merged fields from the table below:

   Figure 1.45 shows the Customize Address List window, while figure 1.46 shows the Mail Merge Recipients.

Sales Acknowledgement

Countryside Timber Leisure Building Company

We would like to acknowledge receipt of your order for a *{insert Contract merge fields}*. This is being managed by *{insert Project Manager merge field}* who you should contact with any queries. The total cost of the order is *{insert Value merge field}*.

Yours sincerely,

{insert your own name}
Managing Director

3 Create a header and footer and enter your own name in the header.

4 Change the format of the sales acknowledgement so that it has:

- heading (i.e. Sales Acknowledgement) – centred and enboldened

- heading (i.e. Countryside Timber Leisure Building Company) – left-aligned and emboldened

  Select a font, character size and margins to present the document in the most effective way.

5 Save the master document with the file name Acknowledgement. Figure 1.47 shows one of the merged acknowledgements.

6 Print the document.

7 Password (Sales1) protect the file from modification.

8 Save the file with the name Acknowledgement.

9 Close the file and exit Microsoft Word®.

Activity 2

During the assessment you will often be asked to take a screen print as evidence that you have completed a task. In this activity you will have an opportunity to practise this task.

1 Open Acknowledgement which you created in activity 1.

2 Use the screen capture facility to demonstrate that you have set password protection. Figure 1.48 shows what you should capture.

3 Print the screen capture.

4 Query your data source to locate the contract for a garden office. You need to select the Tools menu, highlight the Letters and Mailings option and click on Mail Merge Wizard. This opens the Mail Merge recipients – Sales Recipients. Select the Edit recipient list to open the Mail Merge

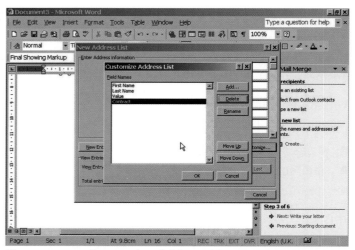

Figure 1.45 Customize Address List

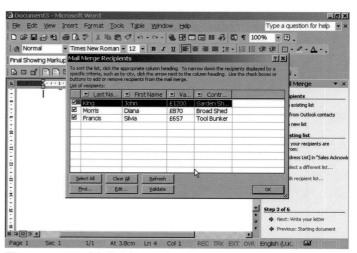

Figure 1.46 Mail Merge Recipients

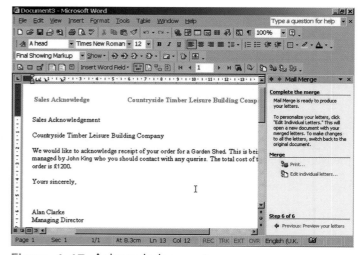

Figure 1.47 Acknowledgement

Recipients List window. Next click on the Edit button to reveal figure 1.49, then choose the Filter and Sort button, which opens the Filter and Sort window (figure 1.50).

5 Print the result.
6 Close the file and Microsoft® Word.

Activity 3

In this activity you are asked to create a sales letter. This will involve combining two files. The files are:

Timber Leisure Buildings

CountryLogo

1 Open the Timber Leisure Buildings document or enter it.

Dear
Timber Leisure Buildings

Do you have enough space? A cost effective solution to the problem of a lack of space to work, store equipment and garden furniture is a timber building. We can supply a wide range of building to meet your needs. These include:

Garden Office®
This building is available in several sizes and is designed to provide a room from which you can operate a business.

Tool Bunker
A problem that many people face is where to store garden and other tools. Our tool bunker provides a secure store for expensive items.

Broad Shed
For many gardeners a simple tool bunker is not sufficient. The broad shed is designed to offer a way of storing tools, furniture and sports equipment safely and securely.

Figure 1.48 Password protection

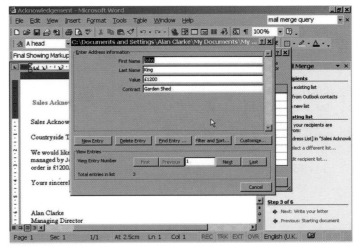

Figure 1.49 Edit Mail Merge Recipients

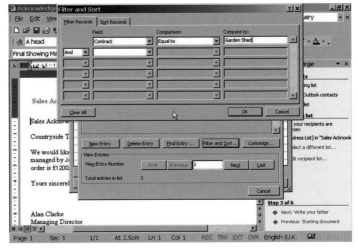

Figure 1.50 Filter and Sort

Please contact Countryside Ltd for more details of our products or visit us at our show site at Country First on the A46.

Yours sincerely,

Managing Director

2   Format Timber Leisure Buildings as follows:

> Paper size – A4
> Orientation – portrait
>
> Alignment – left
> Font – Tahoma
> Character size – 10
> Line spacing – single

3   Format the Timber Leisure Buildings headings as follows:

> Alignment – centred and emboldened
> Font – Times New Roman
> Character size – 14

4   Format the three other subheadings (i.e. Garden Office, Tool Bunker and Broad Shed) as follows:

> Alignment – left and emboldened
> Font – Times New Roman
> Character size – 12

5   Save the file as Direct Sales.

6   Insert the image CountryLogo in the top right-hand corner of the letter. You will need to resize the image, but it must not be distorted by the process. Figure 1.40 shows the document.

7   Add a header and footer to the document, then insert your name in the header and the automatic date in the footer.

8   Save the file as Direct Sales.

9   Close the file and Microsoft Word®.

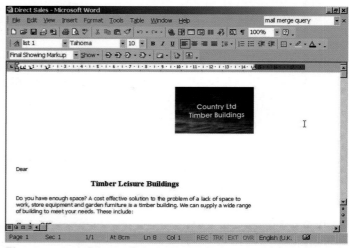

Figure 1.51 Direct Sales document

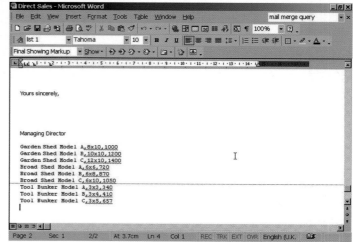

Figure 1.52 Imported table

Activity 4

The sales letter needs to include a table of the timber buildings' specifications and costs. These are provided as the data file in CSV format. This requires the file specification.

1 Open the Direct Sales document.

2 Insert the file Specification.csv below the last line in the letter, after 'Managing Director'.

3 The file will appear, as shown in figure 1.52. Each item of information is separated by a comma.

4 Format the imported information to form a table (Table menu and Convert option). Figure 1.53 illustrates the converted text.

5 Add a new row to insert three column headings, Product, Size and Cost, to the table. Format the table contents to Arial, with a character size of 12. Centre the table.

6 Embolden the column headings and centre them. Apply a shading of your choice to the heading (ie across the new row).

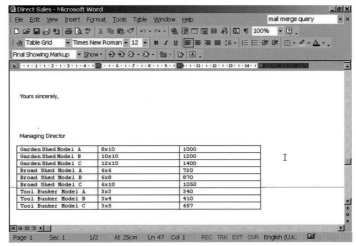

Figure 1.53 Converted text

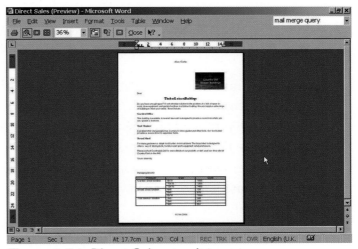

Figure 1.54 Direct Sales preview

7 Merge the cells in the left-hand column so that three new cells are produced (i.e. all Garden Office® cells togther, all Tool Bunker cells together and all Broad Shed cells together). Edit the new cells so that they read Garden Shed Models, Broad Shed Models and Tool Bunker Models).

8 Proofread the document and check you have carried out all the instructions.

9 Check that the layout of the letter is acceptable using the Print Preview function and print a copy of the letter. Figure 1.54 shows the letter in preview.

10 Save Direct Sales.

11 Close the file and Microsoft Word®.

Activity 5

This activity involves creating an information leaflet for the Garden Shed product. The basic text has already been produced and is available from the website or, alternatively, you can enter the text.

Garden Shed

The Garden Shed has been designed for the many people who need to work from home but have little space within their houses to establish an office. The building is available in three sizes:

- Version A, 8ft × 10ft at £1000
- Version B, 10ft × 10ft at £1200
- Version C, 12ft × 10ft at £1400

All models are constructed out of seasoned timber with an inner lining to provide sound and temperature insulation. The roof is constructed using a rubberised process to ensure that it is waterproof. The door and windows are provided with security locks to ensure that the building is safe.

The Garden Shed is provided as a flat pack so that you can assemble it yourself on a concrete base. Alternatively, we can construct the building for you. The costs are available on application to Country Ltd.

1 Open the file Garden Shed product in Microsoft Word®.
2 Format the whole document as Arial, size 10 and centre the headings as character size 12, emboldened.
3 Delete the phrase 'to ensure that the building is safe'.
4 Replace the word 'Version' with 'Model'. Make sure that the first letter is a capital.
5 Insert a copyright symbol at the bottom of the leaflet – © Country Ltd.
6 Spellcheck the document and proofread.
7 Insert a header with your name and a footer with an automatic file name.
8 Save the file as Garden Shed Revised.
9 Print a copy of your document,
10 Close the file and Microsoft Word®.

Activity 6

1 Archive all the source files: Timber Leisure Buildings, Garden Office® product, Contracts, Specification and CountryLogo.
2 Produce evidence that you have undertaken the archiving by using the screen capture function.
3 Print a copy of the screen capture.

SUMMARY

1 Files and folders

All information stored on a computer is held in a file. All files have an individual name and they are stored within folders. Folders can also be stored in other folders. Folders are sometimes called directories.

2 Open files

Files can be opened by double-clicking on them with the mouse pointer. The files will only open if an application which is able to read the file is present on the computer system. If the application is not present, Microsoft Windows® will display a window asking you to locate the appropriate application since the operating system cannot find it.

3 Windows® Explorer

Windows® Explorer provides you with the tools to create new folders and delete, rename, move, copy and save files and folders. These functions are available on the File menu and toolbar. To open Windows® Explorer, click on the Start button and highlight the All Programs option to open another menu. Highlight the Accessories item to open a menu with Windows® Explorer option.

4 Read-only

Highlight the file within Windows® Explorer, select the File menu and the Properties option to open the Properties window. Click on the General tab and in the Read-only radio button.

5 Archive files

Highlight the file or folder within Windows® Explorer and select the Properties option in the File menu. In the General tab is a button labelled Advanced . If you click on it, the Advanced Attributes window opens. This provides an option to create archive files by clicking on the appropriate radio button.

6 Types of files

There are many different types of files. File names normally end with a full stop and three letters (e.g. .doc). This indicates the type of file and helps you to distinguish between them. In addition, the icons show the type of file.

7 Print windows

Press the ALT key and then the Print Screen (sometimes Print Scrn) key. Paste the window image into a document (e.g. Microsoft Word®) and print the document using the normal functions of the application.

To capture the contents of the whole display you need only press the Print Screen key and then paste the image into a document.

8 Spelling and grammar checkers

In Microsoft Word® spelling and grammar checkers are available in the Tools menu as the Spelling and Grammar option.

Automatic checking can be set using the Tools menu and the Options item to reveal the Options window. Choose the Spelling and Grammar tab and configure both checkers. Spelling mistakes are underlined in red and grammar errors in green.

9 Save

Select the File menu and the Save option. This will reveal the Save As dialog window, which allows you to choose where to save your file (e.g. floppy disk) and to name it. After you have saved your file once it will be updated each time you click on the Save option.

10 Save As

Select the File menu and the Save As option. This will let you save your file under a new name or in a new location.

11 Page Setup

Select the File menu and the Page Setup option. This opens the Page Setup dialog window. You can choose the layout of your page (e.g. margins, orientation, size of headers and footers).

12 Headers and footers

Select the View menu and the Header and Footer option, which will open a header area on your document and a toolbar which provides extra options for the header. If you scroll down the page you will find the footer area at the bottom of the page, with the toolbar.

13 Bullets and Numbering

Select the Format menu and click on the Bullets and Numbering option. This will reveal the Bullets and Numbering window.

14 Special symbols

Select the Insert menu and click on the Symbol option. This will open the Symbol window.

15 Search and replace

Select the Edit menu and click on the Replace option to reveal the Find and Replace window.

16 Widows and orphans

Select the Format menu, the Paragraph option and the Line and Page Breaks tab. Click the Widow/Orphan control radio button.

17 Indent text

There are several ways of indenting text:

- Use the tab key on the keyboard. You can set the size of the tab by selecting the Format menu and clicking on the Tabs option, which will open the Tabs window.
- Select the Format menu and click on the Paragraph option. This will reveal the Paragraph window.
- Select the View menu and click on Ruler . By dragging the stops at the end of the ruler you can create first-line and hanging indents.

18 Tables

Select the Table menu, highlight the Insert option and click on the Table option. This will open the Insert Table window.

19 Change column widths

Highlight the columns you want to change. Select the Table menu, highlight the AutoFit option to reveal a range of options, and click on AutoFit to Contents.

20 Presentation of table contents

Highlight the content of the cells you want to change and select the option you desire, such as font, character size, bold, italics, alignment (i.e. left, right and centre).

21 Table alignment

Select the Table menu and click on the Table Properties option. This will reveal the Table Properties window, which has a number of tabs that contain tools to operate on rows, columns and cells.

- Table tab – allows you to align the whole table
- Other tabs let you change height of rows, width of columns and alignment of text in each cell.

22 Borders and Shading

Highlight your table, then select the Format menu and the Borders and Shading option to reveal the Borders and Shading window. This allows you to change the borders of your table by using the Setting, Style, Color and Width of lines options.

23 Layout and formatting

Select the Format menu and click on the Paragraph option to open the Paragraph window. This enables you to change alignment, line spacing and indentation.

24 Import charts, images, data and text

The Copy, Cut and Paste functions let you move charts, images, data and text between Microsoft Office® applications.

Alternatively, select the Insert menu and click on File option, or highlight the Picture option to reveal a sub-menu which enables you to choose an image from Clip Art or From File (i.e. a file stored on the computer).

25 Mail Merge

The Mail Merge function is accessed by selecting the Tools menu, highlighting the Letters and Mailing item to reveal a sub-menu with the option Mail Merge Wizard. Click on the Mail Merge Wizard to open the Mail Merge task pane on the right of the work area. The Mail Merge task pane offers you a step-by-step method of undertaking a mail merge.

Manipulating Spreadsheets and Graphs

This chapter will help you to:

- identify and use spreadsheet and graph software correctly

- enter, edit and manipulate data

- create formulae and use common functions

- format and present data

- link live data from one spreadsheet to another

- select and control data sources

- present data using graphs and charts

- format axes and labels

- format the presentation of graphs and charts

- use graphs to extrapolate information to predict future values

- use spreadsheets to solve problems and project results.

This chapter covers unit 2 (Manipulating Spreadsheets and Graphs). There is no precondition for studying this unit. However, its content does assume that you have the skills and understanding that are provided by the OCR Level 1 ICT course New CLAiT (e.g. Unit 2: Creating Spreadsheets and Graphs and Unit 1: File Management and e-Document Production).

Assessment

After studying unit 2, your skills and understanding are assessed during a three-hour practical assignment. This is set by OCR and marked locally. However, the marking will be externally moderated by OCR. This ensures that the standard is being applied correctly across the many different providers of OCR CLAiT Plus. If you are unsuccessful, you can be reassessed using a different assignment.

An alternative approach is for you to be assessed by an assignment set by OCR or designed by your centre. These assignments cover all the assessment objectives included in the unit. You will need to complete an OCR evidence checklist, explaining how each assessment objective has been covered.

Font families

CLAiT Plus uses font families in its assessments rather than font names. In chapter 1 font families are explained, along with how they relate to font names (see page 7). As you undertake each exercise, consider which font family the font you are using belongs to. For example:

Serif: Courier New and Times New Roman
Sans serif: Tahoma and Arial.

Spreadsheet applications

This chapter is based on Microsoft Excel® XP, which is a modern package that you can employ to create spreadsheets. It also provides you with the means of converting data from your spreadsheet into a graph or chart. Figure 2.1 shows the Microsoft Excel® application interface. Its main feature is a grid of columns and rows. This is the work area of the spreadsheet. The columns are designated with a letter (A, B, C, etc.), while the rows are numbered (1, 2, 3, etc.). The intersection of columns and rows produces a rectangular area called a cell. Each cell is known by the letter and number of its column and row (A1, B2, C3, etc.).

When you click in a cell it is highlighted. In figure 2.1, cell A1 is highlighted. You will also see that the highlighted cell reference is given at the left end of the formula toolbar. At the bottom of the grid, in the left-hand corner, three are tabs, called Sheet 1, Sheet 2 and Sheet 3. These allow you to move between three spreadsheets, which combined are called a workbook. The sheets are often related (e.g. sales figures for three different products).

To the right of the work area is the task pane, which you can switch off and on. This provides a range of options to help you undertake different tasks. When the application opens, the task pane offers options to help you create a new spreadsheet workbook. The task pane changes, depending on what you are attempting to do.

The work area is surrounded by an interface, which is broadly similar to many other Microsoft Office® applications. It has a menu bar and a number of toolbars providing access to the many different functions available within Microsoft Excel® to create, amend and manipulate spreadsheets.

The two main ways of loading Microsoft Excel® are:

■ Click on the Start button in the bottom left-hand corner of the Microsoft Windows® desktop. A

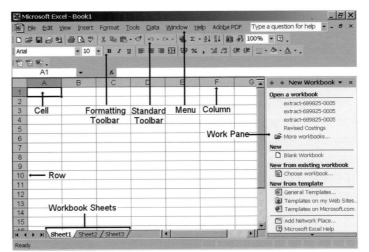

Figure 2.1 Microsoft Excel® XP

menu will pop up. If you highlight the All Programs item a new menu will appear alongside it. If you click on the item shown as Microsoft Excel®, the application will load.

- Double-click on the Excel® icon shown on the desktop.

A variety of exercises are included in this chapter. Their prime purpose is to help you understand how to create and use spreadsheets. They are simplified representations of the world and are not intended to be tutorials on accountancy, but rather explanations of Microsoft Excel®.

The primary purpose of a spreadsheet is to analyse numerical information to assist an organisation's management. They may be used to consider the sales of a product, wage costs, overheads and many other issues. However, one key factor essential for all spreadsheets is numerical accuracy. Data entered must be correct and calculations need to be checked to ensure they are perfect. When creating a spreadsheet you must devote a lot of time to checking that all data and formulae are accurate.

Modelling

A key role for spreadsheets is to model information and enable you to explore what would be the result of a change. For example, you might create a spreadsheet showing the production costs of manufacturing a component. The spreadsheet would let you explore what would be the effect of changing the process (e.g. investing in a new machine which allows you to manufacture the component using half the workforce).

You could create a spreadsheet showing the relationship between sales staff and profit. You might explore the effects of increasing or decreasing the number of staff.

You might develop a spreadsheet showing the relationship between commission and sales volumes. This would allow you to consider the influence of changing the rates of commission.

Create a spreadsheet

To create a new spreadsheet requires that you understand the nature of the information you are going to model and how you want to present the spreadsheet.

The first step is to establish the structure or layout of the spreadsheet. This is important in that it will influence the way the information it contains is accepted. Senior managers will only act on the results of a spreadsheet if they are persuaded that it is quality work. A sheet that is well presented, with an effective structure, will go a long way towards demonstrating that it is worth considering. You can start a spreadsheet with an initial structure and then amend it later to improve its appearance.

The structure of a spreadsheet can be established using the Page Setup

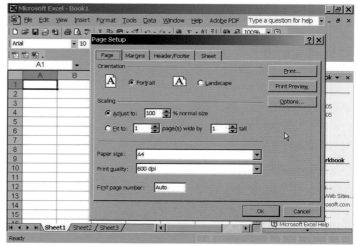

Figure 2.2 Page Setup

option, which is available from the
File menu. If you click on the
Page Setup option it will reveal the
Page Setup window (figure 2.2). This is
divided by a series of tabs into Page,
Margins, Header/Footer and Sheet.

The Page tab lets you set the
orientation of the sheet (i.e. portrait
or landscape). It also provides access
to the scaling feature, which lets you
fit your spreadsheet on to a specified
number of pages when you are
printing it, by scaling the size of the
sheet. For both options, click on the
relevant radio buttons.

The Margins tab (figure 2.3) provides
the means of changing the size of the
four margins (i.e. top, bottom, left and
right). The window demonstrates the
orientation of the sheet and the four
margins. Using the up and down
arrows near each box you can
increase or decrease the margins. The
same display also allows you to set
the size of the header and footer and,
finally, to centre the sheet on the
page either horizontally or vertically.
This can improve the appearance of
the spreadsheet.

The Header/Footer tab (figure 2.4)
enables you to customise the
information that heads and foots the
sheet. By clicking on the
Custom Header or Custom Footer
buttons you will reveal the Header or
Footer window (figure 2.5).

Headers and Footers

Using the Header and Footer windows,
you can insert text which will appear
at the top or bottom of the sheet. In
addition, you can add a number of
automatic fields that will change,
depending on the sheet, when they
appear (e.g. number of the page, new date and a change of file name). The font, character size
and style of text can be changed using the text button. The other buttons allow automatic

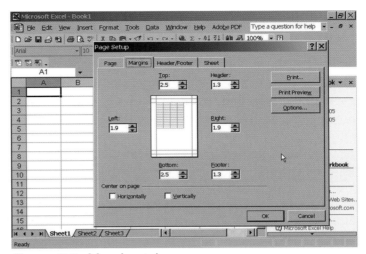

Figure 2.3 Margins tab

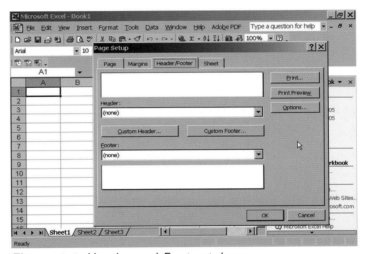

Figure 2.4 Header and Footer tab

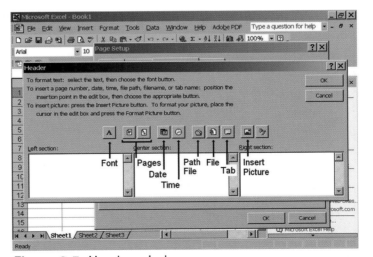

Figure 2.5 Header window

fields to be inserted. The text and automatic fields are inserted at the cursor in the left, right or centre of the header or footer.

Figure 2.5 shows the icons that appear on the Header window (and also on the Footer) and identifes their purpose. Place the cursor in your chosen location or highlight the text, and then click on the icon. The first icon allows you to format the text, while the remaining icons provide you with the means of inserting an automatic field into the header or footer.

Exercise 8

Create a spreadsheet structure

1 Load Microsoft Excel® using either the All Programs menu or the Excel® icon on the desktop. Close the Workbook task pane (button in right-hand corner).

2 Set the orientation of the sheet to landscape, margins to 2 cm – right and left, and 2.5 cm – top and bottom, and the header and footer to 1.5 cm (select File menu and Page Setup option).

3 Insert header to read: 'Sales Forecast' (Arial font and character size 14 bold, in the Center section)

4 Insert automatic fields in the footer:

File name – Left section
Page number – Center section
Date – Right section

5 Enter the table of information below to form your first spreadsheet. Start Item in cell B5. You can use any font and character size that you want to. I selected Arial, character size 10 for the headings and Tahoma, character size 10 for the items.

Item	January	February, etc. (all 12 months of the year)
Hand Tools		
Power Tools		
Wood		
Metal		
Fastenings		
Paint		
Wallpaper		
Electrical		
Garden		
Kitchen		
Garage		

6 Check that you have entered the data accurately and correct any mistakes. If you click in the cell which contains the error, you can amend the mistake by pressing the delete key and re-entering. Alternatively, the contents of a selected cell appear on the formula bar and can be edited if you click on the bar and then use the arrow keys and keyboard.

7 It is good practice to save your work early and update the file as you make changes and enhance the spreadsheet. Insert a floppy disk into the A: drive and select the File menu, then click on the option Save to reveal the Save As window. Change the Save in : box to select the floppy disk and add the file name Sales Forecast in the File name box. Click on the Save button. You will probably hear the floppy drive and your spreadsheet will be saved as the file Sales Forecast. The top line of Microsoft Excel® will change to read 'Microsoft Excel® – Sales Forecast'.

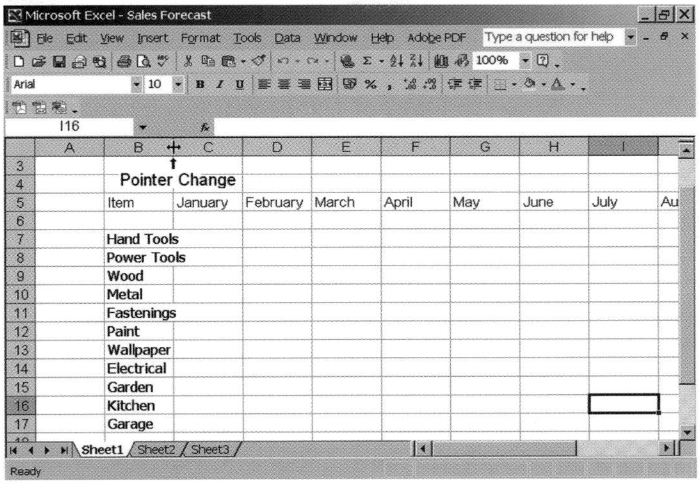

Figure 2.6 Sales forecast

8 You have probably noticed that some of your titles are too large for the cell in which they have been placed (e.g. Hand Tools, Power Tools and September). You can change the size of a column by placing the mouse pointer on the line between the two columns (its appearance will change – figure 2.6), and if you hold down the left mouse button, you can drag the column wider. Make columns B and K wider.

9 Check the appearance of your spreadsheet as a printed document by selecting the File menu and the Print Preview option. This will show you how the sheet will appear if printed. If the text is too small, click on the Zoom button. If it is then too big, click on it again. The preview will allow you to check the content and presentation of the header and footer, sheet and margins and orientation. If you click on the Setup button you can see the settings, and clicking on Margins will reveal them. Explore the different options and ensure you have produced the sheet accurately.

10 Save your sheet by selecting the File menu and clicking on the Save option. The Save As window will not appear since the application assumes you simply want to update your file stored on the floppy disk.

11 Close Microsoft Excel® by selecting the File menu item and clicking on the Exit option or by clicking on the Close button in the top right-hand corner of the application window.

Saving

You can choose to save a spreadsheet in a variety of formats. In the Save As window is a box called Save as type, and there is a down arrow at the side of this box. If you click on this button, a list of formats in which you can save your spreadsheet appears. They include:

■ Microsoft Excel® Workbook – current Microsoft Excel® 2000 format

Manipulating Spreadsheets and Graphs

- Web Page – your sheet is going to be presented on a website
- Microsoft Excel® 4.0 Work – older version of Microsoft Excel®
- other spreadsheet applications.

You need to select which format will serve your purpose. Do you want your work to be read easily on an earlier version of Microsoft Excel® or another application, presented on a website or simply used on Microsoft Excel® XP? The decision has consequences: if you save the sheet in the format suitable for an earlier version of Microsoft Excel® you may lose some presentation aspects or other features. If you are in doubt, you should save in the format of the current version of Microsoft Excel® (Microsoft Excel® Workbook).

Formulae

One of the key features of a spreadsheet is that it can undertake mathematical calculations. It can total columns of figures, add, subtract, multiply and divide the contents of cells. It can carry out complex mathematical operations using formulae which you can devise.

The mathematical operators used in Microsoft Excel® are:

+	add
-	subtract
*	multiply
/	divide
<	less than
<=	less than or equal to
>	more than
>=	greater than or equal to

Brackets are also important in that they tell Microsoft Excel® to calculate anything in the brackets first, before going on with the remaining parts of the calculation. A simple formula could be:

=B2+B3 – this means add the contents of cell B2 to the contents of cell B3
=B2-B3 – this means subtract the contents of cell B3 from the contents of cell B2
=B2/B3 – this means divide the contents of cell B2 by the contents of cell B3
=B2*B3 – this means multiply the contents of cell B2 by the contents of cell B3.

These simple operators can be used to produce more complex formulae and hence carry out complex mathematical actions. For example:

=(B2+B3)/4 – add the contents of cells B2 and B3 together and divide the total by 4
=(B2*10)-(B3/B2)-20 – multiply the contents of cell B2 by 10 and subtract from it the contents of cell B3 divided by the contents of cell B2, then subtract 20 from the total.

When a formula consists of several arithmetical operators (e.g. add, subtract, multiply or divide), Microsoft Excel® works them out according to a standard rule. It will work out multiplication and division first, and addition and subtraction second. If the formula contains multiplication and division or addition and subtraction, it works out the calculation from left to right. However, also remember that anything enclosed in brackets will be calculated first.

Standard formulae

There are a variety of standard functions available to Microsoft Excel® users. These include:

- SUM – this function totals the contents of a group of cells
- AVERAGE – this function produces the average of a number of values (e.g. a column of figures)
- COUNT – this function counts the number of entries in a group of cells that contain numbers
- COUNTA – this function counts the number of cells in a given range with any contents
- COUNTIF – this function counts the number of cells that are equal to a criterion in a range of cells (e.g. M2:M5 holds nails, screws, tacks, screws therefore COUNTIF(M2:M5, "screws")=2).
- MIN – this identifies the minimum value of the contents of a group of cells
- MAX – this identifies the maximum value of the contents of a group of cells
- SQRT – this function calculates the square root of a number (or the contents of a cell)
- IF – this allows you to set a condition so that an action is only carried out if it is satisfied, for example, IF (G4 >=50, "Pass", "Fail" – this means that if the contents of cell G4 are equal to or greater than 50 then the word Pass will appear). This could be the outcome of entering examination marks into a spreadsheet. If G4 is less than 50 then the word Fail will appear. The example shows that there are two outcomes of an IF function – one if the condition is true (i.e. Pass) and one if the condition is false (Fail). If you do not specify the false outcome, the word False will appear if the condition is not met. This can be confusing in some situations.

Here are some examples:

=SUM(A2:A8) – produces the total of the contents of the cells A2, A3, A4, A5, A6, A7 and A8

=AVERAGE (A2:A5) – produces the average of the contents of the cells A2, A3, A4 and A5 (i.e. (A2+A3+A4+A5)/4)

=COUNT (N11:N17) – counts the number of cells between N11 and N17 inclusive which contain numbers

=COUNTA (N11:N17) – counts the number of cells between N11 and N17 inclusive which hold content

=COUNTIF (N11:N17, "Car") – counts the number of cells between N11 and N17 inclusive which equal Car

=SQRT(A7) – if A7 is 25 the function produces the square root of 25, which is 5

=IF (A3>40, A3/10) – if the contents of cell A3 is greater than 40, then divide A3 by 10.

These functions involve identifying a list of cells. This is called the range of cells and can be selected by highlighting them on the spreadsheet, or by writing the first and last cell, separated by a colon, to designate that all the cells between the two are included. They are enclosed in brackets. At the beginning of the function an equals sign tells Microsoft Excel® to carry out the calculation.

A full list of all the functions can be accessed by clicking on the down arrow next to the Sum function button on the Standard toolbar. This reveals a list of functions and the button More Functions (figure 2.7). If you click on More Functions, you open the Insert Function window. If you highlight a function, its definition is given at the bottom of the window. Functions serve a wide range of purposes. Some are linked to mathematical operations, while others provide the means of testing logic (e.g. IF). The Insert Function window allows you to insert the function into the sheet, but you can also simply enter the function from the keyboard or double-click on the function in the list or window. When you enter a function, a new window will sometimes appear called Function Arguments. This allows you to enter any ranges or other information required by the function. However, in other cases the function will be entered with space for you to insert the range (figure 2.8).

Function Arguments asks you to set the parameters for the function. Figure 2.9 illustrates the window for the AVERAGE function. The window provides a short explanation of what is required. For some functions, the requirements are similar to AVERAGE in that a range of cell references is needed. In some cases, Microsoft Excel® will offer you a range, depending on the cell in which you are inserting the function. However, you should always check if it is correct.

The example below shows the use of functions and their mathematical values for a short column of figures (D6 to D9) in column D of a spreadsheet.

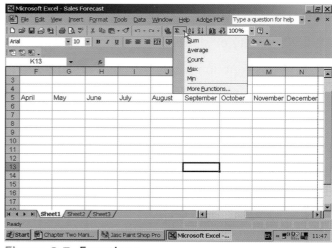

Figure 2.7 Functions

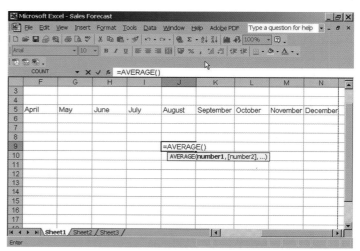

Figure 2.8 Insert a function

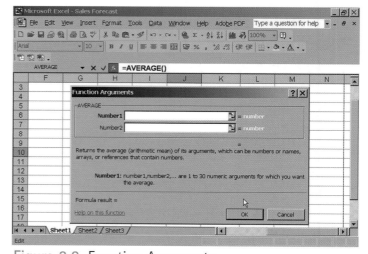

Figure 2.9 Function Arguments

Example:	Value	
D6	78	78
D7	56	56
D8	34	34
D9	56	56
D10	=AVERAGE(D6:D9)	56
D11	=MIN(D6:D9)	34
D12	=MAX(D6:D9)	78
D13	=SUM(D6:D9)	224
D14	=COUNT(D6:D9)	4
D15	=COUNTA(D6:D9)	4
D16	=COUNTIF(D6:D9,34)	1
D17	=SQRT(D9)	7.48

Name

Some of these functions you could design yourself (e.g. SUM (H3:H6) is the same as H3+H4+H5+H6). However, there is always the risk that you will make an error with your own formulae, and in many cases they require more information to be entered from the keyboard. The standard functions are a better guarantee of success.

An alternative approach to defining a range is to highlight the cell or cells and then to select the Insert menu and highlight the Name option to reveal a short menu. Click on the Define option to reveal the Define Name window (figure 2.10). The highlighted cells referenced are shown in the box at the bottom of the window. The name of the cells is entered into the top box. By clicking on the Add button you create the name, and you complete the task by clicking on the OK button. The group of cells is defined by the name.

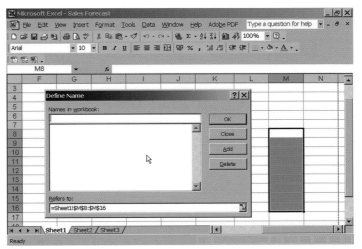

Figure 2.10 Name

To delete a name select the Insert menu, highlight the Name option and select the Define option to reveal the Define window. A list of the names is shown in the middle box. Highlight the name you want to remove and click on the Delete button.

Logical operators/functions

Using the IF function, you can ask questions of your data. It checks if a defined condition is true and then causes an action to take place. Its format is:

IF (Condition, true, false) – that is, if the condition is correct, then the true statement will take place. If it is not true, then the false statement will take place.

For example, you could establish a function so that if a sales person exceeded his target he would receive a bonus:

=IF(A10>55,B12*1.20,B12*0.95)

If cell A10 (containing the number of items sold) is greater than 55 (the sales target) then the contents of cell B12 (sales person's salary) is multiplied by 1.20 (i.e. salary is increased by 20 per cent). If the content of cell A10 is not greater than 55 then the contents of B12 are multiplied by 0.95 (i.e. salary is reduced by 5 per cent).

The IF function is not the only way of testing conditions. There are also three logical operators. These are:

OR   OR(condition1, condition2) This returns true if one or more of the conditions is true; otherwise it returns false.

NOT   NOT(condition) This reverses the value of the condition.

AND   AND(condition1 and condition2) This returns the value true if both the conditions are true; otherwise it returns the value false.

These operators are often useful when combined with the IF function.

In our earlier example, the salespersons only had to sell more than their target to achieve their bonus. If the conditions were that they had to sell more than the target for two consecutive periods, the formula would be:

$$=IF(AND(A10>55,A9>47),B12*1.20,B12*0.95)$$

A9>47 represents the sales target in the previous period.

The OR operator can also be used if the condition for receiving the bonus was to exceed the sales target in either period.

$$=IF(OR(A10>55,A9>47),B12*1.20,B12*0.95)$$

Logical operators can be confusing initially for many people, but can be very useful in carrying out complex tasks.

An important issue with formulae, which may seem obvious, but is often a source of confusion, is that if you change data on a spreadsheet and the data is used within a formula, then the value of the formula will also change. In complex spreadsheets with several interdependent formulae, a single change in data can lead to a series of changes across the sheet. This is the key advantage of a spreadsheet model in that you can see the effects of changes in data on outcomes. You can therefore explore different options (e.g. increase in price, a change in transport costs).

Error messages

In any mathematical calculation you can make an error, and Microsoft Excel® provides a number of messages to tell you about mistakes. These are:

This occurs when the formula or function produces a number greater than can fit in a cell.

#VALUE   The formula contains a mistake in one of its components (i.e. a cell or mathematical operator).

#DIV0!   This is a common error in that the formula involves division by zero. Often you have not entered a value into a cell which is being used to divide another value. You need to check to ensure all the cells have a value.

#NAME?	A meaningless term is included in the formula.
#N/A	This results from a formula requiring data from a cell which does not contain the information at that moment.
#REF!	The formula has an incorrect cell reference.
#NUM!	The formula contains an incorrect number.
#NULL!	The formula has an incorrect cell reference.

In all cases you need to check that the function is correct, you have specified the correct range of cells and that the cells have had the correct contents entered.

It is critical when constructing formulae that they are perfect. Once a spreadsheet is produced, its results are assumed to be accurate. An error in a formula will often be overlooked. When a formula is initially developed it should be checked carefully to ensure it is correct. An error in a formula may not be noticed once a spreadsheet is in use and its results may have a considerable influence on business decisions.

References

It is critical when using a spreadsheet to be able to specify which parts of the sheet you want to work on. This can be a single cell, which is shown by combining the column letter with row number (e.g. A4), or a groups of cells, which is shown by giving the first and last cells, separated by a colon. When a cell name or a range of cells is inserted into a formula or function it is called a reference. This means the formula or function is referring to the contents of that cell or range of cells. If the content changes, the value of the formula or function changes.

There are three types of reference:

■ relative
■ absolute
■ named.

The relative reference is the normal one you encounter when you use Microsoft Excel®. If you move the cells (e.g. delete or insert rows or columns) then the reference in the formula changes to allow for the new position.

The absolute reference is one which remains unchanged no matter what happens. You create an absolute reference by using the $ symbol (e.g. SUM (A2:A5) is a relative reference, while SUM ($A$2:$A$5) is an absolute reference).

A mixed reference combines both relative and absolute references within the same formula or function (e.g. H5+$G$3).

References are especially important when you copy and paste blocks of your sheet. This is called replication and it automatically changes the relative references to allow for their new position. This is very useful if you want to copy formulae or functions, since they will be accurate in their new places. Replication can save a great deal of checking and changing, which would be needed if you had to undertake it manually.

When you highlight a cell, its reference is shown in the left-hand box of the formula bar. You can employ this reference name box to move to any cell of the sheet by entering its reference in the box and pressing enter.

Using the name box, you can give an individual cell, or group of cells, an individual name. Highlight the cell or area and enter the chosen name into the box and then press the enter key. If you enter this name into the reference box in future, the cell or area will be selected.

The four types of references can be combined in formulae to give you many different options. Named references allow you to specify a particular cell or group of cells within a formula. Relative references allow formulae to be replicated, therefore saving time and avoiding creating errors; while absolute references provide you with the option to use an unchanging reference. You can mix different types of reference to maximise the possibilities to solve particular problems or to meet different needs.

Replication and accuracy

Replication is the spreadsheet function that allows data and formulae to be copied to new areas of the sheet. If a formula employs relative references, the formula will change itself to conform to its new position. When you replicate formulae, sometimes zeros will be added to cells that do not contain any data. It is important to remove them to avoid errors, such as dividing by zero, when the formulae are calculated.

Replication has the advantage of ensuring that the formulae and data are accurately entered, as well as saving time. Numerical accuracy is vital to spreadsheets; in fact, perfection is required. Spreadsheets are concerned with modelling numerical data to predict trends, analyse data and identify outcomes. Organisational decisions will often be based on the spreadsheet analysis, so if the data is incorrect, the outcomes will also be wrong and thus will lead to poor decisions. It is therefore critical to the success of spreadsheets that the data is entered accurately. It is good practice to check data at all stages of entering to ensure it is correct.

References and formulae

The application of relative cell references is not difficult to understand. It obviously helps to copy formulae accurately from one part of a spreadsheet to another. However, absolute cell references are not so obvious. They are useful when you need to include standard values in formulae, so it is important to keep them in a single set of locations. If you were producing a spreadsheet to calculate export prices you might wish to include the exchange rates in a series of cells and then link to them through absolute references. In engineering you are often dealing with mathematical constants (e.g. density of iron), and in statistical calculations there are often constants that need to be used. These could all be placed in cells with absolute references.

Figure 2.11 illustrates formulae that use both absolute and relative references. The formulae have been replicated to show the changes to the relative references. The spreadsheet shows a simple calculation of the price of an export product. The euro exchange rate is located in cell D3.

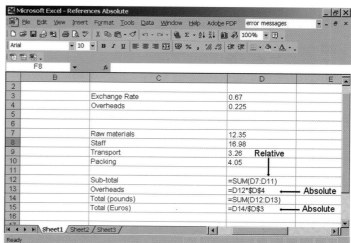

Figure 2.11 Formulae

Overheads are calculated on the basis of 22.5 per cent of the total cost (i.e. the sum of raw materials, staff, transport and packing costs). The cost in pounds is a simple total, while the cost in euros is the cost in pounds divided by the exchange rate.

Figure 2.12 shows the same calculation, but using a named reference instead of an absolute reference, and, once again, it has been replicated to illustrate the changes and the constants. A significant advantage of named references is that you can give them a meaningful

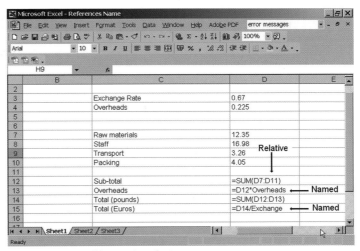

Figure 2.12 Named reference

name. In this example, 'exchange' will have a meaning to the people using the spreadsheet, whereas D3 will not. If it needs to be amended months or years after being created, it will be easier with a name, and the chance of making mistakes will be reduced.

Exercise 9

Entering data and creating formulae

1 Insert your floppy disk into the A: drive.

2 Load Microsoft Excel® using either the All Programs menu or the Excel® icon on the desktop. Open the file Sales Forecast by selecting the File menu, then clicking on the Open option to reveal the Open window. Change the Look in: box to select the floppy disk and the file name will appear in the work area. Double-click Sales Forecast or single-click it and then click the Open button. The spreadsheet will open in Microsoft Excel®.

3 Enter the data shown below.

Item	January	February	March	April	May	June	July	August	September	October	November	December
Hand Tools	12000	13500	12120	9890	10675	10950	11500	10125	10975	11100	10760	15600
Power Tools	32000	27540	27895	26450	26860	27125	27450	26875	24800	25230	25780	37800
Wood	15000	14760	13890	12300	12860	13200	12900	11500	11800	12700	13500	13250
Metal	2300	2150	1980	1875	2050	2300	1550	1250	2300	2100	2050	1950
Fastenings	4750	5050	4430	3675	3980	4100	3500	3250	3300	3400	3050	3100
Paint	17800	18230	16760	16980	19870	22345	20125	16500	17900	19500	18500	17500
Wallpaper	22900	23175	22980	21870	20760	19650	18900	17500	17900	19850	20300	23500
Electrical	14500	16800	15120	13870	14320	13760	13750	14100	13575	13900	14500	16750
Garden	2100	1900	2700	4500	5500	5700	7800	4600	3800	2800	1450	1900
Kitchen	3300	3760	3580	4125	4580	4875	5120	4980	4570	3900	4300	6700
Garage	7900	8800	5780	6750	6890	7200	7500	8000	6875	6800	6500	9100

4 Carefully check the accuracy of your data, since you are going to depend on it once you begin to calculate trends and other useful information. The validity of the calculations is totally dependent on the initial correctness of the data. It is worth spending a lot of time checking the entries.

5 Save your sheet by selecting the File menu and clicking on the Save option. It is good practice to save your work every few minutes.

6 You are going to total each monthly column and each item row. There are several ways of doing this, but the most straightforward involves using the AutoSum function on the Standard toolbar. Highlight the column from cell C7 to C18 and then click on the AutoSum icon on the toolbar and you will see the total of the column appear, 134,550. Click elsewhere in the sheet to remove the highlighting, and then on the total, and you will see the formula appear on the formula toolbar, =SUM(C7:C17).

7 Once you have successfully produced the total for the January column, you can replicate it to the other columns. Highlight C18, select the Edit menu and click on the Copy option, then Paste the contents to D18. If you highlight D18 you will see the formula =SUM(D7:D17). This shows you that in copying the formula the references have been changed to fit the new position. This is called replication and the references are relative. Repeat this process for the remaining columns.

8 Now total the first row (Hand Tools) by highlighting from C7 to O7 and clicking on the AutoSum icon on the Standard toolbar. This will produce the total 139,195 and the formula =SUM(C7:N7). If you highlight cell O7, you will see the formula appear on the toolbar. Edit the formula to make the references absolute =SUM($C$7:$N$7). Replicate (copy) this formula to cell O8 and you will notice that the new total is still 139,195 and the formula remains =SUM($C$7:$N$7). The absolute references are not changed by replication. Now use Undo to remove the formula and the changes that made the cell O7 formula absolute.

9 Replicate the formula =SUM(C7:N7) to O8 and the other rows. Total for Power Tools is 335,805 and formula =SUM(C8:N8).

10 Check the formulae are all correct and then save your sheet by selecting the File menu and clicking on the Save option.

11 Now total all the columns in cell O18 – the total is 1534975. If ####### appears it means that the number is too large to be shown in that cell. The formula is =SUM(C18:N18). Insert the name Total in B18 and O5.

12 Print your sheet by selecting the File menu and Print Preview. Figure 2.13 shows the appearance of the printout. It shows that the gridlines are missing and that some of the spreadsheet is absent. This is because it will be printed on a second sheet – Preview: Page 1 of 2 at left-hand bottom corner of figure 2.13.

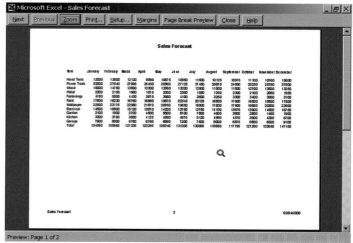

Figure 2.13 Print preview

13 To add the gridlines you need to select the Setup button in the print preview window to reveal the Page Setup window. Select the Sheet tab and click in the Gridlines and Row and column headings boxes so ticks appear. Click on the OK button when you are are finished and you will see the window disappear and a new print preview appear, showing gridlines and headings (figure 2.14). When you want to print the sheet,

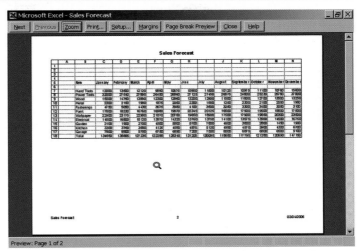

Figure 2.14 Print preview – Gridlines and headings

click on the Print button. To remove the options, repeat the actions and click in the ticked boxes to see the ticks disappear.

14 Print the sheet without gridlines or row and column headings, and then with them.

15 Save your sheet by selecting the File menu and clicking on the Save option.

16 Close Microsoft Excel® by selecting the File menu item and clicking on the Exit option or by clicking on the Close button in the top right-hand corner of the application window.

Printing

You can also print parts of a spreadsheet rather than the whole sheet by highlighting the section you require, selecting the File menu and the Print option. This will reveal the Print window. In the window is a section called Print what, with three options:

- Selection – print areas that are highlighted
- Active sheet(s) – print all the selected sheets
- Entire workbook – print all the sheets within the workbook.

Selection is a useful option if you are seeking to show changes and their effects.

There is a Preview button at the bottom of the Print window with which you can reveal the print preview and access the Page Setup to allow you to print gridlines and row and column headings. You can print the selection or whole sheet by clicking on the Print button in the preview window or by clicking the OK button in the Print window.

The printouts you have considered so far have shown the actual values of calculations. It is also useful to print out the sheet showing the formulae that are being used. This serves several purposes, not least that it is easier to check the accuracy of the formulae on a printout than on the screen.

To print the formulae you must select the Tools menu and the Options option. This will reveal the Options window (figure 2.15). In the View tab is a section called Window options. You can select to print the formulae by clicking in the Formulas box. This is also an alternative way of selecting Gridlines and Row & column headers. When you have made your choices, click on the OK button to enact them.

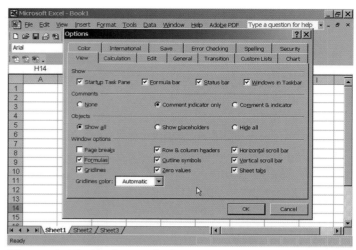

Figure 2.15 Options window

The formulae are now shown instead of their values, and if you select the Print Preview option you will see the spreadsheet showing them. It is useful when printing formulae also to print the row and column headers, since these allow you to interpret the references within the formulae.

Changing format

The Formatting toolbar (figure 2.16) provides a variety of tools to enhance the format of your spreadsheet. They all operate in a similar way. You highlight the cell or cells you need to change and select the appropriate tool from the toolbar. You can:

- change the font
- alter the character size
- embolden the entry
- change to italics
- underline the entry
- align the contents to the left, right or centre
- present the numbers as currency (e.g. £100,000.00)
- present the numbers as a percentage (e.g. 10000000%)
- present the numbers in a comma style (e.g. 100,000.00)
- increase or decrease the number of decimal places (e.g. 100,000 increased by two places becomes 100,000.00)

Spreadsheets are heavily concerned with numerical data and provide you with a variety of ways of formatting data (e.g. percentage, date, time, negative, currency, scientific and general). To select a particular format, you must initially highlight the cell or cells you want to change and then

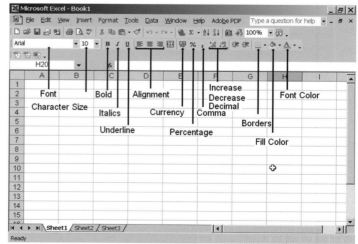

Figure 2.16 Formatting toolbar

select the specific icon from the toolbar. Formats are important since formulae will be designed to calculate values based on the format of the data. An important issue is that the format will control the appearance of the cell contents, but does not change their actual values, which are used in calculations.

For example, if a format has been chosen that limits decimal places to two, then 12.346 will be presented as 12.35, while when it is part of a calculation its actual value will be used, so that if the cell is multiplied by 10 its presented and actual value will be 123.46. However, this will appear to be wrong since 12.35 multiplied by 10 equals 123.50. This confuses many spreadsheet users.

If you enter a date or time in the correct way, Microsoft Excel® recognises it automatically as a date or time. Date formats that Microsoft Excel® accepts are shown by selecting the Format menu and the Cells option to reveal the Format Cells window. For example: 12-hour clock – 3.00pm; 24-hour clock – 15.00. In the Number tab, the Date and Time options show a list of accepted formats (e.g.12/12/2002 or 12 December 2002). Microsoft Excel® treats time as a number, so it is important to enter it correctly. Time can be entered in a 12- or 24-hour format. If you enter a 12-hour number, it must be followed by an 'a' or a 'p' to show if it is a.m. or p.m., respectively.

Microsoft Excel® can calculate time if the data is entered correctly. Date and times can be entered in a single cell providing they are separated by a space.

Borders

The appearance of a spreadsheet can be important in persuading people (e.g. senior managers) to accept its value as a useful business tool. To enhance the spreadsheet's appearance you have a variety of tools, including the Borders tool, with which you can enclose an individual cell, a selection of cells or the whole sheet within a border. Figure 2.17 shows the Borders tool options, available within the Formatting toolbar. When the icon is clicked, a small window of options appears. By clicking on an option you will add it to the cell, selection or whole sheet that you have highlighted.

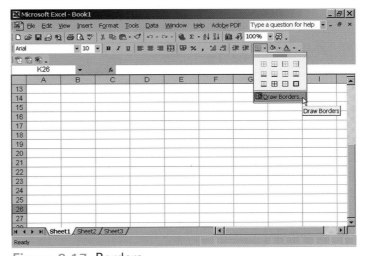

Figure 2.17 Borders

Exercise 10

Enhancing the spreadsheet

1 Insert your floppy disk into the A: drive.

2 Load Microsoft Excel® using either the All Programs menu or the Excel® icon on the desktop. Open the file Sales Forecast by selecting the File menu, clicking on the Open option to reveal the Open window. Change the Look in: box to select the floppy disk and the file name will appear in the work area. Double-click Sales Forecast or single-click it and then click the Open button. The spreadsheet will open in Microsoft Excel®.

3 You can insert additional rows and columns. Click on the row 4 heading and you will see the entire row is highlighted. Click on the Insert menu and select the Rows option. A new row will be inserted and the spreadsheet will change.

4 Now change the character size of the columns headings (e.g. January, February) to 14, centred and embolden them. Highlight the cells and click on the Formatting toolbar options required. You will notice that they change in size and are too large for the column widths. Adjust the widths so that the headings are visible (i.e. January, February, August, September, October, November and December).

5 Now change the character size of the row headings (Items, Hand Tools, etc.) to 14 and embolden them. You will notice that they change in size and are too large for the column width. Adjust the width so that the headings are visible.

6 Now change the total row and column to currency (e.g. £ 100,000.00). Again, the change may be too large for the column width and you will need to make changes.

7 Now change the data by centring all the figures except the totals.

8 Save your sheet by selecting the File menu and clicking on the Save option. Figure 2.18 shows the appearance of the spreadsheet.

9 You are now going to calculate the monthly average for each item. In cell P8 insert =Average(C8:N8) – that is, the Average function and the range C8:N8, which are the monthly figures for Hand Tools. When you are finished, click elsewhere on the sheet to see the formula enacted. You should see the value appear.

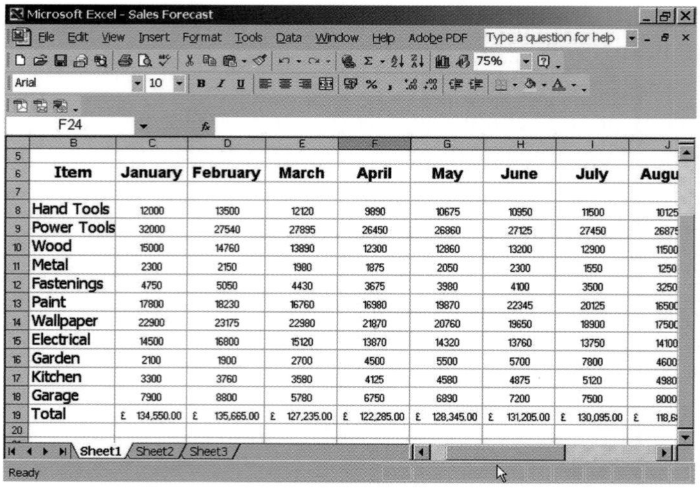

	B	C	D	E	F	G	H	I	J
5									
6	Item	January	February	March	April	May	June	July	Augu
7									
8	Hand Tools	12000	13500	12120	9890	10675	10950	11500	10125
9	Power Tools	32000	27540	27895	26450	26860	27125	27450	2687
10	Wood	15000	14760	13890	12300	12860	13200	12900	11500
11	Metal	2300	2150	1980	1875	2050	2300	1550	1250
12	Fastenings	4750	5050	4430	3675	3980	4100	3500	3250
13	Paint	17800	18230	16760	16980	19870	22345	20125	16500
14	Wallpaper	22900	23175	22980	21870	20760	19650	18900	17500
15	Electrical	14500	16800	15120	13870	14320	13760	13750	14100
16	Garden	2100	1900	2700	4500	5500	5700	7800	4600
17	Kitchen	3300	3760	3580	4125	4580	4875	5120	4980
18	Garage	7900	8800	5780	6750	6890	7200	7500	8000
19	Total	£ 134,550.00	£ 135,665.00	£ 127,235.00	£ 122,285.00	£ 128,345.00	£ 131,205.00	£ 130,095.00	£ 118,6
20									

Figure 2.18 Enhancing spreadsheet

10 Replicate the formula for the other items and change their format to currency. You will need to change the column width to ensure everything is visible. In P6 enter the heading Average in character size 14 and embolden.

11 Print the whole spreadsheet, first showing the actual values of the calculations (using the File menu and the Print option), and then showing the formulae in full, using the Tools menu, Options option, View tab and Formulas box.

12 Highlight the headings across the top of your sheet (i.e. row 6). Select the border icon on the toolbar and click on the All Borders option (if you place your pointer over the options they will be named) and the row will be enclosed in a border.

13 Save your sheet by selecting the File menu and clicking on the Save option.

14 Print using the Selection option in the Print window, the headings enclosed in their border to show the changes you have made. You will need to highlight the headings.

15 An important thing to consider with any spreadsheet is the effect of changing some of the assumptions. If in our spreadsheet we decide to have a marketing campaign on selected products at Christmas, how would that impact on our national averages? Our public relations company has suggested the following new sales figures for December:

Power Tools: 65,000

Electrical: 38,000

Kitchen: 18,500

Enter these new values in the spreadsheet and see the averages and totals change. Are the changes significant? You could consider other predicted amounts. You might want to be more or less optimistic than the public relations company. When you enter the new data and click elsewhere, you should see the Calculated values updated. If this does not happen, click on the equals sign on the Formula taskbar and on the OK button in the window that appears. This will recalculate the formulae.

16 Print the outcomes of your changes, using the Selection option in the Print window. You will need to highlight the new sales figures for December and the new averages and totals.

17 Close Microsoft Excel® by selecting the File menu item and clicking on the Exit option or by clicking on the Close button in the top right-hand corner of the application window.

Hiding rows and columns

Within the Format menu are a number of functions which operate on cells, rows, columns and sheet. The Row and Column options reveal options to change the width of a column or the height of a row and to hide or unhide rows or columns.

It may not seem sensible to hide a row or column, but it is useful if, say, you want to show a customer the costs of a project without revealing confidential information.

Column widths

In earlier exercises you have adjusted the width of columns by using the mouse pointer to drag them. However, Microsoft Excel® provides you with the means to set exact column widths. To set widths, select the Format menu and click on Column to reveal a sub-menu with the option Width. Clicking on the Width option reveals the Column Width window. To change widths, enter a figure and then click the OK button. The function operates on the column or area of the sheet you have highlighted.

Orientation of text

When you enter text into a spreadsheet it is normally left-justified. To change its orientation, select the Format menu and click on the Cells option to reveal the Format Cells window (figure 2.19). The Alignment tab provides options to:

- align the text both horizontally and vertically (the options are available by clicking on the down arrow buttons at the end of the boxes)
- Wrap text – this allows you to enter multiple lines of text in a cell
- Shrink to fit – this reduces the size of text so that it fits into a cell
- Merge cells – this turns two or more cells in a single larger cell
- change the angle of orientation of the text (i.e. slope the text).

These functions work in the normal way (i.e. highlight your chosen cells and choose the desired options).

The other tabs provide extra functions. The Border tab provides an alternative way of selecting borders. The Number tab allows you to select the format of the figures, and the Font tab to choose different fonts, character sizes and the other functions available on the toolbar.

It is important to align spreadsheet data (columns of figures are normally shown perfectly aligned) so that readers can understand the information presented. Even small differences in the alignment can make

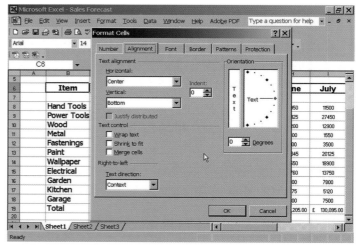

Figure 2.19 Format Cells window – Alignment tab

it difficult to understand a sheet of numbers. Often, important organisational decisions are based on spreadsheet analysis (e.g. signing contracts, setting prices, agreeing pay rises) – part of the decision is influenced by being persuaded that the information is accurate. This is certainly affected by the presentation. If a sheet is a mess it will not persuade managers to take key decisions. One that presents a quality image will help managers to accept the information it is offering. Microsoft Excel® provides the means to align data both vertically and horizontally so that you can produce high quality presentations.

Another useful device that is offered within the Format Cells window is the ability to merge cells. This is helpful when you want a title or label to cover more than one column or row.

Again, this is useful to develop a quality presentation of your information. The importance of a quality product should not be underestimated.

Sorting data

There are occasions when you want to sort your data into order, and Microsoft Excel® provides a straightforward way of sorting a column of data into either ascending or descending order. This function also operates on text, whereby the list is sorted alphabetically.

The sort functions are available on the Data menu or the Standard toolbar. The Sort functions on the toolbar allow you to sort on one column, while the function available from the Data menu enables you to sort on

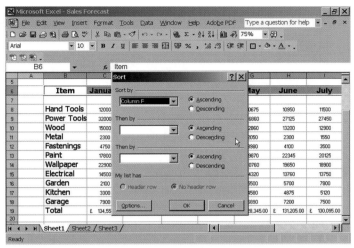

Figure 2.20 Sort window

more than one column of data. Select the Data menu and click on the Sort option to reveal the Sort window (figure 2.20). You can then select a series of columns to sort by and choose either ascending or descending order.

Autofilter

Filtering lets you focus only on items that meet a set criteria. With Microsoft Excel® you can filter a list to show only the rows that meet the criteria (e.g. a spreadsheet of employees could be filtered to show only staff employed in a particular team). One of the options in the Data menu is Filter. If this is highlighted, a new menu appears with the option AutoFilter. To use AutoFilter, make sure that the pointer is within the sheet (i.e. a cell is highlighted). When you select the option AutoFilter you will see that a button with a down-pointing arrow is added to top row of your spreadsheet (figure 2.21). If you select the down arrow button you will see a list of the unique items in the column (figure 2.21). If you choose an item, all the other rows

that do not match the item will be hidden. You have filtered the list to show only the items you wish to study.

The dropdown list also offers three other options:

- All – essentially, this removes the filter and shows the whole sheet of information.

- Top 10 – this allows you to filter against some numeric factor, such as the 6 products with the lowest value of sales or the 5 items with the highest profit. Top 10 is just a

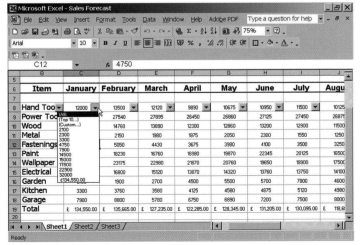

Figure 2.21 AutoFilter

name; it does not limit you to 10 items. When you select Top 10, a window appears enabling you to select the top or bottom, the number of items and items or per cent.

- Custom – this allows more complex filtering to be used.

Tracking changes

In many organisations, people work in teams and a spreadsheet may be used by a variety of people. A very useful feature of Microsoft Excel® and other modern spreadsheets is the ability to show changes that have been made. This is available by selecting the Tools menu, the Track Changes option and the Highlight Changes option, which, when clicked, will open the Highlight Changes window (figure 2.22).

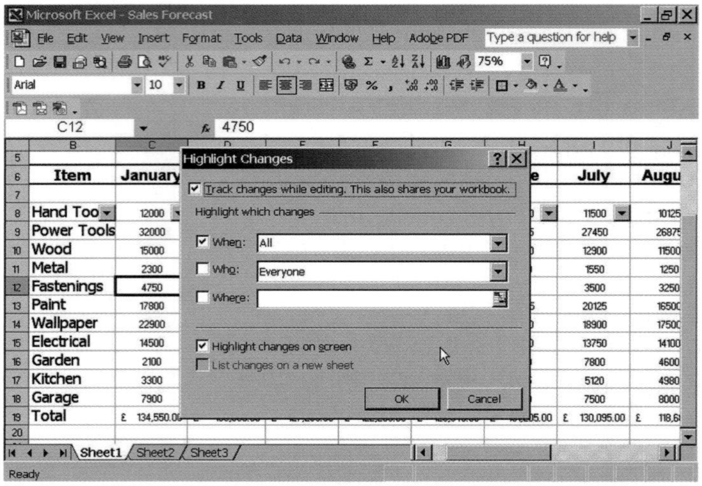

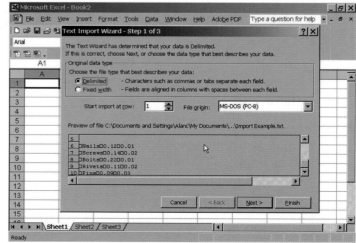

Figure 2.22 Highlight Changes window

You select the options by clicking in the boxes and a tick appears. When you then edit the spreadsheet, the changes are shown by the cells being enclosed by a coloured border. If the spreadsheet is printed, the changes are also shown.

Importing files

There are several ways of importing or opening information/data from other applications within Microsoft Excel®. The most straightforward is to use the Copy and Paste functions, which are available in all Microsoft Office® applications. An alternative is to use the Open option within the File menu. The file types which can be imported into Microsoft Excel® are shown in the Files of type box. It is often puzzling when you see files in a range of types. The type depends on the application software used to create it. This determines its purpose and what it is compatible with. Some generic file formats are designed to allow the file to be opened by a wide range of applications. An example of this is a text file shown by the extension .txt. The file

you want to import is located using the Look in: box to identify the floppy disk, hard drive or folder. The files and folders are shown in the work area and are selected by either highlighting the file with a single click and then clicking on the Open button, or by double-clicking on the file.

The chosen file then needs to be converted into Microsoft Excel® format. To undertake this task, you are helped by a Microsoft Excel® Wizard, shown in figures 2.23, 2.24 and 2.25. The Wizard opens automatically when

Figure 2.23 Wizard Step 1

you try to import a file. If the file you have selected is not one of those that Microsoft Excel® can import, you will see an error message appear. This will say that the file format is not valid. A valid file will open the Wizard, but you may have to select the correct file in the Files of type box for the file you are importing.

Figure 2.23 shows the initial Wizard window, and this asks you to select if the file you are importing is delimited or fixed column width. The file can be seen in the scroll box for you to check. A delimited file is one in which the data is separated by commas or tabs, while a fixed width is one where the data is aligned into columns. When you have made your selection, click on the Next button to move to step 2 of the Wizard (figure 2.24).

Figure 2.24 illustrates how you define the delimiter used if your file is of this type. Click on the Next button when you have finished. Step 3 (the final step) of the Wizard gives you the opportunity to adjust the type of each column (figure 2.25).

By using the scroll box you can see the changes to the data and check how it will appear in a spreadsheet.

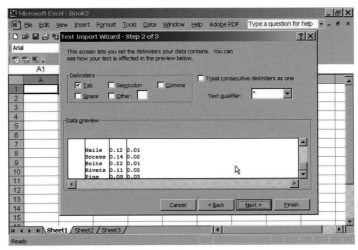

Figure 2.24 Wizard Step 2

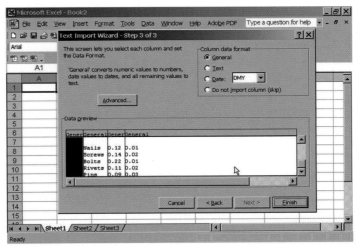

Figure 2.25 Wizard Step 3

Exercise 11

Importing data

1 Insert your floppy disk into the A: drive.

2 Create a data file (figure 2.26) using the Notepad application (Start, All Programs, Accessories and Notepad). Use the tab key to position the information in Notepad (i.e. one tab, enter Item, one tab, enter Cost, etc.). Save the file as Import Data on your floppy disk. It will appear as Import

Import Data - Notepad

File Edit Format View Help

This is a test file to demonstrate importing data into Microsoft Excel.

Item	Cost	Profit
Pens	0.17	0.04
Pencils	0.08	0.03
Ink	0.05	0.01
Refills	0.24	0.07
Staples	0.14	0.04

Figure 2.26 Notepad

Data.txt to show it is a text file. (In the CLAiT Plus assessment you will be provided with data files to import and you will not need to create them. The file is also available from the Hodder Education website – www.hodderclait.co.uk).

3 Load Microsoft Excel® using either the All Programs menu or the Excel® icon on the desktop.

4 Select the File menu and the Open option. Change the Look in: box to choose floppy disk and you should see your files. If you do not, then it is likely that you need to change the Files of type box to read Text Files or All Files. Double-click on Import Data.txt file and the Wizard Step 1 will appear (figure 2.27). The file is delimited, so click on the Next button. Figure 2.28 shows the appearance of the data in Wizard Step 2.

5 If the data is not laid out correctly you will need to adjust its presentation by using the different delimiters. Experiment with different combinations if you do not know what was used. The best is a combination of tab and space, but you may find it is either space or tab on its own if this was the way the file was created. Figure 2.28 shows you the Wizard view of the data once the correct delimiters were selected. In this example, this should be produced automatically.

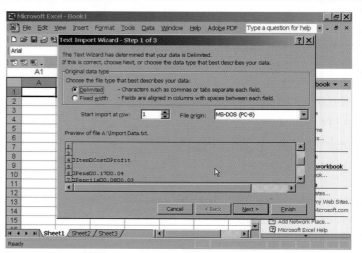

Figure 2.27 Wizard Step 1

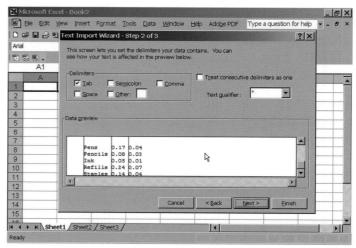

Figure 2.28 Correct delimiters selected

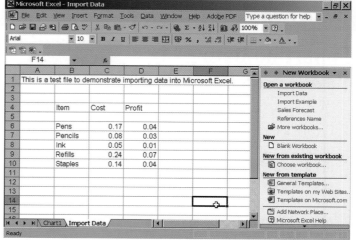

Figure 2.29 Imported data in Microsoft Excel®

continued

6 Click on **Next** in Wizard Step 3 to import the file into the spreadsheet. Figure 2.29 shows the result of importing the file. The process is complex, so you may need to practise this operation several times. Create new files of test data using different delimiters and experiment with the method until you are confident that you can import a data file.

7 Close Microsoft Excel® by selecting the **File** menu item and clicking on the **Exit** option, or by clicking on the **Close** button in the top right-hand corner of the application window.

House styles

In many organisations, spreadsheets are used by large numbers of staff. In order to ensure the quality of their presentation and use, many organisations have produced standards which are called house styles. Microsoft Excel® provides the means of establishing styles using the **Format** menu and the **Style** option.

This allows you to set a style covering factors such as:

- number formats
- fonts
- alignment
- borders
- patterns
- protection.

When you select the **Format** menu and click on the **Style** option, you open the Style window. This is shown in figure 2.30. If you click on the **Modify** button, the Format Cell window is opened, which allows you to choose different formats for your style.

A new style is applied by highlighting the spreadsheet, selecting the style and clicking the **OK** button. There is obviously an alternative way of applying a house style, which is simply to follow the standard as you create the spreadsheet, or amend each element, one by one. Creating a style helps you automate the process and reduce the potential for errors.

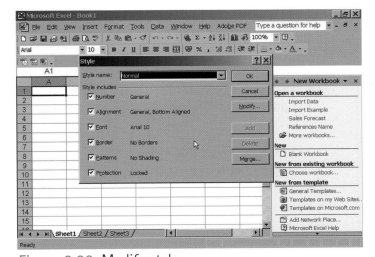

Figure 2.30 Modify style

Linking spreadsheets

In many cases, you will have a number of interrelated spreadsheets dealing with the same area of work. You may need one sheet showing the manufacturing costs, one showing transport costs and one indicating the costs of staff. If you study each of these separately, you will obviously benefit in that you can take more informed decisions. However, each of these areas depends on the others. Ideally, they should be linked directly so that a change in one will have immediate effects on the others. In this way you can see the consequences of any change.

The linked data can be included in formulae so that it can be used to solve problems, identify trends or any of the many other uses of formulae. In Exercise 12 you will link two sheets. The link is between a cell in which a formula has totalled a column of figures to a cell in another sheet. This cell, in turn, is part of a column which is totalled by a formula. This ability to include links into formulae is very useful in developing more complex relationships within spreadsheets.

Exercise 12

Linking spreadsheets

1 Insert a floppy disk into the A: drive.

2 Load Microsoft Excel® using either the All Programs menu or the Excel® icon on the desktop.

3 Set the orientation of the sheet to portrait, margins to 3 cm – right and left, and 2 cm – top and bottom, and header and footer to 1.5 cm (select File menu and Page Setup option).

4 Enter the spreadsheet shown in Figure 2.31. Use the SUM function to total rows and columns. This spreadsheet shows the costs of each factory in January.

5 Select the File menu and click on the option Save to reveal the Save As window. Change the Save in: box to select the floppy disk and add the file name First in the File name box. Click on the Save button. The top line of Microsoft Excel® will change to read 'Microsoft Excel® – First'.

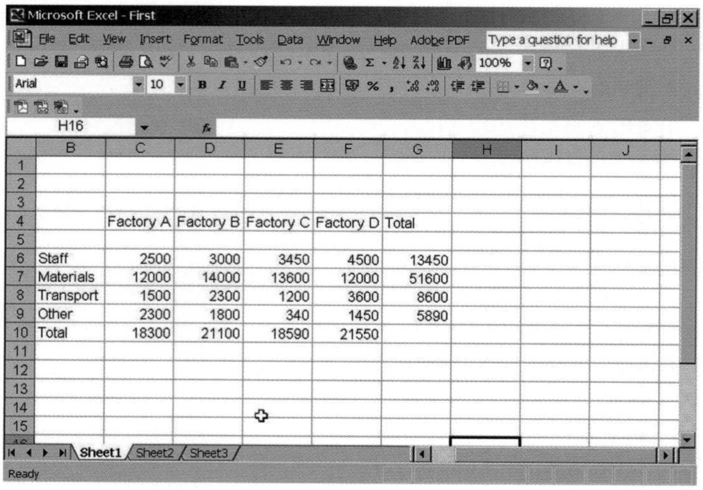

6 Select the File menu and click on the New option to reveal the New Workbook task pane window on the right of the work area (if this pane is already open then nothing will change). Select the Blank workbook option in the

Figure 2.31 First spreadsheet

New Workbook pane and click on the OK button. A new blank spreadsheet will appear. Enter the spreadsheet shown in figure 2.32. Use the SUM function to total rows and columns. This spreadsheet represents the staff costs of each factory.

7 Select the File menu and click on the option Save to reveal the Save As window. Change the Save in: box to select the floppy disk and add the file name Second in the File name box. Click on the Save button. The top line of Microsoft Excel® will change to read 'Microsoft Excel® – Second'.

8 Inspection of the two spreadsheets shows that cell C6 of First should equal cell C11 of Second (i.e. staff costs of Factory A in January). You could transfer the information manually, of course, but it is very straightforward to link the two cells.

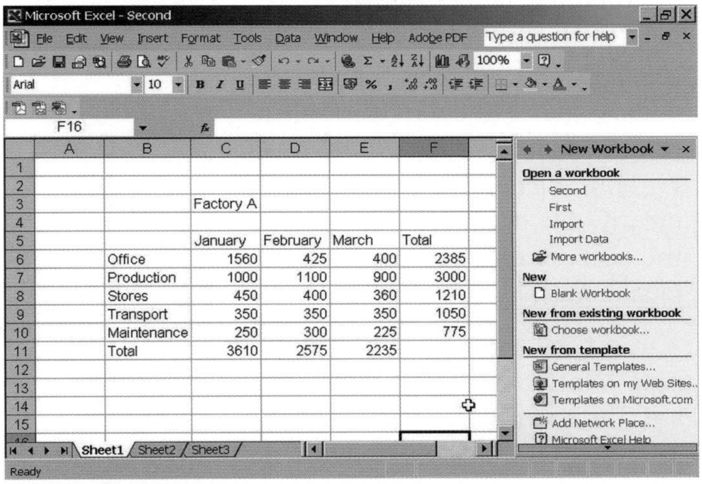

9 In cell C6 of First spreadsheet insert = [Second.xls]sheet 1!C11. To make the new formula calculate, click the mouse away from the formula. You will see value change to 2610. Change the values in Second and see how the link operates.

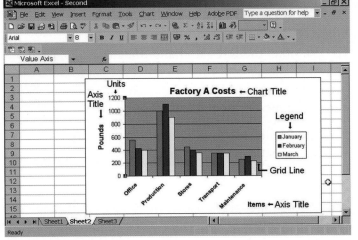

Figure 2.32 Second spreadsheet

10 To link two cells you simply enter the workbook name, sheet number, an exclamation mark and the cell reference. Practise making more links between the worksheets until you are satisfied that you understand the process.

11 Save the spreadsheets as Link.

12 Close Microsoft Excel® by selecting the File menu item and clicking on the Exit option or by clicking on the Close button in the top right-hand corner of the application window.

Graphs and charts

Often numbers are more easily understood if presented in a visual form. Microsoft Excel® provides the means of converting data into a graph or chart. Figure 2.33 illustrates a chart and shows the different labels that can be applied to it.

The main chart or graph labels are:

- Title – this is optional in a Microsoft Excel® chart or graph and provides a name for the chart. The title should relate to the content of the chart or graph.

- Axis titles – these identify the units that measure the chart or graph.

Figure 2.33 Chart

- Labels – these are used to identify the different elements in a chart or graph (eg. label the slices of a pie chart).
- Legend – this provides the key to understanding the data series (e.g. colour coding in a bar chart). Without a legend to correctly identify the displayed data series, the chart or graph is effectively meaningless.

You can set the chart or graph labels by using Microsoft Excel®'s Chart Wizard. The exercises in this chapter will help you to understand how to do this. The main types of charts and graphs are:

- pie charts
- bar/column charts
- line graph charts
- XY scatter graphs.

You can also present information by combining line graphs with column charts.

Figure 2.34 shows the Chart Wizard for Pie charts, which is obtained by selecting the appropriate data in your spreadsheet, then the Insert menu and clicking on the Chart option to reveal the Chart Wizard.

Pie charts are a very effective means of visually presenting a set of values. There is, however, more than one type. For example, the left-hand and middle charts in the second row of choices are exploding and three-dimensional exploding pie charts (figure 2.34).

Figure 2.33 illustrates a column chart; figure 2.35 shows a bar chart; figure 2.36 illustrates a line graph; and figure 2.37 shows a scatter graph. A bar or column chart is useful in comparing a range of results side by side (e.g. rainfall for different months of the year), while a line graph is used to show the relationship between two variables (e.g. how income changes over a period of time).

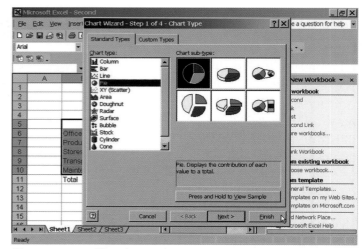

Figure 2.34 Pie charts

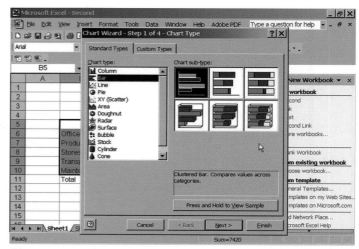

Figure 2.35 Bar chart

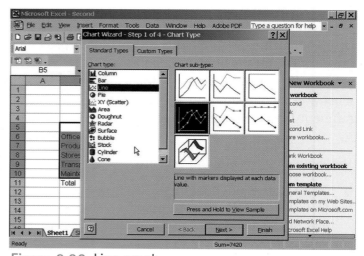

Figure 2.36 Line graph

A scatter graph presents two sets of variable data compared to each other. Often they do not show an obvious relationship, in that, as the name suggests, the data points are scattered over an area. However, it is possible to draw a line through the points to illustrate the trend of the variables against each other.

Selecting data sets

The charts and graphs that you create depend on the data you select to base them on. You are free to select a

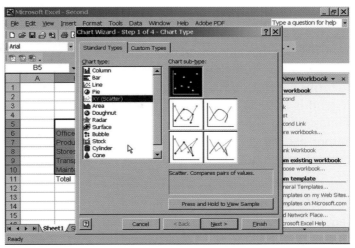

Figure 2.37 Scatter graph

whole spreadsheet, a subset of the data or data from non-adjacent areas. To select data you need to highlight it. If you click in the top left-hand corner of the data you want to select, and hold down the mouse button, you can drag the mouse to the bottom right corner of the data. The subset of data is highlighted when you release the mouse button.

In order to select data from non-adjacent areas you need to highlight the first area using the method described above, and then hold down the Ctrl key while repeating the highlighting operation on the second area. Both areas will be highlighted.

An alternative way of selecting data is to import it from another application. There are several ways of importing or opening information/data from within Microsoft Excel®. The most straightforward is to use the Copy and Paste functions if you are importing data from another Microsoft Office® application. An alternative is to use the Open option within the File menu to reveal the Open window. Microsoft Excel® can import files in a variety of formats. The file format depends on the application that was used to create it. The compatible formats are shown in the Files of type box in the Open window. The file you want to import is located using the Look in: box to identify the floppy disk, drive or folder. The files and folders are shown in the work area and are selected by either highlighting the file with a single click and then clicking on the Open button, or by double-clicking on the file. The chosen file needs to be converted into Microsoft Excel® format. To undertake this task you are helped by a Microsoft

Excel® Wizard, which opens automatically when you import a file. The use of the Wizard was explained earlier in this chapter (see page 64).

Earlier (Exercise 8) you created a spreadsheet called Sales Forecast. You are going to use this information to practise choosing different data sets and creating charts.

Setting parameters

What makes a chart or graph meaningful are the titles, data labels,

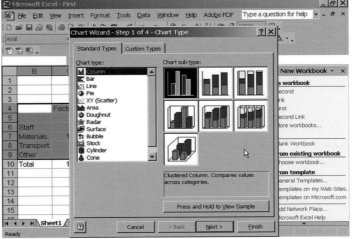

Figure 2.38 Chart Wizard Step 1

legend and units that you employ. The legend is particularly important in that it is specifically intended to provide a key to the colours used to identify different data series. If a legend is missing or incorrect, it is almost impossible to understand. It is rather like showing in black and white a chart which uses colour coding.

The Chart Wizard allows you to enter the title and position, show the legend and select data labels. The initial step in using the Wizard is to select the data set and then the Insert menu and click on the Chart option. This opens the Chart Wizard. Figure 2.38 shows Step 1 of 4 of the Wizard, in which you select the type of chart or graph you want to create. By clicking on the Next button you move to Step 2, and, subsequently, to Steps 3 and 4. In several of the steps there are tabs which provide access to other functions. In Step 2 (figure 2.39) the Series tab allows you to name, add and remove different data series. The data series can be added or removed and named in the bottom half of the window in the Titles area.

In Step 3 (figure 2.40) of the Wizard you are provided with a series of tabbed windows which provide access to different functions. The Titles tab allows you to give the chart or graph a title, as well as naming the axis.

If you click on the Legend tab, you reveal a window which allows you to show or remove the legend and also to select where to position it (i.e. Bottom, Corner, Top, Right and Left) by clicking on the various checkboxes and radio buttons.

If you click on the Data Labels tab,

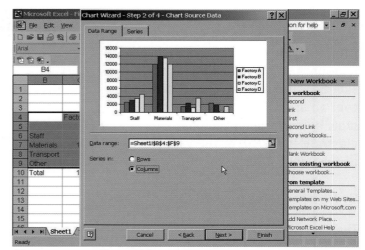

Figure 2.39 Chart Wizard Step 2

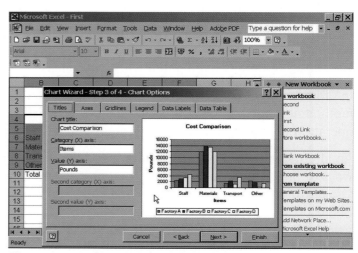

Figure 2.40 Chart Wizard Step 3

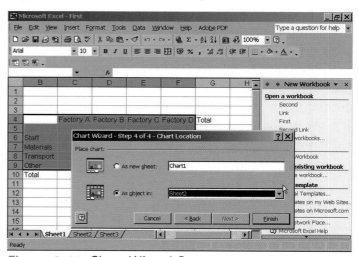

Figure 2.41 Chart Wizard Step 4

you reveal a window which enables you to choose not to apply data labels or to choose between different types of label (e.g. names or values). When you have finished then you can move to step 4 (figure 2.41). This offers you the choice of combining your chart or graph with the associated data or presenting it on a separate sheet.

Exercise 13

Creating an exploding pie chart

1 Insert your floppy disk which contains the Sales Forecast file into the A: drive.

2 Load Microsoft Excel® using either the All Programs menu or the Excel® icon on the desktop. Open the Sales Forecast file by selecting the File menu and clicking on the Open option to reveal the Open window. Change the Look in: box to select the floppy disk and the file name will appear in the work area. Double-click Sales Forecast or single-click it and then click the OK button. The spreadsheet will open in Microsoft Excel®. If you have saved the spreadsheet with the AutoFilter on, you will need to switch it off to avoid obscuring the data (Data menu, highlight Filter and select AutoFilter to remove tick).

3 Highlight the first two columns (i.e. Items and January), excluding the Total row. Select the Insert menu and the Chart option. Click on the Pie chart option and either the two- or three-dimensional exploding items (i.e. the left-hand or middle options of the second row). Check the chart by clicking and holding down the mouse button on the Press and Hold to View Sample button. This allows you to see the chart. Release and click on the next button to move to step 2 of the Chart Wizard (figure 2.42).

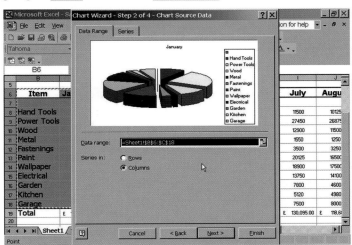

Figure 2.42 Pie Chart Wizard Step 2

4 Consider the data range =sheet1!$B$6:$C$18, which translates to the area in the top left-hand corner, cell B6 to cell C18. The chart shows a blank item in the legend above Hand Tools. This corresponds to the blank row 7, so change the range to B8 to C18 (i.e. =sheet1!$B$8:$C$18), by clicking, deleting and entering new values.

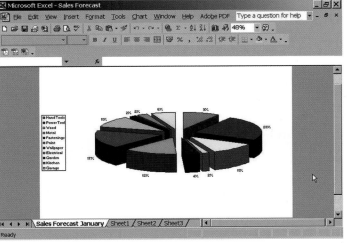

Figure 2.43 Sales Forecast January chart

5 Click on the Next button to reveal Step 3.

6 Click on the FileTitles tab and enter Sales Forecast January. Click on the Legend tab and select left. Click on the Data Labels tab and select the Percentage option. Click on the Next button to reveal step 4.

continued

7 Click on the `As new sheet` option and enter Sales Forecast January. Click on the `Finish` button. The exploding pie chart will appear (figure 2.43) on a new sheet linked to your Sales Forecast Data. If you place your mouse pointer on any of the segments of the pie chart you will see an explanation of what the data represents (e.g. Series 1 "Wood" Value 15,000 11%). Take a moment to consider the image and notice how a three-dimensional exploding pie chart is a powerful representation of the data. The size of each segment is shown in relation to the others so that its value is emphasised.

8 Save your chart by selecting the `File` menu and the `Save As` option to reveal the Save As window. Save your file as Sales Forecast January on your floppy disk.

9 Close Microsoft Excel® by selecting the `File` menu item and clicking on the `Exit` option or by clicking on the `Close` button in the top right-hand corner of the application window.

Rows and columns presentation

In step 2 of the Chart Wizard (figure 2.39) are two options, `Rows` and `Columns`. These options change the presentation of the chart. Figure 2.44 shows the same chart in row presentation. In Column presentation the bars reflect the column values of January, February and March, while the axis shows the row items. In Rows presentation the bars reflect the row values while the axis shows the column items (i.e. the bars are grouped by month).

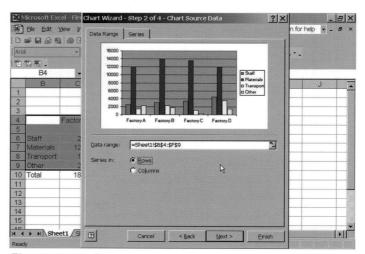

Figure 2.44 Rows presentation

Exercise 14

Selecting data sets

1 Insert your floppy disk into the A: drive.

2 Load Microsoft Excel® using either the `All Programs` menu or the `Excel®` icon on the desktop. Open the file Sales Forecast January by selecting the `File` menu and clicking on the `Open` option to reveal the Open window. Change the `Look in:` box to select the floppy disk and the file name will appear in the work area. Double-click on the Sales Forecast January or single-click it and then click the `OK` button. Select `Sheet 1` to reveal the spreadsheet data.

3 You are going to produce a bar chart for three months of data to compare the different results. Highlight the columns Item, January, February and March, excluding the Total row.

4 Select the Insert menu and the Chart option. Click on the Column chart. Notice that in Chart Wizard Step 2 there is an area of the window called Series in: and two choices:

■ Rows

■ Columns.

Explore what happens when you select rows. When you are finished, select columns.

5 Now work through these steps:

a) Name the chart Quarter Comparison

b) X axis – Items

c) Y axis – Amount

d) Legend – on top

e) No data labels

e) Place chart as a new sheet (i.e. Quarter Comparison Chart).

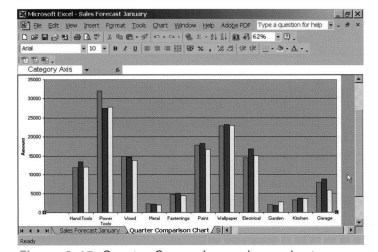

Figure 2.45 Quarter Comparison column chart

6 Save the chart, by selecting the File menu and the Save As option, as the file Quarter Comparison Chart on your floppy disk or a location of your choice.

7 Figure 2.45 illustrates the Quarter Comparison Chart.

8 Repeat this process, but select the columns Item and the months June, July and August. Highlight the Item column and then, holding down the Ctrl key, highlight the other three columns, excluding the

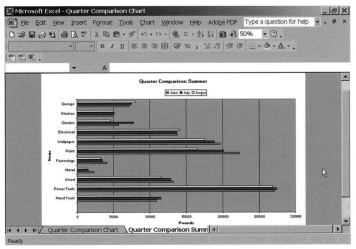

Figure 2.46 Bar chart

Total row. Select the Chart option. Create a bar chart. Use the same axis and legend position, and entitle the column chart Quarter Comparison Summer.

You have created a chart using data from non-adjacent columns.

9 Figure 2.46 shows the bar chart.

10 Save the chart, by selecting the File menu and the Save As option, as the file Quarter Comparison Summer on your floppy disk or a location of your choice.

11 You can present the chart in either portrait or landscape mode by selecting the File menu and clicking on the Page Setup option to reveal the Page Setup window. Click in the appropriate radio button. To check how the chart would appear if printed, click on the Print Preview button. To print the chart, click on the Print button to reveal the Print window.

12 Print your bar chart in both portrait and landscape modes.

13 Close Microsoft Excel® by selecting the File menu and clicking on the Exit option or by clicking on the Close button in the top right-hand corner of the application window.

Line graphs

A line graph shows the relationship between two variables. If you plotted the sales forecast for Hand Tools against months you would obtain a line graph showing how sales of these products fluctuated across the 12 months. It is also possible to combine a line graph with a column chart so that both appear together.

Exercise 15

Line and column graphs

1 Insert your floppy disk into the A: drive.

2 Load Microsoft Excel® using either the All Programs menu or the Excel® icon on the desktop. Open the file Sales Forecast January by selecting the File menu and clicking on the Open option to reveal the Open window. Change the Look in: box to select the floppy disk and the file name will appear in the work area. Double-click Sales Forecast January or single-click it and then click the OK button. Select Sheet 1 to reveal spreadsheet data.

3 Highlight the top three rows of Sales Forecast (Items, Hand Tools and Power Tools), excluding Total and Average columns, and then select the Insert menu and click on the Chart option. Select one of the line graphs (whichever appeals) and create it using the Wizard. However, select:

a) Not to show the legend

b) Title – Tools

c) X axis – Months

d) Y axis – Amount

e) No gridlines

f) No data labels

g) As a new sheet called Tools.

4 Figure 2.47 shows the line graph that you have created.

5 Save the chart, by selecting the File menu and the Save option, as the file Tools on your floppy disk or a location of your choice.

6 Print your line graph in either portrait or landscape.

7 You are now going to produce a graph displaying both a line and columns. Highlight columns Item and October, November and December, excluding the Total row. Remember that to highlight non-adjacent columns you need to hold down the Ctrl key. With the columns highlighted, select the Insert menu and click on the Chart option.

8 Select the Custom Types tab and the Line and Column chart (figure 2.48). Follow the Chart Wizard. Choose the title to be Quarter Comparison Autumn, X axis – Items, Y axis – Amount, Legend – Bottom, and as a new sheet called Quarter Comparison Autumn.

9 Figure 2.49 illustrates a line and column graph. October and November are shown as columns, while December is displayed as a line.

10 Save the chart, by selecting the File menu and the Save As option, as the file Quarter Comparison Autumn on your floppy disk or a location of your choice.

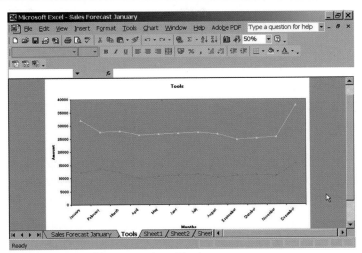

Figure 2.47 Line graph – Tools

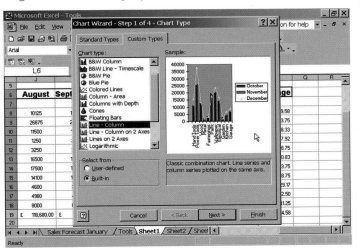

Figure 2.48 Line and column type – Custom

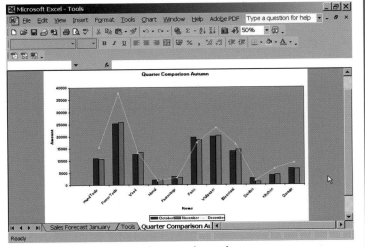

Figure 2.49 Quarter Comparison Autumn

Manipulating Spreadsheets and Graphs

continued

11 Print your line and column graph in either portrait or landscape.

12 Close Microsoft Excel® by selecting the File menu item and clicking on the Exit option or by clicking on the Close button in the top right-hand corner of the application window.

XY scatter graph

XY scatter graphs are used to plot the values of two or more variables against each other in order to show the relationship between them. They are often used to present the results of engineering, laboratory or other experimental work.

Exercise 16

XY scatter graphs

1 Normally you will be provided with the data on which your charts and graphs will be based. In this exercise, the table below shows the relationship between actual and predicted rainfall at monthly intervals.

2 Load Microsoft Excel® using either the All Programs menu or the Excel® icon on the desktop. Enter the data below and save the spreadsheet to a floppy disk as a file called Rainfall.

Months	Predicted Rainfall	Actual Rainfall
January	12.50	10.00
February	16.25	15.50
March	23.75	26.55
April	14.15	18.90
May	12.50	11.75
June	9.85	12.55
July	8.65	5.50
August	4.75	3.55
September	15.75	11.85
October	18.75	17.25
November	19.85	25.95
December	15.65	17.45

3 Highlight the whole of the information except the title line. Select the Insert menu and click on the Chart option. Select one of the XY scatter graphs and create it using the Wizard. You will need to use the Series tab in step 2 to change the names of Series 1 to Predicted and Series 2 to Actual. However, select:

a) Title – Rainfall

b) X axis – Months

c) Y axis – Inches

d) Y Major gridlines

e) Legend – Corner

f) No data labels

g) As a new sheet called Rainfall.

4 Figure 2.50 shows the XY scatter graph that we have created. Notice that you appear to have 14 months in a year. We will edit the graph to remove this error later.

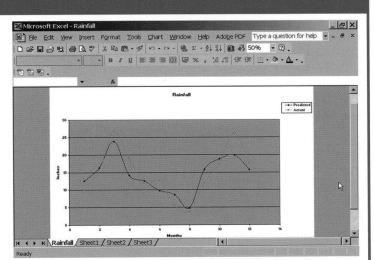

Figure 2.50 Rainfall

5 Save the chart, by selecting the File menu and the Save option, as the file Rainfall on your floppy disk or a location of your choice.

6 Print your XY scatter graph in either portrait or landscape.

7 To help understand the graph, it is possible to add a trendline by selecting the Chart menu to open the Add Trendline window. Select the Linear Trend/Regression type and the

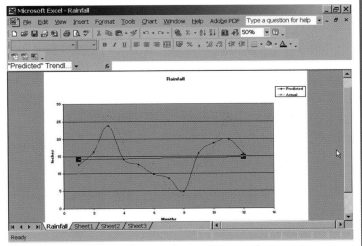

Figure 2.51 Trendline and scatter graph

series the line is based on (i.e. Predicted or Actual Rainfall). Figure 2.51 shows the scatter graph with a trendline. The line helps you to predict the rainfall across the year, or to predict future rainfall by extending the line, while the actual line allows you to consider the variation across the year.

8 It is possible to display the equation by clicking on the trendline so it is highlighted (i.e. each end of the line will have a square handle). Select the Format menu and click on the Selected Trendline option to reveal the Format Trendline window. Select the Options tab and click on the Display equation on chart radio button. The trendline equation is displayed near the graph. In New CLAiT Plus 2006 you will not be assessed on adding a trendline or its equation, but since they are sometimes useful we have included them in the chapter.

9 Save the chart by selecting the File menu and the Save option on your floppy disk or a location of your choice.

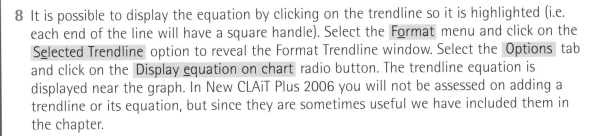

Manipulating Spreadsheets and Graphs

10 Print your XY scatter graph with trendline and equation in either portrait or landscape.

11 Close Microsoft Excel® by selecting the File menu item and clicking on the Exit option or by clicking on the Close button in the top right-hand corner of the application window.

Page setup

You can adjust the display of your charts and graphs by selecting the File menu and the Page Setup option to reveal the Page Setup window (assumes chart and graph is being displayed). This allows you to adjust all four margins – top, bottom, left and right. In addition, you can change the size of the header and footer.

By clicking on the Header/Footer tab you can add them to your chart or graph.

Text box

Although an image is often said to be worth a thousand words, it can be enhanced by the addition of some text. Charts and graphs are useful ways of presenting information, but in many cases they need a short statement to help your audience to fully understand their content. Words can be added to charts and graphs using a text box. Click on the Text Box icon on the Draw toolbar to reveal a new mouse pointer. Draw a box by holding down the mouse button and dragging the box open (figure 2.52). Text then can be added to the open box.

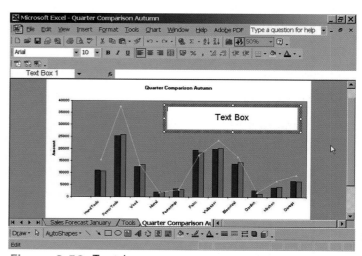

Figure 2.52 Text box

House style

In order to ensure consistency in organisational documents and publications, house styles are often developed. These provide a series of guidelines for staff to follow. An example is given below. House styles are often employed to ensure that a minimum standard of quality is adhered to by employees.

Example house style guidelines:

Pie Charts

Font (typeface)	serif (e.g. Times New Roman)

Character (text) size

Title	20, bold
Subtitle	20, bold
Data Labels	14
Legend	14

Bar/column, line and XY scatter charts and graphs

Font (typeface)	serif (e.g. Times New Roman)

Character (text) size

Title	20, bold
Subtitle	20, bold
X axis title	14, bold
Y axis title	14, bold
Other text/numbering on the X axis	12
Other text/numbering on the Y axis	12
Legend	12
Text box labels	12, border invisible
Trendline equation	12

Headers and footers

During your assessment you will be often asked to insert your name and centre number in either the header or footer. Organisations often use the header and footer to record titles, dates and file names.

Formatting graphs and charts

It is possible to edit your charts and graphs employing the techniques that you have learned from using other Microsoft Office® applications. You can change the fonts, character sizes and effects (e.g. bold), apply superscript and subscript effects, change the style and thickness of lines and alter the colours of your charts and graphs.

To edit a chart or graph you must double-click on the element that you are seeking to change. A window will appear (e.g. Format Chart Title, Format Axis, Format Plot Area, Format

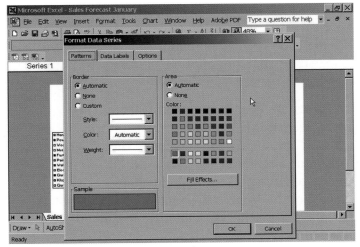

Figure 2.53 Format data series

Legend, Format Data Labels, Format Data Series). Figure 2.53 illustrates the Format Data Series for the Sales Forecast January exploding pie chart that you created earlier. The element that you have double-clicked will be highlighted by being enclosed in a frame with small black squares.

The format window is divided into three tabs – Patterns, Data Labels and Options. Each of these is similarly divided, but in a way appropriate to the element. In the case of Patterns you can alter the colours, fill effects and lines. In the Data Labels tab you can adjust the labels, while in Options you can change the angle of the pie slices. You should notice that the options are customised to the type of chart or graph.

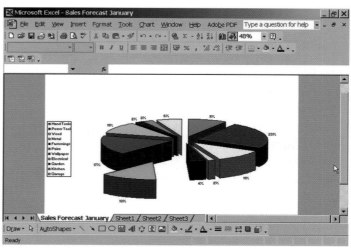

Figure 2.54 Dragging a slice

You can move the various slices of the pie by clicking on a segment and holding down the button to drag it. This is a useful way to emphasise that slice (figure 2.54).

If you click on the axis, the Format Axis window will open. This allows you to change the upper and lower limits, intervals on the axis and numeric formatting. The different functions are grouped together under the various tabs across the top of the window. Figure 2.55 shows the Format Axis for the Quarter Comparison Autumn Chart – notice the tabs of Patterns, Scale, Font, Number and Alignment. The Data Labels Number tab provides you with a wide range of numeric formats for the axes (e.g. fractions, currency, decimal places, date, negative signs and minus signs). The Patterns tab provides you with the means to change the markers on the chart or graph lines, using the options indicated by radio buttons on the right side of the window.

If you select the Font tab, which is available in many of the Format windows, you will reveal the options to change the fonts, including type, style, size and effects. The effects include choosing Strikethrough, Superscript and Subscript, by clicking on the appropriate checkboxes.

If you double-click in the plot area, you will open the Format Plot Area window. This allows you to change the background colour of the plot or to choose to have no background colour (i.e. select the None option radio button). You select the colour by clicking on those displayed in the palette and you are shown a sample of the colour. There is also a Fill Effects button, which provides access to a variety of fills. When you wish to apply the changes to the background, click on the OK button.

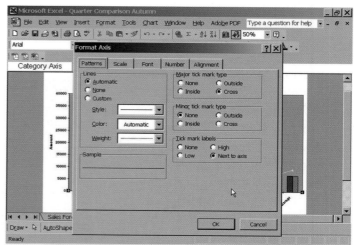

Figure 2.55 Format Axis – Quarter Comparison Autumn

CLAiT Plus 2006 for Office XP

In a similar way to changing the background colour of the chart or graph, you can change the colour of the bars of a data series by double-clicking on one of the bars. This will open the Format Data Series window (figure 2.56). The new bar colour is chosen from the palette or from the Fill Effects options. To apply the new colour or fill, you need to click on the OK button. Compare figure 2.56 with figure 2.53, since both are called Format Data Series. The difference is that they are customised for different types of chart.

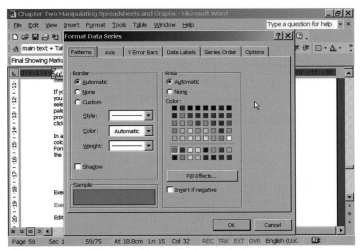

Figure 2.56 Format Data Series window

Exercise 17 provides you with the opportunity to explore many of these options.

Exercise 17

Editing a chart

1 Insert your floppy disk into the A: drive.

2 Load Microsoft Excel® using either the All Programs menu or the Excel® icon on the desktop. Open the file Quarter Comparison Chart by selecting the File menu and clicking on the Open option to reveal the Open window. Change the Look in: box to select the floppy disk and the file name will appear in the work area. Double-click Quarter Comparison Chart or single-click it and then click the OK button.

3 Select the Quarter Comparison Chart by clicking on the tab. You are now going to edit this chart. Double-click on the title to open the Format Chart Title window, and click on the Font tab to show the options. Select the Times New Roman font, character size 20 and embolden the text. You should also explore the other options. When you have completed the changes to conform with the house style, click on the OK button.

4 Double-click on the legend to open the Format Legend window and select Times New Roman and size 14.

5 Double-click on the X and Y axes titles in turn and change them to Times New Roman, emboldened and size 14.

6 Double-click on the text along each axis and change it to Times New Roman and size 12.

7 Once you have made the changes, take the opportunity to explore some other editing possibilities.

8 If you double-click in the plot area you will open the Format Plot Area window, which will allow you to change the background colour or remove it. Experiment with different options until you find one you prefer.

9 If you double-click on the Amount Axis line, you will open the Format Axis window. This provides five tabs – Patterns , Scale , Font , Number and Alignment . Explore the different options. You can select specific numeric formats for your axis. This can be very useful in other charts. In the Patterns tab you will notice three sets of marks (e.g. Major tick mark type). Experiment with the different options.

10 Double-click on one of the data bars and you will open the Format Data Series window. Explore the different options, but choose a new colour for this bar and the other two. Also change the line thickness using the same windows.

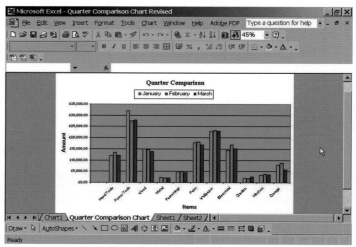

11 Make any other changes that you feel will improve the chart. Figure 2.57 illustrates the changes we have made. Compare your own efforts

Figure 2.57 **Chart edited**

with it. There is no need to be identical, except in respect of the earlier instructions.

12 Save the chart, by selecting the File menu and the Save As option, as Quarter Comparison Chart Revised on your floppy disk or a location of your choice.

13 Print your edited chart in either portrait or landscape.

14 Close Microsoft Excel® by selecting the File menu item and clicking on the Exit option or by clicking on the Close button in the top right-hand corner of the application window.

Editing an XY scatter graph

In Exercise 16, the final chart (Figure 2.51) appears to show that there are 14 months in the year. This can be removed using the editing options.

Exercise 18

Editing XY scatter graph

1 Insert your floppy disk into the A: drive.

2 Load Microsoft Excel® using either the All Programs menu or the Excel® icon on the desktop. Open the file Rainfall by selecting the File menu and clicking on the Open option to reveal the Open window. Change the Look in: box to select the floppy disk and the file name will appear in the work area. Double-click Rainfall or single-click it and then click the OK button.

3 Select the Rainfall chart by clicking on the tab. You are now going to edit this chart.

4 Click on the X axis to open the Format Axis window and select the Scale tab. Change maximum from 14 to 12 and click on the OK button. You will see the scale change to 12.

5 Click on one of the scatter points and the Format Data Series window will open. Select the Patterns tab and change the marker style to one you prefer. Repeat the action, selecting the other series of points. Try to make the scatter graph more legible.

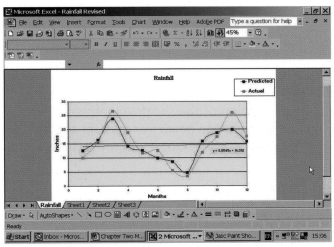

6 Explore the different options and try to improve the clarity of the chart. Our efforts are shown in figure 2.58. However, there is no need to produce an identical copy.

Figure 2.58 Rainfall chart revised

7 Save the chart, by selecting the File menu and the Save As option, as Rainfall Revised on your floppy disk or a location of your choice.

8 Print your edited chart in either portrait or landscape.

9 Close Microsoft Excel® by selecting the File menu item and clicking on the Exit option or by clicking on the Close button in the top right-hand corner of the application window.

Prediction

Graphs and charts are useful ways of presenting numerical information. They can make complex data understandable. Pie, column and bar charts allow you to compare different sets of information so that it is straightforward to understand. However, graphs can also help with prediction, by extending or extrapolating the lines into the future. This requires a graph or chart with one axis being time (e.g. hours, days, months or years).

It is possible to extend the trendline for the actual and predicted rainfall lines and thus estimate rainfall. However, you always need to consider what the data represents. In this case, rainfall is likely to be seasonal, so simply extending the lines may be inaccurate. You need to compare the extended line with the actual values of the months and consider how close the match is.

It is often helpful to extend lines into the future as long as you are careful when considering the context of the information. In this case, there is a distinct cycle to the rainfall throughout the year, which, if you consider it alongside the extrapolations, will provide greater accuracy in your predictions. Weather forecasts are often limited to a few days ahead.

More practice

In the assessment you may be provided with a series of files representing some partly completed spreadsheets and data that you need to import. These additional exercises often require that you enter information to create the spreadsheet. They are also available on the Hodder Education website (www.hodderclait.co.uk) linked to this book, so you can use them rather than having to input the information.

Activity 1

1 Insert a floppy disk into the A: drive.
2 Load Microsoft Excel® using either the All Programs menu or the Excel® icon on the desktop.
3 Set the orientation of the sheet to landscape, margins to 2.5 cm – right and left, and 2.5 cm – top and bottom, and header and footer to 2 cm (select File menu and Page Setup option).
4 Insert a header to read: Sports Results (Arial font and character size 14 bold – in the Centre section).
5 Insert automatic fields in the footer:

   File name – Left section
   Page number – Centre section
   Date – Right section

6 Enter the table of information shown in figure 2.59 to form your first spreadsheet of the average performances of sports club members during the last six months.
7 Check that you have entered the data accurately and correct any mistakes. If you click in the cell that contains the error, you can amend the mistake.
8 Select the File menu and click on the option Save to reveal the Save As window. Change the Save in: box to select the floppy disk and add the file name Sport in the File name: box. Click on the Save button. The top line of Microsoft Excel® will change to read 'Microsoft Excel® – Sport'.

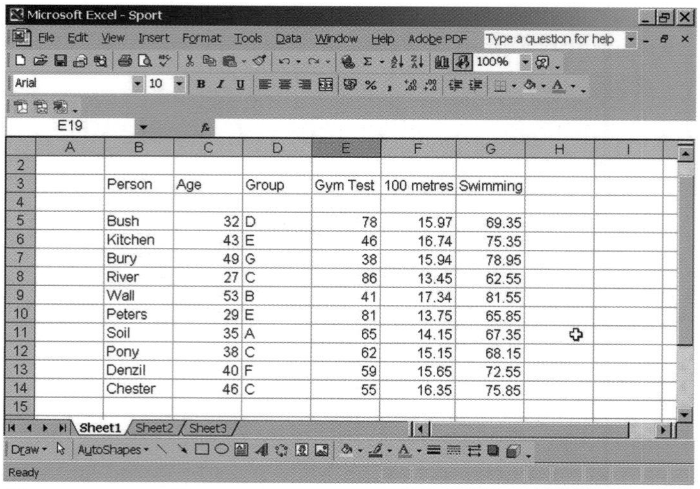

Person	Age	Group	Gym Test	100 metres	Swimming
Bush	32	D	78	15.97	69.35
Kitchen	43	E	46	16.74	75.35
Bury	49	G	38	15.94	78.95
River	27	C	86	13.45	62.55
Wall	53	B	41	17.34	81.55
Peters	29	E	81	13.75	65.85
Soil	35	A	65	14.15	67.35
Pony	38	C	62	15.15	68.15
Denzil	40	F	59	15.65	72.55
Chester	46	C	55	16.35	75.85

Figure 2.59 Sports

9   Change the size of the columns so
    that you can see the contents
    clearly. Use the AVERAGE function
    to average the columns, and add
    the name Average to the row.

10 Check the appearance of your
    spreadsheet as a printed document
    by selecting the File menu and the
    Print Preview option.

11 Click on Sheet 2 to create a new
    spreadsheet. Enter the table of
    information in (figure 2.60) to
    form a second spreadsheet. This
    shows Bush's last four scores at
    the three disciplines.

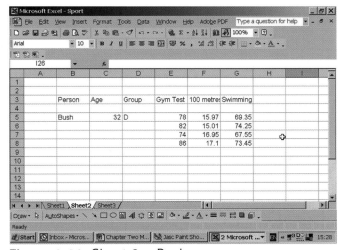

Figure 2.60 Sheet 2 – Bush

12 Change the size of the columns so that you can see the contents clearly. Use the AVERAGE
    function to average the rows. Name the row Average.

13 Link the three Bush averages to the Sports spreadsheet (i.e. sheet2!E9, sheet2!F9 and
    sheet2!G9).

14 Save your sheet, by selecting the File menu and clicking on the Save As option, as file
    Sport Revised.

15 Return to Sheet 1 and in column H create an IF function to decide if the individual
    members are fit or unfit, depending on their Gym Test score. Fitness is determined by
    scoring more than 60 (=IF(E5>60,"Fit","Unfit"). Insert a column heading Fitness.

16 Adjust all the figures in Sheet 1 so they are to two decimal places. Change the font to Arial
    and character size to 12. Embolden all the headings and centre all the data. You will need
    to adjust the column widths accordingly.

17 Use the formula for fitness to produce an overall estimate of the fitness of the members.
    Name this cell Fitness.

17 Figure 2.61 shows the new sheet.

18 Print the sheet without gridlines
    and row and column headings,
    and then with them.

19 Print the sheet showing the
    formulae.

20 Save your sheet by selecting the
    File menu and clicking on the
    Save option.

21 Close Microsoft Excel® by
    selecting the File menu item and
    clicking on the Exit option or by
    clicking on the Close button in
    the top right-hand corner of the
    application window.

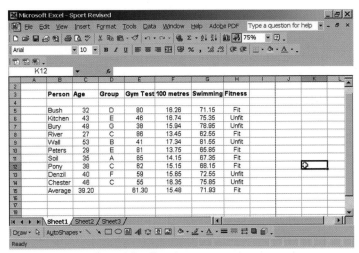

Figure 2.61 Sport Revised

Activity 2

Pie chart

1 Insert a floppy disk into the A: drive.

2 Load Microsoft Excel® using either the All Programs menu or the Excel® icon on the desktop. Open the file Sport Revised by selecting the File menu and clicking on the Open option to reveal the Open window. Change the Look in: box to select the floppy disk and the file name will appear in the work area. Double-click Sport Revised or single-click it and then click the OK button.

3 Using the names of the members and the Gym Test scores, create an exploded pie chart.

   a) Title – Fitness

   b) Label each segment with the member's name.

   c) Do not display the legend.

   d) Create the chart on a separate sheet to the data. Title – Fitness.

   e) Drag Bush's segment out from the others.

4 Add your name to the header.

5 Edit the chart to ensure everything is clear and legible.

6 Print a copy of the pie chart. Figure 2.62 shows the pie chart we created.

7 Save your sheet by selecting the File menu and clicking on the Save option. Call the file Sport Revised Fitness.

8 Close Microsoft Excel® by selecting the File menu item and clicking on the Exit option or by clicking on the Close button in the top right-hand corner of the application window.

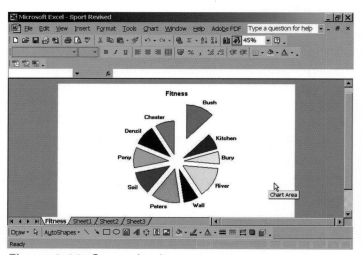

Figure 2.62 Sport pie chart

Activity 3

Scatter graph

1 Insert a floppy disk into the A: drive.

2 Load Microsoft Excel® using either the All Programs menu or the Excel® icon on the desktop. Open the file Sport Revised by selecting the File menu and clicking on the Open option to reveal the Open window. Change the Look in: box to select the floppy disk and the file name will appear in the work area. Double-click Sport Revised Fitness or single-click it and then click the OK button. Sheet 1 contains the spreadsheet data.

3 Using the names of the members and data from 100 metres and swimming, create an XY scatter graph:

a) Title – Relationship

b) Change series names to 100 metres and Swimming.

c) Display the legend at the top.

d) Label X axis – members, and Y axis – seconds.

e) Create the chart on a separate sheet to the data. Title – Relationship.

4   Add your name to the header.

5   Edit the chart to ensure everything is clear and legible.

6   Print a copy of the scatter graph. Figure 2.63 shows the scatter graph we created.

7   Save your sheet by selecting the File menu and clicking on the Save option. Call the file Sport Revised Relationship.

8   Close Microsoft Excel® by selecting the File menu item and clicking on the Exit option or by clicking on the Close button in the top right-hand corner of the application window.

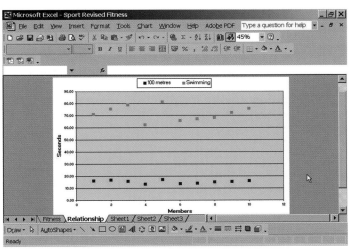

Figure 2.63 Scatter graph – Relationship

Activity 4

Sort and filter

1   Insert a floppy disk into the A: drive.

2   Load Microsoft Excel® using either the All Programs menu or the Excel® icon on the desktop. Open the file Sport Revised by selecting the File menu and clicking on the Open option to reveal the Open window. Change the Look in: box to select the floppy disk and the file name will appear in the work area. Double-click Sport Revised Relationship or single-click it and then click the OK button. Select Sheet 1.

3   Chester has left the sports club, so his records need to be deleted.

4   Filter the data to locate all members who are judged to be fit. Print a copy of the filtered spreadsheet, with row and column headings.

5   Filter the data to locate members with a swimming score less than 71.49 (i.e. use Custom option). Print a copy of the filtered spreadsheet (figure 2.64), with row and column headings.

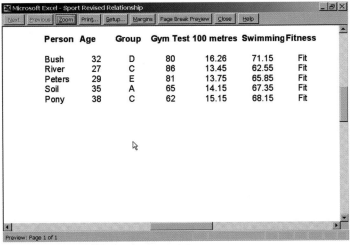

Figure 2.64 Filtered spreadsheet

6 Sort the data into descending order of member names.

7 Create a header. Add your name and file name.

8 Save your sheet by selecting the <u>File</u> menu and clicking on the <u>Save</u> option. Call the file Sport Revised Filter.

9 Close Microsoft Excel® by selecting the <u>File</u> menu item and clicking on the <u>Exit</u> option or by clicking on the Close button in the top right-hand corner of the application window.

Activity 5

1 Insert your floppy disk into the A: drive.

2 Create a data file using the Notepad application (<u>Start</u>, <u>All Programs</u>, <u>Accessories</u> and <u>Notepad</u>). Separate the data only with commas:

```
Staff,January,February,March
Squires,300,700,1200
Johnson,100,300,500
Singh,300,1200,2100
Patel,150,340,800
Gordon,230,560,600
Davies,270,450,560
```

3 Save the file as Sales Data. (In the CLAiT Plus assessment you will be provided with data files to import and will not need to create them. Sales Data is available on the Hodder Education website – www.hodderclait.co.uk).

4 Load Microsoft Excel® using either the <u>All Programs</u> menu or the <u>Excel®</u> icon on the desktop.

5 Import the file Sales Data. The delimiter is a comma. Figure 2.65 shows the spreadsheet.

6 Enter a formula to total the columns B, C and D and rows 2, 3, 4, 5, 6 and 7. Enter the formula once for a row and once for a column and then replicate it. Insert row and column title – Total.

Figure 2.65 Sales

7 Enter a new column heading in F1 called Commission – adjust column widths appropriately. Commission is paid quarterly, at a rate of 9 per cent of sales. Devise a formula to calculate the quarterly commission (i.e. divide quarterly total by 100 and multiply by 9). Enter the formula.

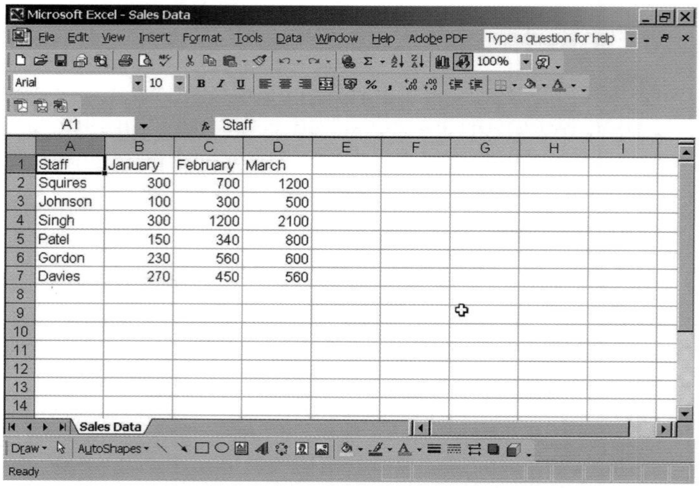

8 Centre and embolden the column headings.

9 Change the format of the commission column to currency.

10 Change the font of the whole spreadsheet, except the column headings, to Times New Roman and character size 12.

11 Insert a new sheet by selecting the <u>Insert</u> menu and clicking on the <u>Worksheet</u> option. A <u>Sheet 1</u> tab will appear alongside the Sales Data sheet. Click on the <u>Sheet 1</u> tab and enter

the data below or import them from the file Sales Data Squires (www.hodderclait.co.uk). This sheet shows the sales performance of Squires, who is also featured in the Sales Data spreadsheet.

Products	Tyres	Brakes	Oil	Filters
January	75	125	50	50
February	125	200	150	225
March	350	250	350	250

12 Total each monthly row using a standard function.

13 The monthly totals for Squires are the same as the content of each entry in the Sales Data sheet (i.e. cells B2, C2 and D2) so link the two sheets. Click away from the fomula to calculate it. Figure 2.66 shows the spreadsheet.

14 Print the sheet without gridlines and row and column headings, and then with them.

15 Print the sheet showing the formulae.

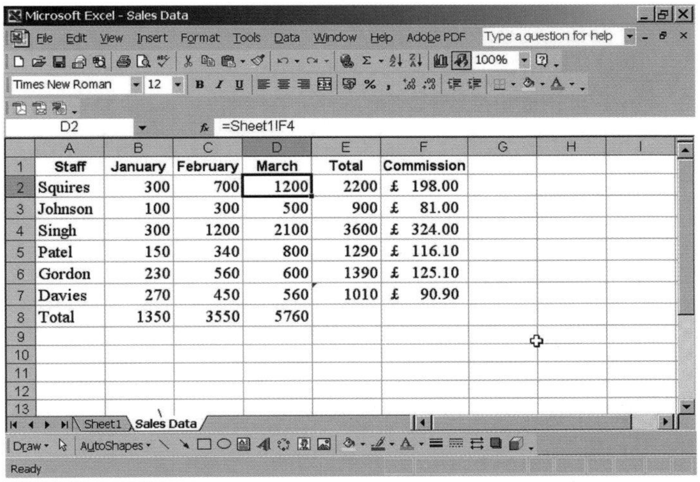

Figure 2.66 Sales Data linked spreadsheet

16 Save your sheet, by selecting the File menu and clicking on the Save option, as a Microsoft Excel® file with the name Sales Data.

17 Close Microsoft Excel® by selecting the File menu item and clicking on the Exit option or by clicking on the Close button in the top right-hand corner of the application window.

Activity 6

Pie chart

1 Insert a floppy disk into the A: drive.

2 Load Microsoft Excel® using either the All Programs menu or the Excel® icon on the desktop. Open the file Sales Data by selecting the File menu and clicking on the Open option to reveal the Open window. Change the Look in: box to select the floppy disk and the file name will appear in the work area. Double-click Sales Data or single-click it and then click the OK button.

3 Using the names of the sales staff and the value of the commission, create an exploded pie chart.

   a) Title – Commission
   b) Label each segment with the commission earned.
   c) Display the legend on the left.
   d) Create the chart on a separate sheet to the data. Title – Commission.
   e) Drag the largest segment out from the others.

4   Add your name to the header.

5   Edit the chart to ensure everything is clear and legible.

6   Print a copy of the pie chart.

7   Save your sheet by selecting the File menu and clicking on the Save As option. Call the file Sales Data Commission.

8   Close Microsoft Excel® by selecting the File menu item and clicking on the Exit option or by clicking on the Close button in the top right-hand corner of the application window.

Activity 7

Column chart

1   Insert a floppy disk into the A: drive.

2   Load Microsoft Excel® using either the All Programs menu or the Excel® icon on the desktop. Open the file Sales Data by selecting the File menu and clicking on the Open option to reveal the Open window. Change the Look in: box to select the floppy disk and the file name will appear in the work area. Double-click Sales Data or single-click it and then click the OK button.

3   Using the names of the sales staff and data from January, February and March, create a column chart:

   a)   Title – Sales

   b)   X axis – Staff, and Y axis – Amount

   c)   Display the legend at the bottom.

   d)   Do not display any gridlines.

   e)   Create the chart on a separate sheet to the data. Title – Sales.

4   Add your name to the header.

5   Edit the chart to ensure everything is clear and legible.

6   Print a copy of the column chart.

7   Save your sheet by selecting the File menu and clicking on the Save As option. Call the file Sales Data Sales.

8   Close Excel® by selecting the File menu item and clicking on the Exit option or by clicking on the Close button in the top right-hand corner of the application window.

Activity 8

Sort and filter

1   Insert a floppy disk into the A: drive.

2   Load Microsoft Excel® using either the All Programs menu or the Excel® icon on the desktop. Open the file Sales Data by selecting the File menu and clicking on the Open option to reveal the Open window. Change the Look in: box to select the floppy disk and the file name will appear in the work area. Double-click Sales Data or single-click it and then click the OK button.

3   A sales person has joined the team. Insert a new row and the following information.

     Jenkins   125, 450 and 670

4 Calculate a new row total and commission for Jenkins.

5 Filter the data to locate staff who earned more than £115.20p commission (i.e. use **Custom** option). Print a copy of the filtered spreadsheet (figure 2.67) with row and column headings.

6 Sort the data into ascending order of staff names.

7 Create a header. Add your name and file name.

8 Save your sheet by selecting the **File** menu and clicking on the **Save As** option. Call the file Sales Data Filter.

9 Close Microsoft Excel® by selecting the **File** menu item and clicking on the **Exit** option or by clicking on the **Close** button in the top right-hand corner of the application window.

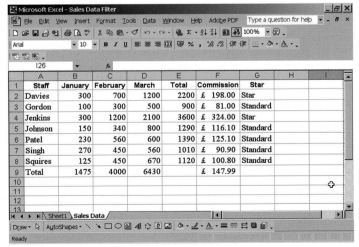

Figure 2.67 Filtered Data

Activity 9

Functions

1 Insert a floppy disk into the A: drive.

2 Load Microsoft Excel® using either the **All Programs** menu or the **Excel®** icon on the desktop. Open the file Sales Data by selecting the **File** menu and clicking on the **Open** option to reveal the Open window. Change the **Look in:** box to select the floppy disk and the file name will appear in the work area. Double-click Sales Data Filter or single-click it and then click the **OK** button. Remove the filter.

3 Add a new heading in column G – Star. In this column, create a formula to identify sales staff who earned more than £150 per quarter, since these are star sales staff. Other staff should be identified as standard.

4 Average the commission earned and name the cell Average. Figure 2.68 shows the revised spreadsheet.

5 Print the sheet without gridlines and row and column headings, and then with them.

6 Print the sheet showing the formulae.

7 Save your sheet by selecting the **File** menu and clicking on the **Save As** option. Call the file Sales Data Star.

8 Close Microsoft Excel® by selecting the **File** menu item and clicking on the **Exit** option or by clicking on the **Close** button in the top right-hand corner of the application window.

Staff	January	February	March	Total	Commission	Star
Davies	300	700	1200	2200	£ 198.00	Star
Gordon	100	300	500	900	£ 81.00	Standard
Jenkins	300	1200	2100	3600	£ 324.00	Star
Johnson	150	340	800	1290	£ 116.10	Standard
Patel	230	560	600	1390	£ 125.10	Standard
Singh	270	450	560	1010	£ 90.90	Standard
Squires	125	450	670	1120	£ 100.80	Standard
Total	1475	4000	6430		£ 147.99	

Figure 2.68 Revised spreadsheet

Other resources

1   The table below shows the orders received from five companies in terms of their number and value in 2006.

These resources will allow you to practise creating formulae to total columns, calculate profit and identify the most profitable company. In addition, it is the basis to produce a pie chart and it will also allow you to sort and filter the data.

	Orders	Value	Profit
Company A	156	45000	
Company B	345	230000	
Company C	198	123000	
Company D	112	56000	
Company E	234	97000	
Total			

2   The table below shows the actual hours of sunshine in each month of 2006, compared to the predicted amount.

These resources will allow you to practise creating formulae to identify the average number of hours of sunshine (i.e. actual and predicted) and to identify the month with the most sunshine. It is also the basis to produce a scatter graph, as well as enabling you to sort and filter the data.

Months	Hours of Sunshine Actual	Hours of Sunshine Predicted
January	5.00	4.25
February	4.50	3.25
March	6.50	3.75
April	9.50	4.50
May	10.50	9.50
June	13.50	12.75
July	15.00	16.50
August	14.50	15.75
September	12.25	14.50
October	9.50	7.25
November	7.50	5.65
December	5.75	4.50

3   The table below shows the relationship between sales, costs, fixed assets and annual profit.

These resources will allow you to practise creating formula to total columns, calculate profit and identify the most profitable company. It is also the basis to produce a column/bar chart and to sort and filter the data. It will provide you with the means to link two spreadsheets using the second table of information.

Organisation	Sales	Cost	Assets	Profit
A	230000	178000	198000	
B	340000	212000	430000	
C	390000	234000	357900	
D	410000	395000	230000	
E	440000	340000	178000	
F	560000	456000	76000	
Total				

Organisation A				
A	Sales	Cost	Assets	Profit
Product 1	78000	48000	68000	
Product 2	23000	17000	34000	
Product 3	35000	33000	41000	
Product 4	65000	55000	27000	
Product 5	29000	25000	28000	
Total	230000	178000	198000	

SUMMARY

1 Open Microsoft Excel®

There are several ways of loading an application in Microsoft Windows®. These include:

- clicking on the Start button, highlighting the All Programs item and clicking on Microsoft Excel®
- double-clicking on the Excel® icon on the desktop.

2 Open a file

Select the File menu, click on the Open option to reveal the Open window. Change the Look in: box to select the folder and the file name will appear in the work area.

3 Page layout

Select the File menu and click on the Page Setup option to reveal the Page Setup window. There are four tabs:

- Page – to set the orientation of the sheet (portrait and landscape) and scale your spreadsheet on to a specified number of pages when you are printing it
- Margins – to set the size of all four margins (i.e. left, right, top and bottom) and the header and footer

- Header/Footer – to insert the content of the header and footer, including automatic fields
- Sheet

4 Adjust column width

Change the width of a column by placing the mouse pointer on the line between the two columns. The pointer's appearance will change and you can drag the column wider.

Alternatively, select the Format menu and click on either the Row or Column option, revealing options to change the width of a column or the height of a row.

5 Save

Select the File menu and click on the option Save to reveal the Save As window. Change the Save in: box to select the floppy disk or other drive/folder, and add the file name in the File name: box. Click on the Save button.

6 Close

Select the File menu item and click on the Exit option or click on the close button in the top right-hand corner of the application window.

7 Mathematical operators

The mathematical operators used in Microsoft Excel® are:

+	add
–	subtract
*	multiply
/	divide
<	less than
<=	less than or equal to
>	more than
>=	greater than or equal to

8 Mathematical rules

When a formula consists of several arithmetical operators, they are worked out in a standard way. Everything enclosed in brackets is calculated first, then multiplication and division, and, finally, addition and subtraction. If a formula contains multiplication and division or addition and subtraction, it works out the calculation from left to right.

9 Standard functions

Microsoft Excel® provides a number of standard functions. These include: SUM, AVERAGE, COUNT, MIN, SQRT, MAX and IF. A full list of all the functions can be accessed by clicking on the down arrow next to the Sum function button on the Standard toolbar. This reveals a list of functions and the button More Functions . Click on More Functions to open the Insert Function window.

The Insert Function window allows you to insert the function into the sheet. When you enter a function, a new window will sometimes appear called Function Arguments. Function Arguments asks you to set the parameters for the function.

10 References

The cell reference is given by combining the column letter with the row number (e.g. A4). There are three types of reference:

- relative
- absolute
- named.

The relative reference is the one you normally encounter when you use Microsoft Excel®. If you move the cells (e.g. delete or insert rows or columns), the reference in the formula changes to allow for the new position.

The absolute reference is one which remains unchanged no matter what happens. You create an absolute reference by using the $ symbol (e.g. SUM (A2:A5) uses relative references, while SUM ($A$2:$A$5) uses absolute references).

A mixed reference combines both relative and absolute references within the same formula or function (e.g. H5+$G$3).

Named cell references are created by highlighting a cell or area and entering its name in the left-hand box of the formula bar and pressing Enter.

11 Print

Select the File menu and click on the Print option.

12 Print preview

Select the File menu and click on the Print Preview option to reveal the Print Preview window.

13 Print gridlines, row and column headings

Select the File menu, click on the Print Preview option to reveal the Print Preview window. Click on the Setup button to reveal the Page Setup window. Select the Sheet tab and click in the Gridlines and Row and column headings boxes so ticks appear. Click on the OK button when you are finished and you will see the window disappear and a new print preview appear, showing gridlines and headings.

14 Print options

Select the File menu and click on the Print option to reveal the Print window. In the window is a section called Print What, with three options:

- Selection – print areas that are highlighted
- Active sheet(s) – print all the sheets you have selected
- Entire workbook – print all the sheets within the workbook.

15 Print formulae

Select the Tools menu and click on Options to reveal the Options window. The View tab shows a section called Window options. Clicking on the Formulas box will print the formulas. There are also boxes to select the Gridlines and Row & column headers. When choices have been made, they are enacted by clicking on the OK button.

16 Change format

The Formatting toolbar provides you with a variety of tools to enhance the format of your spreadsheet (e.g. fonts, character sizes, bold, italics, underline and change alignment). They are selected by highlighting the cell or cells and selecting the appropriate tool from the toolbar.

17 Borders
Click on the Borders icon on the Formatting toolbar to reveal a small window of options.

18 Hide Rows and Columns
Select the Format menu and click on either Row or Column options, revealing the options to hide or unhide rows or columns.

19 Orientation of text
Select the Format menu and click on the Cells option to reveal the Format Cells window. The Alignment tab provides options to:

- Align the text both horizontally and vertically
- Wrap text
- Shrink to fit
- Merge Cells
- Change the angle of orientation of the text (i.e. slope the text).

20 Sort data
Select the Data menu and click on the Sort option to reveal the Sort Window, or select either of the two sort icons on the Standard toolbar.

21 Filtering
Select the Data menu, highlight the Filter option and click on AutoFilter.

22 Track changes
Select the Tools menu and highlight the Track Changes option to reveal the Highlight Changes option, which, when clicked, will open the Highlight Changes window.

23 Import files
Use the Copy and Paste functions which are available in all Microsoft Office® applications.

Alternatively, select the File menu and click on the Open option. Select the file you want to import. A Wizard will help you convert your file into the Microsoft Excel® format. It opens automatically when you try to import the file.

24 Logical operators/functions
The three logical operators are:

OR   OR(condition1, condition2) This returns true if one or more of the conditions is true; otherwise it returns false.

NOT   NOT(condition) This reverses the value of the condition.

AND   AND(condition1 and condition2) This returns the value true if both the conditions are true; otherwise it returns the value false.

25 Link spreadsheets

To link two cells, simply enter the sheet number, an exclamation mark and the cell reference. For example:

Sheet1!cell reference (e.g. sheet2!D6)

26 Style

Select the Format menu and click on Style to reveal the Style window. Click on the Modify button to open the Format Cell window to select format options.

27 Select data

Highlight the whole area of data.

28 Chart Wizard

a) Select the Insert menu and the Chart option. Click on the chart/graph type.
b) Check the chart by clicking on and holding down the mouse button on the Press and Hold to View Sample. Click on the Next button to move to Step 2 of the Chart Wizard.
c) Consider the data range (e.g. =sheet1!$B$6:$C$18 translates into the area at the top left-hand corner, cell B6 to cell C18). Click on the Next button to reveal Step 3.
d) Click on the tab of your choice (e.g. Legends). Click on the Next button to reveal Step 4.
e) Click on the radio button of your choice. Click on the Finish button.

29 Trendline

With the Chart visible, select the Chart menu and click on the Add Trendline option to open the Add Trendline window. Select the equation type for the series the line is based on.

30 Header and footer

With the chart or graph visible, select the File menu and the Page Setup option to reveal the Page Setup window. Click on the Header/Footer tab.

31 Text box

Click on the Text Box icon in the Draw toolbar to reveal a new mouse pointer, which allows you to draw a box by holding down the mouse button and dragging the box open.

32 Format graphs and charts

Double-click on the chart or graph element, then the Format window will appear (e.g. Format Chart Title, Format Legend, Format Data Labels and Format Data Series).

33 XY scatter graph – joining points

Double-click on a point to open the Format Data Series window. Select the Custom radio button to choose the Style, Color and Weight (thickness) of the line.

34 Types of charts and graphs

There are several different types of charts and graphs. The main ones are:

■ pie charts – useful way of visually presenting a range of results (e.g. sales results for four quarters of a year)

- bar/column charts – useful way of comparing results side by side (e.g. car sales by garage)
- line graphs – useful way of showing the relationship between two variables
- XY scatter graphs – useful way of comparing two variables which do not have an obvious relationship.

Creating and Using a Database

This chapter will help you to:

- create a database file, set up fields and enter a range of data
- import data files, update and interrogate database using complex search criteria
- plan and produce database reports in a variety of report formats
- format and present database reports.

This chapter covers unit 3 (Creating and Using a Database). There are no preconditions for studying this unit. However, its content does assume that you have the skills and understanding which are provided by the OCR Level 1 ICT course CLAiT 2006 (e.g. Unit 3: Database Manipulation and Unit 1: File Management and e-Document Production).

Assessment

After studying unit 3, your skills and understanding are assessed during a three-hour practical assignment. This is set by OCR and marked locally. However, the marking will be externally moderated by OCR. This ensures that the standard is being applied correctly across the many different providers of OCR CLAiT Plus 2006. If you are unsuccessful, you can be reassessed using a different assignment.

An alternative approach is for you to be assessed by an assignment set by OCR or designed by your centre. These assignments cover all the assessment objectives included in the unit. You will need to complete an OCR evidence checklist, explaining how each assessment objective has been covered.

Font families

CLAiT Plus uses font families in its assessments rather than font names. In chapter 1 font families are explained, along with how they relate to font names (see page 000). As you undertake each exercise, consider which font family you are using.

Databases

Databases are used extensively, but are often invisible to individuals, who can be unaware when they make contact with them. When you telephone your bank, for example, the staff member dealing with your enquiry is looking at your records stored on a database. This is equally true of almost any financial transaction (e.g. building society, insurance and credit cards). Many organisations keep records on a database of customers details, preferences, order patterns, contacts, and so on. Supermarkets will maintain a database of their stock, while employers are likely to hold information about employees' salary, working hours, rates of pay and holidays on a database.

Databases are extremely useful in organising information. They allow you to manipulate the data to compare different pieces of information and extract any combination of records to aid decision-making. Managers can see the relevant information before they decide what to do. When you tax your car online the system checks several databases (e.g. car insurance) to ensure your vehicle complies with the legal conditions to drive on the road. This happens with amazing speed compared with the alternative of gathering your documents together and visiting a post office to have them checked.

Database applications

This chapter is based on Microsoft Access® XP, which is a modern package that you can employ to create databases. Figure 3.1 shows the Access® application interface. When the application initially loads it shows the New File task pane on the right of the display. This provides a range of options, such as:

- create a new blank database – New section, Blank Database option
- open an existing database – Open a file section, file name of existing database

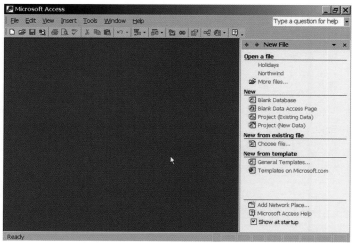

Figure 3.1 Microsoft Access®

- create a new database based on a template – New from template section

New database

With any application, it is always tempting to rush ahead and begin to construct something immediately. Modern software applications provide many powerful tools to edit and enhance the outcome and allow you to start straightaway. However, this can produce poorly designed and structured databases. It is not easy to restructure or amend a database once you have constructed it. It is good practice to plan your database before trying to develop it – a few minutes spent planning will save you many problems later.

We are going to develop a database for a sports club, showing the performance of some of the members. We will need to consider what information the database will hold. There are three terms that it is important to remember:

- field – this is an individual piece of information or data (e.g. surname)
- record – a group of fields with a common purpose (e.g. information about a single individual)
- table – a set of records (e.g. information about all the club's sprint runners).

The normal process is to consult the people who are going to use the database in order to identify what information it should contain and how it should be structured. This consultation has taken place and we have been requested to construct a database containing the following information:

- club membership number, date of membership, fees paid, title, first name, surname, street, town and postcode
- sporting events
- career best performance in an event.

When you have identified the information, you need to decide what sort of data it is (i.e. numbers or text). This is vital because the database needs to be able to sort and manipulate the information, so it must be sure what form the data takes. Microsoft Access® needs to know the type of data and how large it is so that it can reserve enough space to hold the information. Microsoft Access® allows you to define nine types of data:

- Text: a text field can hold up to 256 characters, which can be letters, numbers or special characters
- Memo: this allows you to store items such as sales reports, customer details, product information, and so on
- Numbers: a Microsoft Access® database can store numbers and also carry out calculations (e.g. calculate salary based on hours worked and pay rates)
- Date/time: a standard format is provided for dates and times
- Currency: this is a special number type designed for currency
- Autonumber: creates a unique number so that records can be numbered
- Yes/No: a simple type of data that can only be yes or no (e.g. Invoice paid yes/no)
- OLE Object: provides the means of including in the database other Microsoft Windows® objects (e.g. graphic image, spreadsheets and Microsoft® Word® files). When you click on the object, the appropriate application is opened and you can view that object.
- Hyperlink: provides the means to link the database to a website.

For our sports database we need to decide the data type of each field. Table 1 shows the type of each piece of data. There is an important practical issue with regard to dates in that different formats are used across the world. This can cause confusion. For CLAiT Plus 2006 you must use the English format (i.e. day, month and year).

Table 1 Sport data types

Field Name	Data Type
Club membership number	Autonumber – this field will automatically be incremented for each new member
Date of membership	Date
Fees paid	Yes/No
First name	Text – 20 characters
Last name	Text – 50 characters
Event	Text – 50 characters
Career Best performance	Number

In addition to deciding on the data types, you would also consider querying the data (i.e. asking the database questions – how many members ran the 100 metres faster than 12 seconds?), designing standard reports that the people using the database will need (e.g. who has not paid their membership fee?), and also input forms to provide an efficient data entry process. We will consider these issues later.

A key to the usefulness of any database is an obvious one, but is sometimes overlooked. The information contained in a database must be accurate. Potential errors are inserted into a database during data entry. It is essentially that data is entered accurately. It takes far longer to correct an error than any time gained by rushed entry. Inaccurate data can produce misleading reports and queries and lead to poor decisions.

Exercise 19

Creating a database

1 Load Microsoft Access® by selecting Start , highlighting the All Programs menu and clicking on the Microsoft Access® item or click on the Access® icon on the desktop.

2 Microsoft Access® will load (figure 3.1). Select Blank Database option in the task pane. The File New Database window opens to enable you to save your new database. Create the database as a file called Sports on a floppy disk (i.e. change Save in: box to floppy disk, File name: to Sports and click on Create button).

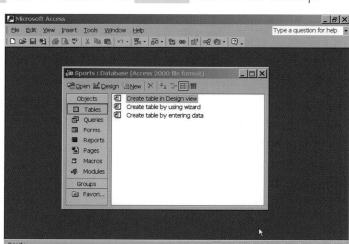

Figure 3.2 Sports Database window

The Sports Database window (figure 3.2) shows three options with the Tables object on the left-hand side selected:

- Create table in Design view

- Create table by using wizard

- Create table by entering data

3 Double-click on Create table in Design view and the table window opens.

4 You need to insert your field names and their types. If you enter Club membership in Field Name box and click in the corresponding Data Type box, a small down arrow will appear revealing a list of types. Select autonumber and click in the next Field Name box, then enter Date of Membership. Complete the table, as shown in figure 3.3.

5 When you enter a type, you should observe that in field size a value (e.g. 50) will appear with a text type and long integer with a number type. The value 50 indicates the number

of characters that the field can store, while a long integer is a whole number (i.e. no decimal places). Change First Name to 20 characters, but leave the other text items at 50 characters. If you wanted to show real numbers (i.e. with decimal places) then you would need to click in the Long Integer box to produce a down arrow which, if clicked, gives you other options. In this case, Career Best performance needs to include decimal places, so select the decimal option and insert 2 in the Scale and decimal places fields. This will allow data containing two decimal places to be entered (e.g. minutes and seconds).

You can also add a brief description alongside each field. This can be useful if you need to make changes later. It can be very difficult to understand your own decisions even a few months later.

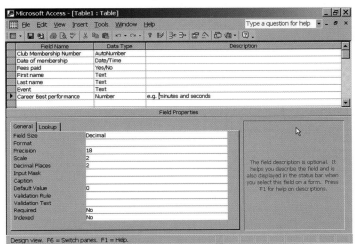

6 You need to save your table. If you select the File menu and the Save As option, the Save As window appears. Enter Membership and click on the OK button. If you try to close the window without saving, a

Figure 3.3 Table

warning message appears to offer you the option of saving your table.

7 A warning message will now appear asking you if you need a primary key. In this case you do not need to define one, so click on the No button. A primary key is a unique number which allows different tables to relate to each other. The table window reappears and you should close it by clicking on the close button in the top right-hand corner of the table window. You can now see the Sports Database window, but with an extra item added – membership.

8 Double-clicking on membership allows you to begin entering the data. We will return to this table to enter the data later. Close the window by clicking on the close button in the top right-hand corner of the Sports Database window.

9 Unless you wish to carry on with the next exercise immediately, close Microsoft Access® by clicking on the close button in the top right hand corner of the main application window or select the File menu and the Exit option.

Entering data

This unit stresses the importance of entering data accurately. The value of a database relies on its contents being accurate. Data errors considerably reduce the value of a database and can lead to wrong conclusions being reached and to poor business decisions. Correcting a single error takes considerably longer than entering many items of data, so accuracy is more important than speed of entry.

Table 2 Data input

Date of membership	Fees paid	First name	Last name	Event	Career Best performance
12/01/89	Yes	Michael	Doherty	MA	183.56
15/03/89	Yes	Brian	Dowling	SH	6.4
23/05/89	Yes	Hari	Ghorbani	SP	12.95
30/10/89	Yes	John	Gibbins	TW	120.50
12/12/89	Yes	Clive	Groom	HI	1.80
08/01/90	Yes	Peter	Hanson	SP	12.56
26/02/90	No	Hazel	Hill	TR	13.55
14/05/90	Yes	Jane	Hopwood	MA	200.85
17/09/90	No	Bill	Johnson	MD	14.05
09/12/90	Yes	Latia	Rannie	LO	6.25
03/01/91	Yes	Alice	Luckhurst	MD	16.15
22/02/91	Yes	Cheryl	Ludden	SP	15.75
11/04/91	Yes	Mark	Ludlow	SP	12.15
16/05/91	Yes	Asghar	Malik	HI	1.82
27/07/91	Yes	Christine	Morris	TR	13.10
14/11/91	Yes	Kevin	Steele	TW	118.55
12/01/92	Yes	Gary	Newhouse	MA	175.75
02/02/92	No	James	Night	MA	177.55
07/06/92	Yes	Richard	Palmer	SP	12.68
10/08/92	Yes	Julie	Pandey	MA	203.45
11/10/92	Yes	Pannu	Rasmussen	SP	12.10
04/01/93	Yes	Steven	Salt	TW	110.45
05/03/93	Yes	Rao	Palk	LO	5.95
17/05/93	Yes	Mathew	Peek	SP	12.85
19/07/93	Yes	Paula	Pitman	HI	1.56
23/09/93	No	Paul	Pecan	TW	122.85
30/11/93	Yes	Karl	Polkowski	MA	165.85
05/02/94	No	Oliver	Randall	TW	118.65
09/05/94	Yes	Alan	Rider	TR	15.65
13/07/94	Yes	Linda	Rose	LO	6.05
20/09/94	Yes	Fred	Scrim	SP	13.05
12/02/95	Yes	Kate	Scott	MD	15.35
25/07/95	Yes	Murray	Smith	TW	117.50
29/08/95	Yes	Ben	Sibley	TR	16.05
03/01/96	No	Peter	Swain	MI	3.58
16/05/96	Yes	John	Sutton	JA	55.34
21/09/96	Yes	Susan	Taylor	SH	5.6
22/10/97	Yes	Tom	Turner	HU	18.95
17/03/98	Yes	Dorothy	West	SP	15.65
18/06/98	Yes	Tim	Wilson	LA	52.35

The event column codes are:

- 100 and 200 metres – SP
- 110 and 400 metres hurdles – HU
- 400 metres – LA
- 800 metres – TW
- 1500 metres – MI
- 5000 metres – MD
- Marathon – MA
- Shot – SH
- Javelin – JA
- Discus – DI
- Long Jump – LO
- Triple Jump – TR
- High Jump – HI

Table 2 shows the records of 40 members of the club. The event column shows a two-letter code rather than the full name of the event (e.g. MA – Marathon). This type of encoding is frequently used to save time during data input. Only a few seconds are saved for each entry, but when you are inputting hundreds or even thousands of records, the saving is significant. Errors are also reduced since less needs to be entered. However, this is only half the story in that databases are also concerned with presenting, comparing and contrasting information. A code is of little benefit if it is not understood by the database users. An effective code is one that users recognise and can convert to the full terms. This also helps users enter the data since they are easily able to recognise errors and it is always easier to enter meaningful data than a meaningless set of numbers and letters. A set of random numbers is unlikely to be helpful unless users have a reason to memorise them (e.g. product codes widely used in the company). Database reports that contain encoded information need to be meaningful to the reader or their value will be diminished by the need to translate them into the actual terms. The example in Table 2 shows encoding based on an attempt to use the first two letters of the event name or something relating to the name (e.g. 100 and 200 metres SP or sprint, SH – Shot, 1500 metres – metric mile MI, and 5000 metres – middle distance MD). They are therefore shorter and reasonably meaningful to a sports club user.

Once you have created a database that reflects your needs, it is important that your data is aligned with the types of data you have specified. If the data is different, you will waste time and perhaps produce confusing results. An example of potential confusion is that there are several alternative ways of showing dates (e.g. American – month, day and year). It is important to present dates in the format that your users understand. In the case of Great Britain, this is day, month and year. Often users will wish to search for data relating for a particular date; this will be seriously impaired if dates have been entered in the wrong format. An American format 2/09/02 means 9 February 2002. It is therefore vital that dates are entered correctly. This type of error is difficult to detect and so it is important to ensure accurate and correct input.

Exercise 20

Entering data

1 Load Microsoft Access® by selecting Start, highlighting the All Programs menu and clicking on the Microsoft Access® item or click on the Access® icon on the desktop. Insert your floppy disk into the drive.

2 The New File task pane (figure 3.1) offers you the choice of:

- opening an existing database file
- creating a new blank database.

If you have only recently created the Sports database (see previous exercise), you should see it listed in the Open a file section. If not, select the More files option, which will reveal the Open window to allow you to locate the file Sports and load it.

3 The Sports: Database window should open (figure 3.4). By double-clicking on the membership table item, it will open for data entry.

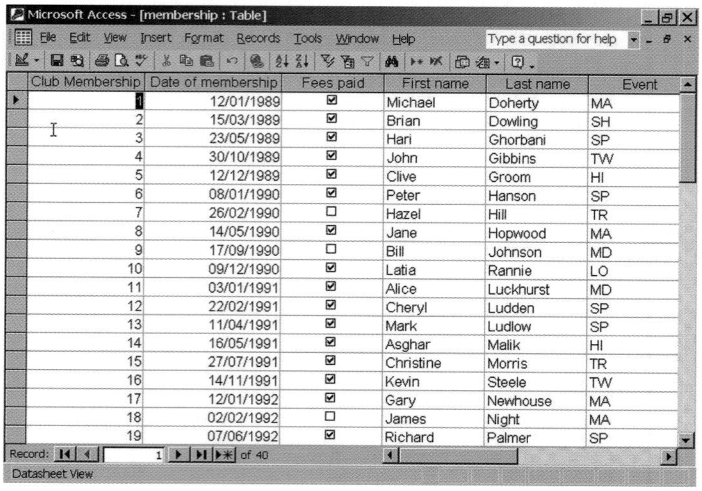

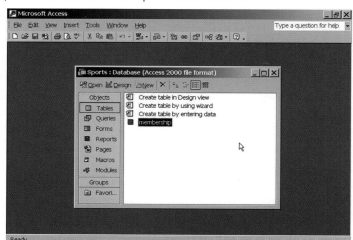

Figure 3.4 Sports database – Membership table

4 Some of the columns are too small to show the whole title. You can adjust the size by placing your mouse pointer over the line separating the columns and it will change shape to form a double arrow. If you hold down the mouse button, you can drag the column line to widen it. Change the column widths so that their titles can be seen.

Club Membership	Date of membership	Fees paid	First name	Last name	Event
1	12/01/1989	☑	Michael	Doherty	MA
2	15/03/1989	☑	Brian	Dowling	SH
3	23/05/1989	☑	Hari	Ghorbani	SP
4	30/10/1989	☑	John	Gibbins	TW
5	12/12/1989	☑	Clive	Groom	HI
6	08/01/1990	☑	Peter	Hanson	SP
7	26/02/1990	☐	Hazel	Hill	TR
8	14/05/1990	☑	Jane	Hopwood	MA
9	17/09/1990	☐	Bill	Johnson	MD
10	09/12/1990	☑	Latia	Rannie	LO
11	03/01/1991	☑	Alice	Luckhurst	MD
12	22/02/1991	☑	Cheryl	Ludden	SP
13	11/04/1991	☑	Mark	Ludlow	SP
14	16/05/1991	☑	Asghar	Malik	HI
15	27/07/1991	☑	Christine	Morris	TR
16	14/11/1991	☑	Kevin	Steele	TW
17	12/01/1992	☑	Gary	Newhouse	MA
18	02/02/1992	☐	James	Night	MA
19	07/06/1992	☑	Richard	Palmer	SP

Figure 3.5 Membership table

5 Enter the data shown in table 2. Remember that the membership number is entered automatically by Microsoft Access®. Click in the field Date of Membership and enter the date. You can enter data into any field providing you click into that field first. The Fees paid field shows a small rectangle that you click in to indicate that the fees have been paid. It is left blank if the fees have not been paid.

6 Figure 3.5 shows the completed table in full screen view. It is very important to check that each record has been entered accurately. If you find a mistake, click on the appropriate field and enter your correction.

7 Save your data by selecting the File menu and the Save option.

8 Close the membership: Table window by clicking on the close button in the top right-hand corner of the window.

9 Close Microsoft Access® by clicking on the close button in top right-hand corner of the main application window or select the File menu and the Exit option.

Reports

The information stored in a database is only part of the story. The real value of databases lies in accessing the information in a form that is useful to you. This involves designing reports, which are the means of presenting selected data. Microsoft Access® provides two ways of helping you extract information in the form of a report. They are:

■ using the Access® Wizard to assist your design (i.e. Create report by using wizard)

■ developing the report manually (i.e. Create report in Design view).

If you look at the Sports Database window you will see that down the left-hand side is a series of buttons. If you select Reports, figure 3.6 will appear, showing you the two approaches to creating reports.

Figure 3.7 is an example of a simple report listing all the members of the Sports Club in order of their membership number.

Reports are intended to present information to users. It is therefore

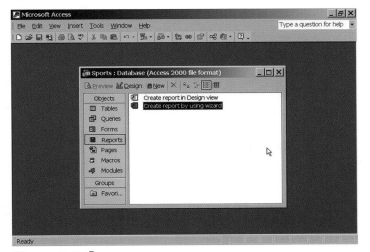

Figure 3.6 Reports

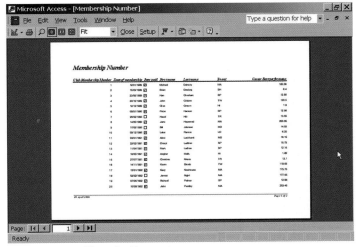

Figure 3.7 Simple Report

important that the information is displayed effectively so that it is easy to understand. This means that you need to control the alignment of the data and how it is presented. The presentation and alignment of a report can be changed by highlighting the report you wish to amend and clicking on the Design icon on the toolbar. This will open the report showing the structure (figure 3.8). If you click on the text boxes and headers you will see they are enclosed in a frame with small rectangles; these allow you to resize and move them. You can also use the Format menu Align option to align the text (i.e. left, right, top, bottom and to grid).

When you print or review a report on the screen you will sometimes notice that the fields are not printed or shown in full. This is sometimes the result of different text boxes overlapping, so you need to move and resize them. This is important because:

■ It avoids confusing readers of the report, who may be misled by shortened title or data. This is important if decisions are being taken on the basis of the information.

■ Presentation of a report will help convince managers that they need to act on the information it contains. A poorly presented report will not help to persuade managers to treat the information with the importance it deserves.

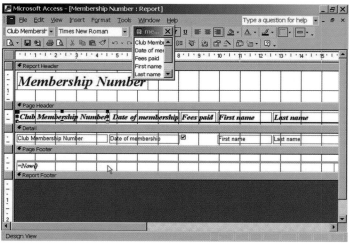

Figure 3.8 Edit reports

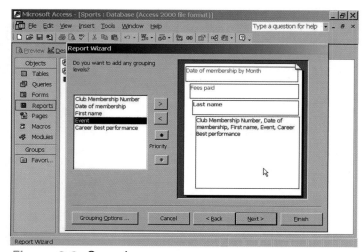

Figure 3.9 Grouping

An important approach to presenting a report is to group records together with some common characteristic. This could be the year when the members joined the sports club or any other characteristic (i.e. a specific field). Using the Report Wizard you are offered the opportunity to group your information by a specific field. Figure 3.9 shows this aspect of the Wizard.

For example, comparing the presentation of grouped information with a list of the same information:

List of Orders

1999 Order ABC
2001 Order BHK
2000 Order DGH
2000 Order HJY
1999 Order JCF
2001 Order JKY

Orders Grouped by Year

1999

Order ABC
Order JCF

2000

Order DGH
Order HJY

2001

Order JKY
Order BHK

The Report Wizard provides a systematic process to the design of reports. The first step is to identify the fields that will be included in the report. Figure 3.10 shows the Wizard's first step. This window allows you to select the table or query on which to base the report. We will consider queries later in the chapter. Once a table or query has been selected, you can choose the individual fields from it to include in the report.

The second step is to choose how to group the fields. This is shown in figure 3.9. The third step is to order your fields and this is shown in figure 3.11.

The fourth step in creating a report is to select its layout. There are three options Columnar, Tabular and Justified. The layout associated with each presentation type is shown in the window. This window also provides you with the option to select the orientation of the report (i.e. Portrait or Landscape) and adjust the field widths so they all appear on the page. Figure 3.12 shows the fourth step.

Step 5 (figure 3.13) offers you a variety of styles in which to present your report. The sixth and final step (figure 3.14) allows you to name your report and modify the report.

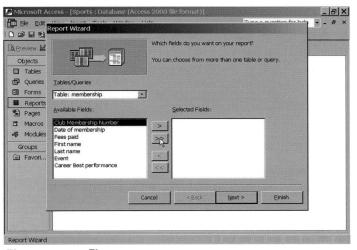

Figure 3.10 First step

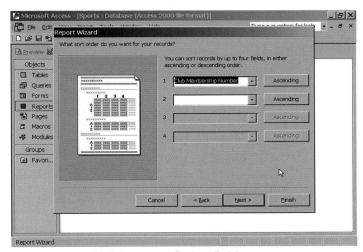

Figure 3.11 Third step – Order fields

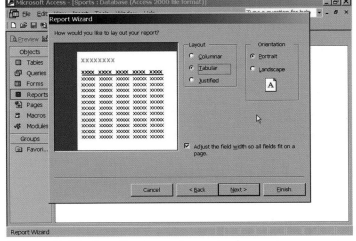

Figure 3.12 Fourth step – Layout of report

When you open a report by clicking on it in the database report window, a small (dialog) window will open sometimes called Enter Parameter Value. Simply click on the OK button to proceed.

Printing

You will often need to print a report or a table of information in order to provide the information to a wider audience than those who have direct access to the database. Presentation of the information is important, so you should preview the document before you print it to check it. The Print Preview option is available from the File menu and operates in the same way that it does in other Microsoft Office® applications. You are presented with an image of the report or table as it will appear when printed. Sometimes, because of the density of the information, you will need to use the zoom function (i.e. a magnifying glass) on the toolbar to see the detail.

If the preview is acceptable, you can either print it directly from the

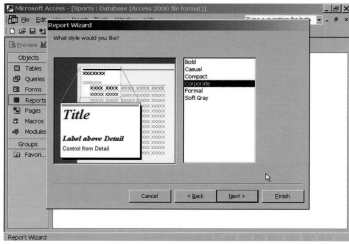

Figure 3.13 Fifth step – Styles

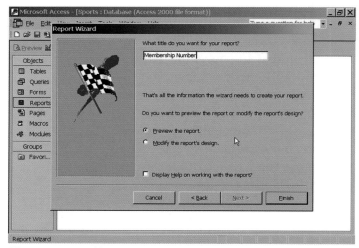

Figure 3.14 Name report

preview window by selecting the Print icon on the toolbar, or close the window and select the File menu and then the Print option to reveal the Print window. By clicking on the OK button the report or table will be printed. If the preview is not satisfactory you may need to select the File menu and Page Setup to change the margins, orientation and column settings. If you are printing a report you may have to use the Design option to move and resize the boxes.

Exercise 21

Reports

1 Load Microsoft Access® by selecting the Start button, highlighting the All Programs option and clicking on the Microsoft Access® item or click on the Access® icon on the desktop. Insert your floppy disk into the drive.

2 The New File task pane (figure 3.1) offers you the choice of:

- opening an existing database file
- creating a new blank database.

If you have only recently created the Sports database (see previous exercise), you should see it listed in the Open a file section. If not, select the More files option, which will reveal the Open window to allow you to locate the file Sports and load it.

3 If the Reports button is not pressed, click on it to show the two options for creating a report.

4 Select Create report by using a wizard and the Report Wizard window (figure 3.10) will appear. This shows the table that the report will be based on in the box below the Tables/Queries title. It allows you to change the table or to select a query on which to base your report. The process is the same in both cases. This window allows you to select which fields you wish to include in your report. You select a field by highlighting it and clicking on the single arrow button pointing towards the right-hand box. If you click on the double arrow button you will select all the fields. If you accidentally select a field by mistake you can correct it by highlighting it and using the left-pointing arrow button.

5 Select Club Membership, First name and Last name to produce a report which is essentially a list of the members.

6 When you have successfully selected your fields, click on the Next button to reveal the next window that allows you to group your information by again highlighting the item and using the arrow button. Experiment with different groupings. However, return to the original state when you have finished and click on the Next button. You should note that there is a Back button that lets you to return to the previous window if you have made an error.

7 The next window enables you to sort your records into ascending or descending order. In this example we do not wish to sort the records, so simply click on the Next button. This allows you to change the orientation of the report from portrait to landscape, as well as selecting the layout of the report – Columnar, Tabular or Justified. You can explore these options since this window provides you with a preview facility. Select Portrait and Tabular and click on the Next button.

8 The next window offers you a choice of styles and you can explore the options by watching the preview area. Select Formal and click on the Next button.

9 You are now approaching the end of the Wizard process and by using the window you can choose the title of your report – enter Membership List. You can preview your report or modify its design. Click on the Finish button. The report will now appear (figure 3.15).

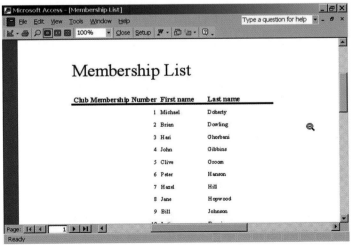

Figure 3.15 Membership report

continued

10 Select the File menu and the Print Preview option to check the report. Print the report by selecting the File menu, clicking on the Print option and then clicking on the OK button to print with the default settings or select the printer icon in the Print Preview window. Before you print, check that the printer is switched on and has paper.

11 Close the Report window using the control buttons in the top right-hand corner of the window. You will now see the Sports database window with the new report, Membership List, included.

12 If you wish to stop now, close the Sports: Database window using the Close button in the top right-hand corner of the window; to move to the next exercise ignore this step.

13 Close Microsoft Access® by clicking on the close button in the top right-hand corner of the main application window or selecting the File menu and the Exit option.

Amending a report

Although you have created a report using the Wizard it is possible to make changes to the layout and presentation. You can alter the report's:

- margins (i.e. left, right, top and bottom)
- orientation (i.e. portrait or landscape)
- headers and footers
- automatic fields (i.e. date, page and file name).

Exercise 22

Amending the report

1 Load Microsoft Access® by selecting the Start button, highlighting the All Programs option and clicking on the Microsoft Access® item or by clicking on the Access® icon on the desktop. Insert your floppy disk into the drive.

2 The New File task pane (figure 3.1) offers you the choice of:

- opening an existing database file
- creating a new blank database.

If you have only recently created the Sports database, you should see it listed in the Open a file section. If not, select the More files option, which will reveal Open window to allow you to locate the file Sports and load it.

3 If the Reports button is not pressed, click on it to show the Membership List report. Click on Membership List to reveal the report. Investigate the report – move to page 2. Notice that at the bottom of page 2 the date is shown, as well as page 1 of 2. These are produced by automatic fields, inserted into the report by the Wizard, that calculate the date and page length.

4 It is straightforward to change the report's margins and orientation by selecting the File menu and the Page Setup option, or if the report is open, select the Setup button. Both methods will open the Page Setup window (figure 3.16), allowing you to change the margins; if you select the Page tab, you can alter the orientation. You can also select the size of paper that the report will be printed on.

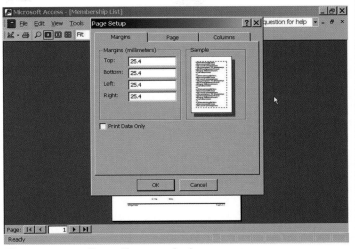

Figure 3.16 Page Setup window

5 Change all four margins to 34.99 mm and the orientation to landscape. Inspect the result of these changes. Close the Report window using the control buttons in the top right-hand corner of the window.

6 Microsoft Access® also provides tools to alter the details of the report. If you highlight Membership List and click on the Design icon on the toolbar, the structure of the report is revealed (figure 3.8). You can now manipulate the various elements of the report. Investigate changing the structure by resizing and moving the boxes, and use the Align option in the Format menu to change alignment. For example, resize the Membership List text box so it fills the whole width, and explore different alignments. Continue until you are confident.

7 If you click on the element Membership List you will see that the title is enclosed in a frame (figure 3.17). This is the equivalent of highlighting it. You can drag the frame and its contents – the mouse pointer changes to a small hand and you can move the frame by holding down the mouse button and dragging it. Move the title Membership List to the centre of the report.

8 With the Membership List enclosed in a frame you can also change the font and character size. Change the font to Arial and character size to 28, using the toolbar. You will need to adjust the size of the frame to this by placing the pointer on the frame edge – it will change to a double-headed arrow. If you hold down the left mouse button you can drag the frame edge to make it larger.

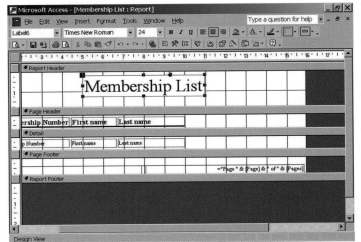

Figure 3.17 Adjust framer

continued

9 Now change the character size of the subheading (Page Header) to 12. You will need to rearrange the three headings. In order to align the information you will also need to align the detail to the Page Header subtitles.

10 If you consider the Page Footer you will see:

=Now() – this is the date automatic field

="Page " & [Page] & "of" & [Pages] – this is the page automatic field

These are inserted using the Insert menu and either the Page Numbers or Date and Time option. If you left or right double-click on the Report Footer, a window will appear providing a range of options. Explore the options and you will notice that you can alter the presentation of the date and pages. In a similar way, Report Header can be changed. Try to add your name to the footer (Right-click to open a pop-up box, select Toolbox and use the Label tool).

11 When you have finished you can close the design view of the report using the control buttons in the right-hand corner of the window. You will be presented with a message window asking you if you would like to save the changes you have made. Click on the Yes button.

12 Close the Sports: Database window using the close button in the top right-hand corner of the window.

13 Close Microsoft Access® by clicking on the close button in the top right-hand corner of the main application window, or select the File menu and the Exit option.

AutoReport

There is another quick way to produce reports other than using the Wizard. This is the AutoReport. This can be accessed by selecting the New button in the Report window. This opens the New Report window, which contains a range of options (figure 3.18), including AutoReport: Tabular and AutoReport: Columnar. In this window you need to select the table or query that the report is based on by using the down arrow.

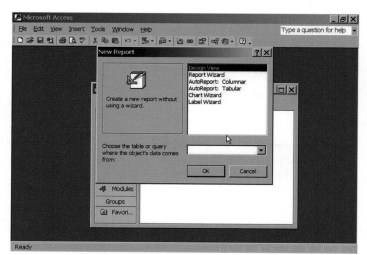

Figure 3.18 AutoReport

If you select one of the AutoReport options, a report showing the contents of the selected table or query will appear in the chosen layout. Figure 3.19 shows the columnar option.

You can give the report a name and save it. The AutoReport can be amended using the Design option in the same way that a report produced using the Wizard can be.

Data entry forms

When entering information into a database, it is important that the source of the data is designed to make data entry as easy as possible. This will improve productivity and reduce errors. The source is normally some type of form. In the example we have been using of a Sports Club, the source document could be the membership application form. A common problem is that the membership form's layout does not correspond to the database table. This is often made worse by the use of abbreviations in the database, so that mistakes can easily be made.

Microsoft Access® allows you to design a data entry form that resembles the source document, to avoid errors and make the process efficient. Figure 3.20 shows Sports: Database in forms view (i.e. the Forms button has been clicked) and the two ways that Microsoft Access® provides of creating forms:

- Create form in Design view
- Create form by using wizard.

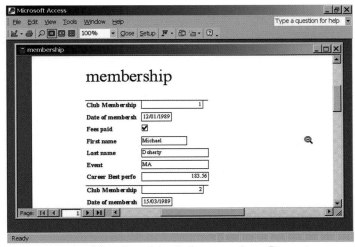
Figure 3.19 Membership Columnar AutoReport

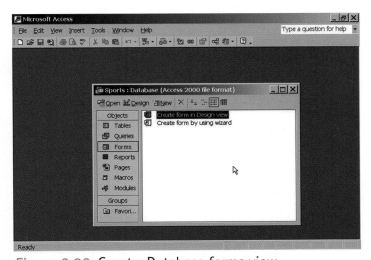
Figure 3.20 Sports: Database forms view

By printing out the data entry form you have created a form which serves both as an input document and as a membership application form. This will minimise errors and reduce the need to transfer data between documents. CLAiT Plus 2006 does not require you to be skilled in the development and use of forms. However, it is included to provide you with the opportunity to understand the use of forms if you wish.

Exercise 23

Data entry form

1 Load Microsoft Access® by selecting the Start button, highlighting the All Programs option and clicking on the Microsoft Access® item or by clicking on the Access® icon on the desktop. Insert your floppy disk into the drive.

2 The New File task pane (figure 3.1) offers you the choice of:

- opening an existing database file
- creating a new blank database.

If you have only recently finished the last exercise, the Sports database will still be listed in the Open a file section. If not, select the More files option, which will reveal Open window to allow you to locate the file Sports and load it.

3 Click on the Forms button on the left-hand side of the window and you will reveal two options to create a form. This is shown in figure 3.20. Click on the Create form by using wizard option to open the Form Wizard window. The fields to include in the form are chosen by highlighting the field and clicking on the single arrow keys. If the double arrow is selected, all the fields are included. In this case, select all the fields (figure 3.21).

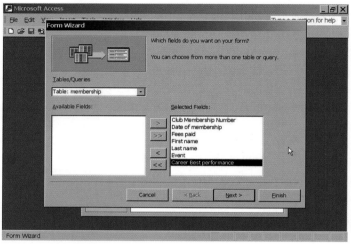

Figure 3.21 Form Wizard

4 Click on the Next button to move to the next stage of the Wizard. This gives you a choice of six layouts. In this case, select Justified and click on the Next button to reveal figure 3.22, which provides you with a variety of style choices.

5 Select the Standard style, but you should also explore the different options. Click on the Next button to reveal figure 3.23. This allows you to select a

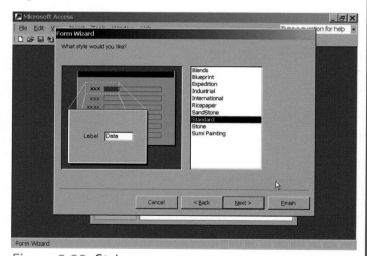

Figure 3.22 Styles

name for your form. Enter Membership Form and complete the process by clicking on Finish button.

6 The Membership Form is shown in the Sports Database window when the Forms button is pressed. By double-clicking on Membership Form you can see the completed form, showing the first record of the membership table (figure 3.24).

7 The forms for all members can be printed out by selecting the File menu, the Print option and the OK button. All the records will be printed in the form layout. Print the data forms. The printout can help administer the Sports Club by allowing you to work manually on the membership list (e.g. copies can be provided for all members of the management team).

8 A blank form can be produced by selecting the Arrow Star button on the bottom line of the form. New members can also be added directly through the form into the database. In this case, you would need to find record 41. The membership number is automatically generated.

9 Close the Sports: Database window using the close button in the top right-hand corner of the window.

10 Close Microsoft Access® by clicking on the close button in the top right-hand corner of the main application window or select the File menu and the Exit option.

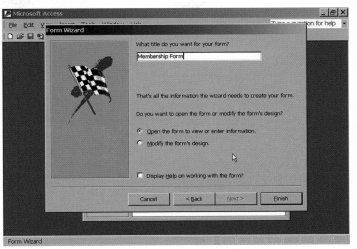

Figure 3.23 Form name

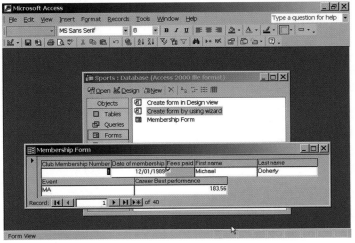

Figure 3.24 Completed Membership Form

Presentation of data – Labels

You have already investigated some of the possibilities of presenting the information contained in a database so that it is more useful to you. Reports and forms allow you to extract data in a way that meets your needs. You can group information, present it as a table, in a column or in justified form. One way that is often required is extracting information in order to produce address labels.

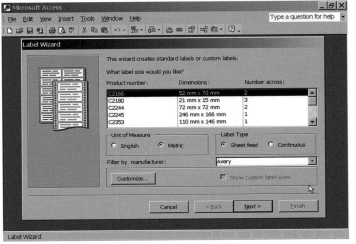

Figure 3.25 Size of labels

If you click on the <u>N</u>ew button in the Report window, a new window will appear called New Report (figure 3.18). This provides access to the Label Wizard, which will assist you to design a label.

In order to use the Label Wizard you need to select a table from which to supply the information. The table can be inserted in the New Report window or selected from the list available if the down arrow button at the end of the box is clicked.

Figures 3.25 to 3.31 show the sequence of steps to produce the labels. Step 1 (figure 3.25) allows you to select the size of lables to match the ones you use.

Step 2 (figure 3.26) allows you to select the font, character size and colour of your text.

Step 3 (figure 3.27) provides you with the means to design your label (i.e. selecting the fields, layout and adding extra text).

Step 4 (figure 3.28) enables you to sort your labels by a chosen field (e.g. membership number or name).

Step 5 (figure 3.29) is the final stage, where you can name your label report, choose to preview it and modify the design.

Figure 3.30 illustrates an example label, based on the membership database table.

When you close the labels window (figure 3.30), the report is saved and added to the window (figure 3.31).

Reports can be designed to present data in many forms, such as a

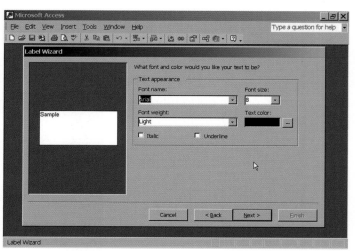

Figure 3.26 Font and character size

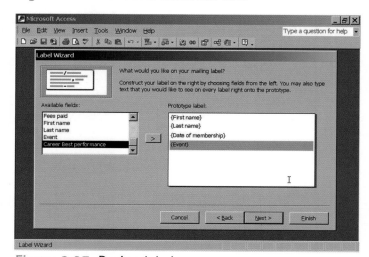

Figure 3.27 Design label

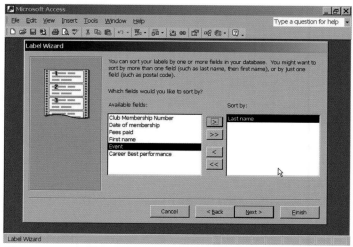

Figure 3.28 Sort labels

particular field order, table/list/group format and summaries. During the Report Wizard process, you select the order of presentation of the fields, the options to present your data in table form or columns and to group the data.

CLAiT Plus 2006 for Office® XP

Queries can also be designed to present the data in your chosen order by using the Query Wizards (i.e. Simple and Crosstab Query Wizard) in a similar way to producing a report. If you produce a query in design view, the order of presentation is determined by the order in which you select the fields. We will consider queries later in this chapter.

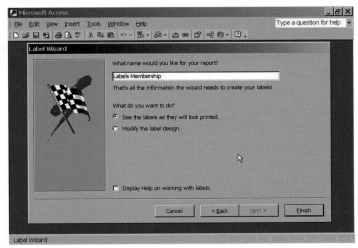

Figure 3.29 Name the label report

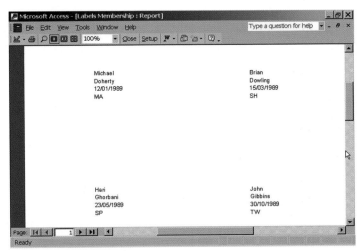

Figure 3.30 Labels

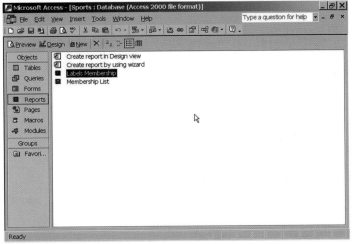

Figure 3.31 Report Window

Importing a Data file

Unit 3 requires that you are able to import or open a data file in Microsoft Access®. Access® provides a standard approach to importing data using the File menu, highlighting the Get External Data and clicking the Import option to reveal the Import Window (figure 3.32). The option is only available when a database window is open, so you will need to create a new database or open an existing one.

The Import Window allows you can select files that can be imported into a Microsoft Access® database. Figure 3.33 shows the spreadsheet files created in chapter 2 that can now be imported into Microsoft Access®. The file is selected by double-clicking on it or by single-clicking on the file and then on the Import button. Microsoft Access® will then guide you through the process of converting the data into a database format. Figure 3.33 shows the Import Spreadsheet Wizard.

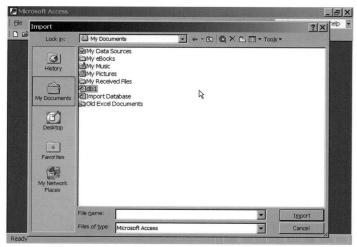

Figure 3.32 Import Window

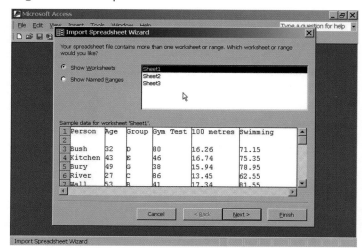

Figure 3.33 Import Spreadsheet Wizard

Exercise 24

Importing a data file

1 Load Microsoft Access® by selecting the Start button, highlighting the All Programs option and clicking on the Microsoft Access® item or clicking on the Access® icon on the desktop. Insert your floppy disk into the drive.

2 The New File task pane (figure 3.1) offers you the choice of:

- opening an existing database file
- creating a new blank database.

Select Create a blank database. The File New Database window opens. Save the database as a file called Import on a floppy disk. An alternative is to open an existing database, in which case, the imported data is saved either in a new table or combined with an existing table.

3 Click on the File menu and highlight Get External Data to reveal the Import option. Click on Import to show the Import Window (figure 3.32). You are going to import one of the spreadsheets you created in chapter 2 – Sales Forecast – so you need to adjust the

continued

Look in: box to the location you saved the spreadsheet (e.g. floppy disk). When Sales Forecast is in the window, double-click on the file to load it into Microsoft Access®.

4 The Import Spreadsheet Wizard will appear with the contents of Sales Forecast within the window. The display shows each spreadsheet sheet. In this case you want to select Sheet 1. Click the Next button to open the next window, which will ask you to select the database fields. Click on the radio button – First Row Contains Column Headings and then on the Next button to see if the row headings are suitable to become the field titles. In this case you will see a warning message that informs you that the first row contains data that cannot be used in valid Microsoft Access® field names. Click on OK. This means that you cannot import the column titles as your field names, but we can correct this later, so go on.

5 The next window to appear asks you to choose between storing the imported information In a New Table or In an Existing Table. In this case, select In a New Table and click on the Next button.

6 The new window that is shown offers you the opportunity to modify the fields in the database table. You select the column of the field by clicking in it. You can now change the fields selected by Microsoft Access® back to those from the imported spreadsheet. Change Field 1 to Item, Field 2 to January, Field 3 to February, and so on, until you have replaced all the fields. Click on the Next button.

7 The next step is revealed. Now you can add a primary key, which is essentially a unique record identifier. However, in this case you do not need a primary key. Select No primary key by clicking in the radio button and then click on the Next button.

8 The final step allows you to complete the process of importing data by clicking on the Finish button. However, you need to name your new table, so enter Sales Office® in the Import to Table: box in the centre of the window and then click Finish. An information window will appear to tell you when you have finished importing the file. Click the OK button on the information window after you have read it.

9 You will now see that your new table has been listed in the database window you created originally. In this case, it was the Import Database.

10 The table you have created by importing the spreadsheet data has been added to the database window as the file Sales Office®.

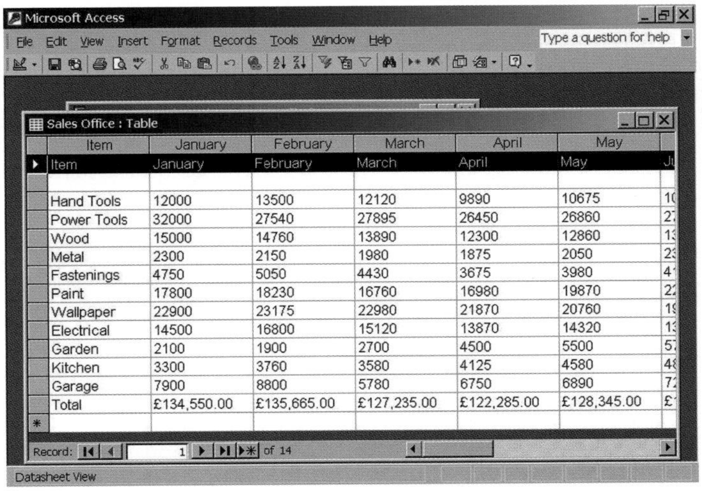

Item	January	February	March	April	May
Item	January	February	March	April	May
Hand Tools	12000	13500	12120	9890	10675
Power Tools	32000	27540	27895	26450	26860
Wood	15000	14760	13890	12300	12860
Metal	2300	2150	1980	1875	2050
Fastenings	4750	5050	4430	3675	3980
Paint	17800	18230	16760	16980	19870
Wallpaper	22900	23175	22980	21870	20760
Electrical	14500	16800	15120	13870	14320
Garden	2100	1900	2700	4500	5500
Kitchen	3300	3760	3580	4125	4580
Garage	7900	8800	5780	6750	6890
Total	£134,550.00	£135,665.00	£127,235.00	£122,285.00	£128,345.00

Figure 3.34 Sales Office® table

11 If you double-click on the file Sales Office®, the table will open and you can see the new data (figure 3.34). There is one final step to take and that is to remove the spreadsheets column headings and blank line. Delete rows 1 and 2 by highlighting them and selecting the Edit menu and the Delete option.

12 Close the window by clicking on the close button in the top right-hand corner of the Sales Office® window.

13 Close Microsoft Access® by clicking on the close button in the top right-hand corner of the main application window or select the File menu and the Exit option.

Maintenance

The maintenance of any database requires that occasionally you need to add, amend and delete records and fields. To amend a field is a straightforward task in that you need to click in it, delete the contents and enter the new data. It is also possible to delete an entire column (i.e. remove a field from all records) or an individual row (i.e. an individual record). By placing your pointer over the column or row heading you will see it change shape to become a thick black arrow. If you click now, the whole column or row is highlighted. To delete the row or column, select the Edit menu and click on the Delete, Delete Record or Delete Column option (figure 3.35). Before the row or column is removed, a message window will ask you to confirm that you want the record or field deleted permanently.

This type of approach is effective if you want to change an individual data item or delete a record or entire field, but if you want to change a recurring piece of the information, then Microsoft Access® provides a more productive method called Find and Replace. If you select the Edit menu and click on Replace, then the Find and Replace window will appear (figure 3.36). This window provides two different functions. It can simply search your data to locate a particular piece of information or it can locate an item and then replace it. The latter is very useful when you have to change an item which occurs in several places in your database. The functions allow you select a particular table to search and specify the degree of match you are seeking (i.e. any part of the field, the whole field or the start of a field).

The Find and Replace function ensures that you find every item that you are seeking to find or

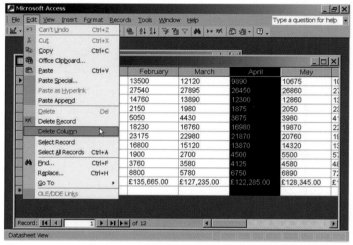

Figure 3.35 Delete a record

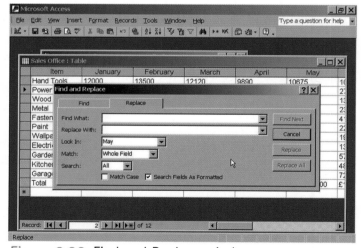

Figure 3.36 Find and Replace window

to replace. A manual search is likely to miss items, so the function is a method of guaranteeing a perfect result. It is also considerably quicker.

Sorting

Microsoft Access® provides a number of ways of presenting information. One of the most straightforward is sorting. Information can be ordered alphabetically or numerically so that it is ascending (i.e. lowest to highest) or descending (i.e. highest to lowest). The sort functions are available on the toolbar.

Figure 3.37 shows the results of sorting the Sales Office® table by descending alphabetical value. Compare the effects on the data of the different types of sorting.

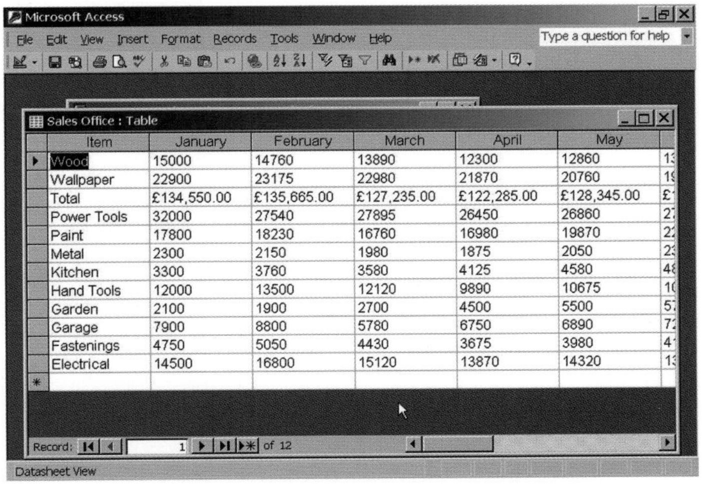

Item	January	February	March	April	May
Wood	15000	14760	13890	12300	12860
Wallpaper	22900	23175	22980	21870	20760
Total	£134,550.00	£135,665.00	£127,235.00	£122,285.00	£128,345.00
Power Tools	32000	27540	27895	26450	26860
Paint	17800	18230	16760	16980	19870
Metal	2300	2150	1980	1875	2050
Kitchen	3300	3760	3580	4125	4580
Hand Tools	12000	13500	12120	9890	10675
Garden	2100	1900	2700	4500	5500
Garage	7900	8800	5780	6750	6890
Fastenings	4750	5050	4430	3675	3980
Electrical	14500	16800	15120	13870	14320

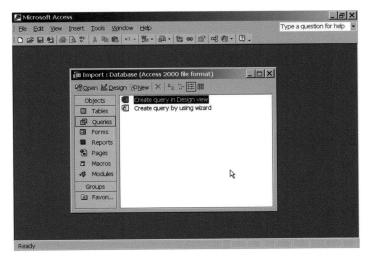

Figure 3.37 Sorted Data

Queries

A major requirement of any database is the ability to extract the information that it contains. Microsoft Access® enables you to find out what information is held within the database in any form or combination you require. Extracting data is called querying the database. The starting point for producing a query is the database window. Figure 3.38 shows the two ways of producing a query which are available once you have selected the Queries button on the left-hand side of window. They are:

- Create a query in Design view
- Create a query using wizard.

Figure 3.38 Creating a query

Exercise 25

Querying data

1 Load Microsoft Access® by selecting the Start button, highlighting the All Programs option and clicking on the Microsoft Access® item or clicking on the Access® icon on the desktop. Insert your floppy disk into the drive.

2 The New File task pane (figure 3.1) offers you the choice of:

- opening an existing database file

- creating a new blank database.

If you have only recently finished the previous exercises, the Sports database will still be listed in the Open a file section. If not, select the More files option, which will reveal Open window to allow you to locate the file Sports and load it. The Sports database window will open. Click on the Queries button to reveal figure 3.38.

3 Select Create query in Design view and you will see an overlaid window Show Table appear. Click on the Add button and you will notice a small window called Membership. Now click on the Close button in Show Table to reveal figure 3.39.

4 The cursor will be flashing in the Field: box, and if you click on the down arrow all the Membership table fields are available for you to select from. Select the Club Membership item by clicking on it and you will see it appear in the Field: box. Now click in the Sort: box and you will see another down-arrow button that provides access to sorting functions. Select the Ascending option.

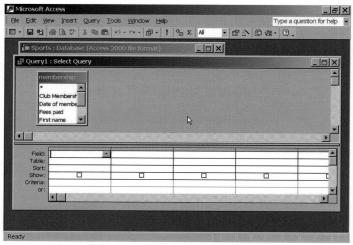

Figure 3.39 Select Query

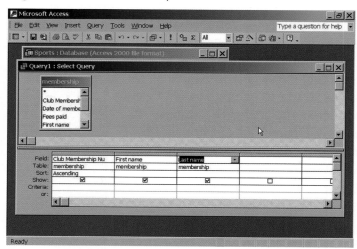

Figure 3.40 Query fields

5 Now click in the next column and select First name in the Field box. Repeat this action in the third column, selecting Last name. Figure 3.40 shows the result you should have obtained.

6 Now close the window using the button in the top right-hand corner. A message window will appear asking you if you want to save the query as Query1. Click on the Yes button and another window (dialog) box will appear, to offer you the opportunity to name your query. Change the name to List and click on the OK button. You will see your query appear in the Sports: database window (assuming the Queries button has been selected).

7 You have created a straightforward query to produce a list of members' names and their membership numbers (i.e. only the fields you have selected will appear in your query). If

you double-click on the query (List), you will see the results of the query appear (figure 3.41).

8 If you need to change your query because, for example, it is producing incorrect results, you need to select the Design icon on the toolbar with List highlighted.

9 Highlight List and click on the Design icon. You are now going to change the list to select only those members who have not paid their membership fees.

10 Select the fourth column and in the Field box insert the fees paid field. Now click in the Criteria row and enter =No. You are telling Microsoft Access® only to present records of members who have a value equal to No (i.e. not paid) in this field (figure 3.42). Fees Paid can only have two values Yes or No. Close the window and you will be asked if you want to save your changes. Click on the Yes button to return to the Sports: Database window with List showing. Double-click on List to see your new query.

11 Close Microsoft Access® by clicking on the close button in the top right-hand corner of the main application window, or select the File menu and the Exit option.

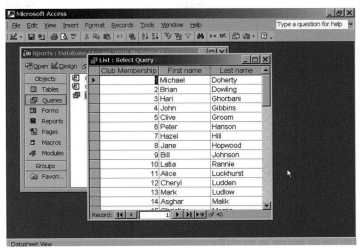

Figure 3.41 List Query

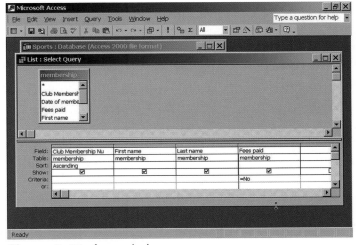

Figure 3.42 Amended query

Criteria

In the previous exercise you had your first experience of using a criterion to select information (e.g. =No). This was relatively simple, but you can use a variety of symbols to be more precise. These are:

> greater than

< less than

>= greater than or equal to

<= less than or equal to

<> not equal to

These symbols are available on the keyboard:

> greater than – hold the shift key down and then the full stop key

< less than – hold the shift key down and then the comma key

>= greater than or equal to – hold the shift key down and then the full stop key, release the keys and press the equal key

<= less than or equal to – hold the shift key down and then the comma key, release the keys and press the equal key

<> not equal to – hold the shift key down, press the comma key and then the full stop key

In addition to these symbols are the logical operators:

- AND
- OR.

AND combines two different criteria, both of which must be true before the action can be undertaken. For example:

Club Membership >=10 AND <=20

This selects records of members who have a membership number greater than or equal to 10 and also less than or equal to 20 (i.e. records for Club Members 10 to 20 inclusive).

OR allows two criteria to be selected so that if either is true, the action can take place. For example:

Fees Paid = No OR Date of Membership <01/01/90

This selects the records of members who have not paid their fees or who were members before 01/01/1990. In this example, notice that we are linking two fields. Both AND and OR can be used within a single field and also combining fields.

Exercise 26

Queries and criteria

1 Load Microsoft Access® by selecting the Start button, highlighting the All Programs option and clicking on the Microsoft Access® item or clicking on the Access® icon on the desktop. Insert your floppy disk into the drive.

2 The New File task pane (figure 3.1) offers you the choice of:

- opening an existing database file
- creating a new blank database.

If you have only recently finished the previous exercise, the Sports database will still be listed in the Open a file section. If not, select the More files option, which will reveal Open window to allow you to locate the file Sports and load it. The Sports database window will open. Click on the Queries button to reveal figure 3.38.

3 Select Create query in Design view and you will see an overlaid window Show Table appear. Click on the Add button and you will notice a small window called Membership appear on the query window. Now click on the Close button in Show Table to reveal figure 3.39.

4 The cursor will be flashing in the Field: box, and if you click on the down arrow all the Membership table fields are available for you to select from. Select the Date of Membership. Click in the Sort: box and you will see another down-arrow button appear that provides access to sorting functions. Select the Descending option.

5 Now click in the criteria row and enter >=01/01/94. You are selecting all members who joined the club on or after 1 January 1994.

6 Now click in the OR row and enter <= 01/01/99. You are adding an extra condition to select members who joined on or before 1 January 1999. If the criteria are too long, press the Shift and F2 keys together, with the cursor in the criteria box. This opens a Zoom window to let you see the whole criterion. Try it.

7 Now click in the next column and select First Name in the Field: box. Repeat this action, selecting Last name in the third column, Fees Paid in the fourth and Event in the fifth. Figure 3.43 shows the result you should have obtained.

8 Now close the window using the button in the top right-hand corner. A message window will appear asking you if you want to save the query as Query1. Click on the Yes button

and another window (dialog) box will appear offering you the opportunity to name your query. Change the name to Fees then click on the OK button. You will see your query appear in the Sports: database window (assuming the Queries button has been selected).

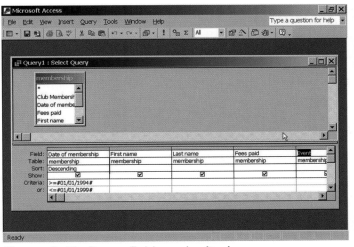

Figure 3.43 **Query fields and criteria**

9 You have created a straightforward query, producing a list of members with a particular range of membership dates. If you double-click on the query (Fees), you will see the results of the query appear (figure 3.44). Print the query you have created.

10 You are now going to change this query by highlighting Fees and clicking on the

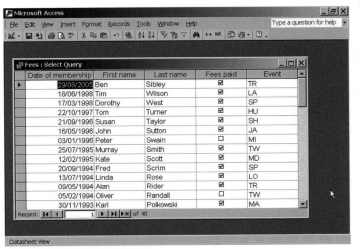

Figure 3.44 **Fees query**

Design icon on the toolbar. You want to select those members who have paid their membership fees, so in the criteria row of the Fees Paid column enter =Yes.

11 Close the window and save the query. Double-click on Fees to see the result of your change. Notice the change in the number of records now selected (i.e. changes from 40 to 34). Print out the new query.

12 We will now change the query by adding an extra criterion to the Event column. Enter =SH (i.e. Shot putting). The results of the new query are shown in figure 3.45.

13 Amend Date of membership column criteria to read >=01/01/94 AND <=01/01/99 and remove the criteria from Event column. Compare the result with the OR criteria. Figure 3.46 shows

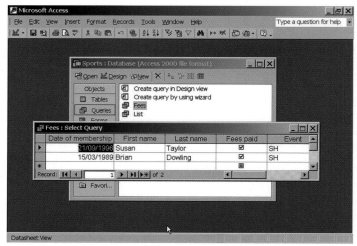

Figure 3.45 Event amendment

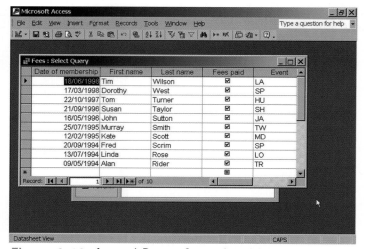

Figure 3.46 Amend Date of membership

the results of the new query. This shows the different effects of AND and OR. Experiment with the logical operators until you are a confident user of them.

14 Close Microsoft Access® by clicking on the close button in top right-hand corner of the main application window, or select the File menu and the Exit option.

Wild Cards

When designing criteria for searching, it is possible to use a device called a wild card. This is useful when you only know part of a name or title. Say you wanted to list all the members in our database beginning with the letter S. This would be shown as S*, the * indicating that any combination of letters is acceptable. * is the wild card.

Calculations

It is sometimes necessary to perform a calculation on information contained in a table. In the Import Database (Sales Office Table) we created earlier we have information about the sales of various items. However, there is no field to calculate VAT(Valued Added Tax). This may be occasionally needed. Microsoft® Access allows you to add an additional field which is known as a calculated field.

In order to add a calculated field you need to enter a calculated field name, a colon and then the calculation when you are creating a query into an empty row. If you include a table field in the calculation it must be enclosed in a square bracket.

Example

VAT:[January]*0.175

The example shows that the sales in January for an item multiplied by 0.175 will produce the VAT for that item. In this example the calculated field name is VAT and since January is a table field it is enclosed in square brackets. The value of sales in January for an item is multiplied by 0.175, the equivalent of 17.5% (i.e. a current VAT rate).

In this example we have used multiplication (*) but you can also use addition (+), subtraction (–) or division (/). It is important to notice that the symbols for the different ma matical operators are different from the conventional ones in some cases.

Exercise 27

Calculated Fields

1 Load Microsoft Access® by selecting the Start button, highlighting the All Programs option and clicking on the Microsoft Access® item or clicking on the Access® icon on the desktop. Insert your floppy disk into the drive.

2 The New File Task Pane (Figure 3.1) offers you the choice of:

- Opening an existing database file

- Creating a new blank database

Select the More files option which will reveal the Open window to allow you to locate the file, import and load it. The Import database window will open. Click on the Queries button.

3 Select Create query in Design view and you will see an overlaid window, Show Table, appear. Click on the Add button and you will notice a small window called Sales Office appear on the query window. Now click on the Close button in Show Table.

4 The cursor will be flashing in the Field: box and if you click on the down arrow all the Sales Office table fields are available for you to select from. Select the item. Click in the Sort box and you will see another down arrow button appear that provides access to sorting functions. Select the Descending option.

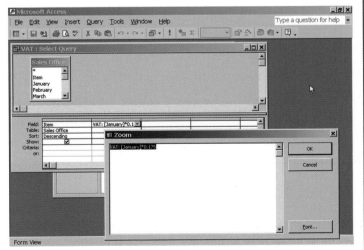

Figure 3.47 Calculated Field (Zoom View)

5 In the next column enter VAT:[January]*0.175 (figure 3.47). The space to enter the expression is limited and if you need more right click and select the Zoom option which will provide you with sufficient space to enter even large complex calculations.

6 Now close the window using the button in the top right hand corner. A message window will appear asking you if you want to save the query as Query1. Click on the Yes button and another window (dialogue) box will appear offering you the opportunity to name your query. Change the name to VAT, then click on the OK button. You will see your query appear in the Import: database window (assuming the Queries button has been selected).

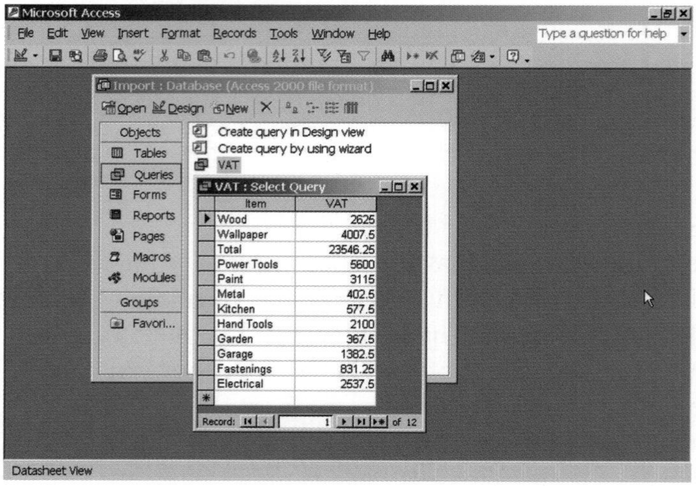

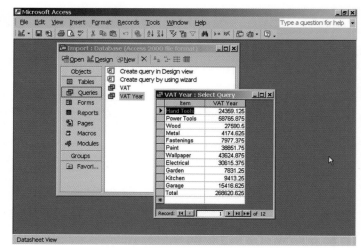

Figure 3.48 VAT

Figure 3.49 VAT Year Query

7 You have created a calculated field in a query to show VAT on the January sales. If you double click on the query (Fees) you will see the results of the query appear (Figure 3.48). Print the query you have created.

8 You are now going to create a new query to add a calculated field in order to calculate the VAT for each item for the whole year. The calculation you need to insert is VAT Year:[Total]*0.175.

9 Explore creating other calculated fields until you are confident.

10 Print out each new query. Figure 3.49 shows the VAT Year.

11 Close Access by clicking on the Close button in the top right hand corner of the main application window or select the File menu and the Exit option.

Summaries

There are many occasions when you want to summarise the information that is held in a database table and Microsoft Access® provides you with a straightforward way of summarising data using a Query. If you select Create a query using Wizard or the Simple Query Wizard (New button), you will reveal the Simple Query Wizard (figure 3.50).

The Wizard allows you to select the fields you want to include in the query by highlighting a field and clicking the arrow button; the field will be moved to the Selected Fields area. When you have completed your selection, you can move forward by clicking on the Next button. As you move through the Wizard, you will be offered the choice of displaying the details of the fields or a summary. If you select Summary and Summary Options, then figure 3.51 will appear, offering you the options to display the Sum, Average, Minimum and Maximum values of the fields.

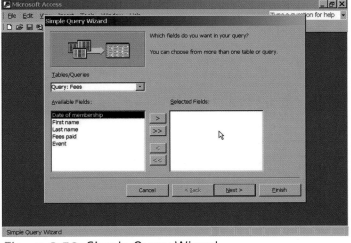

Figure 3.50 Simple Query Wizard

More practice

Activity 1

Database

1 Create a new database called Equipment Orders based on table 3.

Table 3 Equipment Orders

Field Name	Data Type
Customer Reference	Autonumber – this field will automatically be incremented for each new customer
First Order	Date
Name	Text
Address	Text
Equipment Ordered	Text
Cost	Decimal number
Credit Customer	Yes/No

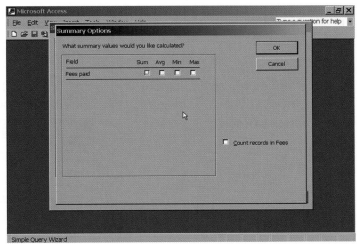

Figure 3.51 Summary Options

2 Enter the data in table 4 into the Equipment Orders database. The equipment ordered is coded to improve speed of input. Call the table Orders.

Table 4 Data Input

First Order	Name	Address	Equipment Ordered	Cost	Credit Customer
01/02/86	Brown	Liverpool	A12	1110	Yes
03/02/87	Clare	Manchester	B67	650	No
06/08/83	Davies	London	K17	230	Yes
11/09/95	Edwards	Brighton	P11	345	Yes
15/05/92	Frame	Leicester	N45	890	Yes
10/04/93	Gornski	Newcastle	A12	1110	No
02/05/89	Davies	Stoke	B34	120	No
21/07/93	Smith	Bristol	A09	560	No
31/01/95	Rao	Poole	B67	650	Yes
18/03/90	Weatherall	Exeter	P11	345	Yes
12/04/99	Weston	London	N45	890	No
16/02/92	Hunter	Manchester	A09	560	Yes

3 Amend your table in the following ways:

Add these new records:

13/02/99	Giles	Bury	A12	1110	Yes
25/08/98	Singh	Halifax	B34	120	Yes
03/11/01	Harris	Manchester	N45	890	No

Delete this record:

| 31/01/95 | Rao | Poole | B67 | 650 | Yes |

Change Credit Customer to No:

| 11/09/95 | Edwards | Brighton | P11 | 345 | Yes |

Change Date of First Order to 12/05/00:

| 12/04/99 | Weston | London | N45 | 890 | No |

4 Systematically check that your data has been entered accurately and then save the database.

Activity 2

Report

1 Open the database Equipment Orders and produce a tabular report using formal style in portrait orientation, showing all the fields, but in the following sequence:

Equipment Ordered

Name

Address

Cost

Credit Customer

First Order

2 Give the report the title Orders List.

3 Sort the information in descending order of First Order.

4 In the header and footer, show the date and add your name to the footer.

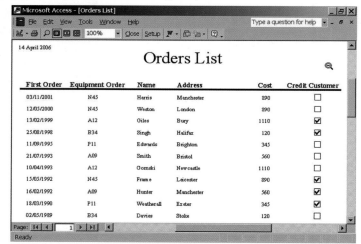

Figure 3.52 Report – Orders List

5 Preview the printout to check that the report is clear and shows all the information. Figure 3.52 shows our efforts. Some text boxes needed to be moved to ensure that columns were aligned. You may have made other choices, so the figure may not be identical to your report.

6 Print the report.

7 Save the report.

8 Create a label for each customer – call the report Customer Labels.

Equipment

Address

First Order

9 Sort the data in order of address.

10 In the footer show:
   Your name
   Page number.
11 Check that all the labels are correct and print them.
12 Close the database.

Activity 3

Query

1 Open the database Equipment Orders and produce a query to identify customers who placed their first order on or after 01/02/93; include all the fields except Customer Reference.

2 Save the query as Date of First Order (figure 3.53).

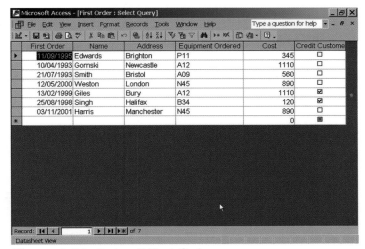

Figure 3.53 Date of First Order query

3 Use the Date query to produce a tabular report in portrait orientation in corporate style, with the title Date of First Order. The report could be sorted on First Order ascending.

4 Show the following fields in this sequence:
   First Order
   Cost
   Equipment Ordered
   Name
   Address
   Credit Customer

5 In the footer show:
   Your name
   Page numbers
   Date.

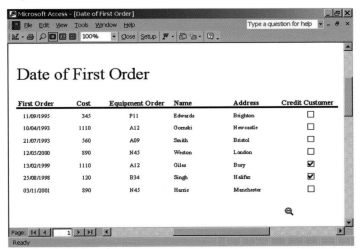

Figure 3.54 Date of First Order report

6 Check the report for clarity and make any necessary changes.

7 Save the report and print. Figure 3.54 shows our effort.

Activity 4

New database

1 Create a new database called Paint, based on table 5.

   Table 5 Paint

Field Name	Data Type
Product Name	Text
Volume	Integer
Type	Text (10 characters)
Unit Cost	Currency
Supplier	Text

2   Enter the data in table 6 into the Paint database. The type of paint is coded to improve speed of input (i.e. E – Emulsion and G – Gloss).

Table 6 Data Input

Product Name	Volume	Type	Unit Cost	Supplier
Light Green	950	E	1.5	Justin
Dark Green	560	G	2.1	King
Red	350	G	2.2	Lord
Light Blue	1200	E	1.7	Lord
Dark Blue	125	E	1.8	Justin
White	550	G	2.0	King
Cream	230	G	1.4	Justin
Yellow	175	E	2.3	King
Black	900	E	1.1	Lord
Brown	750	G	1.6	King

3   Systematically check that your data has been entered accurately and then save the database.

Activity 5

Reports

Using the Import Database (Sales Office® table), create reports which show:

■ a list of items and sales in April, May and June (figure 3.55)
■ a list of items and total sales.

In both cases, explore columnar, tabular and justified layouts.

Activity 6

Queries

Using the Sales Office® database, create queries that present a list of the items and sales in June (figure 3.56)

Explore creating a variety of queries and reports.

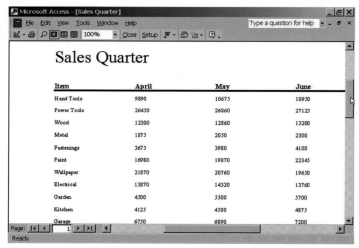

Figure 3.55 Sales Quarter

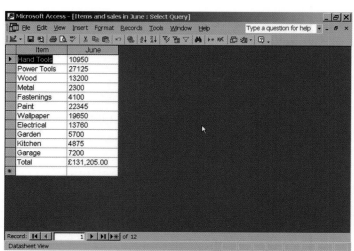

Figure 3.56 Query – Sales in June

SUMMARY

1 Open Microsoft Access®

There are several ways of loading an application in Microsoft Windows®. These include:

- clicking on the Start button, highlighting the All Programs item and clicking on Microsoft Access®
- double-clicking on the Access® icon on the desktop.

2 Create a blank database

Microsoft Access® will load and reveal the New File task pane, which offers you the choice of:

- opening an existing database file
- creating a new blank database.

Select Blank Database. The File New Database will open to enable you to save your new database.

3 Open an existing database

Microsoft Access® will load and reveal the New File task pane, which offers you the choice of:

- opening an existing database file
- creating a new blank database.

If you have only recently created the database, it will be listed in the section. If not, select the More files option, which will reveal the Open window to allow you to locate the file and load it.

4 Create a new table

Once you have saved your new database, the Database window will open to show three options, with the Table object on the left-hand side selected:

- Create table in Design view
- Create table by using wizard
- Create table by entering data.

Double-click on Create a table in Design view and the Table window opens. Insert your field names and their types. If you enter a name in the Field Name box and click in the corresponding Data Type box, a small down arrow will appear, revealing a list of types. Select the appropriate type, and so on, to complete the table.

Save your table by selecting the File menu and the Save As option. The Save As window appears. Enter the table name and click on the OK button.

5 Types of Microsoft Access® data

Microsoft Access® allows you to define nine types of data. They are text, memo, numbers, date/time, currency, autonumber, yes/no, OLE Object and hyperlink.

6 Enter data in a table

Double-click on the table in the Database window and it will open. If it is a new table, the columns may be too small to show the whole field name. Adjust the size by placing your mouse pointer over the line separating the columns and it will change shape to form a double arrow. If you hold down the mouse button, you can drag the column line to widen it.

Click in the fields and enter the data. It is very important to check that each record has been entered accurately. If you find a mistake, click on the appropriate field and enter your correction.

7 Reports

In the Database window, click on the Reports button (left hand side of window) and the two ways of producing a report will be revealed. These are:

- Create report in Design view
- Create report by using wizard.

Reports can be based on tables or queries.

8 AutoReport

In the Reports window, select the New button. This opens the New Report window, which contains a range of options, including AutoReport: Tabular and AutoReport: Columnar).

9 Page setup

Select the File menu and Page Setup. This will open the Page Setup window. Margins can be adjusted and orientation changed by additionally selecting the Page tab.

10 Amend report layout

Highlight the report and click on the Design icon on the toolbar. The structure of the report will be revealed. Clicking on an element will enclose it in a frame. The frame and its contents can be manipulated using the mouse pointer (i.e. pointer changes to a small hand). Items enclosed in a frame can also have their font and character size changed.

11 Header and footer (report)

With the report in Design view, automatic functions – Page Numbers or Date and Time – can be added using the Insert menu. To add your name, right-click on the page footer to reveal a pop-up menu, select Toolbox and use the Label tool.

12 Forms

From the Database window, select the Forms button on the left-hand side of the window and the two options to create a form will be revealed. Click on Create a form using the Wizard. This will help you through the process of producing a form.

13 Labels

From the Database window, with the Reports button selected, click on New on the toolbar and a new window will appear called New Report. This allows you to choose the Label Wizard, which will assist you in designing a label.

14 Import a data file

Select the File menu, highlight the Get External Data item and click the Import option. The option is only available when a database window is open, so you need to create a new database or open an existing one.

15 Query

Select the Queries button in the Database window and click on the
Create query in Design view option.

Alternatively, you can select the Create query by using wizard option. This allows you to
create a summary query.

16 Delete records and fields

Highlight your chosen row or column. Select the Edit menu and click on the Delete option.
Before the row or column is removed, a message window will appear to ask you to confirm
whether you want the record or field deleted permanently.

17 Find and Replace

Select the Edit menu and click on Replace. The Find and Replace window will appear.

18 Update

With the design view grid open, select the Query menu and click on the Update Query
option.

19 Customised calculations

Insert a calculation into an empty field with the design view grid, enter the calculated
field name, a colon and the calculation. If a table field is included in the calculation it
needs to be enclosed in square brackets (e.g. Month: [March] $\times$ 7).

20 Sort

The Sort function is available on the toolbar and allows you to sort data into ascending or
descending order. It sorts on numerical, alphabetical and chronological information.

21 Add calculated field in query

With the design view grid open, add the Total row by clicking on the Totals icon on the
toolbar. The down-arrow button in the Total row gives access to a range of standard
mathematical functions.

Customised calculations can be inserted into an empty field within the design view grid.

e-Publication Design

This chapter will help you to:

- identify and use appropriate software correctly, in accordance with laws and guidelines, keeping risks to self and others to a minimum

- use appropriate techniques to handle, organise and save files

- set up and use master page/template, according to the design brief

- set up page layout grids/guides

- use most tools and techniques appropriately

- import and manipulate text and image files

- amend publication content using proof correction symbols

- produce professional publications/documents

- prepare a publication for press.

This chapter covers unit 4 (e-Publication Design). There are no preconditions for studying this unit. However, its content does assume that you have the skills and understanding which are provided by the OCR Level 1 ICT course CLAiT 2006 (e.g. Unit 4: E-Publication Creation and Unit 1: File Management and e-Document Production).

Assessment

After studying unit 4, your skills and understanding are assessed during a three-hour practical assignment. This is set by OCR and marked locally. However, the marking will be externally moderated by OCR. This ensures that the standard is being applied correctly across the many different providers of OCR CLAiT Plus. If you are unsuccessful, you can be reassessed using a different assignment.

An alternative approach is for you to be assessed by an assignment set by OCR or designed by your centre. These assignments cover all the assessment objectives included in the unit. You will need to complete an OCR evidence checklist, explaining how each assessment objective has been covered.

Desktop publishing

Desktop publishing is an exciting and motivating application. It provides, for example, a means of using your creativity to produce interesting publications in a wide variety of forms. You can design newsletters for your organization or group, or combine illustrations with text to produce publicity material. In a sense, desktop publishing allows you to become your own design studio and printer, without leaving your workplace.

The danger is that the facilities offered to you are so rich in possibilities that you design publications which use too many of the facilities, producing documents that overpower your readers. Good practice suggests that publications should be kept simple and straightforward. This means:

- Do not use too many colours.
- Do not use too many fonts or different character sizes (each should be used for a distinct purpose – e.g. different types of heading). Fonts are sometimes called typefaces.
- Illustrations should complement the text and serve a distinct purpose.
- White (blank) space aids readability, so leave plenty around your text and illustrations – line spacing can aid/improve readability.
- Present a visually balanced publication.
- Ensure consistent presentation.

Copyright

There is a large range of resources available to help you to produce high quality publications. There are many websites that offer images and text that could be included in your designs, as well as CD-ROMs of graphics. It is also straightforward to capture graphics and screen displays. However, it is vital to check who owns these resources, since ultimately someone owns the copyright of all materials not in the public domain. The website or CD-ROM should say how the resource can be used; even when they grant permission, it is often qualified (e.g. only for non-profit educational purposes). If you want to include screen captures of applications, you need to check with the producer of the product, who, again, may only give permission for specific purposes and designate how the images can be displayed. In some cases they will not give permission. If you cannot find out if a resource can be used, you must assume it cannot be included in your publication.

In many ways it is best to use original materials that you have requested for the publication. However, if you are photographing people, it is normal practice to ask the individual's permission to take the photograph and ask them to sign an agreement to that effect.

Font families

CLAiT Plus uses font families rather than font names. Chapter 1 explains font families and gives examples of the fonts that link to them. This chapter will employ font families. For example:

Serif: Courier New and Times New Roman

Sans serif: **Tahoma** and Arial.

House styles

Desktop publishing provides you with a wide range of choices in designing publications. This is a major advantage, but is accompanied by the risk that each document produced will be so different that readers will be confused. In order to provide a consistent appearance in their publications, many organisations have developed standards for documents. These are called house styles.

House styles will often include:

- size of paper
- orientation (portrait or landscape)
- size of margins
- gutter
- header and footer
- font family (e.g. serif)
- character size (e.g. 12)
- different fonts and character sizes for headings and the main body of text
- line spacing (e.g. double).

You may find it useful to identify if your employer or another organisation you are involved in has a house style. Consider what it includes.

Microsoft Publisher®

This chapter is based around the desktop publishing application Microsoft Publisher® XP or 2002. Figure 4.1 shows the opening display of Microsoft Publisher®. The main application is divided into two areas:

- New Publication task pane
- Quick Publications.

The task pane allows you to select different types of publications. If you change the type of publication in the Start from a design dropdown box, the options displayed in the area below and the Quick Publications area will change (e.g. By Design Sets – Master Sets and Blank Publications – Blank Full Page).

If you are developing a newsletter for your company or community, it is likely to be issued many times (e.g. every month), so it is important to present a consistent image to your readers. It is therefore useful to design a master or template for your publication, as this provides a standard layout for your content. It will also save time, since you can use the master over and over again.

The other technique to ensure that your publications are consistent is to define

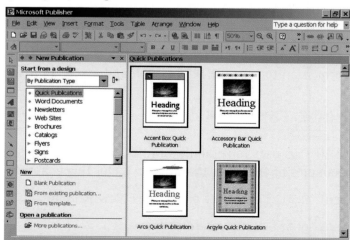

Figure 4.1 Microsoft Publisher®

text styles. These are combinations of text characteristics (e.g. font, character size) that you can apply to your content so that it takes on the style. This is a quick way of formatting your text and providing a consistent look and feel to the document. This technique helps to improve your productivity while maintaining the quality of your publication. Over time you will build up a range of masters and styles.

These standards (i.e. a combination of master document and text style) sometimes represent the organisation's house style.

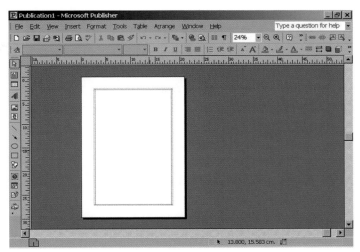

Figure 4.2 Microsoft Publisher® work Area

Figure 4.2 shows the work area of Microsoft Publisher® XP or 2002. This is another Microsoft Office® application, so has the familiar layout and structure that you will probably be aware of. The main difference from applications such as Microsoft Word® are:

- the outline of a document in the work area – this shows you the shape and orientation of your publication (e.g. rectangle in portrait orientation)
- a row of drawing tools down the left-hand side of the application window
- rulers down the left-hand side and across the top of the work area – these help you position your text and images in your publication.

Layout

There are a number of functions and options that you need to be aware of in order to use Microsoft Publisher® effectively. These are:

- Page size – Microsoft Publisher® allows you to select both standard and non-standard pages.
- Columns – A page can be divided into columns so that text flows up and down them (figure 4.3).
- Gutter – There is a small gap between the columns which is called a gutter (figure 4.3).
- Margins – Normally text does not start and stop at the edge of the page. To improve presentation, a margin (gap) is left along right and left edges. Margins are also left at the top and bottom of the page (figure 4.3). You can set margins using the Layout Guides in the Arrange menu.
- Text frames – To enter text into Microsoft Publisher® you must first create a text frame. All text

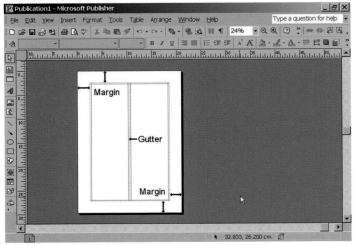

Figure 4.3 Margins, columns and gutters

has to be placed within a frame (figure 4.4).

- Picture frames – In a similar way to text frames, you can create a picture frame in order to place an image precisely in your publication (figure 4.4). It is also possible to insert a picture directly into your publication.
- Headers and footers (figure 4.5) – These are special areas at the top (header) and bottom (footer) of the page in which you can place information which will appear on every page (e.g. copyright statements, author, organisation).
- Orientation (figure 4.6) – Pages can be aligned in landscape or portrait orientation.

People sometimes become confused between page and text frame margins, since you can adjust both of these The difference is that a page margin applies to the whole page, while a text frame margin applies only to the frame. Figure 4.3 shows page margins.

You can choose your document type and size by selecting the File menu and clicking on the Page Setup option. The Page Setup window will appear. Select the Publication type and you can enter the width and height of your document. In some cases (e.g. Business Card) a new window will appear to allow you to select a specific size of document for a particular use or location (e.g. USA, East Asia or Europe). The chosen publication is illustrated in the Preview area. You can also select the orientation of the publication in the Page Setup window.

Layout guides

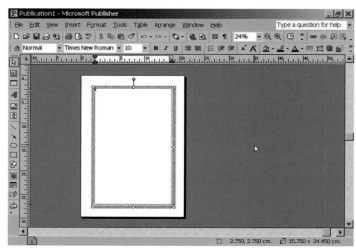

Figure 4.4 Frames

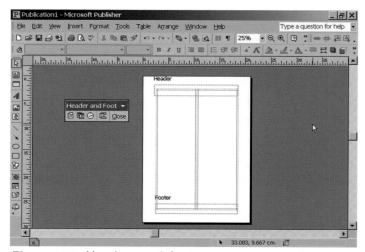

Figure 4.5 Headers and footers

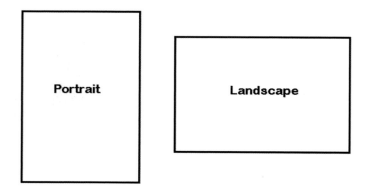

Figure 4.6 Orientation

To ensure consistency, Microsoft Publisher® provides you with layout guidelines that appear on the screen but do not print out. These are rather like pencil marks that act as guides and are then rubbed out when you have finished. You can set margins, columns and rows, and even allow for printing facing pages (i.e. like a book) using the Layout Guides. The first step in designing a publication is usually to provide yourself with guidelines (e.g. for page margins). It is important to remember that these are only guidelines indicating where to insert text, pictures and tables.

To establish some guidelines, select the Arrange menu and click on Layout Guides to reveal the Layout Guides window (figure 4.7). You can set margins or divide the page with columns and rows to help you lay out

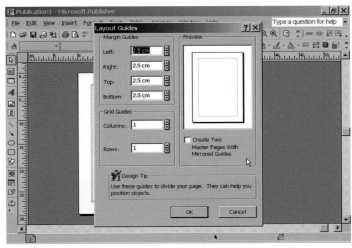

Figure 4.7 Layout Guides window

the design. They appear as pink and blue lines. The pink lines show the exact division of the page in terms of the precise sizes of margins, columns, and so on, while the blue lines allow a small gap from the exact measurements. This gap is called the gutter. When you are positioning text frames and images, you can place them anywhere, but that ignores the value of guidelines. Good practice is to place objects on the blue lines, thereby taking advantage of the safety margin of the gutter.

A text frame can have its own margins, so if you place a frame next to the page margin, then you are increasing the size of the margin to become the sum of the two margins. To ensure that the page margin is accurate, you need to reduce the text frame margin to zero.

Background and foreground

It is useful to understand the nature of foreground and background. Background can be considered as part of the paper, so if you have a watermark in the paper, you can add text on top of it. The text would be foreground, while the watermark is background. When you create headers and footers they are in the background, while the columns, pictures and text which form the content of the publication are mainly in the foreground.

Toolbar

A key feature of Microsoft Publisher® is the toolbar (figure 4.8) down the left-hand side of the application, offering a range of tools to create text and picture frames and draw objects. The tools are accessed by clicking on them. This changes the shape of the pointer (e.g. to cross-hair for text frame).

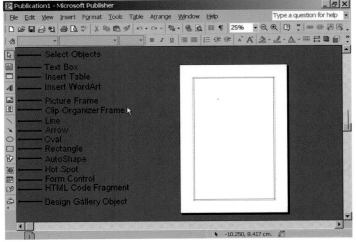

Figure 4.8 Toolbar

Entering text

You can enter text into a text frame from the keyboard. You must first click in the frame and the text will appear at the cursor. Since the publication is shown reduced in size to fit into the work area, it sometimes means that text is too small to see and you need to use the zoom function.

The other option is to import a text file into the frame. Both options are included in the later exercises.

Exercise 28

Master newsletter

1 During this exercise you are going to create a master publication of a newsletter for your company. The newsletter must conform to this design brief. It will be printed on A4 paper in portrait orientation with the default margins (ie. the ones automatically provided by selecting the Full page option). It should have a header and footer in the top and bottom page margins. The header should show the name of the company (i.e. PrePax) and the footer should give page numbers and date of publication in the centre of the page. The body of the newsletter should be divided into three equal columns, with a 0.2 cm gutter and 0.4 cm margins (i.e. left, right, top and bottom of text frame – remember these are the frame margins, not the page margins). The middle of the page should contain a picture overlapping the three columns. Text should wrap around the picture.

2 Load Microsoft Publisher® by selecting Start, highlighting the All Programs menu and clicking on the Microsoft Publisher® item or by clicking on the Publisher® icon on the desktop.

3 Select the Blank Publication option in the task pane and a Full Page publication will appear in the working area.

4 Select the Arrange menu and click on the Layout Guides. Set all the margins to 2.54 cm.

5 Select the Text Box from the toolbar and the pointer will turn into a cross-hair. Position it in the top left-hand corner of the page and then, holding down the mouse button, drag the pointer to the bottom right-hand corner and release the button. A text frame needs to be in place before you can divide it into columns.

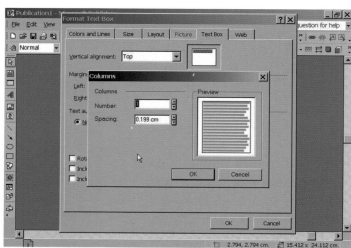

Figure 4.9 Columns

6 The text frame should be highlighted (i.e. the frame is visible). Click on the frame if it is not highlighted. Select the Format menu and click on the Text Box option to reveal the Text Box window. Choose the Text Box tab and the Columns button to reveal the Columns window (figure 4.9).

7 Set the number of columns to 3 and spacing to 0.2 cm (i.e. Columns window), select the Wrap text around objects option (i.e. Layout tab), left and right margins to 0.4 cm and top and bottom margins to 0.14 cm (i.e. Margins tab). Click on the OK button when you have completed your changes.

8 The next step is to insert headers and footers in the area forming the top and bottom margins. Select the View menu and Header and Footer option. The header will appear enclosed in a frame with a toolbar. Scroll down to the footer.

9 Click on the footer to highlight the text frame. Using the Text Box tool, add a text box to the footer. Insert page number by clicking on toolbar icon. A symbol will appear in the bottom left-hand corner of the footer. The symbol will automatically number the pages of the publication. Insert the Date and Time option from the Toolbar. Your footer now has two automatic fields embedded within it, which will automatically number the page and date the publication. Alternatively, you can insert the automatic fields using the Insert menu. This allows you to choose the layout of the date.

10 Now click in the header to highlight it. Using the toolbar, change the font to Tahoma and character size to 36, select the centre option, bold and enter PrePax. Adjust the size of the header by dragging the frame using the pointer, so that the header is visible.

11 Figure 4.10 shows the master document layout. The header overlaps the text frame, so move it up into the margin area.

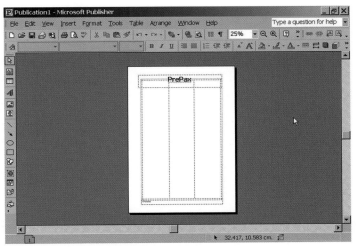

Figure 4.10 Master

12 Now save your master document. Insert a floppy disk into the computer's drive. Select the File menu and click on the Save option. The Save As window will appear. Change the Save in: box to floppy disk, name the file as Master in the File name: box and click on the Save button.

13 The Master publication is shown in figure 4.10. If you select the File menu and the Print option you will reveal the Print window. Click on the OK button and your publication will be printed (assuming your computer is connected to a printer). You should see a blank page produced with only the header text shown (i.e. PrePax), and the page number and date in the footer.

14 Close the application either by selecting the File menu and clicking on the Exit option or by clicking on the close button in the top right-hand corner of the application window.

Text styles

New text styles can be created by selecting the F<u>o</u>rmat menu and clicking on the <u>S</u>tyles and Formatting option to reveal the Styles and Formatting task pane on the left of the work area (figure 4.12). A new style can be created by clicking on the Create new style button. Different options appear in the F<u>o</u>rmat menu depending on whether a text frame is highlighted or not. Figure 4.11 shows the menu with a text frame highlighted.

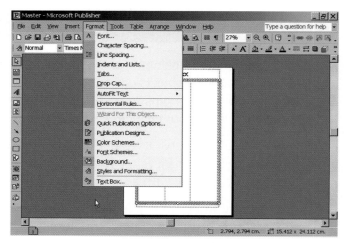

Figure 4.11   Format menu – Frame highlighted

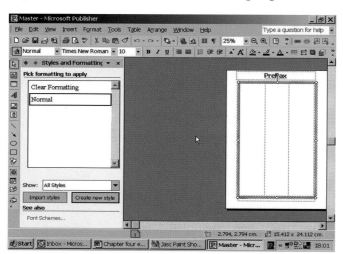

Figure 4.12   Style and Formatting task pane

Exercise 29

Creating a text style

1 Insert your floppy disk into the computer's drive.

2 Load Microsoft Publisher® by selecting Start, highlighting the All Programs menu and clicking on the Microsoft Publisher® item or by clicking on the Publisher® icon on the desktop. If you have recently completed the last exercise, you may see Master listed at the bottom of the task pane in the section Open a publication. Double-click on Master and the document appears in the work area. If Master is not displayed, select More publications to reveal the Open Publication window and select floppy disk and Master file.

3 Select the F<u>o</u>rmat menu and click on the <u>S</u>tyles and Formatting option to reveal the task pane (figure 4.12). Click on the Create new style button and the Create New Style window will open (figure 4.13).

continued

4 Enter News in the new style name box and click on Font and size button. Another window called Font will open. Change the font to Arial and the size to 12, then click on the OK button. You will then return to the Create New Style window. Click on the Indents and Lists button and another window will appear (figure 4.14).

5 Change the alignment to Justified and click on the OK button to return to the Create New Style window. Select Line spacing to reveal figure 4.15. Change the spacing Between lines to 1.5, Before paragraphs to 1 pt and After paragraphs to 1 pt. Click on the OK button when the changes have been made to return to the Create New Style window. In the sample area of the display you should see the style you have created. Click on the OK button to create the style and you will see the News style appear in the Pick formatting to apply area of the task pane. Click on the close button to remove the task pane.

6 On the left-hand side of the Format toolbar is the text style box, which will probably be reading Normal. (The toolbar is only visible if a text frame is highlighted.) If you click on the down-arrow button you will see the News style listed. News is in the text style of the main body of text that will form the newsletter. You could now go

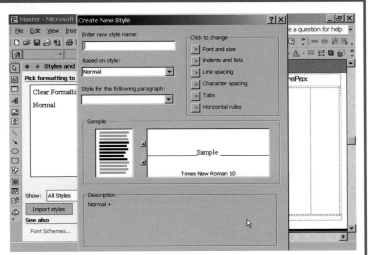

Figure 4.13 Create New Style window

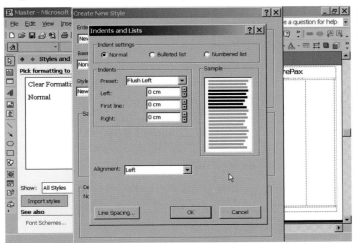

Figure 4.14 Indents and Lists

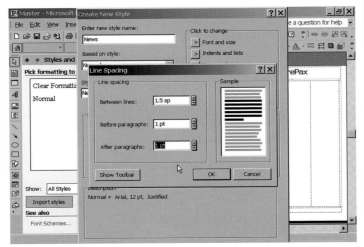

Figure 4.15 Line Spacing window

e-Publication Design

149

on to create other styles, such as main headings, subheadings, lists and so on. Each would have a different name, providing you with the means of creating newsletters consistently.

7 Save the Master publication on to your floppy disk.

8 Close the application by either selecting the File menu and clicking on the Exit option or by clicking on the close button in the top right-hand corner of the application window. Alternatively, proceed to the next exercise.

Exercise 30

Applying a text style

1 Insert your floppy disk into the computer's drive.

2 Load Microsoft Publisher® by selecting Start, highlighting the All Programs menu and clicking on the Microsoft Publisher® item or by clicking on the Publisher® icon on the desktop. If you have recently completed the last exercise, you may see Master listed at the bottom of the task pane in the section Open a publication. Double-click on Master and the document appears in the work area. If Master is not displayed, select More publications to reveal the Open Publication window and select floppy disk and Master file.

This is an opportunity to practise applying styles. You do not need to save your work, so refuse if the application offers you the opportunity to save the file.

3 The Format toolbar is only revealed in full when a text frame is highlighted, so click on a Master publication text frame. Click on the Style box down arrow and select News from the list. Everything you now enter into the frame will follow the News style. The Format toolbar font and size will have changed to show Arial and character size 12.

4 Enter:

This is the first Newsletter of the PrePax Organisation and is intended to help communication between the different departments by explaining new developments, changes in the organisation and presenting news items.

The Newsletter will be published every month and employees are invited to submit ideas for stories or comments on the publication to John Reynolds, Newsletter Editor.

If you cannot see the text, change the Zoom percentage (Standard toolbar).

5 If you click anywhere within an individual paragraph and then select a style, the style of the paragraph will change. Select the second paragraph by clicking within it, then change the style to Normal and you will see the paragraph change. Now select News and watch the style change back to News. Figure 4.16 illustrates the text in the News style. Notice that the pointer has changed shape because it is positioned over the frame handle.

6 Experiment with changing the styles until you are confident.

7 Close the application by either selecting the File menu and clicking on the Exit option or click on the close button in the top right-hand corner of the application window. There is no need to save your practice, so when you are prompted to save the file, decline by clicking on the No button.

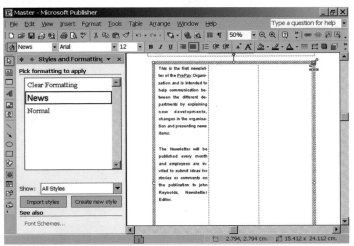

Figure 4.16 News style text

Template

The exercises have allowed us to create a master document for a newsletter. A template serves a similar purpose to a master document. It is a foundation document for a particular purpose (e.g. a newsletter, a flyer and a poster) and contains basic formatting and layout, but there are no precise rules so it could also contain graphics (e.g. organisation logo). It is intended to provide a standard document in which content can be added, thus improving productivity, quality and standardisation. Microsoft Publisher® allows you to save a template in a file format called Publisher® Template.

When you want to use a template, select the File menu and New option to display the New Publication task pane. This provides access to a wide range of templates, such as websites, newsletters and brochures. If you highlight a category, a range of choices will appear in the work area to the right of the task pane. Figure 4.17 illustrates newsletter templates.

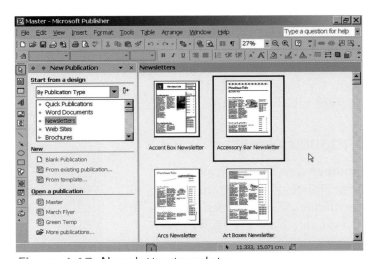

Figure 4.17 Newsletter templates

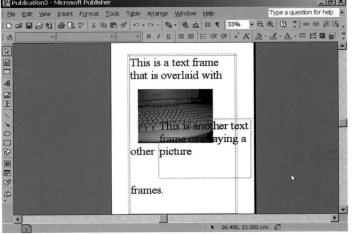

Figure 4.18 Layering of objects

Layering

An interesting function of Microsoft Publisher® is that it lets you overlap pictures and text. This is called layering and it is similar to placing objects on top of each other (figure 4.18). If you are able to layer pictures and text in an effective way, you can produce very eye-catching and professional publications. Figure 4.18 illustrates three objects overlapping with each other – they are a text frame overlaid with a picture, which is in turn overlapped by another text frame.

Background

Microsoft Publisher® provides functions to help you create a coloured or textured background or to use a picture as the background of your publication. If you select the Format menu and Background option, the Background task pane is opened, giving you many colour choices. In addition, if you click on More Backgrounds, a new window Fill Effects is opened, which offers choices of textured and patterned backgrounds, as well as a picture to form the background within the Picture tab (figure 4.19).

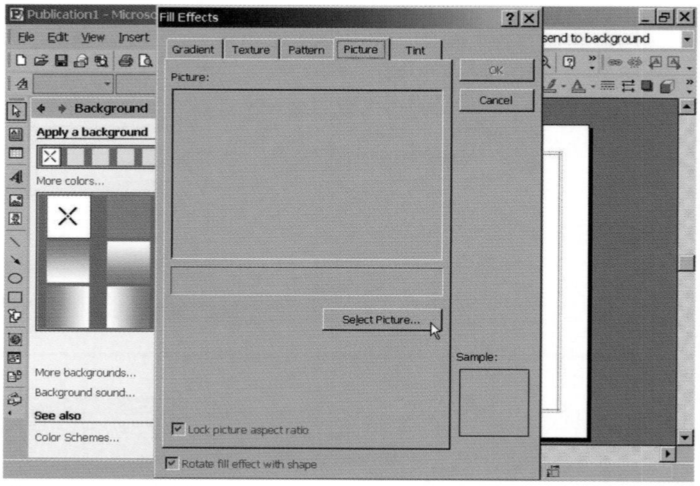

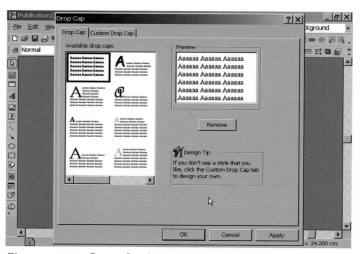

Figure 4.19 Picture tab

Dropped capital

Another way of enhancing the appearance of text is to use a technique called dropped capitals. This is available from the Format menu when a text frame is highlighted, by clicking on the Drop Cap option. This reveals the Drop Cap window (figure 4.20) which allows you to choose a fancy first letter (Capital letter) to draw the reader's attention. If you are not happy with any of the standard dropped capitals, you can create your own by clicking on the Custom Drop Cap tab in the Drop Cap window.

Figure 4.20 Drop Capital window

Resources

Normally when you are creating a desktop publication, you will already have produced the text and pictures that will form the content of the document. It is possible to enter text from the keyboard into a publication, but it is better to use a word-processed document and assemble it using Microsoft Publisher®.

In order to practise importing text and pictures into a publication, you need access to a word-processed document and one is provided below to use with our master document. You should either create this as a word-processed document (save the file as Newsletteron1.doc on to your floppy disk) or use some other resources of your own. During your assessment, the imported text files and images will be provided.

Newsletter One

This is the first Newsletter of the PrePax Organisation and is intended to help communication between the different departments by explaining new developments, changes in the organisation and presenting news items.

The Newsletter will be published every month and employees are invited to submit ideas for stories or comments on the publication to John Reynolds, Newsletter Editor. This edition is essentially an introduction to the organisation for new staff.

There are five departments within PrePax. These are:

- Manufacturing
- Sales
- Transport
- Support
- Policy

Manufacturing

This is the largest department of the company and is responsible for producing all the packaging products which we are famous for making. 350 people work in the manufacturing department.

Sales

The sales staff are based in many different locations across Great Britain. Each sales representative is responsible for a distinct geographical area and liaison with the customers in that patch.

Transport

The transport department is responsible for delivering orders to our customers either through our own fleet of lorries and vans or using subcontractors. We offer all customers a 72-hour delivery service.

Support

Support consists of the many small teams who ensure that everything works well behind the scenes. They are personnel, accommodation, finance and office staff.

Policy

Policy is the smallest department. It comprises the directors and their assistants who plan the company's activities, ensuring that we maximise our opportunities to make a profit.

Inserting pictures

Images are a major way of both communicating information and adding interest to your publications. To add an image to a document you need to create a picture frame in the same way that you do with text. Select the Picture Frame icon and the pointer will change shape to a cross-hair to allow you to position the image accurately on the page. Click on the position of the top left-hand corner of the image and drag the frame open. Release the mouse button

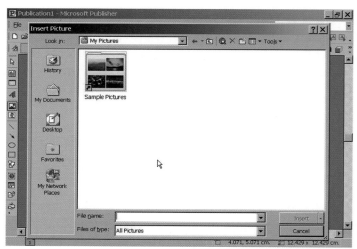

Figure 4.21 Insert Picture window

when you are ready and the Insert Picture window (figure 4.21) is revealed. This allows you to identify an image from your files, CD-ROM or other source. The picture file is selected in the same way that you open any other file in an application.

The picture frame can be moved and resized in the same way as a text frame.

An alternative way of adding an image is to select the Clip Organizer frame, which enables you to add Clip Art to the document. This works in a similar way to the Picture Frame approach, except that you select a Clip Art image rather than a picture file.

Exercise 31

Manipulating text and image files

1 Insert your floppy disk into the computer's drive.

2 Load Microsoft Publisher® by selecting Start, highlighting the All Programs menu and clicking on the Microsoft Publisher® item or by clicking on the Publisher® icon on the desktop. If you have recently completed the last exercise, you may see Master listed at the bottom of the task pane in the section Open a publication. Double-click on Master and the document appears in the work area. If Master is not displayed, select More publications to reveal the Open Publication window and select floppy disk and Master file.

3 The PrePax master document should be visible in Microsoft Publisher® work area. The first step is to add an image to the Master publication. Select the Picture Frame or Clip Organizer Frame if you do not have access to a suitable image and create a new frame in the middle of the document, overlapping all three columns. If you select the Clip Organizer Frame, the Insert Clip Art task pane will appear. You may be asked to carry out an organisation task, but select the later option. You can search for an image of your choice using the task pane. In order to insert a Clip Art image you need to click on it. A menu bar will appear down the image side which offers you options. Select the Insert option. You can then position the Clip Art on the page. Figure 4.22 shows an inserted image.

4 Save the new Master file, since we will use the picture on future additions of the newsletter. Select the File menu and the Save option. Close the task pane.

5 You are now going to insert your file Newsletteron1.doc into the publication. Click on the

text frame and you will see the cursor appear. Select the Insert menu and the Text File option. This will open the Insert Text window. Change the Look in: box to the folder in which you saved Newsletter on 1 file (e.g. floppy disk) and double-click on the text file.

A message will appear warning you that your text does not fit into the chosen box (i.e. it is too much for a single-page publication). It will offer you the opportunity to use Autoflow. Click on the Yes button. A second message will appear, asking if you want Microsoft Publisher® to create new text boxes automatically. Again, click on the Yes button. A final message appears, informing you that a second page has been created and you are viewing it.

An alternative approach to allowing the application to create a new page is to create a second page before inserting

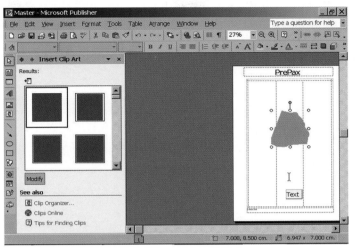

Figure 4.22 Picture

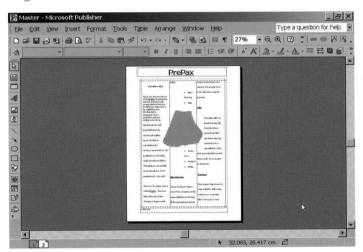

Figure 4.23 Imported text page 1

the text file, by selecting the Insert menu and the Page option to reveal the Insert Page window. You need to insert one new page, after the current one, and duplicate all objects on the page (i.e. you are copying the master page's layout on to the new page). In the bottom left-hand corner of the Microsoft Publisher® display you will see the numbers 1 and 2, with 2 highlighted. To move to the first page click on the figure 1.

6 The text will now cover parts of two pages and will flow around the picture on page 1. You can move between the two pages by clicking on the numbers 1 and 2 in the bottom left-hand corner of the work area.

7 Save your newsletter as the file PrePax News 1 on your floppy disk, by selecting the File menu and clicking on the Save As option.

8 Figures 4.23 and 4.24 show the two pages of your newsletter. At the top of the second page is a button with an arrow which, if clicked, returns you to the first page. The first page has a similar button at the bottom of the page, linking you to the second page. Notice that the text you have imported has flowed up and down the columns and around your picture frame.

9 Microsoft Publisher® reduces the size of the publication so that it is easier to see the whole layout. You can increase the size of the image using the zoom function on the Standard toolbar. Experiment with different sizes to check the presentation of your newsletter. Use the News text style to change the text. Adjust the text and image so that your publication is presented effectively. You may need to reduce the size of the image so that the text flows around the picture without leaving large gaps, or adjust line spacing so that you achieve the required layout. Explore the different ways of adjusting your publication until you are confident that you can achieve the desired results.

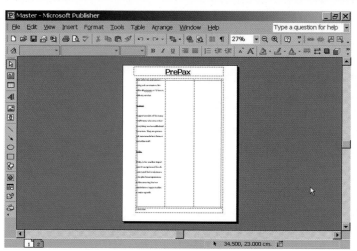

Figure 4.24 Imported text page 2

10 During your inspection of the publication you will notice widows and orphans. These are examples of single words or phrases being left behind on a page (or column) or pushed on to a new page or column (e.g. a single word on a new page). When you make a change to your publication, you need to check that you have not created widows or orphans. There are various ways of removing them, such as changing line spacing, increasing white space, and so on.

11 Select an appropriate drop capital for your publication.

12 When you are happy with the presentation, select the File menu and click on the Print option, then on the OK button in the Print window. This will print the newsletter with the printer's default settings. Figure 4.25 shows my efforts. The printout is another means of checking your publication to see if the results are what you desire.

13 Save your publication again.

14 Close the application either by selecting the File menu and clicking on the Exit option or by clicking on the close button in the top right-hand corner of the application window.

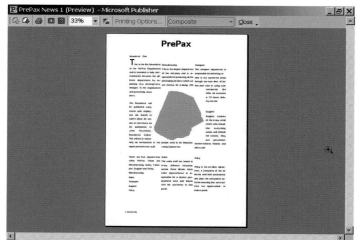

Figure 4.25 PrePax Newsletter

Correcting a proof

Although you can amend a publication on a screen, it is sensible to print your document and check the paper copy. These are called proof copies while they are being developed. There are a number of standard symbols which are used to show changes that need to be made. Figure 4.26 shows these correction symbols.

Using the printout of the PrePax Newsletter, check the document and use the symbols to record the changes that are needed.

	Document Mark	Margin
New Paragraph		
Change	the green text	red
Delete	men and and women	
Insert	select File menu	the
Indent	This is the way	1
Punctuation	Sentences must finish with a full stop	⊙
Return to original	Stet	Stet
Close up		
Capitalisation	england	≡
Transpose	way the	

Figure 4.26 Correction symbols

Lines and boxes

The tools (figure 4.8) provide you with the means of adding lines and boxes to different parts of the desktop publication. You could:

- add lines to emphasise the columns
- add a line to separate the header from the rest of the document
- enclose headings in a box.

A line or box is drawn by clicking on the icon in the tool bar, which changes the pointer to a cross-hair

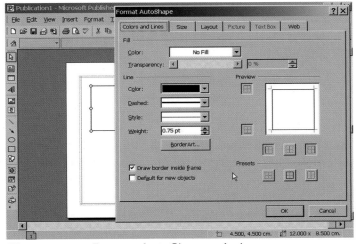

Figure 4.27 Format AutoShape window

that allows you to position the start of your line or the corner of the box. By holding down the left mouse button and dragging the line or box you can form it. It is shown enclosed in small black boxes. In this mode, it can be manipulated (e.g. moved, dragged). The thickness and the style of the line can be adjusted by right-clicking on the box or line to reveal a short menu. Select Format Autoshape option to open the Format AutoShape window, which allows you to change the lines or rectangle sides (figure 4.27).

Cropping an Image

It is a straightforward task to insert a picture file into a publication, but frequently you need to change the size of the image, move it or alter its appearance. Earlier we saw how to change the size, location and shape of an image by using the pointer. This is often called resizing the image. When you resize an image you can change its proportions and therefore reduce its quality (i.e. it becomes distorted). However, you do not lose any of the content of the image as you do with other methods. To resize an image, you position the pointer over one of the handles that make up the frame and drag it. This will alter the size of image. To reduce any distortion, it is best to resize using one of the corner handles. There are two other methods that can be used. These are:

- Masking – that is, covering part of the image with another picture or text frame. In effect, you are hiding some of the image behind the other frame. This can be effective because there is no risk of reducing the quality of the image which resizing can bring. However, masking is probably only suitable if you want to hide one edge of an image, since it can be difficult to mask several different parts of a picture. If you later want to edit the publication, masking can make this more complex.

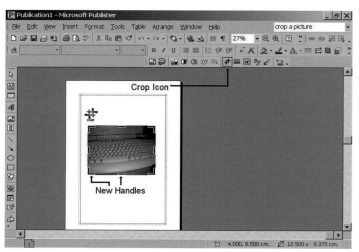

Figure 4.28 Cropping an image

- Cropping – that is, cutting part of the image to remove an unnecessary section. This is an effective method if the image contains elements that you would like to remove permanently. The image is made smaller and the quality of the remaining image is not changed.

Resizing is best when you need to change the size of an image without losing any content; masking allows you hide a small part of an image without resizing and risking any change in quality, and cropping allows you to remove content that is not required.

To crop a picture you need to highlight the image frame which reveals the Picture toolbar. Alternatively, select the View menu, highlight the Toolbars option and click on Picture. Clicking on the Crop icon on the Picture toolbar produces a new pointer (i.e. crossed scissors) and also encloses the image in new shaped handles (figure 4.28). When the pointer is positioned over the edge of the image frame, it changes shape to that of the new handles and the picture can be cropped by holding down the mouse button and dragging to cut the image.

Copyfitting techniques

Copyfitting is a means of fitting text into a particular space. If a headline needs to fit on to a single line, copyfitting will reduce the character size until it fits into the space. You can set Microsoft Publisher® so that copyfitting is automatic. The Autofit functions are available from the Format menu, within the Autofit Text option, which opens a sub-menu of choices when the text frame is highlighted.

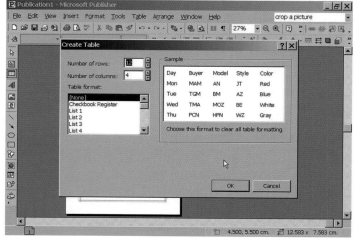

Creating a table

Another type of frame is the Table frame, which is accessed from the

Figure 4.29 Create a table

CLAiT Plus 2006 for Office XP

tools area in the same way as the Text and Picture Frame tools. The frame is inserted into the publication in exactly the same manner. As soon as you have created the frame, the Create Table window opens (figure 4.29) to allow you to set the number of rows and columns that make up the table.

The window gives you access to a range of different table formats which you can explore, since a sample of them is shown each time you highlight one.

Hyphenation

Microsoft Publisher® will automatically insert hyphens, so you may find that hyphens appear in places that you would not have inserted them. At the end of a line, Microsoft Publisher® may split a word, using hyphens, so that gaps do not appear. For example:

With Automatic Hyphenation

This is the first Newsletter of the Pre-Pax Organisation and is intended to help communication

Without Automatic Hyphenation

This is the first Newsletter of the PrePax Organisation and is intended to help communication

To switch automatic hyphenation on or off you need to highlight the text frame or table and then select the Tools menu, highlight the Language option and click on the Hyphenation

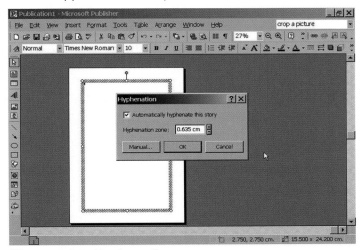

Figure 4.30 Hyphenation

option. Figure 4.30 shows the hyphenation choices. By clicking in the radio button, the automatic hypenation feature can be switched on or off.

Condensed and expanded text

Good presentation of text in desktop publishing is vital. Microsoft Publisher® lets you adjust the space between letters so that you have the freedom to condense or expand text to fit precise spaces. This is available on the Format menu when a text frame or table is highlighted. Click on the Character Spacing option (figure 4.31) and the Condense or Expand options are available under Kerning. When you select one of the options you can adjust the spacing using the box alongside the option, your choice being illustrated in the Sample area at the bottom of the window.

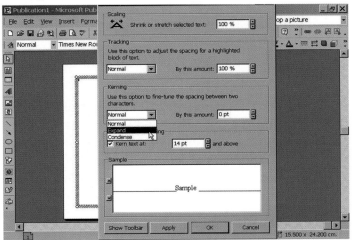

Figure 4.31 Character spacing

Text wrap

In Microsoft Publisher® you can insert pictures, tables and other objects. Once your publication contains an object, you have the choice of wrapping text around the object or not. In the PrePax newsletter you wrapped text around the image frame. It is also possible to wrap text around the actual picture (i.e. not the frame). The image wrapping functions are available on the Picture toolbar when a picture frame is highlighted.

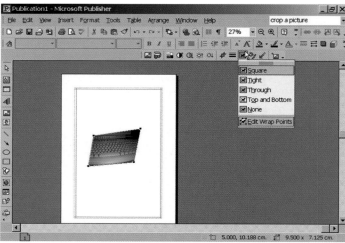

Figure 4.32 Edit Wrap Points

You can select options that will wrap text around the picture frame or around the picture. One of these, Edit Wrap Points (figure 4.32), allows you to manipulate how the text flows around the image. The image is enclosed in an outline with several small black squares that can be dragged by the mouse to change the text wrap.

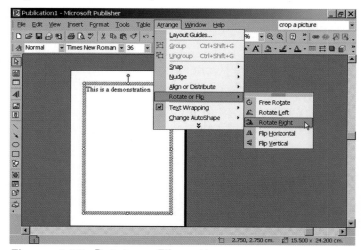

Figure 4.33 Rotate or Flip option

Rotating and reversing text

Microsoft Publisher® provides a variety of means to add interest to your publications by rotating the text or reversing the text's foreground and background colours.

To rotate text you need to highlight the text frame and select the Arrange menu then the Rotate or Flip option (figure 4.33) to reveal a sub-menu with five options: Free Rotate, Rotate Left, Rotate Right, Flip Horizontal and Flip Vertical. The Rotate Left and Right allow you to move the text through 90 degrees. The Free Rotate lets you rotate left or right using a rotational pointer. Flip Horizontal and Vertical essentially flip the text over. You can use the options multiple times to experiment with the look of the text. When you are content, click on the Apply button.

Another straightforward way of enhancing or emphasising text is to reverse the colours of the text's foreground and background (e.g. instead of black text on a white background, reverse the colours to show white text on a black background). To reverse the colours, highlight the text and select the Font Color icon on the toolbar, then change font colour to white. Next select the Fill Color icon and select black. The text colours will be reversed.

Symbols and shapes

There are two tools (figure 4.8) that allow you to add special shapes and symbols to your publications. These are:

- Insert WordArt
- AutoShape.

When you select the AutoShape icon, it opens a window, with a variety of shapes to choose from. Once an image is selected, a frame can be drawn on the publication and the shape inserted. The WordArt icon opens the WordArt Gallery for you to select from. Once you have selected by double-clicking on a choice, a new window opens to allow you to enter your text, select a font and character size. You confirm your choices by

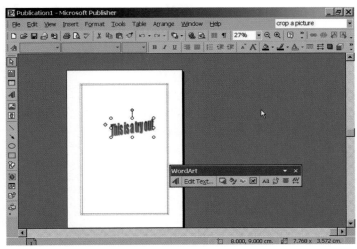

Figure 4.34 WordArt

clicking on the OK button. The selected words and art form appear for you to move into position using the pointer (figure 4.34). WordArt is accompanied by the WordArt toolbar.

Printing

The whole purpose of desktop publishing is to produce a printed document. There are a range of printing choices. These include:

- printing in colour
- printing a spot colour
- printing in black and white
- printing on a local printer
- using a commercial printer.

Microsoft Publisher® supports all these different options. The most straightforward way of printing your document is to use your own printer. You need to check its settings to ensure that it is going to produce a good copy of the publication. These are available if you select the File menu and Print option to open the Print window. Click on the Properties button to reveal the printer's properties. The actual appearance and options will depend on the printer that you are using.

It is always useful to print a single copy to check the appearance of the publication. What shows on the screen is not always reproduced on paper. This check copy is called a proof copy, and a commercial printer will send you a proof before printing the remainder. It is very important to check the publication systematically. You may have to alter the design (e.g. colours are sometimes unsuitable when you see them printed) to ensure that text is legible, or adjust the

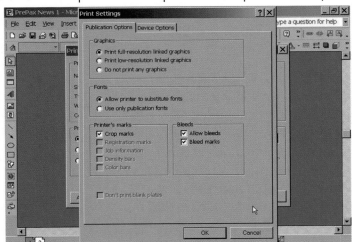

Figure 4.35 Print Settings windows

layout to achieve a balanced image. It is normal to show changes using the correction symbols.

If your publication is smaller than the paper it is being printed on, the printer will produce crop marks on the publication. These show what needs to be cut off to produce the correctly sized document. These can be removed in the advanced settings within the Print window (i.e. File menu, Print option and Advance Print Settings). Figure 4.35 shows the Print Settings window.

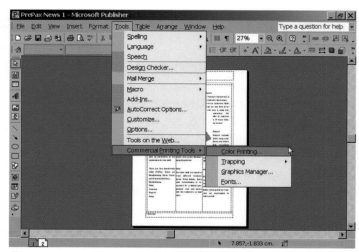

Figure 4.36 Commercial Printing Tools

Commercial printing

Microsoft Publisher® helps you set up your publication so that it is suitable for commercial printing. There are three choices:

- print in black and white
- print as process colours
- print as spot colours.

These options are available by selecting the Tools menu and highlighting the Commercial Printing Tools to reveal a menu of options (figure 4.36).

The Color Printing option provides access to the Color Printing window (figure 4.37):

- Composite RGB sets up the publication for commercial process-colour printing. It is important to check the proofs to ensure the colours are the ones you want to use.
- The Spot color option reveals a dialog window which lets you to choose between Black and White only and Black plus one or two different colours (figure 4.38).

Commercial printers will print a publication in two main ways:

- process colour or CMYK (i.e. Cyan, Magenta, Yellow and Black)
- spot colour.

There are significant differences between the two. Process colour will provide a full range of colours and is more expensive, whereas spot colour is far more limited but cheaper. The choice depends on your publication. If it uses colour photographs and graphics and needs high resolution, process colour is probably required. If you have a simpler design, with only the occasional use of colour for

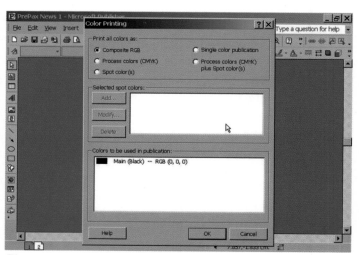

Figure 4.37 Color Printing window

emphasis (e.g. coloured heading), then spot colour printing is probably the best choice. It is often useful to discuss your plans with a commercial printer so that they can advise you. They will often be able to help with the choice of colours to obtain the best results.

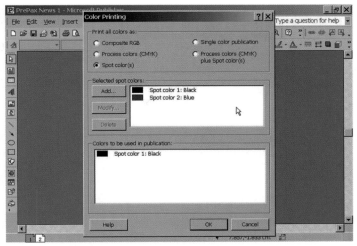

Figure 4.38 Change spot color

You will often want to print proofs yourself before sending your design to the printers. There are again two choices – composite and separation. The options are available in the Print window (i.e File menu and Print option), but you need to have selected the appropriate option in the Color Printing window (figure 4.38). Composite proofs, as the name suggests, include all the colours in one publication. This is useful when you want to check the overall look of the publication. Separation proofs produce the colours on different pages. This allows you to check each colour. Printers can advise you on the basis of proofs and therefore may help you avoid errors.

The last point to understand is that your computer displays colour using the RGB (Red, Green and Blue) system and Microsoft Publisher® changes these colours to the CMYK system to prepare for printing. Occasionally there is not a direct match.

Exercise 32

Inserting tables, cropping and printing

1 Insert your floppy disk into the computer's drive.

2 Load Microsoft Publisher® by selecting Start, highlighting the All Programs menu and clicking on the Microsoft Publisher® item or by clicking on the Publisher® icon on the desktop. If you have recently completed the last exercise, you may see Master listed at the bottom of the task pane in the section Open a publication. Double-click on Master and the document appears in the work area. If Master is not displayed, select More publications to reveal the Open Publication window and select floppy disk and Master file.

3 Insert a new section at the end of your publication using News style:

Growth

PrePax is growing rapidly and the table below shows the increase in our sales volumes over the last three years.

In my case, the text frame for page 2 has been placed over the margin and I have needed to move it back. If this is also true in your case, adjust the frame by dragging the corner handle.

4 You are going to insert a table into your newsletter. The table shows the sales figures for the last three years and illustrates the success of the business:

Year	Volume
1998	66,560
1999	83,470
2000	98,650

5 Select the Table Frame tool and insert a frame below your new text, approximately the width of a column, with four rows and two columns. Complete the table with the information shown above (figure 4.39) using the News style. When you have finished, click in another part of the publication to remove the table surround. You can return to the table by clicking on it.

You can adjust the size and shape of the table in the same way as with a picture. Consider adding a border to your table using the Format menu and the Table option. Remember that your table must be highlighted (i.e. enclosed). Click inside the table to highlight it. To highlight a row or column you need to click in the row or column heading, respectively, once the pointer has changed into a small arrow; or simply click in the respective cell and, holding down the mouse button, highlight the row or column.

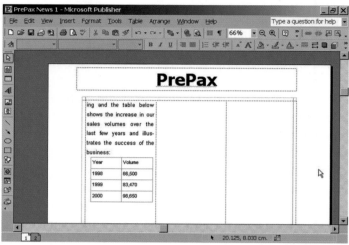

Figure 4.39 Table

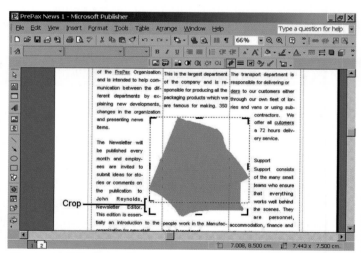

Figure 4.40 Cropping

6 Often you need to crop the images that you insert into publications. First, highlight the image. The Crop icon will appear on the Picture toolbar. Click on this and then place the mouse pointer over the top left or the bottom left-hand corner of the picture. The pointer will change shape to resemble a handle. Hold down the mouse button and move the pointer up or down the image (figure 4.40). When you release the button, the picture will be cut to remove the area you have dragged the pointer over. Practise cropping the image using the Undo button to start again, until you are confident.

7 Create a new text style for the table. Name your style Table. It should employ the Times New Roman font, size 10, bold and with centred text. Apply the new style to the table by highlighting the whole table and then clicking on the Table style (i.e. toolbar style box).

You should see the whole table change.

8 The text wrap needs to be changed so that it wraps around the picture rather than the frame. Highlight the picture frame by clicking on it, then click on the Text Wrapping icon on the Picture toolbar. Explore the different options. Watch the text around the image change.

Figure 4.41 shows the effect of selecting Tight option. Select Edit Wrap Points and the picture's enclosure will now show a surround of small black rectangles. You can adjust the wrap by dragging these rectangles with your mouse (figure 4.42). Experiment with changing the wrap. You can undo changes by clicking on the Undo icon.

9 Consider the presentation of your publication and balance the display. Your changes will have altered the layout. You may have widows and orphans. Adjust the layout to produce an effective publication. Figure 4.43 shows our layout. Try to improve on it.

10 Print your newsletter as a composite proof.

11 Save your publication again.

12 Close the application either by selecting the File menu and clicking on the Exit option or by clicking on the close button in the top right-hand corner of the application window.

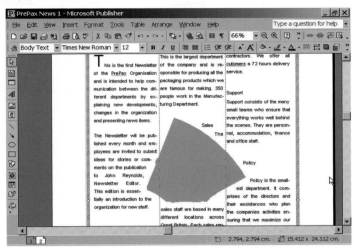

Figure 4.41 Tight

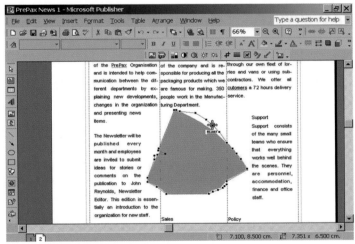

Figure 4.42 Edit Wrap

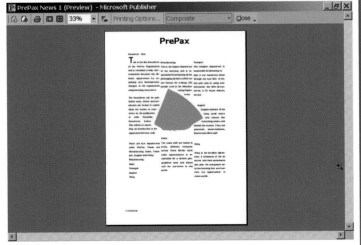

Figure 4.43 Final layout

Group

Once you have created a publication such as a master or template, it is often useful to group together all the objects that make up the document. This simply means that they will act as if they are one object (e.g. moved or copied together). However, you can still edit each object individually. To group objects together, select the Edit menu and the Select All option, then click on the Group Objects button at bottom of the page (Figure 4.44). To ungroup objects you need to click the Ungroup icon.

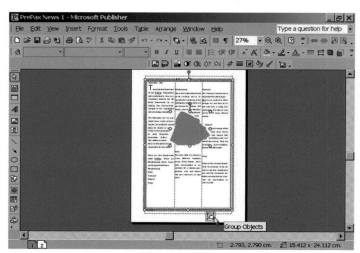

Figure 4.44 Group Objects

Exercise 33

Grouping

1 Insert your floppy disk into the computer's drive.

2 Load Microsoft Publisher® by selecting Start, highlighting the All Programs menu and clicking on the Microsoft Publisher® item or by clicking on the Publisher® icon on the desktop. If you have recently completed the last exercise, you may see Master listed at the bottom of the task pane in the section Open a publication. Double-click on Master and the document appears in the work area. If Master is not displayed, select More publications to reveal the Open Publication window and select floppy disk and Master file.

3 Group all the objects by selecting the Edit menu and the Select All option, then click on the Group Objects icon at the bottom of the page (figure 4.44). The objects should now be grouped.

4 Practice moving the objects.

5 When you are confident that you can move the objects click on the Ungroup Objects icon and then in another part of the document. The objects should now be ungrouped.

6 Repeat the process of grouping and ungrouping.

7 There is no need to save the changes.

8 Close the application either by selecting the File menu and clicking on the Exit option or by clicking on the Close button in the top right hand corner of the application window.

Design Brief

A design brief is a straightforward and clear statement of what is to be designed. When you are creating an e-publication you will often be provided with instructions in the form of a design brief (e.g. size of margins, style of text and alignment). This will indicate the overall appearance of the publication. This is often accompanied by a diagram which shows the text flow throughout the publication (e.g. between pages). For example in a document with two columns the text may flow down the first column until the bottom and then start at the top of the second and flow down it. However, there are other choices. The text flow diagram shows you the one your design must follow. The diagram often indicates the location of headings and position of images as well as the flow of text. Design briefs are often a mixture of instructions and diagrams. The key factor is that they need to be followed.

When you create a master document or template then you are essentially embodying your design brief into the publication. It makes creating future publications within the design brief instructions straightforward and you are less likely to make a mistake. Organisations will often present their house style in the form of a design brief.

In the More Practice Activities you are provided with design briefs in the form of instructions and layout guides (e.g. figure 4.45 and 4.47) for some of the exercises so you can practice working with their guidance. It is important that you follow the design as closely as you can.

Review

It is always important to review your publication, so consider the appearance of the newsletter you have created and decide if it is an effective publication. You might wish to consider issues such as:

- Should it be presented in three columns? Perhaps two or even one would be better?
- Consider the image – is it suitable? Is it positioned in the most useful place?
- Should the columns be separated by a line or a wider gutter?
- Is the text style the best choice?
- Is the table in the correct place or should it appear earlier?

You should systematically consider all the possibilities.

More practice

Activity 1

Template

1 Create a template publication for a publicity flyer for your organisation. The flyer must conform to this design brief. It should be:
   a) A4 document presented in portrait orientation
   b) Page size – width 20 cm and height 25 cm (File menu, Page Setup and Custom Type)
   c) Footer – Insert your name and today's date using the automatic field in the format dd/mm/yy (View menu and Header and Footer option)
2 Use the layout shown in figure 4.45 as a guide.

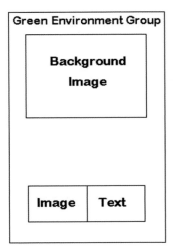

Figure 4.45 Template layout

3 Create a picture frame and import an appropriate Clip Art image or other picture. This is going to provide a background for the top of the publication. You may resize the image, but do not distort the picture.

4 Enter a header at the top of the document and enter the title Green Environment Group. Select a font and character size to emphasise it. Centre the title.

5 Create a text frame over the background picture and over the whole document.

6 Create a text frame in the bottom right-hand corner of the document and enter the text in red:

Contact

Secretary: Mary Mint

Tel. No. 9999 999 999

Enclose the text in a black border.

7 Create a picture frame alongside the text frame in the bottom left of the document. Insert an appropriate Clip Art image or other picture.

8 Save your template with the file name Green Temp.

9 Close Microsoft Publisher® XP.

Activity 2

1 Open the Green Temp template and create a new file based on it.

2 Create a file in Microsoft Word® called Events and import it into the document over the background image.

Events

During March the group have organised a series of events for members:

| 10th March | Country walk to Cropwell in order to continue work on the canal restoration project |
| 17th March | Meeting at village hall to discuss the County Council Plan for the country park |

3 Give your imported text double line spacing.

4 Select a font and colour. Embolden the text.

5 Check that your text is clear and that no words are hypenated.

6 Save your new flyer as March Flyer. Figure 4.46 shows our efforts.

7 Print the flyer in a colour separated form.

8 Check the copies for errors.

9 Save the flyer and close Microsoft Publisher®.

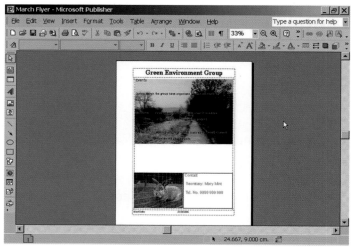

Figure 4.46 March Flyer

Activity 3

1 Handout

Create a handout for distributing at shops. The document must conform to this design brief. It should be:

a) A4 document presented in portrait orientation

b) Page size – width 18 cm and height 20 cm (File menu, Page Setup and Custom type)

c) Footer – Insert your name and today's date using the automatic field, in the format 12/06/99, and centre them

d) Top Margin – 0.75 cm

e) Bottom Margin – 0.75 cm

f) Left Margin – 0.5 cm

g) Right Margin – 0.5 cm

h) Gutter (space) – 0.5 cm

i) 2 columns

2 Use the Layout shown in figure 4.47 as a guide.

3 Content

The handout is intended to inform people about a research project that your organisation is undertaking to investigate the use of a computer search facility you provide in each of your shops. Normally during the assessment, text and image files are provided so that you can concentrate on the design aspects of desktop publishing, without the extra burden of creating the resources.

The text for the handout is given below. Save it as the file Research. The word file and images are available from the Hodder Education website (www.hodderclait.co.uk).

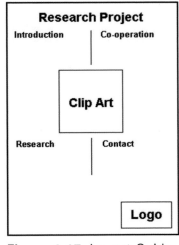

Figure 4.47 Layout Guide

Research Project

Introduction

We have been providing a free computer search facility to allow you to quickly locate any product held by any of our stores in Great Britain. We are now undertaking a review of this service to identify how we could enhance and extend its value to you.

Research

We have commissioned masters, Franks and James, an internationally recognised firm of market researchers, to investigate the use of the service and make recommendations about its future development. They will be working in a sample of our stores and will be approaching some customers to ask if they would cooperate with the research.

Cooperation

If you are willing to help, it will involve no more than a short (20 minutes) discussion with a researcher. To repay you for providing us with your views, we will be offering a £5 gift token to each participant.

Contact

If you are interested in volunteering, please speak to the sales assistant wearing the yellow jacket in the store.

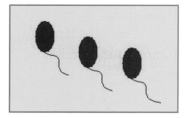

Figure 4.48 Logo

In addition to the text of the handout, you will need to include two images. Image 1 is shown in figure 4.48 and is the logo of your organization. You should also select an appropriate image from the Clip Art provided with Microsoft Office® to add to the flyer.

4   Once you have created the basic layout of the handout, save your work as the file Research Handout.

5   Check your text file and make amendments shown in figure 4.49.

6   Import text and image files.

7   Draw a line to separate the columns. Emphasise the main heading (e.g bold and large character size) and underline the subheadings. Check your handout for widows and orphans and adjust the presentation.

8   Save and print a composite version of your handout. Figure 4.50 shows our efforts.

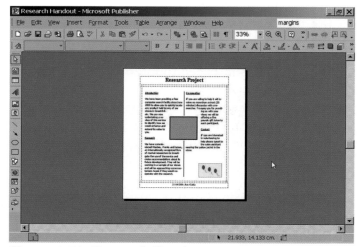

Figure 4.49 Proofread text

Figure 4.50 Research Handout

SUMMARY

1 Load Microsoft Publisher®
Load Microsoft Publisher® by selecting Start, highlighting the All Programs menu and clicking on the Microsoft Publisher® item or by clicking on the Publisher® icon on the desktop.

2 New Blank Publication
Select the Blank Publication option in the task pane and a Full Page publication will appear in the working area.

3 Save
Select the File menu and click on the Save option. The Save window will appear. Change

the Save in: box to the location of your choice (e.g. floppy disk), name the file in the File name: box and click on the Save button.

4 Text frame

Select the Text Box icon from the toolbar and the pointer will turn into a cross-hair, which you position the top left-hand corner of the frame; then, holding down the mouse button, drag the pointer to the bottom right-hand corner and release the button.

5 Columns

A text frame needs to be in place before you can divide it into columns. The text frame should be highlighted (i.e. the frame is visible). Click on the frame if it is not highlighted. Select the Format menu and click on the Text Box option to reveal the Text Box window. Choose the Text Box tab and the Columns button to reveal the Columns window.

6 Header and footer

Select the View menu and the Header and Footer option.

7 Layout guides

Select the Arrange menu and click on the Layout Guides option to reveal the Layout Guides window.

8 New text style

Select the Format menu and click on the Styles and Formatting option to reveal the Styles and Formatting task pane on the left of the work area. A new style can be created by clicking on the Create new style button.

9 Picture toolbar

The Picture toolbar is only revealed when a picture frame is highlighted. To highlight a picture frame, simply click within it.

10 Apply a text style

Highlight a text frame and select the Style box down arrow on the Format toolbar. Select the Style from the list. Everything you now enter into the frame will follow this style.

An alternative approach is to click anywhere within an individual paragraph and then select a style. The style of the paragraph will change.

11 Create a table

Another type of frame is the Table Frame, which is available from the tools area. Selecting the Insert Table icon changes the pointer to a cross-hair to help you position the table. Insert the Table Frame into the publication. When you have created the frame, the Create Table window opens to allow you to set the number of rows and columns that make up the table.

12 Lines and boxes

Select the Line or Rectangle icon from the toolbar, which changes the pointer to a cross-hair that allows you to position the start of your line or the corner of the box. By holding down the left mouse button and dragging the line or box, you can form it. It is shown enclosed in small black boxes. In this mode, it can be manipulated (e.g. moved, dragged). The thickness and the style of the line can be adjusted by right-clicking on the box or line to reveal a short menu. Select the Format Autoshape option to open the Format AutoShape window. This allows you to change the lines or rectangle sides.

13 Insert an image
Select the Picture Frame icon and the pointer will change shape to a cross-hair, which lets you accurately position the image on the page. Click on the top left-hand corner of the image and drag the frame open. Release the mouse button when you are ready and the Insert Picture window is revealed. This allows you to identify an image from your files, CD-ROM or other source.

14 Crop an image
Highlight the image frame, which reveals the Picture toolbar. Clicking on the Crop icon produces a new pointer (i.e. crossed scissors) and encloses the picture in new handles. Position the pointer over the handles and it changes shape again. You can now drag the picture to change its size by holding down the mouse button.

15 Copyfitting techniques
With the text frame highlighted, select the Format menu and highlight the Autofit Text option to reveal a sub-menu of choices.

16 Hyphenation
Highlight the text frame or table and then select the Tools menu, highlight the Language option, and click on the Hyphenation option.

17 Condense and expand text
Highlight the text or table frame. Select the Format menu and click on the Character Spacing option to reveal the Character Spacing window. The condense and expand options are available under Kerning.

18 Text wrap
Highlight the picture frame and select the Text Wrapping icon from the Picture toolbar. You have a range of options. You can use the Edit Wrap Points option to customise the text wrapping.

19 Printing
Select the File menu and click on Print.

20 Commercial printing
Select the Tools menu and highlight the Commercial Printing Tools to reveal a menu of options. Select the Color Printing option to reveal the Color Printing window.

21 Rotate text
Highlight the text frame and select the Arrange menu and the Rotate or Flip option to reveal the sub-menu.

22 Reverse text colours
Highlight the text and select the Font Colour icon, then choose the reverse colour. Select the Fill Colour icon and choose the reverse colour.

23 Document size
Select the File menu and click on the Page Setup option to reveal a window. Select the

Publication type and you can enter the width and height of your document. You can also select the orientation of the publication in the Page Setup window.

24 Line spacing (leading)

Click in the text frame you wish to alter (i.e. highlight it). Select the Format menu and click on the Line Spacing option to reveal the Line Spacing window. To change the spacing between the lines, enter the value in the Between lines box. Click on OK to make the change.

25 Template

Select the File menu and the New option to display the New Publication task pane. This provides access to a wide range of templates, such as websites, newsletters and brochures. If you highlight a category, a range of choices will appear in the work area to the right of the task pane.

26 AutoShapes

Select the AutoShapes icon from the left-hand toolbar to open a window with a variety of shapes for you to choose from. Once an image is selected, a frame can be drawn on the publication with the shape inserted.

27 WordArt

Select the WordArt icon from the left-hand toolbar to open the WordArt Gallery. Select an option, by double-clicking, to reveal a new window in order to enter text, select a font and character size. Click on the OK button and WordArt appears.

28 Background

Select the Format menu and Background option to open the Background task pane. Click on More Backgrounds to open the Fill Effects window. Choose the Picture tab to select a picture as background.

29 Group

Select the Edit menu and select All option , then click on the Group Objects button. To ungroup objects click on the Ungroup button and then in another part of the page.

30 Composite and separation printing

Select the File menu and click on Print option. Select the Composite or Separation options. What is displayed depends on the selectings in the Commercial Printing Tools option in the Tools menu.

This chapter will help you to:

- create a presentation
- set up a master slide
- insert and manipulate data
- control a presentation
- save, print and produce support documents for a presentation.

This chapter covers unit 5 (Design an e-Presentation). There are no preconditions for studying this unit. However, their content does assume that you have the skills and understanding which are provided by the OCR Level 1 ICT course CLAiT 2006 (e.g. Unit 5: Create an e-Presentation and Unit 1: File Management and e-Document Production).

Assessment

After studying unit 5, your skills and understanding are assessed during a three-hour practical assignment. This is set by OCR and marked locally. However, the marking will be externally moderated by OCR. This ensures that the standard is being applied correctly across the many different providers of OCR CLAiT Plus. If you are unsuccessful, you can be reassessed using a different assignment.

An alternative approach is for you to be assessed by an assignment set by OCR or designed by your centre. These assignments cover all the assessment objectives included in the unit. You will need to complete an OCR evidence checklist, explaining how each assessment objective has been covered.

Presentation graphics

Over recent years there has been a large increase in the use of presentation graphics to support business meetings, conferences and teaching. They allow individuals to create a set of slides and handouts quickly to illustrate and support their presentations. These can be projected from the computer through a video (data) projector or printed on transparencies for use with an overhead projector. In either case, high quality visual aids can be produced straightforwardly.

Microsoft PowerPoint® XP is the presentation graphics application on which this chapter is based (figure 5.1). It is a modern tool for creating presentations and offers users a wide range of facilities to combine text and graphics. However, it is good practice to develop a consistent format for your slides that does not overuse colour, images or text effects. Many organisations provide their staff with a house style to follow, which incorporates standard features such as the organisation's logo. Microsoft PowerPoint® provides you with the means of creating a standard template or master for your presentations.

A master/template will include:

- background colour
- standard graphics (e.g. logo)
- slide number
- presenter's name and date (this will help you manage your presentations when you have several)
- heading style (i.e. font, size, colour and style)
- bullet style (i.e. font, size, colour and style)
- sub-bullet style (i.e. font, size, colour and style).

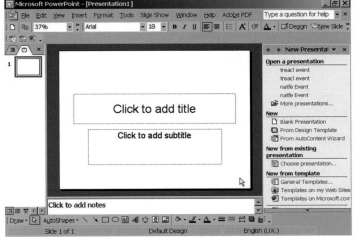

Figure 5.1 Microsoft PowerPoint® XP

It will also specify the location of different elements (e.g. pictures, slide numbering and dates) and the use of Microsoft PowerPoint® effects. Microsoft PowerPoint® and other presentation graphics packages allow you to employ animation techniques to add interest to presentations. However, it is good practice not to overuse these effects.

In exercise 34 you are going to create a master style. The house style that you are going to follow is:

Master slide

Feature	Colour	Position	Comments
Background	none		
Graphic		Left corner of text area	
Number slides		Bottom right-hand corner of the slide	
Text (footer)		Bottom centre of the slide	Enter your name and centre
Date		Bottom right-hand corner of the slide	
Timings			Each slide 60 seconds
Transitions			1 effect on every slide
Builds			1 effect on every slide

Text

Style name	Typeface	Point size	Feature	Alignment
Heading	Sans serif	40	Bold/blue	Centre
Bullet (level 1)	Serif	28	Include bullet character	Left
Sub-bullet (level 2)	Serif	24	Include bullet character	Left
Sub-bullet (level 3)	Serif	20	Include bullet character	Left

Table

Style name	Typeface	Point size	Feature	Colour	Alignment
Text	Serif	24	No bullet characters	Black	Left
Currency					Use decimal tabulation

Typeface (font)

The house style sheets use the term typeface, which is an alternative to the term font. There are two types of font (or typefaces), sans serif and serif. A serif type font has small projections on the ends of the characters, while a sans serif type font does not. You might say that serif fonts have more fancy characters or that sans serif fonts have plain characters. You need to experiment with your choice of fonts to find the ones that you like. For example:

Serif

Courier New
Serifa BT
Times New Roman

Sans serif

Arial
Helvetica

Microsoft PowerPoint®

Figure 5.1 shows the initial view of Microsoft PowerPoint® when it loads. It shows a display divided into four main areas. Across the top are a series of menus and toolbars, which are similar to those provided by other Microsoft Office® applications. A further toolbar (i.e. Drawing) is shown across the bottom. On the right-hand side is the New Presentation task pane. On the left-hand side is an Overview pane, showing the slides that you have created in the presentation – at the moment, one blank slide. In the middle is the work area, showing a blank slide and an area to add notes for your presentation.

Exercise 34

Starting a new presentation master slide

1 Insert a floppy disk into the computer's drive.

2 Load Microsoft Publisher® by selecting Start , highlighting the All Programs menu and clicking on the Microsoft PowerPoint item or by clicking on the PowerPoint icon on the desktop.

3 Select the Blank Presentation option from the New Presentation task pane on the right of the display. This will display the Slide Layout task

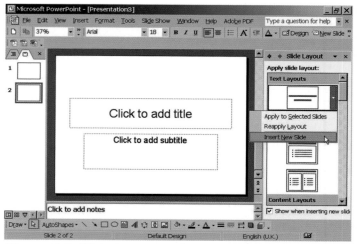

Figure 5.2 Slide Layout task pane

pane (figure 5.2), which offers you a variety of outline slides in a scrolling box to choose from. If you place the pointer on an outline, a button with a down arrow will appear on the right of slide (figure 5.2), along with a description of the slide type. The first outline is a title slide, which is identical to the opening display. Scroll down the outlines and explore the options, then return to the first one and click on the button to reveal a short menu. Select Insert New Slide (figure 5.2).

4 The title slide will appear in the work area of Microsoft PowerPoint®. However, since it is identical to the original display, you will only notice a flicker as the display is refreshed.

5 You are now going to create a master slide for this presentation. Select the View menu, then highlight the Master option to reveal a sub-menu (Figure 5.3). Click on the Slide Master option. The master slide template will show in the Microsoft PowerPoint® work area (figure 5.4). A small Slide Master View toolbar will also appear. If you drag the toolbar down to the Drawing toolbar, it will merge with it.

6 To edit the master (i.e. to change the characteristics) you need to click on the different slide features (e.g. Title). However, before you start to change the master, you should decide on the

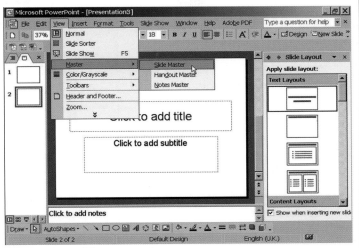

Figure 5.3 Master option

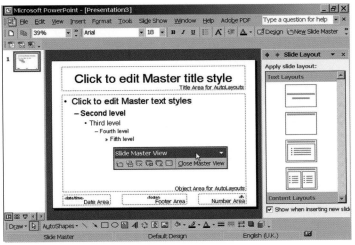

Figure 5.4 Master slide template

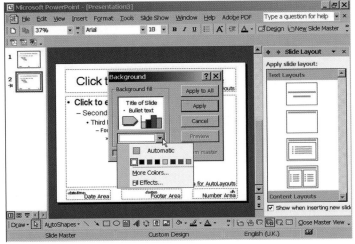

Figure 5.5 Background

background colour for the slide. Select the Format menu and click on the Background option to reveal the background window (figure 5.5). This allows you to choose a background colour for your slides. If you click on the down-arrow button you are given access to more choices. In this case, we will select no colour and click on Apply to All.

7 Click on the Master title style and from the toolbar choose Tahoma (font), size 40, bold and centred (figure 5.6). Click on Master text style (i.e. first-level bullet point) and choose Times New Roman, size 28 and left-justified. Click on Second level and choose Times New Roman, size 24 and left-justified. Click on Third level and choose Times New Roman, size 20 and left-justified. Delete the fourth and fifth levels.

8 The bottom left-hand side box contains the date (i.e. date/time) and is left-justified. Click on the box and highlight the date and time. Select the Insert menu and click on the Date and Time option to reveal the Date and Time window (figure 5.7). Select the layout dd/mm/yyyy and click the automatic update radio button.

9 Click on the footer to highlight it and enter your

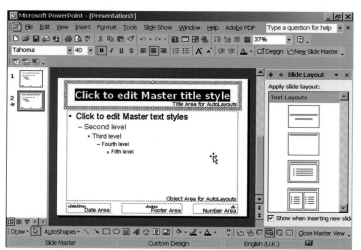

Figure 5.6 Master title

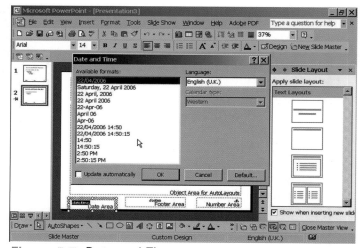

Figure 5.7 Date and Time

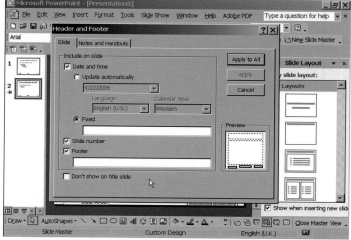

Figure 5.8 Header and Footer window

name, which should be centred.

10 Click on the right-hand box Number Area. Select Insert menu and click on Slide Number. This will reveal the Header and Footer window (figure 5.8). Click in the Footer radio button to show the footer you have created on the slides. Click on the radio button Slide number and then the Apply to All button. The Preview area will show positions of date/time, footer and number boxes.

11 The next step is to select a font colour. The default colour is black, which is acceptable, except for the title, so click in the title box and then select the Font Color icon on the Drawing toolbar (figure 5.9). Choose blue.

12 The last step is to place a graphic image in the bottom right-hand corner of the text area. Select the Insert menu,

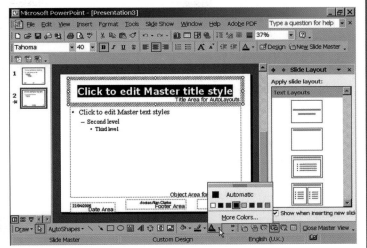

Figure 5.9 Drawing toolbar

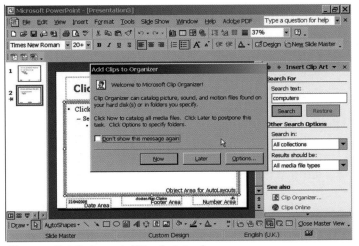

Figure 5.10 Insert Clip Art task pane

highlight Pictures to reveal the sub-menu and click on Clip Art. This will open the Insert Clip Art task pane (figure 5.10). A message will overlay the display (Add Clips to Organizer). Click on Later to remove the message.

13 The Insert Clip Art task pane lets you search for an image to fit your presentation theme. The results of a search are displayed in the task pane in a scrolling box. Explore the pictures. When you place the pointer over the image, a description of it will appear, as well as a button with a down arrow along the right edge of the picture. When you click the button, a menu of options appears. Select the Insert option to add an image to the master slide.

14 The Clip Art image will appear on the slide, enclosed in a frame, with small rectangles at the corners and centres of the lines. These allow you to change the shape and size of the image. You can move the image by positioning the mouse over the image, holding down the mouse button and dragging the image around. The mouse pointer is shaped

like crossed arrows. To resize or change the shape of the image, position your mouse over one of the rectangles and it will change to a double-headed arrow. By holding down the mouse button and dragging, you can change the shape and size of the picture. Experiment, but remember that changing its shape and size may distort the image, so you need to ensure the image's proportions are acceptable when you have finished.

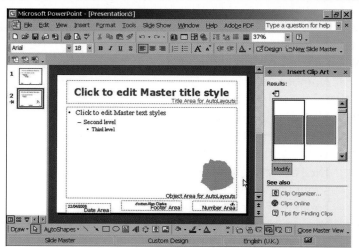

Figure 5.11 Master slide

15 You have now established your master and need to save it. Select the File menu and the Save option. The Save As window will appear. Save the master as a file called Presentation1 on your floppy disk. You will need to change the Save in: box to floppy disk and enter the file name in the File name: box.

16 The master is shown in figure 5.11. Notice that in overview pane it shows that we have two slides. This is simply the result of the process we have followed and the first slide is the original default master before the changes we have made. We therefore need to remove it, otherwise presentations developed using our master will default to the original design. Click on the first slide in the overview and press the delete key. The slide will be removed, leaving your revised master. Save this again.

17 Close the application either by selecting the File menu and clicking on the Exit option or by clicking on the Close button in the top right-hand corner of the application window.

Transition and other effects

A slide show is a presentation of a set of individual slides. Microsoft PowerPoint® allows you to control the change from one slide to the next by using transition effects. For example, you can slowly dissolve the closing slide and gradually reveal the next one. These effects can add considerable interest to a standard presentation. Among the transition effects is the control of time, so you can display each slide for a set period and then change it. This is very useful for providing a continuous presentation for an exhibition stand or similar function.

The transitions are accessed by selecting the Slide Show menu and clicking on the Slide Transition option to reveal the Slide Transition task pane (figure 5.12). This lets you select the type of transition and either have a standard change for the whole presentation or a different transition between each slide.

In figure 5.12 you will notice that there is a down-arrow button which you need to click to reveal the rest of the task pane. At the top of the pane, in the Apply to selected slides: area, is a scroll box that gives you a choice of different transition effects. Below this area is Modify transition, which allows you to vary the speed of change and also to add sound effects. Below this section is one called Advance slide, which gives the choice of manually controlling the move from one slide to the next by clicking your mouse button, or allowing the slides to change automatically after a set time.

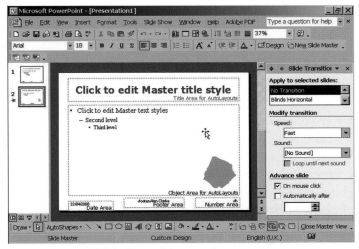

Figure 5.12 Slide Transition task pane

If you click on the down-arrow button at the bottom of the pane you reveal a series of choices of which slides to apply the transition effect to:

- Apply to Master (only appears when you are working on the master slide)
- Apply to All Slides
- Play (so you can see effect)
- Slide Show.

At the top of the pane, an up arrow will appear to allow you to return to the original display.

In addition to adding transitions to each slide, you can also add animation to the individual slide elements (e.g. title). The main effects are available by selecting the Slide Show menu and clicking on the Custom Animation option. This reveals the Custom Animation task pane.

Although Microsoft PowerPoint® provides a wide variety of effects, it is good practice to limit their use since they can distract from your overall message. One or two carefully chosen effects can enhance your presentation, whereas too many can leave your audience confused.

Charts

When starting a new presentation or inserting a new slide, you are offered the choice of a variety of different layouts (figure 5.2). Among the choices is to have slides which are:

- text only
- graphics (picture) only
- text and graphics
- charts only
- text and charts
- organisational charts
- organisational charts and text.

When you scroll down the outline they are divided into sections, and the charts are displayed in the Other layout section. If you select either the chart only or text and chart slides, you will see a chart placeholder, which, if you double-click it, will reveal a chart with its corresponding data in the form of a datasheet (figure 5.13). The datasheet contains sample information indicating where you can enter your own information to create a new chart. If you enter information, you will see the chart change in a corresponding way. When you have completed entering your data, just click away from the chart or datasheet and you will see the datasheet disappear and the new chart will be inserted into the slide.

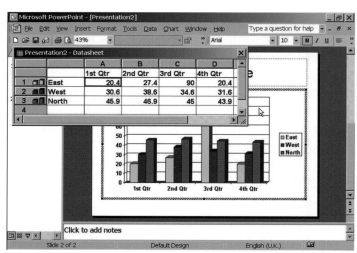

Figure 5.13 Chart

You can also insert a Microsoft Excel® chart into a slide by selecting the Insert menu and clicking on the Object option to reveal the Insert Object window. This provides you with two choices: to create a new object or select an existing one. An object is a file produced by a variety of applications. The Insert Object window displays a list of suitable applications.

Microsoft PowerPoint® also provides a special type of chart called an organisational chart. If you select the organisational chart slide, you will see an organisational chart placeholder. If you double-click on it, the Diagram Gallery window will be revealed (figure 5.14). Select the top left-hand corner option (i.e. Organization chart) to reveal the Organization toolbar and slide (figure 5.15). You can enter your own labels into the chart and then extend it by using the toolbar options.

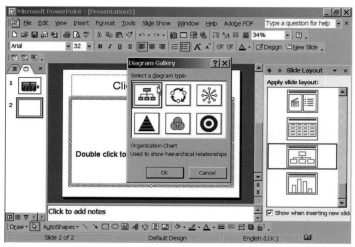

Figure 5.14 Diagram Gallery

Create a presentation

You have created a master slide or a template for your slides. You now need to employ it to guide you

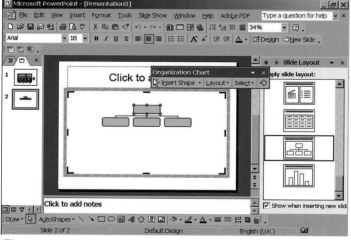

Figure 5.15 Organisation Chart

through producing a slide show. Your master can still be amended or adapted. When you have used Microsoft PowerPoint® for a period you will begin to develop a library of presentations and different master slides to suit different purposes.

You are going to create a presentation for a senior manager who is demonstrating a new product to the company directors. It is always useful to plan your presentations before you rush to create the slides. Outline what you would like to say, what the objectives of the presentation are and how long you plan to speak. People often produce more material than they can fit into the time available. Consider carefully what are the key things you need to say and how best to present them. It is often appropriate to finish early to allow time for questions. Few audiences appreciate speakers who finish late or have to rush their final slides in order to keep to time.

For this presentation, the manager wants to:

- introduce himself (1 slide)
- explain the new product (2 slides)
- discuss prices (1 slide)
- discuss sales approach (1 slide)
- discuss customers (1 slide)
- forecast chart (1 slide)
- conclude the presentation (1 slide).

Your final presentation will consist of eight slides. These will be based on the master you have already developed.

Exercise 35

Creating a presentation

1 Insert a floppy disk into the computer's drive.

2 Load Microsoft Publisher® by selecting Start, highlighting the All Programs menu and clicking on the Microsoft PowerPoint® item or by clicking on the PowerPoint® icon on the desktop.

3 If you have only recently completed exercise 34, then you may see Presentation1 in the Open a presentation section of the New Presentation task pane. If it is not visible, click on the More presentations option to reveal the Open window. Change the Look in: box to floppy disk to locate Presentation1. Double-click on Presentation1 to load it.

4 The master slide Presentation1 will load into the Microsoft PowerPoint® work area. It is useful now to save the presentation under a new name to avoid overwriting the master slide, which you may want to use later for a different presentation. Select the File menu and the Save As option. This will open the Save As window. Change the Save in: box to floppy disk and enter New Product into the File name: box, then click on the Save button.

5 You now need to create your presentation. Select the View menu and click on the Normal option. The master slide will be replaced by the Title slide in the master slides style. Enter AMEX STATIONERY in the Click to add title area. In this case, you do not have a subtitle, so select the Insert menu and click on the New Slide option.

6 The Slide Layout task pane will appear. Select a text-only layout with a single column, and use

the Apply to Selected Slides option to change the new slide to this layout. Click on Click to add title and enter Leather Bound Notebook. Click on Click to add text and insert Pocket Size, then press the enter key. The cursor will move to the next line and a new bullet will appear. Enter Desk Size and then press the enter key to move to a new line. Enter Different Formats. Figure 5.16 shows the result.

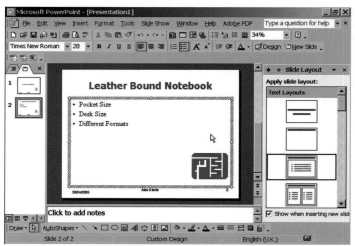

Figure 5.16 Initial Slide 2

7 Figure 5.16 shows that your bullet point text is presented on the left side of the slide. The text area is enclosed in a box, with small squares at the corners and in the centre of each side. These squares allow you to change the shape of the text area and adjust the position of the text. If you place your mouse point on the enclosure lines, but not on the squares, the pointer changes shape to a star. If you hold down the mouse button while the pointer is in this shape,

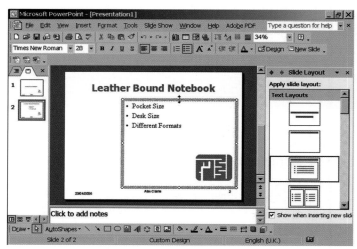

Figure 5.17 Slide 2

you can move the whole text area. Try to move the text area, but return it to its original place when you have finished.

8 If you place your mouse over a square, the mouse pointer changes to a double-headed arrow. If you hold down the button you can drag the text area to change its size and shape. Experiment changing the shape until you are content with the new appearance. Figure 5.17 shows the method.

9 Select Insert menu and click on the New Slide option. The Slide Layout task pane will appear. Select the Text in Two columns layout and use the Apply to Selected Slides option to change the new slide to this layout. Insert the title Options. Insert in the left-hand column: Lined Paper, Squared Paper and Plain Paper; and in the right-hand column: Address Book, Diary and Folder. You will notice that each column is enclosed so that it can be moved, resized or its shape adjusted. Change the columns to improve the presentation of the slide.

10 Now create a further four slides:

Slide 4 – Text slide: the title of the slide is Price; add a WordArt image of the pound symbol to represent money, and in the text column add Wholesale, Retail, Independent and Chains.

Alternatively, select a slide with a text column and a Clip Art column and then insert a clip to represent money. When inserting Clip Art you may be asked to insert the Microsoft Office® CD-ROM containing the Clip Art if this has not been installed on the hard disk.

Slide 5 – Text only slide: the title of the slide is Sales Staff; add to text National Sales Manager, Regional Sales Manager and Sales Representatives; again, position the text box to conform with your earlier decisions.

Slide 6 – Text only slide: the title of the slide is Customers; add the text Independent Stationers, Chains, Bookshops, General Retail, Wholesale and Postal; again, position the text box to conform with your earlier decisions.

Slide 7 – Chart only slide: the title of the slide is Forecast; the data sheet for the slide is:

	1st Quarter	2nd Quarter	3rd Quarter	4th Quarter
Address	15	16	21	23
Diary	27	22	31	26
Folder	8	11	9	12
Notebook	35	34	30	32

Slide 8 – Text only slide: the title of the slide is Conclusions; add to the text Product Launch, Advertising and Sales Effort.

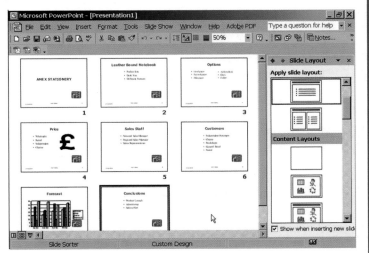

11 Adjust the layout to improve the appearance of all slides. When you are adjusting the shape and size of a graphic, there is a danger that you will alter its proportions so that a poor image results. Figure 5.18 shows the whole presentation. As you created your presentation, you will have noticed an overview of the presentation appear in the left-hand column of the work area. If you select the first tab (Outline), an overview of the text appears (figure 5.19).

Figure 5.18 **Slides 4 to 8**

12 Save your presentation by selecting the File menu and clicking on Save. No window will appear since the system assumes you are saving in the current location, using the same file name.

continued

13 Close the application by either selecting the File menu and clicking on the Exit option or by clicking on the Close button in the top right-hand corner of the application window.

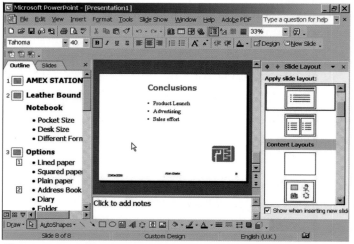

Figure 5.19 Outline

Exercise 35A

Create Timings

1 Insert a floppy disk into the computer's drive.

2 Load Microsoft PowerPoint® by selecting Start, highlighting the All Programs menu and clicking on the Microsoft PowerPoint® item or by clicking on the PowerPoint® icon on the desktop.

3 If you have only recently completed Exercise 35 then you may see New Product in the Open a presentation section of the New Presentation Task Pane. If it is not visible then click on the More Presentations option to reveal the Open window. Change the Look in: box to Floppy Disk to locate New Product. Double click on New Product to load it.

4 The presentation will load into the PowerPoint® work area. You are now going to set times between slides so that they will change automatically. This is useful if you are running a presentation as part of an exhibition.

5 Select the Slide Show menu and the Slide Transition option to open the Slide Transition task pane. In the section Advance Slide is a radio button Automatically which you need to click in order to insert a tick. Immediately below the button is a box in which you can enter times either from the keyboard or by clicking on the up or down arrows. Enter 15 seconds.

6 Click on the Apply to All Slides button which you may need to scroll down to.

7 Now run the presentation by selecting the Slide Show menu and View Show option. Watch as the slides change automatically every 15 seconds.

12 Save your presentation as New Product Automatic by selecting the File menu and clicking on Save. No window will appear since the system assumes you are saving in the current location using the same file name.

13 Close the application by either selecting the File menu and clicking on the Exit option or by clicking on the Close button in the top right hand corner of the application window.

Editing a presentation

Microsoft PowerPoint® provides functions so you can edit the presentation. You are able to:

■ change the order of the presentation
■ delete slides
■ insert new slides
■ edit individual slides (e.g. text, graphics)
■ hide slides.

You can gain an overview of the whole presentation by selecting the View menu and clicking on the Slide Sorter option. This reveals a display showing a small (thumbnail) picture of each slide. Slides can be dragged around the presentation by clicking on them to highlight them. A highlighted slide is enclosed in a rectangle. Highlighted slides (figure 5.20) can be dragged to new positions in the presentation, or deleted by pressing the delete key. New slides can be added by clicking the position (figure 5.21) you would like to add a new slide to, and then selecting the Insert menu and clicking on the New Slide option.

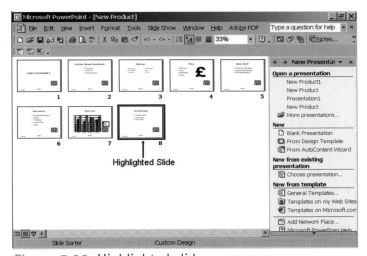

Figure 5.20 Highlighted slide

An alternative approach is to scroll through the slides from the work area. You can return from the Slide Sorter display by selecting the View menu and clicking on the Normal option. Slides can be inserted using the Insert menu and clicking on New Slide or deleted by selecting the Edit menu and clicking on the Delete Slide option.

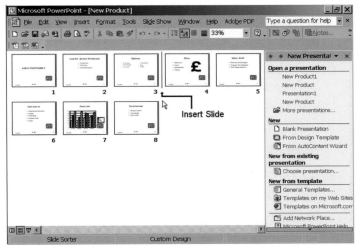

Figure 5.21 New slide

It may seem a little odd that you would want to hide a slide, but there are occasions when you want to show different information to different groups. For example, you may have created a presentation for internal staff that you later need to show some customers. Hiding slides allows you to change the presentation quickly.

To hide a slide, select the View menu and click the Slide Sorter option. Click on the slide you want to hide to highlight it, and select the Slide Show menu, click the Hide Slide option. The slide is now hidden. This is indicated by the slide number being crossed. To reverse the process, click on the Hide Slide option.

You can create a link from another slide to the hidden one so that by clicking on a word, image or button, you can present the hidden slide. The Hyperlinks section explains how to create links to hidden slides.

Exercise 36

Editing

1 Insert a floppy disk into the computer's drive.

2 Load Microsoft Power Point® by selecting Start, highlighting the All Programs menu and clicking on the Microsoft PowerPoint® item or by clicking on the PowerPoint® icon on the desktop.

3 If you have only recently completed exercise 35, you may see New Product in the Open a presentation section of the New Presentation task pane. If it is not visible, click on the More presentations option to reveal the Open window. Change the Look in: box to floppy disk to locate New Product. Double-click on New Product to load it.

4 You are going to insert an additional slide between slides 5 and 6, showing the organisation of the sales staff. Select the View menu and click on the Slide Sorter option. You will see all eight slides appear as small images. Click between slides 5 and 6 and you will see a line appear between them.

5 Select the Insert menu and click on the New Slide option. A new slide will appear in the position you have selected and the Slide Layout task pane will be displayed. Select the organisational chart layout from the task pane and click on the Apply to Selected Slides option.

6 Double-click on the new slide and you will return to the work area, with the new slide occupying the display. The slides are automatically renumbered so that the new one is now number 6.

7 Double-click on the slide to reveal the Diagram Gallery window (figure 5.14). Select the Organization Chart image in the left-hand corner to insert the organisational chart.

8 The Organization Chart toolbar is opened with the blank organisation chart (figure 5.15). This allows you to create a chart. Click on the top box of the chart and enter National Sales Manager. Now move to the next row down. Enter into each box Regional Sales Manager (three times).

9   Click on the centre Regional Sales Manager box and then on the down arrow on the Insert Shape option on the toolbar. Select the Subordinate option and a new box will be added, linked to the central Regional Sales Manager box. Click in the new box and enter Sales Representative. Your chart should now look like figure 5.22.

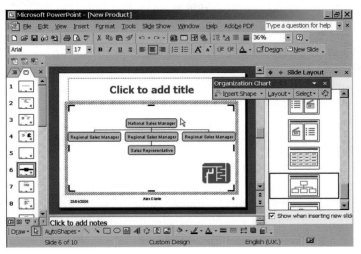

Figure 5.22 **Sales organisational chart**

10 Close the Organization Chart toolbar.

11 Click on the Title and enter Sales Organisation.

12 Save your new presentation by selecting the File menu and clicking on the Save option.

13 Select the View menu and click on Slide Sorter. You are going to change the order of the slides by moving slide 4, Price, to appear after slide 7, Customers. Click on the Price slide to highlight it (enclose it) and, holding down the mouse button, drag the slide to the new position. A line will appear in this new position. You can then release the button.

14 Save your new presentation by selecting the File menu and clicking on the Save option.

15 Close the application by selecting either the File menu and clicking on the Exit option or by clicking on the Close button in the top right-hand corner of the application window.

Hyperlinks

Hyperlinks are the means by which you can add extra slides to your presentation which only appear if you click on a sensitive area or the button on an existing slide. This allows you to customise a presentation to meet the needs of different audiences or to provide more control over the presentation. Figure 5.23 shows the connection between the main presentation slides and the hyperlink ones. Hyperlinks can also link your presentation to a document, a website, an intranet location or an e-mail address.

To add a hyperlink, select the text on the slide, click on the Insert menu and select the Hyperlink option. The Insert Hyperlink window will appear, which allows you to link the

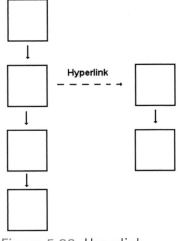

Figure 5.23 **Hyperlink**

slide to a chosen location where the other slides or documents are stored. If you are linking to other slides and want to return to the original presentation, you must create a second hyperlink back to your original slide. The link text will change colour and be underlined to show the hyperlink.

You can add standard hyperlink buttons to a slide by clicking on the Slide Show menu and highlighting the Action buttons option to reveal a small menu of buttons. Click on the button of your choice and the pointer changes to a cross to let you position it on the slide. Once it is located, the Action Settings window opens to allow you to select the action which will take place when the button is pressed. You can establish buttons to link you to the previous, next, first or last slides, giving you considerable control over the presentation.

Earlier we discussed hiding slides to protect confidential information. It is possible to create links to hidden slides so that you have the option of showing the slide. You need to highlight the text or image, then select the Insert menu and click on the Hyperlink option. This will reveal the Insert Hyperlink window (figure 5.24). Select the Place in This Document button to reveal a list of the slide titles. To complete the link, choose the hidden slide by clicking on it. The hidden slide will appear in the Preview area. Click the OK button to finish the task. This

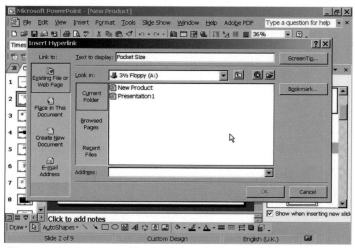
Figure 5.24 Insert Hyperlink window

method can be used to establish links within a presentation, not simply to hidden slides.

Using blank slides

One of the major difficulties in designing a presentation is to time the slide show. You do not know how many questions you will be asked or if a previous presenter will not arrive and you will have more time than you planned for. One way of maintaining control is to insert blank slides into the presentation.

This gives you the opportunity to pause or to stop if time runs out. Blanks should be inserted at logical places to allow you to pause, perhaps to provide an opportunity for questions or comments.

Tables

One of the layout options is a table, which you can select from the Slide Layout task pane and a table slide is placed within the presentation (figure 5.25). Click on the Insert Table icon to

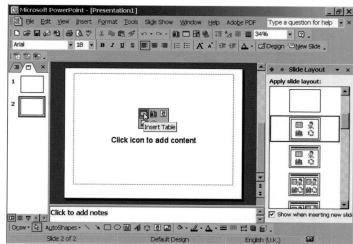
Figure 5.25 Table slide

CLAiT Plus 2006 for Office® XP

open the Insert Table window in which you can choose the number of rows and columns. When you have selected the size of the table and clicked on the OK button, you will see the table on the slide, and the Tables and Borders toolbar (figure 5.26) appears (alternatively, View menu, highlight Toolbar and Tables and Borders option). This lets you change the appearance of the table. When you have made your selections you are presented with an empty table in which to enter your information. The mouse pointer looks like a pen.

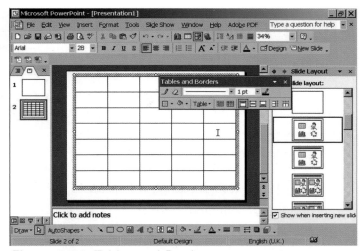

Figure 5.26 Tables and Borders

You can also insert a table into an existing slide by selecting the Insert menu and the Table option to reveal the Insert Table window, which allows you to set the number of rows and columns. This will produce a table for you to enter text into. The table can be resized and moved using the mouse pointer to position it on the slide.

Tables are one means of aligning information on a slide, but you can also use the tab key. The justification icons on the toolbar also let you align the text left, right and centre, in the same way that text is aligned in Microsoft Word®.

Exercise 37

Transitions and effects

1 Insert a floppy disk into the computer's drive.

2 Load Microsoft PowerPoint® by selecting Start, highlighting the All Programs menu and clicking on the Microsoft PowerPoint® item or by clicking on the PowerPoint® icon on the desktop.

3 If you have only recently completed Exercise 36, you may see New Product in the Open a presentation section of the New Presentation task pane. If it is not visible, click on the More presentations option to reveal the Open window. Change the Look in: box to floppy disk to locate New Product. Double-click on New Product to load it.

4 You are now going to apply a transition effect to each slide of the presentation. Select the Slide Show menu and click on the Slide Transition option to reveal the Slide Transition task pane (figure 5.12). Click on the down-arrow button below Apply to selected slides to display a list of transition options. Select an option and you will see it demonstrated on the slide in the work area. Explore the options and choose one you feel is effective. You are also provided with three speeds as transitions (i.e. slow, medium and fast). To select a new speed, click on your choice. You will again see it demonstrated in the work area.

5 In the Advance Slide area you are going to set the presentation to change slides automatically. The house style sets 60 seconds as the time for each slide, so click in the automatic box and adjust the time to read 60 seconds or 1 minute. Both the On Mouse Click and Automatically after options now have a tick in them, so you can manually change slides or they will change themselves after a minute. Now click on the Apply to All button (you may need to click on the down arrow to reveal the options).

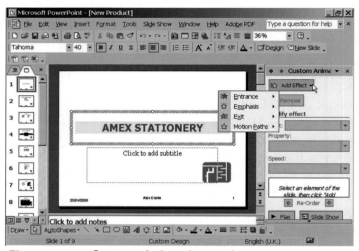

Figure 5.27 Custom Animation task pane

6 You are now going to add animation effects to each slide. The house style is for one effect for each slide. Scroll through the slides until you reach the title one. Click on the title to highlight it (i.e. enclosed in a frame). Select the Slide Show menu and the Custom Animation option to reveal the Custom Animation task pane. Click on the down arrow of the Add Effect box to reveal a series of options (figure 5.27). Choose Entrance and the Fly In option. The option will be demonstrated on the working slide as soon you select it. You can modify the effect using the other parts of the task pane.

7 Repeat the process for each slide.

8 Save your new presentation by selecting the File menu and clicking on the Save option.

9 Two other ways of enhancing your presentation are by using hyperlinks and hiding slides. You may want to use this presentation for external audiences and some slides will not be appropriate (e.g. forecasts of income). Let us hide the Forecast slide. Select the View menu and click on the Slide Sorter option. Thumbnail images of each slide will appear. Click on the Forecast slide to highlight it (i.e. it will be enclosed in a rectangle). Now select Slide Show menu and click on the Hide Slide option. The number of the slide will be crossed.

10 In some cases you may want to show the hidden slide. This can be achieved by using hyperlinks. Move to the slide prior to the Forecast slide and highlight the text you want to make the link (e.g. Slide Title). Select the Insert menu and click on the Hyperlink option to reveal the Insert Hyperlink window (figure 5.24). Click on the Place in This Document button, since you are linking to a slide in this presentation. A list of slide titles will appear. Double-click on the Forecast slide and you will return to the slide working area. You have linked the slides.

11 Save your revised presentation by selecting the File menu and clicking on the Save option.

12 Close the application either by selecting the File menu and clicking on the Exit option or by clicking on the Close button in the top right-hand corner of the application window.

Importing text and graphics

Microsoft Office® applications enable you to cut, copy and paste text and graphics between applications. It is possible to cut or copy text from Microsoft Word® and paste it into PowerPoint®. You can also send text from Microsoft Word® to Microsoft PowerPoint® directly, using the option Send To, which is available from the File menu. This reveals a sub-menu with the option Microsoft PowerPoint. This will change the file into a Microsoft PowerPoint® presentation.

Graphics can be inserted into Microsoft PowerPoint® by selecting the Insert menu and highlighting the Picture option to reveal a sub-menu of options (figure 5.28). This provides you with a series of choices, including inserting Clip Art or selecting a graphic image from a file, a scanner or a digital camera.

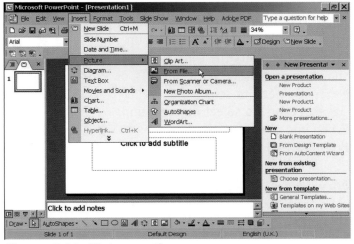

Figure 5.28 Picture option

Find and replace

When you need to make changes to a presentation, you can do it manually by locating the slide, deleting the text and then inserting the replacement text. Alternatively, you could employ the Replace function, available by selecting the Edit menu and clicking on the Replace option (figure 5.29). This lets you search for a word or phrase and replace it throughout the whole presentation.

Spellchecker

One of the most frequent problems with presentations is showing a misspelt word to an audience. They will see the error immediately, and

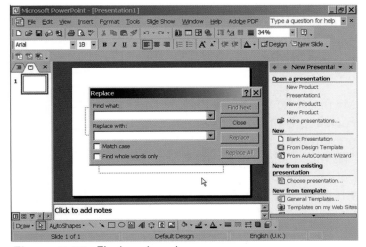

Figure 5.29 Find and replace

often you are only aware of it when someone tells you after the presentation. Microsoft PowerPoint® provides a spellchecker and it is good practice to check your completed presentation. The spellchecker is available by selecting the Tools menu and clicking on the Spelling option. However, you should not simply rely on the checker, but also proofread your slides.

Showing a Presentation

There are several ways of running a presentation. These are:

1   Select the View menu and click on Slide Show option.

2 Select the Slide Show menu and click on the View Show option (figure 5.30).

3 Click on the Slide Show button in the bottom left-hand corner of the display (figure 5.30). This shows the presentation from the slide in the work area.

Microsoft PowerPoint® allows you to save your slides in the Presentation format, which lets the slide show be shown immediately. With Save As or Save, you need to select the Save as type: to select Presentation. When you double-click on the Presentation, the slides open immediately.

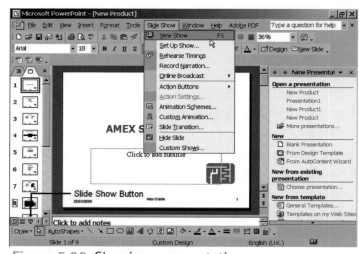

Figure 5.30 Showing a presentation

Moving a presentation to a new computer

The computer on which the presentation is created is frequently not the one used for actually showing it. Therefore you need to move the presentation. You can simply transfer the file using a memory stick or other portable method. However, this does assume the new computer will

have all the resources that you need to run the show (e.g. images, sounds and fonts). You do not want to discover that it does not during a presentation.

Microsoft PowerPoint® provides a Pack and Go facility to ensure your presentation is complete. Select the File menu and the Pack and Go option. This opens a Wizard, which will take you through the process step by step (figure 5.31).

To install the pack presentation on the new computer, you need to double-

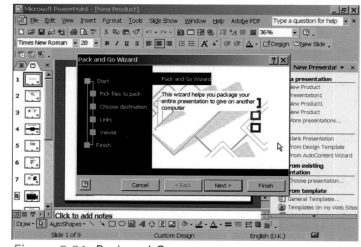

Figure 5.31 Pack and Go

click on Pngsetup (i.e. Pack and Go setup file) and select the folder in which you want to save the presentation, then click on OK. The system will tell you when the unpacking is successful. You can then run the presentation in the normal way.

Exercise 38

Showing a presentation

1 Insert a floppy disk into the computer's drive.

2 Load Microsoft PowerPoint® by selecting Start , highlighting the All Programs menu and clicking on the Microsoft PowerPoint® item or by clicking on the PowerPoint® icon on the desktop.

3 If you have only recently completed exercise 37, you may see New Product in the Open a presentation section of the New Presentation task pane. If it is not visible, click on the More presentations option to reveal the Open window. Change the Look in: box to floppy disk to locate New Product. Double-click on New Product to load it.

4 Run the presentation using one of the options. You will see the slide occupy the whole screen. You may need to click your mouse to see the transition effects. Observe what happens when you move between slides. Try waiting for 60 seconds to see the slides change automatically. The precise change will depend on your previous choice of effects.

5 Run the presentation several times, including linking to the hidden slide.

6 Close the application either by selecting the File menu and clicking on the Exit option or by clicking on the Close button in the top right-hand corner of the application window.

Printing supporting documents

As well as producing slides using Microsoft PowerPoint®, you can also create a variety of printed documents to support the presentation. The slides themselves can be printed on to transparencies for use with an overhead projector. In addition, you can print:

- copies of individual slides
- a set of notes for the presenter
- handouts which allow audience to add notes
- a copy of the presentation in outline view.

These are all available by selecting the File menu and clicking on the Print option to reveal the Print window (figure 5.32). This gives you a variety of options. In the Print what: area you can select from a list. The Handouts options lets you print copies of slides as small thumbnail images in a number of different formats (e.g. six images to a page). You can also print

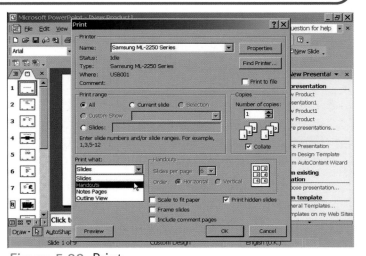

Figure 5.32 Print

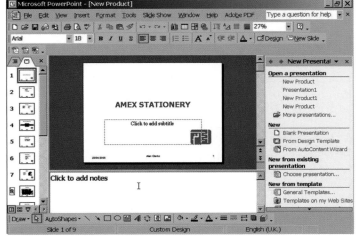

Figure 5.33 Speaking notes

full-size copies of individual slides, groups or the whole presentation, using the Print range options.

When you are creating your slides you can also produce a set of speaking notes to accompany them, using the Slide notes area below the working area (figure 5.33).

Screen prints

Microsoft Windows® provides you with the means of capturing the display on the computer screen. To do this, press the PrtSc (Print screen) button. The display is captured and stored in a special area of the computer's memory called the clipboard. If you open Microsoft Word® or another suitable application, you can paste the captured display into the document. This is useful in that you can capture the slides as they appear on the screen, so you can document the build-up of the slide and other special effects. CLAiT Plus 2006 requires that you use screen prints as evidence of transitions, builds and hyperlinks.

Exercise 39

Printing

1 Insert a floppy disk into the computer's drive.

2 Load Microsoft PowerPoint® by selecting Start, highlighting the All Programs menu and clicking on the Microsoft PowerPoint® item or by clicking on the PowerPoint® icon on the desktop.

3 If you have only recently completed exercise 38, you may see New Product in the Open a presentation section of the New Presentation task pane. If it is not visible, click on the More presentations option to reveal the Open window. Change the Look in: box to floppy disk to locate New Product. Double-click on New Product to load it.

4 Notice that under the slide is an area labelled Click to add notes. Click in this area, since you are going to produce a set of speaker's notes. In slide 1 enter:

Good morning. I am pleased that you were able to find the time in a busy day to attend my presentation. I am sure that you will find its contents beneficial.

In the final slide, Conclusions, enter:

This is an exciting new product that will potentially generate substantial profits for the company. However, it requires an effort from everyone in this room in order to be successful.

Now enter appropriate text for the other slides to produce a full set of notes.

5 Select the File menu and click on the Print option to reveal the Print window. Print:

- copies of all slides – full size

- handouts with six, four and two copies of the slides on each page

- notes pages

- outline view.

Explore all the options until you are confident that you can produce the desired documents.

6 Now run the presentation and practise capturing the screen displays using the PrtSc key. Paste your captures into Microsoft Word® or Microsoft Windows® Paint. Print the resulting document. Continue until you are confident.

7 Close the application either by selecting the File menu and clicking on the Exit option or by clicking on the Close button in the top right-hand corner of the application window.

Importing data

You can import information from other Microsoft Office® applications into PowerPoint®. There are many occasions when you need to show an audience information from your company. The obvious way is to copy and paste information between the applications. The copied object is transferred to Microsoft PowerPoint®. However, you can also transfer an object and maintain a link with its original application. It is therefore able to change as it is updated. This is useful when you are presenting a spreadsheet that will change. Your presentation is automatically kept up to date.

In order to establish the link, you need to copy the object (e.g. spreadsheet) and select Paste Special to reveal the Paste Special window (figure 5.34). If you use Paste Special without establishing a link, it is still useful, since the table is transferred to the slide. When you simply use paste, the data but not the table is transferred.

Once you have imported an object you can edit it by double-clicking on it. You will return to the original application if the object is linked to it and can therefore edit it. If the object is not linked, it is enclosed in a spreadsheet frame, allowing you to edit it. To return to Microsoft PowerPoint®, select the File menu and the Exit option in the linked case, and simply click away from the table when not linked.

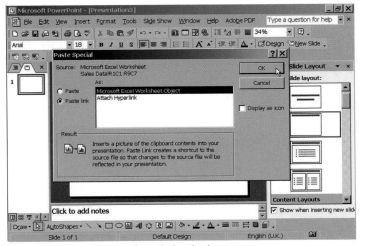

Figure 5.34 Paste Special window

More practice

Activity 1

Master slide

1 Create a master slide based on the specification below:
Orientation is landscape

Master slide

Feature	Colour	Position	Comments
Background	none		
Graphic		Bottom right corner of text area	
Number slides		Bottom right hand corner of the slide	
Text (footer)		Bottom centre of slide	Enter your name
Date		Bottom left hand corner of the slide	
Timings			Each slide 30 seconds
Transititions			1 effect on every slide
Builds			1 effect on every slide

Text

Style name	Typeface	Point size	Feature	Alignment
Heading	Sans serif	44	Bold/red	Centre
Bullet (level 1)	Serif 36	Include bullet character	Left	
Sub-bullet (level 2)	Serif 32	Include bullet character	Left	

2 Save the master presentation as News. Figure 5.35 shows the master slide.

3 Close Microsoft PowerPoint® or proceed to activity 2.

Activity 2

1 Create a presentation for a manager who wants to explain some changes to the employees of a company. The structure and text is shown below:

- introduction (1 slide)
- explain the changes (3 slides)
- current organisation (1 slide)
- new organisation (1 slide)
- invite questions (1 slide)
- conclude the presentation (1 slide).

Text for the slides

Slide 1	Kingston Computing Ltd
Slide 2	Changes Global Competition More Efficient Structures Reduce Costs
Slide 3	Changes Flexibility Team Working Learning Organisation Insert a Clip Art image alongside the text relevant to change
Slide 4	Changes Streamline Organisation Reduce Management More Delegation

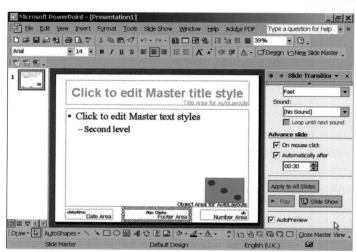

Figure 5.35 Master slide

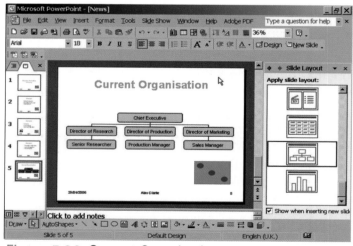

Figure 5.36 Current Organisation

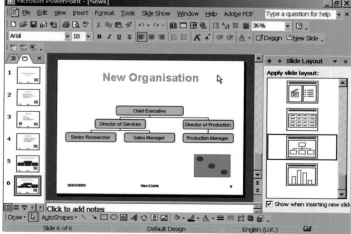

Figure 5.37 New Organisation

Slide 5	Current Organisation Insert organisation chart (figure 5.36)
Slide 6	New Organisation Insert organisation chart (figure 5.37)
Slide 7	Questions Please ask any questions
Slide 8	Conclusion Change Cooperation Thank you

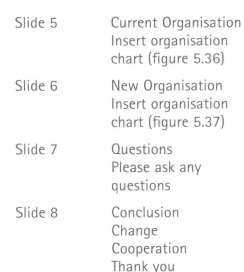
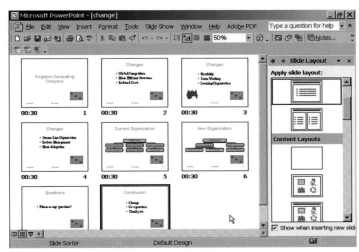

Figure 5.38 Change presentation

2   Figure 5.38 shows the presentation slides.

3   Save the presentations as Change.

4   Close Microsoft PowerPoint® or proceed to activity 3.

Activity 3

1   Create an additional slide between the existing slides 1 and 2, showing the current financial position of the company.

2   The new slide is based on the spreadsheet shown below and saved as Finance.

	Income	Expenditure	Profit
2003	22.30	21.80	0.50
2004	21.90	21.65	0.25
2005	21.20	21.35	−0.15

Import data from spreadsheet and display on new slide 2.

3   Insert slide title – Financial Position.

4   Format the table:
column headings – sans serif, character size 16, bold
row headings – sans serif, character size 14, bold
data – sans serif, character size 12.
(Tip: double-click on the table)

5   Figure 5.39 shows the imported table.

6   Save the revised presentation.

7   Close Microsoft PowerPoint® or proceed to activity 4.

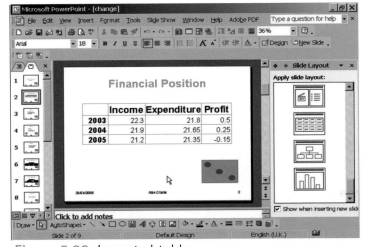

Figure 5.39 Imported table

Activity 4

1 Slide 2 of the Change presentation contains sensitive information, so hide the slide with a hyperlink from slide 1 so that the presenter can choose when to show it.

2 Hide slide 2.

3 Create a hyperlink from slide 1 to hidden slide.

4 Test the link (figure 5.40).

5 Add the speaker's notes below to the slide 1:

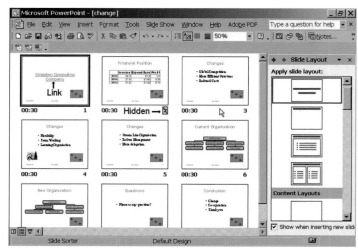

Figure 5.40 Hyperlink and hidden slide

Thank you for coming along at short notice. I would like to explain the nature of my presentation and what it will include. The company has been struggling for several years to maintain its profit margins and is now making a loss. It is therefore important to take action to bring us into profit. In the next few minutes I plan to give an overview of the financial position and explain the nature of the changes we want to introduce to save costs and make us more efficient.

6 Save your revised presentation as Change.

7 Close Microsoft PowerPoint® unless you are going on to activity 5.

Activity 5

Transitions and animation

1 Revise the Change presentation to add a single transition between each slide and a single animation in each slide.

2 Test the presentation transitions and animations.

3 Now print:
   - all the slides as handouts – four slides per page
   - outline view
   - speaker's notes on slide 1.

4 Save the presentation as Change.

5 Close Microsoft PowerPoint®.

SUMMARY

1 Loading Microsoft PowerPoint®

Select Start, highlight the All Programs option and click on the Microsoft PowerPoint® item or click on the PowerPoint® icon on the desktop.

2 Save

Select the File menu and the Save option. The Save As window will appear.

3 Blank presentation

Select the Blank presentation option from the New Presentation task pane on the right of the display. This will display the Slide Layout task pane, which offers you a variety of outline slides in a scrolling box to choose from.

4 Master slide

Select the View menu, highlight the Master option to reveal a sub-menu. Click on the Slide Master option. The Master Slide template will appear in the Microsoft PowerPoint® work area.

5 Edit master

To edit the master (i.e. to change the characteristics) you need to click on the different slide features (e.g. Title) and select the new characteristics (e.g. font, text colour and character size).

6 Background colour

Select the Format menu and click on the Background option to reveal the Background window. This allows you to choose a background colour for your slides.

7 Date and time

Select the Insert menu and click on the Date and Time option to reveal the Date and Time window.

8 Page numbers

Select the Insert menu and click on the Slide Number option to reveal the Header and Footer window.

9 Font colour

Select the Font color icon on the Drawing toolbar and choose your colour.

10 Hyperlinks

Select slide text, click on the Insert menu and select the Hyperlink option.

To add hyperlink buttons, click on the Slide Show menu and highlight the Action buttons option. Select a button, position it on the slide and select an action from the Action Setting window.

11 Transitions

Select the Slide Show menu and click on the Slide Transition option. This will reveal the Slide Transition task pane.

12 Animation

Select the Slide Show menu and click on the Custom Animation option. This will reveal the Custom Animation task pane.

Alternatively, Select the Slide Show menu and highlight the Animation Scheme option to reveal the Slide Design task pane options.

13 Open an existing presentation

Presentation may be visible in the Open a presentation section of the New Presentation task pane. If it is not, click on the More presentations option to reveal the Open window.

14 New slide

Select the Insert menu and click on the New Slide option.

15 Manipulate text and graphics

The text and graphic areas are enclosed in a box, with small squares at the corners and in the centre of each side. These squares allow you to change the shape of the text area and adjust the position of the text or graphics.

Placing your mouse pointer on the enclosure lines, but not on the squares, changes its shape to a star. If you hold down the mouse button while the pointer is in this shape, you can move the whole text area.

If you place your mouse pointer on the squares, it will change shape to a double-headed arrow. If you hold down the mouse button, you can drag the enclosure to change the shape and size of the area.

16 Overview

Select the View menu and click on the Slide Sorter option.

17 Manipulate slides in slide sorter

Highlight a slide, then drag it to a new position in the presentation or delete it by pressing the delete key. New slides can be added by clicking at the position in which you would like to add a new slide and then selecting the Insert menu and clicking on the New Slide option.

18 Organisation chart

Select the Organization Chart layout from the Slide Layout task pane.

19 Import text

Cut or copy text directly between Microsoft Word® and PowerPoint®.

Send text from Microsoft Word® to PowerPoint® directly by using the option Send To, which is available from the File menu in Microsoft Word®. This reveals a sub-menu with the option Microsoft PowerPoint. This will change the file into a Microsoft PowerPoint® presentation.

20 Import graphics

Select the Insert menu and highlight the Picture option to reveal a sub-menu of options.

21 Find and replace

Select the Edit menu and click on the Replace option to reveal the Replace window.

22 Spellchecker

Select the Tools menu and click on the Spelling option.

23 Show a presentation

Select the View menu and click on the Slide Show option.

Alternatively, select the Slide Show menu and click on the View Show option.

OR, click on the Slide Show button in the bottom left-hand corner of the display.

24 Printing

Select the File menu and click on the Print option to reveal the Print window.

25 Close application

Select the File menu and click on the Exit option or click on the close button in the top right-hand corner of the application window.

26 Chart/graph

Select a chart slide from the Slide Layout task pane and click on the chart/graph placeholder to reveal a chart and its corresponding datasheet. Enter your data to produce a new chart.

To insert a Microsoft Excel® chart, select the Insert menu and click on the Object option to reveal the Insert Object window.

27 Speaker's notes

Click on the area below the slide working area, labelled Click to add notes. Enter your notes.

You can print your notes by using the Print option in the File menu. Print what: allows you to select Notes Pages.

28 House styles

Many organisations have developed standards for their presentations. This ensures consistency and quality in the use of them. To ensure standards, it is often useful to develop a master slide. Many organisations provide this to ensure their standards are adhered to. Standards are often called house styles.

29 Microsoft PowerPoint® show

Select Save As or Save and choose Save as type to select PowerPoint Show.

30 Pack and Go

Select the File menu and the Pack and Go option. This opens a Wizard which will take you through the process step by step.

31 Unpack

Double-click on Pngsetup (i.e. Pack and Go setup file) and select the folder in which you want to save the presentation, then click on OK. The system will tell you when the unpacking is successful.

32 Import spreadsheet file

Copy the highlighted object in the application and select the Edit menu in Microsoft PowerPoint® to reveal the options. Choose the Paste Special option to reveal the Paste Special window. This lets you simply paste in the object or link the object to the original file.

33 Edit object (spreadsheet table)

Double-click on the object. If linked, the object will transfer the display to original application (i.e. spreadsheet), in which you can edit it before returning by selecting File menu and Exit option. If the object is not linked, then it is enclosed in a frame and you can edit it within Microsoft PowerPoint®.

e-Image Manipulation

This chapter will help you to:

- identify and use appropriate software correctly, in accordance with laws and guidelines, keeping risks to self and others to a minimum

- use appropriate techniques to handle, organise and save files

- use most tools and techniques appropriately

- import and manipulate text and image files

- create artwork incorporating text and images in layers

- edit and retouch images

- use a variety of graphic effects

- create an animated image for electronic media

- prepare artwork for print/electronic publishing

- save files in an appropriate format.

This chapter covers unit 6 (e-Image Manipulation). There are no preconditions for studying this unit. However, its content does assume that you have the skills and understanding which are provided by the OCR Level 1 ICT course CLAiT 2006 (e.g. Unit 6: e-Image Creation and Unit 1: File Management and e-Document Production).

Assessment

After studying unit 6 your skills and understanding are assessed during a three-hour practical assignment. This is set by OCR and marked locally. However, the marking will be externally moderated by OCR. This ensures that the standard is being applied correctly across the many different providers of OCR CLAiT Plus. If you are unsuccessful, you can be reassessed using a different assignment.

An alternative approach is for you to be assessed by an assignment set by OCR or designed for your centre. These assignments cover all the assessment objectives included in the unit. You will need to complete an OCR evidence checklist, explaining how each assessment objective has been covered.

CorelDRAW®

This chapter is based on CorelDRAW® 10, which is a vector-based graphics package. This means that you can create artwork using a variety of tools. You can produce posters, book covers, web page graphics and animations, as well as a variety of other illustrations. CorelDRAW® 10 consists of three applications. These are: CorelPHOTO-PAINT® 10, CorelDRAW® 10 and Corel R.A.V.E.™ You need to use all three as part of this chapter.

Figure 6.1 shows the CorelDRAW® interface. This resembles many other Microsoft Windows®-based applications, in that it consists of:

- a work area
- a menu bar
- toolbars (figures 6.2, 6.3 and 6.4).

The major visual difference is that there are toolbars down both edges of the work area. The left-edge toolbar consists of a series of drawing tools (figure 6.3) while the right toolbar is a colour palette (figure 6.2).

CorelDRAW® allows you to measure precisely the size of artwork that you are creating. Figure 6.2 shows that you can set the dimensions of the artwork in terms of page sizes (e.g. A4) or in exact measures in a wide variety of units, including millimetres, centimetres, inches and pixels. The page size is adjusted using the small down arrow next to the page size box, which reveals a list of options. These are chosen by clicking on them. The dimensions can be adjusted using the up and down arrows, which change them directly. The toolbar also allows you to change the orientation of the page between portrait and landscape. This toolbar changes to provide other options when different drawing tools are chosen. Explore the different options when you load the application.

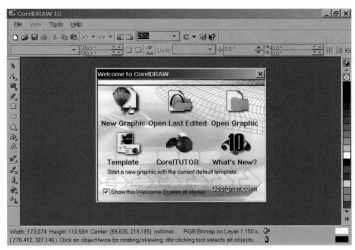

Figure 6.1 CorelDRAW®

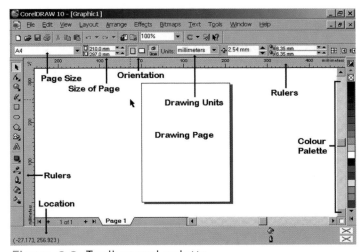

Figure 6.2 Toolbar and palette

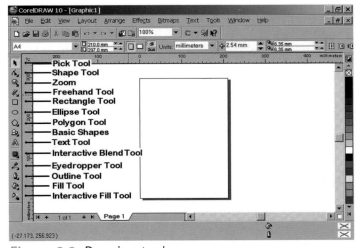

Figure 6.3 Drawing tools

The quality of an image is dependent on its resolution. A high resolution will allow the image to convey fine detail. However, to convey fine detail on paper requires a good printer. The quality of a printer is given in the number of dots per inch (dpi). This is frequently given as 300 dpi. There are printers that can produce far higher dots per inch. Clearly, the more dots that can be printed, the higher quality the image. However, a high quality printer will not overcome a low resolution image. To produce the best quality requires both a high resolution image and a good printer.

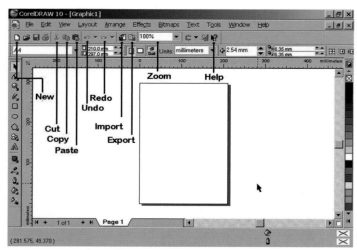

Figure 6.4 Standard toolbar

Artwork is not only designed to be displayed on paper, but also for web pages. Images for web pages are specified in the form of pixels. The maximum practicable width of an image for a web page is 640 pixels, since this allows most users to see it without horizontal scrolling. You can make it far wider, but viewers will need to scroll from side to side to see the whole picture.

Figure 6.4 shows the standard functions, many of which appear on Microsoft Windows® applications, such as new, open, print, cut, copy, paste, undo and redo. In addition, you can also import and export images using other tools. A useful function is Help, which will provide you with an explanation of the tool's purpose.

Figure 6.2 shows you the range of drawing tools. CorelDRAW® assists you to draw straight and curved lines, rectangles, ellipses, polygons and other shapes. You can add colour to your drawings (e.g. Fill Tool) as well as text. In essence, you can do many tasks which would normally require a skilled artist, even though you lack many of his skills. The colour palette (figure 6.2) is a natural companion to the drawing tools in that you select the colours for your lines and fills from the palette. At the bottom of the palette is a down-arrow button that allows you to scroll down the list of colours, and a left-pointing arrow which will reveal the whole palette as three lines of colours. Explore these options when you load the application.

CorelPHOTO-PAINT® also has a toolbar down the left-hand side of the work area and you should explore this when you first encounter it. In both applications, some tool icons have an arrow in the bottom right-hand corner. This indicates that if you click on the icon, a series of other tools will pop out. These are all related, but it is sometimes puzzling to locate a tool until you become familiar with the application.

Image size

CorelDRAW® allows you to set the size of your artwork in terms of the page size. However, it is also possible to create an image and define its precise size. In order to do this, you need to use CorelPHOTO-PAINT® 10. When the application loads it displays an overlay window with six choices, similar to CorelDRAW®; click on New Image to reveal the Create a New Image window.

The window allows you to define the size of the image, using the Width, Height and Resolution boxes. The higher the resolution, the more detail that the image can show when it is printed. The image can be copied and pasted into a CorelDRAW® document.

Design brief

The creation of artwork is often controlled by a design brief, which specifies the nature of the images, layout and structure. Figure 6.5 shows a simple design brief. This suggests that a background image will provide a foundation on to which two text boxes and an image are placed. All these different objects are part of a single layer. They can be moved around and even stacked on top of each other. More layers can be added to form the artwork. This has the advantage that each individual layer can be edited separately. Complex designs can be created using layers.

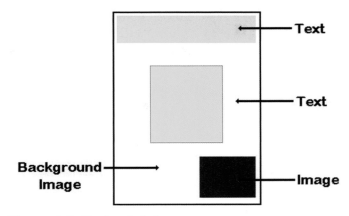

Figure 6.5 Design brief

Copyright

There are a large range of resources available to help you to produce high quality images. There are many websites that offer graphics that could be included in your designs, as well as CD-ROMs. It is also straightforward to capture images. However, it is vital to check who owns these resources, since ultimately someone owns the copyright of all materials in the public domain. The website or CD-ROM should say how the resources can be used, but even when they grant permission it is often qualified (e.g. only for non-profit purposes or for educational purposes). If you want to use screen captures, you need to check with the producer of the product, who, again, may only give permission for specific purposes and designate how their images can be displayed. In some cases they will not give permission. If you cannot find out if a resource can be used, you must assume it cannot be included in your publication.

In many ways it is best to use original materials. However, if you are photographing people it is normal practice to ask the individual's permission to take the photograph and ask them to sign an agreement to that effect.

Exercise 40

New artwork

1 CorelDRAW® is opened either by selecting the Start button, highlighting the All Programs option, then highlighting the CorelDRAW® option, to reveal a sub-menu and clicking on the CorelDRAW® 10 item, or by double-clicking on the CorelDRAW® icon on the Microsoft Windows® desktop.

2 The initial display is shown in figure 6.1, which reveals an overlay with six options in the form of icons. If you place your mouse pointer over the icons, a brief explanation of each is displayed. Click on the New Graphic icon, since we are going to take the first steps in producing a poster. This will open a page within the working area of the application (figure 6.2).

3 Notice that the size of the page is A4 (i.e. 210 × 297 mm). The position of the pointer is shown on the rulers (i.e. across the top and left side of the work area) as a dotted line, which moves as the pointer does. This assists you to place objects accurately on the page. The location of the pointer is also indicated by numbers in the bottom left-hand corner of the display. This uses a system similar to a graph, with two axes (e.g. x and y).

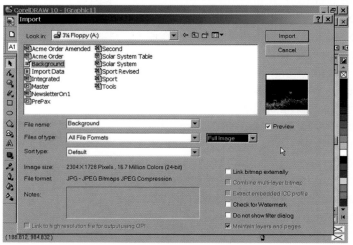

Figure 6.6 Import window

4 You are going to create a poster, so the size of the page needs to change. Click on the down-arrow button alongside the page box (i.e. A4) to reveal a list of options. Choose A1, which is a poster-sized page. The poster is for a village fete. The background is a photograph, taken with a digital camera, near to the village.

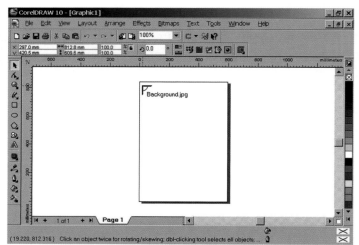

Figure 6.7 Mouse pointer

5 The image can be imported by clicking on the Import icon on the toolbar. This opens the Import window (figure 6.6). Change the Look in: box to the folder in which your background image is stored. In my case, the Countryside image is stored on a floppy disk. Observe the nature of the image – it is 2304 × 1728 pixels and is based on 16.7 million colours. If you have the Preview radio button clicked then you should see the image displayed. To import the picture into the poster you need to click on the Import button again.

6 The Import window will disappear and the mouse pointer will change, as shown as in figure 6.7. This allows you to position the image precisely on the page. Place the new pointer in the top left-hand corner and click. The countryside image will appear enclosed in a frame, which enables you to drag the edges of the image and thus change its size. Figures 6.8 and 6.9 show the beginning and end stages in altering the countryside picture. Figure 6.8 is the initial image. This is expanded by placing the pointer over one of the black squares in the frame. The pointer will change shape to become a double-headed arrow. By holding down the mouse button you can drag the image's edge to form a new

size, filling the top of the page. However, we want the picture to provide a background for the poster, so it needs to grow to fill the bottom of the page. This is again achieved using the pointer to drag the bottom edge of the image. Figure 6.9 shows the final image.

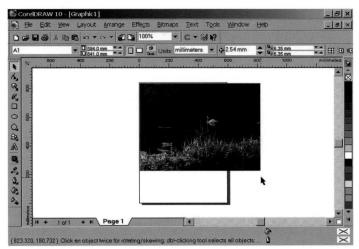

Figure 6.8 Opening image

7 When you drag the image into a shape that is not its natural one the image will distort to some extent. You need to judge the degree of distortion. In this case, you are creating a countryside background so it is not important that leaves or other objects in the picture are elongated. The important thing is that a rural image is presented. If the distortion is too great, you need to think again about your design.

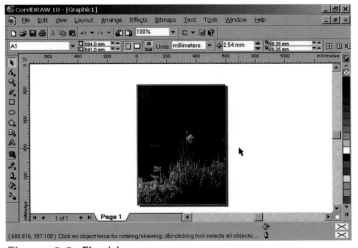

Figure 6.9 Final image

8 If you place your mouse pointer on the centre of the image (the centre is marked to help you locate it) you will see the pointer change shape to a star. If you hold down the mouse button, you can move the whole image and position it precisely.

9 Save the poster by selecting the File menu and clicking on the Save option. The Save Drawing window will appear. You need to change the Save in: box to the location you want to store the poster. Enter Posterbackground.cdr into the File name: box and then click on the Save button.

10 The design brief asks you to insert an image in the bottom right-hand corner of the poster. This is the logo of the Village Fete committee. The logo can be imported by clicking on the Import icon on the toolbar. This opens the Import window (figure 6.6). Change the Look in: box to the folder in which your logo is stored, then locate and highlight it. In my case, the logo image is stored on a floppy disk. To import the picture into the poster you need to click on the Import button.

e-Image Manipulation

11 Position the logo in the bottom right-hand corner of the poster using the pointer to adjust its size and position.

12 The design brief requires that you place two text boxes on the poster. The Text Tool is available on the Drawing toolbar (left-hand side of the work area). Click on the Text Tool and the pointer will change to a cross-hair and the letter A. The cross-hair allows you to position the text box by clicking and holding down the button and dragging the box open. Position the boxes as shown in the design brief (figure 6.5).

13 You can now enter text into the boxes. If you place your pointer into the box, it changes shape to a cursor to let you select where to enter text by clicking. A cursor flashes at the chosen position. The text boxes are shown by a broken outline. If you click on the text box, it becomes enclosed in a frame with small black squares (Figure 6.10). This allows you to reshape and move the text box in the same way you move an image. Select the colour yellow for your text – click on the yellow colour on the palette (right-hand side of work area) – select a font and set the character size to 200. Enter across the top of the poster – Village Fete. Centre the text, using the horizontal alignment icon on the toolbar (figure 6.11), and embolden the text.

14 Now enter the following text into the central text box in yellow, character size 150, using a font of your choice, and embolden the text. On separate lines enter:

Saturday

17th June

2 to 5 pm

Notice that the lines of text are separated by a blank line. The final poster should look like figure 6.12.

15 Save the poster by selecting the File menu and clicking on the Save As option. The Save Drawing window will appear. You need to change the Save in: box to the location you want to store the poster and enter Poster.cdr into the File name: box, then click on the Save button.

16 Close the application by selecting the File menu and click on the Exit option or click on the close button in the top right-hand corner of the application.

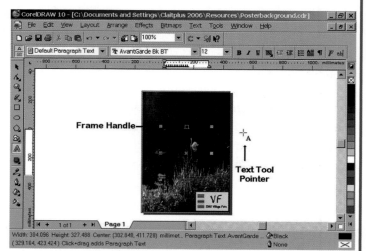

Figure 6.10 Village poster

Layers

In producing the Village Fete poster you have created a layer. Figure 6.13 shows the layer and its different objects (e.g. logo).

Objects can be moved over each other and, when combined, are useful devices to create artwork. Extra layers can be added with varying degrees of transparency, so that different things can be seen through from other layers. You might have created your poster with a background layer, a text layer and a logo layer. Each could then

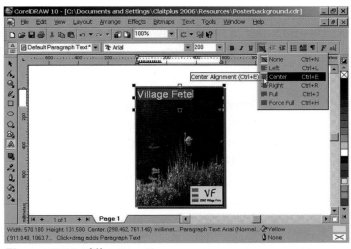

Figure 6.11 Alignment

be edited independently. This is rather like designing three overhead transparency slides and placing them on top of each other to create complex images.

It is possible to create a master layer containing the images that would appear on every page of a long document (e.g. logo, copyright statements). This would save time and guarantee a consistent image.

Layers can be managed using the Object Manager, available by selecting the Tools menu and clicking on the Object Manager, which will open the Object Manager window (figure 6.14). If you click on the different components of the layer, you will see that they are framed on your poster.

The Object Manager shows the single layer and the objects associated with it. You can add layers by selecting the New Layer icon in the bottom left-hand corner. The figure displays a blank master layer.

Against each layer in the Object Manager you will notice some icons. If you place your pointer over them you will see that they are labelled. In order, they are Visibility, Printing, Editing and Master. You can select to make your layer visible, editable, and so on.

Figure 6.12 Village Poster

Masking

Masking is another method, like layers, that allows you to develop complex and engaging artwork. It lets you hide parts of a layer or allow other layers to be seen. Masks work by varying the degree of transparency across the layer. A mask can have holes in it so that you can edit the visible areas. In some cases, you might want to remove a portion of your image. Once you delete an area, it is essentially permanently removed, whereas a mask allows you to change your mind or make small adjustments.

If you have a multiple-layer image, with each layer having an associated mask, you can build up very complex graphics. However, to achieve this level of skill will require a great amount of practice.

There are a number of different types of masks, such as:

- empty masks which cover the whole underlying image
- selection masks, which are empty masks with a hole in them, so you can see a part of the underlying image (e.g. you might create a mask with a circular hole through which the image can be seen)
- image masks, which are those made from another image, so one image will overlay another; you can create complex effects by placing one image on top of another and employing the transparency tools.

Exercise 41

Stacking and masking

1 CorelDRAW® is opened either by selecting the Start button, highlighting All Programs option, then highlighting the CorelDRAW® option, to reveal a sub-menu and clicking on CorelDRAW® 10 , or by double-clicking on the CorelDRAW® icon on the Microsoft Windows® desktop.

2 The initial display shows an overlay, with six options in the form of icons. If you place your mouse pointer over the icons, a brief explanation of each is displayed. Click on the Open Graphic icon to reveal the Open Drawing window. Change the folder in the Look in: box to the one in which you stored the Poster artwork. Enter Poster.cdr in the File name: box and click on the Open button.

3 The Poster artwork will appear in the work area of CorelDRAW®.

4 Click on the centre of the middle text box (i.e. Saturday). The pointer will change shape to a star and you can move the box by holding down the mouse button. Move the box until it overlays the logo. Notice what happens – you should be able to see through the text box while the text appears to be on top of the logo. This illustrates the stacking effect (figure 6.15).

5 Experiment with moving the logo on top of the text box, and any other combinations, until you are clear about moving images and text boxes and understand the nature of stacking.

6 Do not save the changes.

7 You are now going to practise adding a new layer to the poster by selecting the Tools menu and clicking on the Object Manager option. This will open the Object Manager window on the right of the work area. Click on your poster to highlight it (i.e. enclose it), then select the New Layer icon in the bottom left-hand corner of the window (figure 6.14).

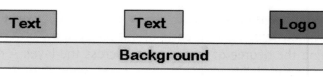

Figure 6.13 Layer

Layer 2 will be added to the window. No obvious change will happen to your poster, since the layer is transparent.

8 Next let us import an image of some balloons into the poster in the bottom left-hand corner of your new layer. Select the Interactive Blend Tool to reveal a menu of options. If you place your pointer against each one, a pop-up label will tell you the name of the tool. Click on the Interactive Transparency Tool(figure 6.16) and the pointer will change shape. Click with it on the top left-hand corner of the balloons image. Holding down the mouse button, drag the pointer to the bottom right-hand corner. The pointer will change shape to a black square and an arrow, and a diagonal line will be drawn across the rectangle. A white bar will be placed across the line and the transparency of the image will have changed. If you click on the bar you can drag it along the diagonal line to increase or reduce transparency and reveal the layer below (figure 6.17). This illustrates the potential of adding layers and masking images.

9 If you want to apply a uniform level of transparency across an image, you need to select the Uniform transparency type from the toolbar (having selected the Interactive Transparency Tool in

Figure 6.14 Object Manager

Figure 6.15 Stacking effect

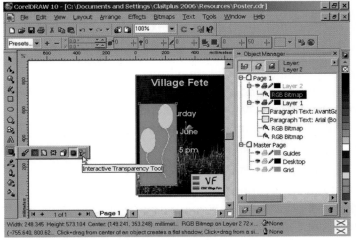

Figure 6.16 Interactive Transparency Tool

figure 6.16) and the Starting Transparency level (e.g. 50%). Notice that by selecting a tool a new toolbar appears (figure 6.18). This is often the case and can be confusing initially. Try varying the degree of transparency using the slider control on the toolbar. There are a variety of other transparency tools to explore. Try the different options.

10 There is no need to save your revised poster, but you are free to save it to another file name.

11 Layers, stacking and masks all require a considerable amount of practice to develop your skill. Experiment with the tools and the poster or another image you have. Add layers, vary the transparency and mask the images. Try to be creative, but keep notes of what is effective.

12 Close the application by selecting the File menu and clicking on the Exit option or by clicking on the close button in the top right-hand corner of the application.

Capturing an image

CorelDRAW® allows you to scan images and import pictures from a digital camera, if you have a scanner or camera connected to your computer. If you select the File menu and highlight Acquire Image , you will reveal a sub-menu. Click on the Select Source option and a list of sources will appear. You select the option (e.g. scanner) you intend to use.

If you select a scanner to import an image, select the File menu, highlight Acquire Image and click on the Acquire option to reveal the Scan using (whatever scanner you are linked to). Figure 6.19 shows my window (Scan using Hewlett-Packard OfficeJet G85 Scanner).

The window provides you with a range of options for scanning different content:

- Color picture
- Grayscale picture
- Black and white picture or text
- Custom Settings.

Greyscale is a colour picture with each colour shown by a different shade of grey. The options available will depend on the type of scanner that you have attached to your computer.

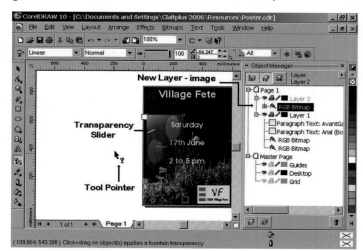

Figure 6.17 Change Transparency

There is also an option to adjust the quality of the scanned image. If you click on this option, Advanced Properties window will appear in which you can adjust the resolution (dots per inch), brightness and contrast. If you move the sliders, you can see the effects immediately in the Appearance area.

If you select a camera to import an image, select the File menu, highlight Acquire Image and click on the Acquire option to reveal a window showing the images stored on the digital camera.

Scanning an image

1 CorelDRAW® is opened either by selecting the Start button, highlighting the All Programs option, then highlighting the CorelDRAW® option, to reveal a sub-menu and clicking on CorelDRAW® 10 item, or by double-clicking on the CorelDRAW® icon on the Microsoft Windows® desktop.

2 The initial display is shown in figure 6.1, which reveals an overlay with six options in the form of icons. Click on the New Graphic icon. This will open a page within the working area of the application. The scanning options are only available when a graphic is being created.

3 Select the File menu, highlight Acquire Image and click on the Select Source option to reveal the Select Source window. Select the scanner of your choice.

4 Select the File menu, highlight Acquire Image and click on the Acquire option to reveal the Scan window. If you have a preview option, employ it to view your image. Adjust the scan options to produce the image of your choice. Scan the image as a colour picture. You will probably see a variety of messages telling you that data is being transferred.

5 When the transfer is completed, you will see your scanned images appear on the artwork page (figure 6.20).

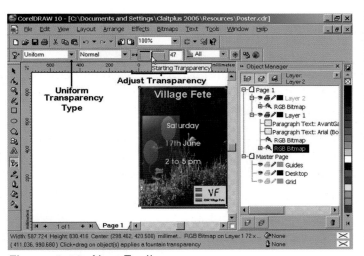

Figure 6.18 New Toolbar

6 In our case, the image of the swan includes a large area of blank space, which needs to be removed. This is achieved using the Shape Tool, by clicking on it. The image will change to show small squares at each corner, and the pointer will take the form of an arrow. If you click on the small squares, you can move them to new positions, cropping the image.

7 Save the scanned image by selecting the File menu and clicking on the Save option. The Save Drawing window will

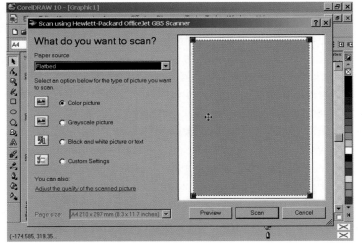

Figure 6.19 Scanner

appear. You need to change the Save in: box to the location you want to store the picture and enter Scanned.cdr into the File name: box, then click on the Save button.

8 The image can be edited by selecting the Bitmaps menu and clicking on Edit Bitmap. This opens the editing window (figure 6.21). This is within CorelPHOTO-PAINT 10 and provides access to more tools and effects.

9 When you scan old pictures they are often scratched and/or dusty. CorelPHOTO-PAINT® provides the means to remove these marks. Select the Effects menu, highlight the Noise item and click on Dust and Scratch to reveal the Dust and Scratch window (figure 6.22). The window asks you to set two variables – threshold and radius. These are interactive settings so that as you move the slider with the mouse you can see the effects on the picture below the window. Experiment with the two controls. There is a slight delay between moving the sliders and seeing the change. In my case, the best setting for radius is 1 and for threshold is 0.

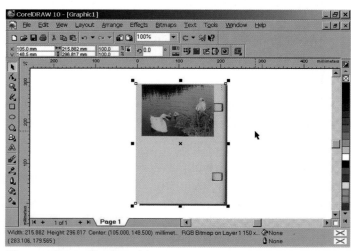

Figure 6.20 Scanned image

Figure 6.21 Bitmap editor

10 Many photographs show red-eye (i.e. light reflected from the person's or animal's eyes make them look red). You can remove this by replacing the red with another colour. Select the Effects menu, highlight the Color Transform item and click on Red Eye Removal. A warning message will tell you that you need a mask, which is an area of the image that you have designated. You can select the whole image as a mask from the Mask menu and the Select All option, or identify an area using the Rectangle Mask Tool, which provides a variety of other ways of defining an area. This tool is on the left-hand toolbar (figure 6.23).

11 Several of the tools have a small diagonal arrow head that tells you a range of other options are available if you place your pointer on the icon and hold down the button.

12 Explore the different tools (if you place your pointer over each tool, it will be labelled). Try to add colour using the different paint brushes, and experiment with the transparency tools and the mask tools. The Effects brush is particularly interesting, while the Clone brush is also worth exploring. Use the undo and redo tools on the toolbar to correct any errors. There is a wide range of tools, so systematically consider what happens with each one. You can apply colour by clicking on the palette and then the brush or fill tool. When you select a tool, you will notice that the horizontal toolbar changes, providing even more options. Those associated with the Paint Tools are also worth exploring (e.g. many different paint effects).

13 Explore the different colour effects within the Effects menu and Color Transform option.

14 Explore the other options within the Effects menu.

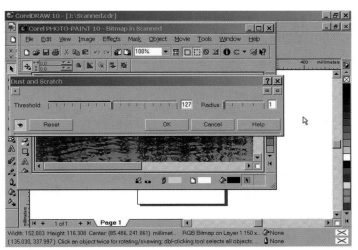

Figure 6.22 Dust and Scratch

15 It is often necessary to remove the background from pictures. CorelPHOTO-PAINT® provides a variety of methods to undertake this task. One useful tool is the Color Transparency Tool (figure 6.24), which samples a colour and replaces it anywhere in the picture with transparency. This tool does not require that you click and drag. Simply click on the colour you want to replace. You can use the tool multiple times to turn several colours transparent. Experiment with this tool on an image with a background (e.g. lots of sky). Create a new image and import a suitable picture into it.

16 A colour consists of three components – hue, saturation and lightness. With CorelPHOTO-PAINT® you can alter each of them.

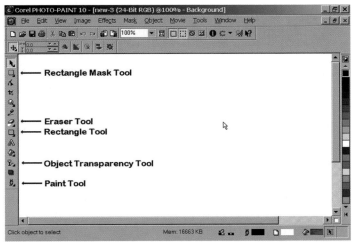

Figure 6.24 CorelDRAW PAINT Tools

Select the Image menu and highlight Adjust, then click on Hue/Saturation/Lightness to reveal the Hue/Saturation/Lightness window (Figure 6.25). As you move the three sliders, you can see the changes both in the Before and After images and in the scanned image. Experiment with the different combinations.

17 You can correct colours (i.e. change a colour) using the Image menu, Adjust and then options such as Color Tone, Color Hue and Replace Colors. Explore – Hue and Tone allow you to experiment.

18 There are many different tools and options to try, so experiment until you are confident that you are able to locate each tool and understand its purpose. If you create any impressive images, save them and keep notes of your experiments.

19 Close the application by selecting the File menu and click on the Exit option or click on the Close button in the top right-hand corner of the application.

Filters

CorelDRAW® and CorelPHOTO-PAINT® contain a wide variety of filters to allow you to carry out a task automatically. In the previous exercise you have encountered two filters – Dust and Scratch and Red Eye. Explore what the others filters can do for you (Effects menu).

Format text (colour and shape)

You have already seen that you can enter text in a wide variety of fonts, character sizes and colours. In addition, you can rotate, sketch, skew and transform text.

Exercise 43

Text

1 CorelDRAW® is opened either by selecting the Start button, highlighting the All Programs option, then highlighting the CorelDRAW® option, to reveal a sub-menu and clicking on CorelDRAW® 10 item, or by double-clicking on the CorelDRAW® icon on the Microsoft Windows® desktop.

2 The initial display is shown in figure 6.1 and reveals an overlay, with six options in the form of icons. Click on the New Graphic icon. A new page will be inserted within the working area of the application.

3 Click on the Text tool and create a text frame across the top of the page, occupying about a quarter of the page. Select a font and set the character size to 72. Enter This is a test. Highlight the text and select the

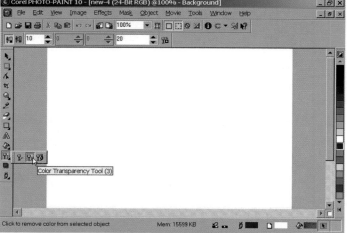

Figure 6.24 Colour Transparency Tool

colour red from the palette – you will see your text change colour. Centre the text using the HorizontalAlignment Tool.

4 You can rotate text by selecting the Pick tool and clicking with it on to the text frame. The text frame will now be enclosed, with arrows at the corners showing how to rotate the box by dragging with the mouse – the pointer changes to a circle. Figure 6.26 shows the box being rotated.

5 There are also double-headed arrows in the middle of the top and bottom lines of the text box; with these you can skew the text using the mouse – the pointer changes to two opposed arrows. By combining rotating and skewing, you can produce interesting effects.

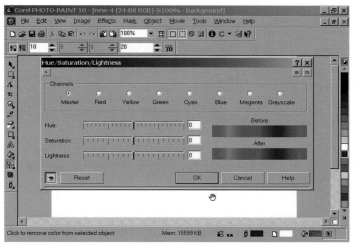

Figure 6.25 Hue/Saturation/Lightness Window

6 You can also transform your text by selecting the Arrange menu and highlighting Transformations to reveal a sub-menu of options.

7 Explore the options.

8 Continue to experiment until you are confident that you can rotate, skew and transform text.

9 You can also enter text using the Freehand tool. Essentially, you are sketching with an electronic pen. This

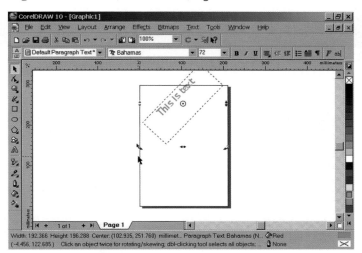

Figure 6.26 Rotating Box

can be very effective if you adjust the width of the tool's nib (i.e. the outline width tool on the horizontal toolbar or the Artistic Media Tool – figures 6.27 and 6.28). Explore the options until you are satisfied you can draw text this way.

10 Close the application by selecting the File menu and clicking on Exit or click on the Close button in the top right-hand corner of the application.

Artistic text

CorelDRAW® also contains another form of text called artistic text. Select the Text Tool and simply click within the drawing area and enter your text. A cursor like a line will appear to show you where the text will be entered. This is called an insertion marker. Once you have finished entering text, it will be enclosed in a frame. This allows you to move, rotate and skew your text in the normal way. If you drag artistic text you can produce remarkable effects.

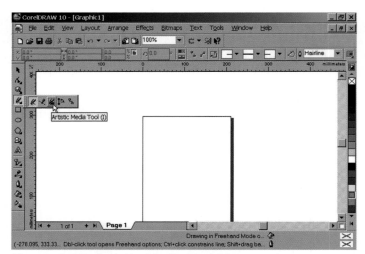

Figure 6.27 Artistic Media Tool Menu

You can change text from one type to the other by clicking on the text with the Pick tool and selecting the Text menu, then Convert to Paragraph Text or Convert to Artistic Text.

You can apply special effects to artistic text. One of the most interesting is extruding text, with which you can turn 2D text into what appears to be 3D. To extrude text you need to select the Interactive Extrude Tool. You click and drag on the text and you will see the text extend (figure 6.29).

Exercise 44

Graphic effects

1 CorelDRAW® is opened either by selecting the Start button, highlighting the All Programs option, then highlighting the CorelDRAW® option, to reveal a sub-menu and clicking on CorelDRAW® 10 item, or by double-clicking on the CorelDRAW® icon on the Microsoft Windows® desktop.

2 The initial display reveals an overlay, with six options in the form of icons. Click on the New Graphic icon. A new page will be inserted within the working area of the application.

3 Set the size of the page to 120 × 100 mm, using the toolbar controls.

4 Click on the Rectangle Drawing tool and draw a rectangle covering the whole area of the page. Ensure that it is enclosed in a frame (i.e. highlighted so the fill tool can operate on the

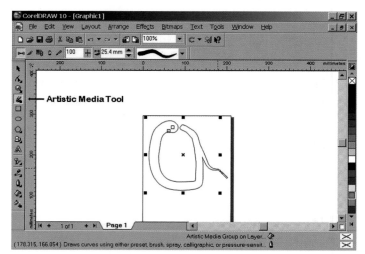

Figure 6.28 Artistic Media Tool

rectangle). Click on a colour in the palette and you will see the rectangle fill with the chosen colour. Remove the colour using the Undo icon on the toolbar.

5 Click on the Fill tool and hold down the mouse button. You will see a number of different Fill options (figure 6.30). Select the Pattern Fill option and you will reveal Pattern Fill window, which provides a

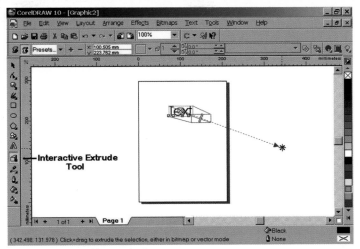

Figure 6.29 Extruded text

variety of patterns to fill the rectangle. Pick one and click on the OK button. The rectangle will fill with that pattern. Undo this fill using the Undo icon and explore the other options.

6 Finally, fill the rectangle with a solid colour. Now select the Bitmaps menu and click on Convert to Bitmaps to reveal a small window, Convert to Bitmap. Click on the OK button, select Bitmaps menu and click on Edit Bitmap. CorelPHOTO-PAINT® will open. Maximise the windows to fill the display.

7 Select the Rectangle tool and draw a small rectangle in the middle of your image. Enclose it in a frame (i.e. highlight it). Fill the rectangle with another colour. Now select the Object Transparency Tool. The pointer will change to a cross-hair with a small wine glass. Place the pointer in one corner of the new rectangle and, holding down the button, drag the pointer to the opposite diagonal corner. Right-click your mouse button and a menu will appear. Click on Apply. You will see that your rectangle now has different degrees of transparency across the diagonal. This is essentially a masking technique.

8 Close CorelPHOTO-PAINT® (select the File menu and the Exit option) to return to CorelDRAW®.

9 There are various other effects. One of the most used is Drop Shadow. If you open a new page (select the File menu and click on the New option), a blank page will appear in the middle of the work area. Set the size of the page to 100 3 100 mm.

10 Click on the Ellipse tool and draw a circle in the top left-hand corner of the page. With the circle highlighted (i.e. enclosed in a frame), click on the yellow colour and the circle will fill with yellow. Now select the Text tool and draw a rectangular text box across the circle. Enter the word SHADOW in a font and size that will fit the box. Embolden your text if it looks better.

11 With the text box highlighted (i.e. enclosed in a frame), select the Interactive Drop Shadow Tool. The pointer changes to a large arrow and rectangle. Click on the left-

hand corner of the text box and, holding down the mouse button, drag the pointer down and diagonally. This will produce the shadow of the text and allow you to change the angle to produce the effect you desire. Experiment and see what you can create. If you are not happy, remember that you can use undo to start again.

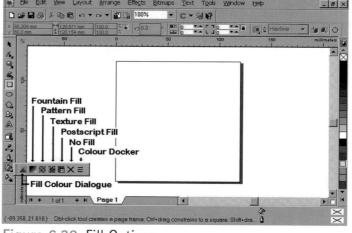

Figure 6.30 Fill Options

12 You can also form shadows of objects other than text. Click on the circle to enclose it in a frame. Select the Interactive Drop Shadow Tool . Click on the edge of the circle, hold down the button and drag the pointer away to produce a circle shadow. Figure 6.32 shows my efforts.

13 Save the image by selecting the File menu and clicking on the Save option. The Save Drawing window will appear. You need to change the Save in: box to the location you want to store the picture and enter Effects.cdr into the File name: box then click on the Save button.

14 Experiment with the different effects until you are confident.

15 Close CorelDRAW® (select the File menu and the Exit option).

Image editing

Earlier we considered features of CorelDRAW® that help you repair scratches and remove red-eye from a photograph. CorelDRAW® also offers considerable assistance to help you edit images to remove or disguise aspects of a photograph that you do not want to include. Figure 6.33 shows a photograph of a ship which also includes, on the right-hand edge, part of another ship's rail and a lamp. You could crop the image to remove these aspects, but obviously this

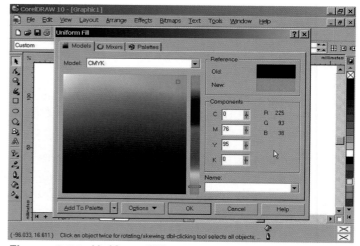

Figure 6.31 Uniform Fill

reduces the content of the picture. Alternatively, you can employ the Clone Tool , available from CorelPHOTO-PAINT®, to disguise the rail and lamp.

Figure 6.34 shows the Clone brush, which allows you to capture part of the background, in this case the sea or sky, and paint it across the parts you want to hide. You click with the left mouse button to capture part of the background, and then, by holding down the left button, you can paint the background over another part of the image. The application allows you to change the size of the brush so that you are able to judge what is needed.

Figure 6.35 shows that you have two brushes on the screen as you are cloning the background. Figure 6.36 shows what you can achieve with a few minutes' effort. Cloning is most effective when you have time to work carefully on the image.

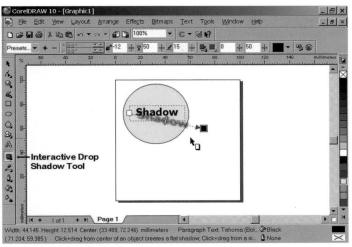

Figure 6.32 Drop Shadow

Figure 6.33 Photograph

Figure 6.34 Clone tool

Exercise 45

1 CorelPHOTO-PAINT® is opened either by selecting the Start button, highlighting All Programs option, then highlighting the CorelDRAW® option, to reveal a sub-menu and clicking on CorelPhoto-Paint® , or by double-clicking on the CorelDRAW® icon on the Microsoft Windows® desktop.

Figure 6.35 Cloning

2 The initial display reveals an overlay, with six options in the form of icons. Click on the New Image icon and the Create a New Image window appears (figure 6.37). Change the size of the image to 250 width, 200 height and resolution 150. The display changes to present a new blank image.

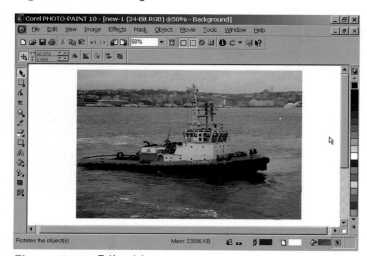

Figure 6.36 Edited image

3 Import (File menu, Highlight Import option and click on Import option) the image balloon1 or another of your choice. Balloon1 is available from the Hodder Education website (www.hodderclait.co.uk). Figure 6.38 shows the image.

4 Use the Clone tool to remove some of the small balloon images. Explore different ways of using the tool (e.g. painting compared to single-clicking); also consider different sized brushes and the use of the left and right mouse buttons. You will need to consider what part of the background you are cloning; if you make a mistake, you can go over the area with another part of the background. Explore and it will become clear.

Once you are confident about cloning, close CorelPHOTO-PAINT® (select the File menu and the Exit option).

Animation

CorelDRAW® has an additional feature to allow you to create animations using the Corel R.A.V.E.® (Real Animated Vector Effects) tool. Figure 6.39 shows the application. It is almost identical to the CorelDRAW® application except that at the bottom of the application window is the timeline with which you can control the speed of the animation.

Animations are composed of a series of individual frames (i.e. images) which are quickly changed so that a movement effect is produced. The aim is to produce an attractive and eye catching display. They are often placed on websites to advertise features or products. Figure 6.40 shows a series of frames.

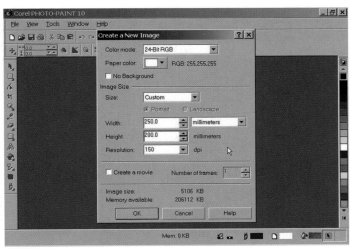

Figure 6.37 Create a New Image Window

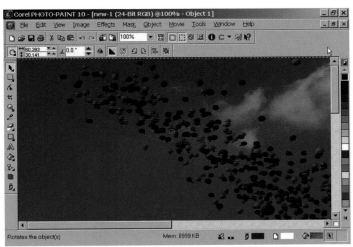

Figure 6.38 Balloons

Exercise 46

Simple animation

1 Corel R.A.V.E.™ is opened by selecting the Start button, highlighting All Programs option, then highlighting the CorelDRAW® option, to reveal a sub-menu and clicking on Corel R.A.V.E.™ 1.0. Alternatively, load CorelDRAW® and select the Application Launcher (figure 6.41) to reveal the Corel family of applications. Click on Corel R.A.V.E .

Figure 6.39 Corel R.A.V.E™

2 The initial display reveals an overlay, with four options in the form of icons. Click on the New Movie icon. This will open a page within the working area of the application.

3 Set the size of the frame to 500 × 500 pixels.

4 CLAiT Plus does not require you to produce the graphics and text that you will use to create individual frames. They will be provided for the assessment, along with a design brief for you to follow. However, in this exercise you will be producing some simple frames around which to develop the animation.

5 Select the Rectangle tool, draw a rectangle covering the whole frame and click on the yellow colour to fill it (remember that the rectangle must be highlighted – enclosed in its frame).

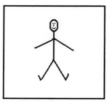

Figure 6.40 Frames

6 Now observe the timeline at the bottom of the display. You will see a rectangle has been added to the left of the timeline and a black circle to the timeline items. Figure 6.42 illustrates the effect.

7 Now click on the black spot which represents the yellow rectangle and drag it right to the fifth line. This makes the yellow rectangle the background for the other frames.

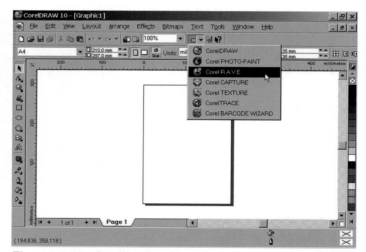

Figure 6.41 Application launcher

8 To create the second frame, click on the next column in the timeline (figure 6.43). The yellow rectangle will remain in the timeline.

9 Add a text box covering the whole frame and then enter Village Fete in a font and size of your choice on the first line (figure 6.43).

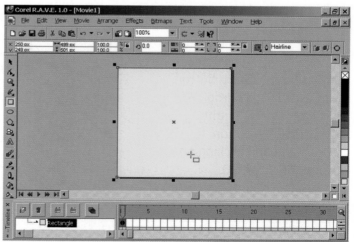

10 To create the third frame, click on the next column in

Figure 6.42 Timeline

the timeline. The yellow Village Fete rectangle will disappear and a yellow frame will appear. Add a text box covering the whole frame. Enter on the third line, two spaces in from the edge, the words Village Fete (figure 6.44).

11 To create the fourth frame, click on the next line in the timeline. A blank yellow frame will appear. Add a text box covering the whole frame. Enter on the fifth line down, four spaces in from the edge, the words Village Fete (figure 6.45).

12 To play your animation, select the Movie menu, highlight the Control option and click on Play Movie. Observe what happens with the frames and timeline. You can stop the animation by selecting the Movie menu, highlighting Control and clicking Stop Movie.

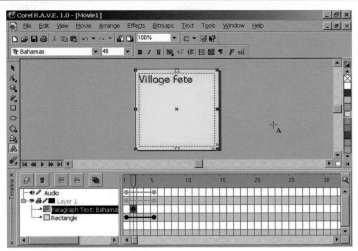

Figure 6.43 Second frame

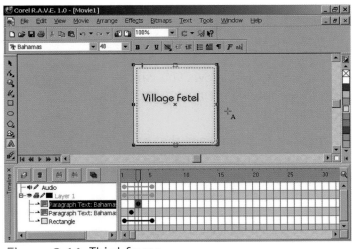

Figure 6.44 Third frame

13 Page through the animation frames by clicking on each line of the timeline. Try this approach to consider each frame.

14 A major part of any animation is its speed (i.e. the number of frames per second). This can be set by selecting the Movie menu and clicking on the Movie Setup option. This opens the Options window (figure 6.46). Change the Frame Rate and run the animation to see what happens. Keep experimenting until you are confident that you can adjust the frame rate. Try comparing slow rates (e.g. 3 frames per second) with faster rates (e.g. 20 frames per second).

15 Save the image by selecting the File menu and clicking on the Save option. The Save Drawing window will appear. You need to change the Save in: box to the location you want to store the picture, enter VillageFeteMovie.clk into the File name: box, then click on the Save button.

16 There is an alternative way to create a background frame. It requires you to open the Options window (figure 6.46) and click on Background (left-hand side of the display)

to open another element of the Options window (figure 6.47). You can set the background as a solid colour or as a bitmap image.

17 Close Corel R.A.V.E.™ and CorelDRAW® by selecting the File menu and the Exit option for each application.

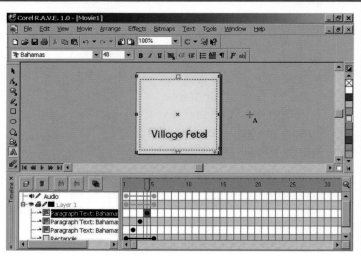

Figure 6.45 Fourth frame

Timing of the Display

Using Corel R.A.V.E.™ allows you can set the frame rate of the animation. For example:

10 frames per second means that each frame is shown for 0.1 second. You can increase this display time for an individual frame by dragging the frame across several time lines, since each one represents 0.1 second. If you drag the frame across ten lines it will display for a second (figure 6.48). You are actually creating ten identical frames, but it has the same overall effect.

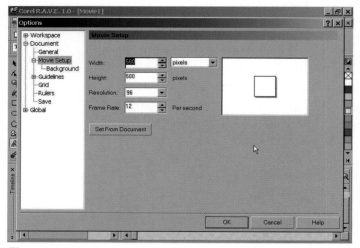

Figure 6.46 Options Window

The display time of each frame depends on the frame rate you have set. For example:

2 frames per second – each line is 0.5 seconds
5 frames per second – each line is 0.2 seconds
10 frames per second – each line is 0.1 seconds.

The bitmaps used in exercise 47 were drawn using Microsoft Windows® Paint. They can be obtained from the Hodder Education website (www.hoddereducation.com).

Importing images

1 Corel R.A.V.E.™ is opened by selecting the Start button, highlighting Programs option, then highlighting the CorelDRAW® option, to reveal a sub-menu and clicking on Corel R.A.V.E. 1.0. Alternatively, load CorelDRAW® and select the Application Launcher to reveal the Corel family of applications. Click on Corel R.A.V.E.

2 The initial display reveals an overlay, with four options in the form of icons. Click on the New Movie icon. This will open a page within the working area of the application.

3 Select the Movie menu and the Movie Setup option. Set the frame rate to 6 per second. Click on Background and Solid. Select red for the background colour and click on the OK button.

4 Click on the second line of the timeline, then on the Import icon to reveal the Import window. Change the Look in: box to the folder in which the graphic image is stored. In my case it is a floppy disk. Highlight the file you want to import and click on the Import

button. The pointer will change shape to a set-square with the file name. Click to insert the graphic and change the shape of the graphic to a suitable size (figure 6.49). Position the graphic in the bottom right-hand corner of the frame.

5 Click on the graphic to enclose it in a frame and copy the image using the Edit menu and the Copy option. Now click on the next line of the timeline and a blank red frame will remain. Paste the graphic on to the frame, slightly above and to the left of the original position. You are going to create an animation of balloons rising up and across the frame.

6 Repeat, creating three more frames.

7 Insert a final frame and create a text frame in the middle. Enter Balloon Festival 2006 in a font and size of your choice (figure 6.50). Centre the text, embolden and adjust it to appear in the

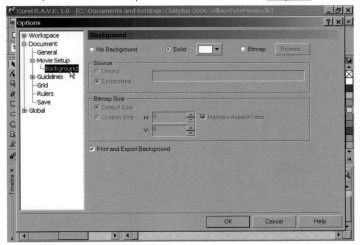

Figure 6.47 Background

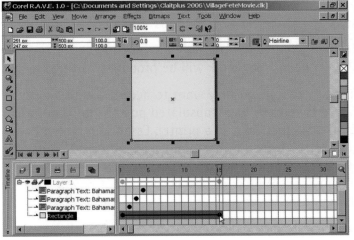

Figure 6.48 Timeline Changes

e-Image Manipulation

centre of the frame. You want this frame to stay on the display for 1 second, so drag the black dot across the next six lines.

8 Save the image by selecting the File menu and clicking on the Save option. The Save Drawing window will appear. You need to change the Save in: box to the location you want to store the picture, enter BalloonFestivalMovie.clk into the File name: box then click on the Save button.

9 Play your animation (Movie menu, highlight the Control option and click on Play Movie). Observe what happens with the frames and timeline. You can stop the animation by selecting the Movie menu, highlighting Control and clicking Stop Movie.

10 Close Corel R.A.V.E.™ and CorelDRAW® by selecting the File menu and the Exit option for each application.

Publishing

CorelDRAW® prints both vector drawings and bitmap images as a series of dots. A high resolution image does not guarantee a good quality printout, since the quality of the printed artwork depends on the printer. An inkjet printer's quality is probably limited to 300 to 600 dpi (dots per inch). Printing on a higher quality printer will produce clearer and better quality artwork. To print your artwork, select the File menu and the Print option to reveal the Print window (figure 6.51). This allows you to preview your work and to select the wide range of options available to you.

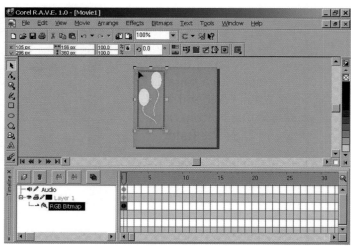

Figure 6.49 Import Graphic

The simplest way of printing your document is to accept the default settings and click on the Print button. Your work will be produced as the preview shows you.

In many cases, you may want to access a high quality external printer. This will require you to convert your file to encapsulated postscript (.eps) format. In order to do this, you need to print to a file rather than to a printer. Essentially, you prepare your document for printing, but send the file to storage rather than to the printer. You can then send your file to the external printer. However, you need to be connected to a postscript printer to generate the file or to the Device Independent Postscript File. If you do not have a postscript printer or file you will need to ask your printer for advice.

To generate an encapsulated postscript file, click in the Print to file radio button in the General tab and choose a postscript printer or Device Independent Postscript File. Click on the Print button to reveal the Print to File window and select which folder to save your file to.

Often when you are printing artwork, you want to examine its quality, and the normal approach is to produce full-colour proofs. To determine what appears on your proofs, select the Misc tab, which contains a proofing options area, where you can choose what appears on the proofs. The options allow you to print vectors, bitmaps and text, as well as producing full-colour proofs.

Outside the proofing options area is one called Rasterize entire page (DPI), with a box alongside letting you adjust the dots per inch of the printed image. Rasterise means that you have converted a vector image into a bitmap. It is now displayed as pixels.

To ensure that the final document is presented accurately, select the Crop/Fold marks in the Prepress tab, which will print marks on the page to indicate where the paper should be cut or folded to produce the finished document.

Exporting animations

You can export the animations created within Corel R.A.V.E.™ in a variety of formats, such as:

- Adobe (formerly Macromedia) Flash® – often forms part of a website
- animated gif – often a way of producing an animation for a website
- Video for Microsoft Windows®
- Adobe QuickTime® Movie.

To export your animation, select the Export icon on the toolbar to open the Export window (figure 6.52). You will be able to select the file format and folder to export your work to.

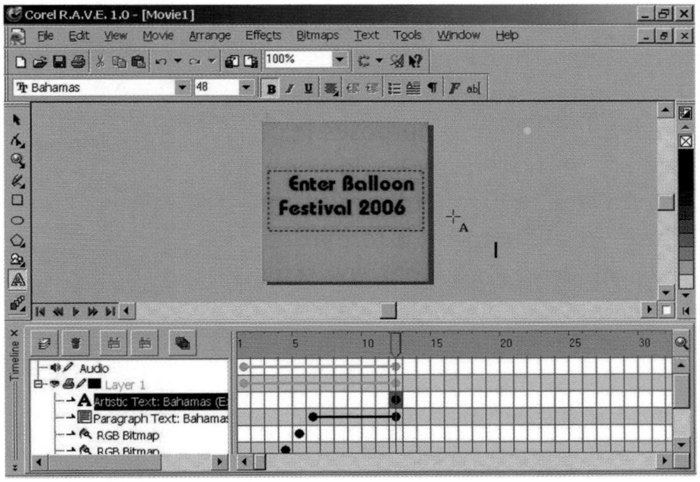

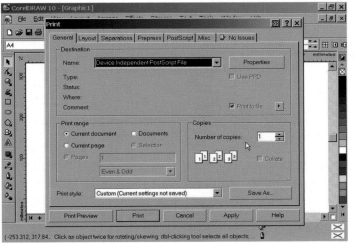

Figure 6.50 Final Frame

Resolution

To change the resolution of your images, you need to be in CorelPHOTO-PAINT® (i.e. Edit Bitmap from CorelDRAW®). Select the Image menu and the Resample option to reveal the Resample window (figure 6.53). You can change the resolution of an image while maintaining its original dimensions if the Identical values radio button is ticked. This is useful should you need to reduce the storage size of an image, but wish to keep to the

Figure 6.51 Print Window

physical design brief size of the artwork. The Anti-alias button smoothes the edges of the image. If you select the Maintain original size button, this maintains the storage size while adjusting the resolution, so that the physical dimensions of the image may alter.

Screen print

If you need to capture what appears on the screen, press the Print Screen key. A copy of your screen display is made and stored on the Microsoft Windows® clipboard. You can then paste the image into an application of your choice, such as Microsoft Windows® Paint, from where you can print the display. If you want to copy only the contents of the active window, press the Alt and Print Screen keys together.

Export/save in appropriate format

CorelDRAW® and CorelPHOTO-PAINT® allow you to export your work in a wide variety of formats. This is important, since different formats are needed for different purposes (e.g. artwork for a website would normally be provided in jpeg(jpg) or gif format). To export an image in a format of your choice requires that you select the File menu, highlight Export and click on Export option or select the Export icon on the toolbar. These open the Export or Export an Image to Disk windows (figure 6.54), respectively.

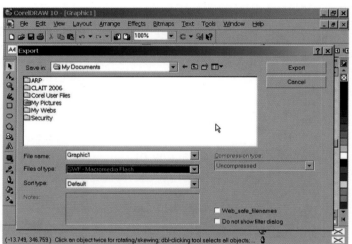

Figure 6.52 Export Window

The main file types that you are likely to encounter are:

- jpeg (jpg) – joint photograph expert group (often associated with websites)
- gif – graphics interchange format (often associated with websites)
- bmp – bitmap (usually associated with Microsoft Windows® systems)
- tiff – tagged image file format (a full-colour format)
- eps – encapsulated postscript (a page layout format).

The examples illustrate the different roles played by each type of format.

More practice

The photographs required for these activities are available from the Hodder Education website (www.hoddereducation.com), or you can select alternative images. During the assessment you will be asked to use the screen capture to provide evidence that you have carried out tasks, so use these exercises to practise taking screen captures.

Activity 1

Create background picture

1 CorelPHOTO-PAINT® is opened either by selecting the Start button, highlighting All Programs option, then highlighting the CorelDRAW® option, to reveal a sub-menu and clicking on CorelPhoto-Paint®, or by double-clicking on the CorelDRAW® icon on the Microsoft Windows® desktop.

2 The initial display reveals an overlay, with six options in the form of icons. Click on the New Image icon and the Create a New Image window appears (figure 6.37). Change the size of the image to 250 width, 200 height and resolution 150. The display changes to present a new blank image.

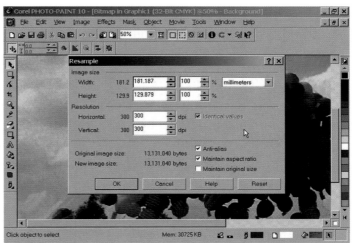

Figure 6.53 Resample Window

3 Import the photograph Balloon2 (figure 6.55). The image shows a balloon release. Remove the man's head to the right side of the bottom edge and three or four of the stray ballons near to him to improve the image. Remember that tools only operate when the image is highlighted/selected.

4 Remove any scratches from the image (Effects menu, highlight Noise option and click on Dust and Scratch). Figure 6.56 shows the revised image.

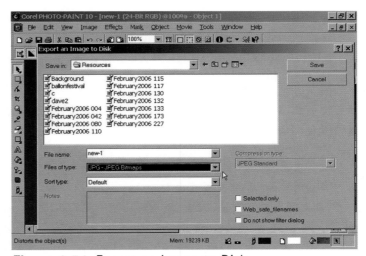

Figure 6.54 Export an Image to Disk

5 Save your revised image as Balloonfestival.jpg (jpeg format). You will need to use the Export option in the File menu. You may get a warning message that you are also saving the background. This means that your image is bordered by a white window. When you import it you will need to crop the image.

6 Print your revised image

7 Close CorelPHOTO-PAINT®.

Activity 2

Poster for Balloon Festival

1   CorelDRAW® is opened either by selecting the Start button, highlighting All Programs option, then highlighting the CorelDRAW® option, to reveal a sub-menu and clicking on the CorelDRAW® 10 item, or by double-clicking on the CorelDRAW® icon on the Microsoft Windows® desktop.

2   The initial display is shown in figure 6.1, which reveals an overlay with six options in the form of icons. If you place your mouse pointer over the icons, a brief explanation of each is displayed. Click on the New Graphic icon, since we are going to take the first steps in producing a poster. This will open a page within the working area of the application (figure 6.2).

3   Notice that the size of the page is A4 (i.e. 210 × 297 mm). Change the size of the page to A5 and the orientation to landscape. Set the resolution to 80 pixels per centimetre. You are going to design a poster for the balloon festival, based on the image you revised in activity 1, in accordance with the design brief (figure 6.57). You will probably need to crop the image during the import process to remove white border.

Figure 6.55 Balloon Release Image

4   Enter Balloon Festival 2006 across the image, in accordance with design brief, as a new layer.

5   Change the colour of the text to yellow.

6   Save your work as the file festivalposter. Figure 6.58 shows our efforts.

6   Print your artwork.

7   Close CorelDRAW®.

Figure 6.56 Revised Image

Activity 3

Edit the poster

1   CorelDRAW® is opened either by selecting the Start button, highlighting the All Programs option, then highlighting the CorelDRAW® option, to reveal a sub-menu and clicking on the CorelDRAW® 10 item, or by double-clicking on the CorelDRAW® icon on the Microsoft Windows® desktop.

2 The initial display is shown in figure 6.1, which reveals an overlay with six options in the form of icons. If you place your mouse pointer over the icons, a brief explanation of each is displayed. Click on the Open Graphic icon and select the Festival Poster file.

3 Use the basic shapes tool to add a callout, with the text 23 May, on to the poster as a new layer.

4 Colour the text blue and the callout background white. Position the 23 May text in the middle of the callout.

5 Save the poster as Festival Poster Revised.

6 Use some form of special effect on the background image to change the poster. Figure 6.59 shows my efforts, using the Interactive Transparency Tool .

7 Print the poster, using a colour printer, showing crop marks.

8 Save the special effect version as Festival Poster Special Effect.

9 Print the poster, using a colour printer, showing crop marks.

10 Close CorelDRAW®.

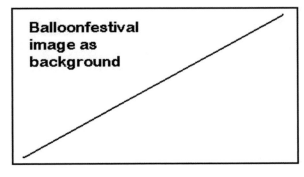

Figure 6.57 Design Brief

Activity 4

Animation

Create an animation showing a set of dice. The six dice images are available from the Hodder Education website (www.hoddereducation.com) or can be created in Microsoft Windows® Paint.

Frame 1 – Blue background

Frame 2 – Number 1 Dice

Frame 3 – Number 2 Dice

Frame 4 – Number 3 Dice

Frame 5 – Number 4 Dice

Frame 6 – Number 5 Dice

Frame 7 – Number 6 Dice

Frame 8 – Unicorn Casino (centred).

Frame rate 6 per second, except that Unicorn Casino should display for 1 second.

1 Corel R.A.V.E.™ is opened by selecting the Start button, highlighting Programs option, then

Figure 6.58 Festival Poster

highlighting the CorelDRAW®
option, to reveal a sub-menu and
clicking on Corel R.A.V.E.™ 1.0.
Alternatively, load CorelDRAW®
and select the Application
Launcher (figure 6.41) to reveal
the Corel family of applications.
Click on Corel R.A.V.E .

2   The initial display reveals an
overlay with four options in the
form of icons. Click on the
New Movie icon. This will open a
page within the working area of
the application.

3   Set the size of the frame to 178 ×
178 pixels.

4   Create the animation.

5   Save animation as CasinoMovie.

6   Close Corel R.A.V.E.

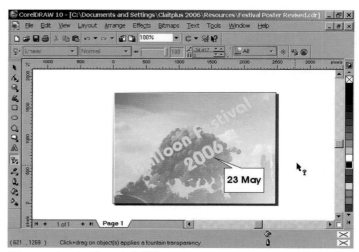

Figure 6.59 Special Effects

cross-hairs enable you to position the text box by clicking and holding down the mouse button and dragging the box open.

7 Enter text

Place your pointer in the text box and the cursor will change shape. Select the location where you want to enter text by clicking. The cursor will flash at the chosen position.

8 Resize and move text box

Click on the text box to enclose it in a frame with small black squares. Placing your mouse on the edges will change the shape of the pointer. Hold down the mouse button in order to drag the edges to resize and reshape the box.

The text box can be moved by placing the pointer on its centre, where the pointer will change shape (star), allowing you to drag the whole box by holding down the mouse button.

9 Scan an image

Select the File menu and highlight Acquire Image to reveal a sub-menu. Click on the Select Source option and a list of sources will appear. Select the option (e.g. scanner) you intend to use.

Select the File menu and highlight Acquire Image to reveal a sub-menu. Click on the Acquire option.

10 Crop a scanned image

Click on the Shape tool. The image will change to show small squares at each corner and the pointer will take the form of an arrow. Click on the small squares and move them to new positions, cropping the image.

11 Edit bitmapped image

Select the Bitmaps menu and click on Edit Bitmap (CorelPHOTO-PAINT® will open).

12 Dust and Scratches (CorelPHOTO-PAINT®)

Select the Effects menu, highlight the Noise item and click on Dust and Scratches to reveal the Dust and Scratch window.

13 Red-eye (CorelPHOTO-PAINT®)

Select the Effects menu, highlight the Color Transform item and click on Red Eye Removal. A warning message will tell you that you need a mask. A mask is an area of the image that you have designated. You can select the whole image as a mask from the Mask menu and the Select All option, or identify an area using the Rectangle Mask Tool, which provides a variety of other ways of defining an area. This tool is on the left-hand toolbar.

14 Adjust colours

Select the Image menu and highlight Adjust, then click on Hue/Saturation/Lightness to reveal the Hue/Saturation/Lightness window.

15 Rotate and skew text

Select the Pick tool. Clicking with it on the text box will enclose the frame, with arrows at the corners. You can rotate the box by dragging with the mouse. The pointer changes to a circle.

There are double-headed arrows in the middle of the top and bottom lines of the text box; use them to skew the text by dragging with the mouse (pointer changes to two opposed arrows).

Alternatively, select the Arrange menu and highlight Transformations to reveal a sub-menu of options.

16 Artistic text
Select the Text tool and simply click within the drawing area, then enter your text. A cursor like a line will appear to show you where the text will be entered. This is called an insertion marker. Once you have finished entering text it will be enclosed in the normal way. This means you can move, rotate and skew your text in the normal way.

17 Convert text types
Select the text with the Pick tool, then select the Text menu and either Convert to Paragraph Text or Convert to Artistic Text .

18 Extruded text
Select the Interactive Extrude tool and click and drag on the text to see it extrude.

19 Sketch/draw text
Click on the Freehand tool. Adjust the width of the tool's nib, using the outline width tool on the horizontal toolbar, and draw your text.

20 Fill
Click on the Fill tool to reveal a number of different Fill options. Select your chosen option.

21 Layer
Select the Tools menu and click on the Object Manager option to reveal the Object Manager window on the right of the work area. Select the New Layer icon in the bottom left-hand corner of the window.

22 Mask transparency
When importing or drawing an image, select the Interactive Transparency Tool and click with it on or near the image. Holding down the mouse button, drag the pointer to the chosen location. The pointer will change shape, to a black square and arrow, and a line will be drawn across the image. A white bar will be placed across the line and the transparency of the image will have changed. The bar can be moved to increase or reduce transparency.

23 Shadow
Select the Interactive Drop Shadow Tool . The pointer changes to a large arrow and a rectangle. Click on the edge of the object frame and, holding down the mouse button, drag the pointer to the chosen position.

24 Open Corel R.A.V.E.
Select the Start button, highlight the Programs option, highlight the CorelDRAW® option to reveal a sub-menu and click on the Corel R.A.V.E.™ 1.0 item. Alternatively, load CorelDRAW® and select the Application Launcher to reveal the Corel family of applications. Click on the Corel R.A.V.E™ option.

25 Form animation background
After creating a background frame, click on the black spot on the timeline and drag it to the chosen position; or select the Movie menu and click on the Movie Setup option to reveal the Options window. Click on the Background option.

26 Play animation
Select the Movie menu, highlight the Control option and click on the Play Movie option.

27 Speed of display
Select the Movie menu and click on the Movie Setup option to open the Options window.

28 Import images
Click on the Import icon to reveal the Import window.

29 Disguise image
Select CorelPhoto-Paint® option, Clone brush and paint the background over aspects of the image you wish to hide.

30 Export image or artwork
Select the File menu, highlight Export and click on Export option or select the Export icon on the toolbar. These open the Export or Export an Image to Disk windows, depending on whether you are using CorelDRAW® or CorelPhoto-Paint®.

Chapter 7

Unit 7

Website Creation

This chapter will help you to:

- create a web page from unformatted source material
- use standard images and formatting to create a consistent house style
- create and format tables, frames and forms
- use meta tags to define content
- set dimensions, alignments and other attributes of page items.

This chapter covers unit 7 (Website Creation). There are no preconditions for studying this unit. However, its content does assume that you have the skills and understanding which are provided by the OCR Level 1 ICT course CLAiT 2006 (e.g. Unit 7: Web Page Creation, Unit 8: Online Communication and Unit 1: File Management and e-Document Production).

Assessment

After studying unit 7, your skills and understanding are assessed during a three-hour practical assignment. This is set by OCR and marked locally. However, the marking will be externally moderated by OCR. This ensures that the standard is being applied correctly across the many different providers of OCR CLAiT Plus. If you are unsuccessful, you can be reassessed using a different assignment.

An alternative approach is for you to be assessed by an assignment set by OCR or designed by your centre. These assignments cover all the assessment objectives included in the unit. You will need to complete an OCR evidence checklist, explaining how each assessment objective has been covered.

Resources

The exercises included in this chapter require text and image files that are provided on the Hodder Education website (www.hoddereducation.com) for you to download. However, if you do not have access to the pack, please use other available text files and images so that you can practise the techniques discussed in the chapter. During the CLAiT Plus assessment, the resources required are provided for your use as part of the process.

Microsoft FrontPage® XP (2002)

Web pages can be created using a variety of tools and systems. Microsoft FrontPage® XP (2002) is an application that provides you with a straightforward way of doing this, without having to understand the HTML (hypertext markup language) which is used to produce them. HTML provides instructions for the structure, presentation and content of the page. These instructions are called tags.

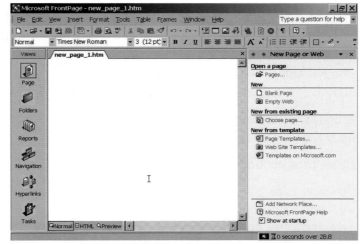

Figure 7.1 Microsoft FrontPage®

Microsoft FrontPage® automatically converts your design into HTML and shows how it appears as a web page.

If you understand HTML you can obviously edit the language yourself, using Microsoft FrontPage®'s HTML view. However, this is not required to produce quality pages, since Microsoft FrontPage® provides templates for a variety of different types of page to improve your productivity and the quality of what you produce.

Figure 7.1 shows the Microsoft FrontPage® interface. It is similar to other Microsoft Office® applications in that it has a work area where you design your pages, toolbars containing a number of tools that other applications employ (e.g. Cut, Copy and Paste), task pane (right-hand side) and a menu bar. The two main visual differences are:

- a toolbar down the left-hand side of the display called Views
- three different views of the page in the bottom left-hand corner of the display (i.e. Normal, HTML and Preview).

The Normal view is used to design your page; the HTML view means you can see the language; and Preview allows you to test your page (i.e. what does it look like on a website). However, it is critical to test your pages using a browser, rather than relying only on Preview. It is essential to test your pages in the real environment.

HTML tags

Although you do not need to know HTML to use Microsoft FrontPage®, it is useful to have a basic understanding of tags. This forms part of the new CLAiT Plus qualification. Figure 7.2 shows some basic HTML language.

<html> marks the start of the HTML commands

</html> marks the end of the HTML commands

<head> marks the beginning of the HTML introduction

</head> marks the end of the HTML introduction

<meta> marks information about the page itself (e.g. author, authoring tool)

<title> marks the start of the title of the page

</title> marks the end of the title of the page (i.e. the title – New Page – appears between the two tags)

<body> shows the start of the main body (i.e. the content of the page)

</body> shows the end of the main body (i.e. end of the content)

Other tags include:

<p> and </p> paragraph of text
<u> and </u> underline
<b> and </b> bold
<a> and </a> hypertext links.

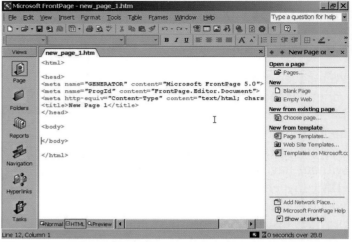

Figure 7.2 Basic HTML

If you consider the HTML in figure 7.2, you will see that there is a definite pattern of tags.

Creating a web page

Microsoft FrontPage® and HTML give you a great deal of freedom in designing web pages. However, some basic good practice is:

- Consistency: many users of the Web complain of getting lost, confused and distracted by the structure and design of websites and web pages. You should be consistent in the layout and presentation of the pages that make up a website. It is important to create standard features that appear on every page, such as navigation bars. This not only aids the use of the site, but also improves the productivity of designing pages in that you have a standard structure to build on.
- Length of a page: there is no limit to how long a web page can be. However, long pages are often difficult to use (e.g. for locating information), so good practice suggests that a maximum length is approximately three A4 pages.
- Users often want to find information quickly and will abandon a site if they cannot immediately find the content they are seeking. It is therefore important to present information in a clear and concise way (i.e. short sentences, lists and illustrations).
- Most users will complain if a page takes too long to download. This is a feature often associated with the use of illustrations, sound and video content. It is always good practice to minimise the size of a page and reduce the download time. One way to do this is to use repetitive content, since after it is downloaded, it is available to the other pages and thus effectively reduces their size.

An essential component of any website are the hyperlinks between the different pages. In later exercises you will have the opportunity to create links, but a fundamental issue is the nature of a link. There are two types:

- relative
- absolute.

A relative link is one which will change if the website is moved from where it was created to a new location. This is the normal process as it is important that links are relative (i.e. they change to allow for a site to be moved).

An absolute link is one which is fixed and will not change. This should only be used if the site will never be moved, otherwise links may fail.

Many organisations have tried to embody a consistent approach in a house style which they ask their web page designers to follow. This is normally accompanied by a design brief, which provides the content for each page.

Character sizes

In most Microsoft Office® applications the character sizes are shown as 10 pts, 12 pts, 24 pts, and so on. HTML has a different size classification. Microsoft FrontPage® shows both sizes to make it easier to transfer your understanding from other applications. The table below compares the different sizes.

HTML character sizes	Microsoft application character sizes
1	8
2	10
3	12
4	14
5	18
6	24

Tables

To insert a table into a web page you need to select the Table menu and highlight the Insert option to reveal a sub-menu. Click on the Table option. This will open the Insert Table window (figure 7.3). You can insert the number of rows and columns, align the contents of the cells (left, right and centre), border size and width of table, either in pixels or as a percentage of page width.

Once you have created a table you can amend it using the options within the Table menu. These allow you to insert or delete extra rows and columns, split or merge cells and change the properties of a cell. The first step is to highlight the row, column, cell or table, and then select the desired option. If you highlight the Table Properties option you will reveal a sub-menu. Click on the Cell option to reveal the Cell Properties window. This allows you to change many features of the cell or cells, including the alignment. For example:

Horizontal – left, right, centre and justify
Vertical – top, middle, baseline and bottom.

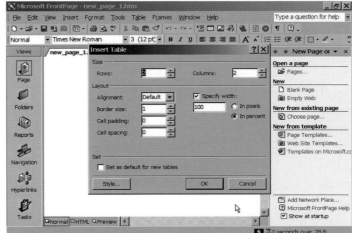

Figure 7.3 Insert Table window

The table inserted in the web page can have a border added using the Borders and Shading option within the Format menu. Alternatively, you can employ the Insert Table window to add a border, using the Border size, Cell padding and Cell spacing when you create a table. If you do not add a border, the table's borders are transparent. This offers the possibility of using the table to lay out the content of a web page. This allows you to control the exact presentation of text and images.

Spreadsheet

An alternative approach to creating a table is to copy one designed in a spreadsheet such as Microsoft Excel®. A major advantage of using a spreadsheet is that it is specifically designed to create complex and attractive tables. You could design a table complete with formatting, borders and colour far easier in Microsoft Excel® and then add it to your page. Alternatively you could simply transfer the contents of a table into the page and use FrontPage's functions to format it.

There are two ways of inserting a spreadsheet table into a web page. It can simply be undertaken using the copy and paste functions available in Microsoft Excel®, or you can insert a spreadsheet table into a webpage using the Insert and File menu option.

In both cases the copied or inserted table may not be enclosed in a border. If you need to add a border you must first select the table by clicking within it and selecting the Table menu, highlight the Select option and click on Table. The imported table will be highlighted. Now select the Borders icon and add one of the border options.

In order to manipulate the contents of the table you follow the normal approach of highlighting and selecting an option. You can employ all functions in FrontPage to manipulate it. Obviously all these actions can be undertaken in Excel and then the completed table can be inserted.

File formats

Creating web pages involves using a variety of resources, so it is important that you are able to recognise the different file types. Most files have an extension made up of three or four letters which indicate their type. Some of the most frequently encountered are:

.txt	–	text file
.doc	–	Microsoft Word® file
.rtf	–	rich text file
.gif	–	graphic file
.bmp	–	bitmap graphic file
.jpg (jpeg)	–	graphic file
.htm	–	web page
.html	–	web page
.pdf	–	Adobe Acrobat® document file
.xls	–	Microsoft Excel® spreadsheet
.mdb	–	Microsoft Access® database file

The house style of the site is often closely associated with the file types. The example house style below illustrates some of the issues:

Site structure:

- All files must be saved to Web Design folder.
- All image files should be stored in sub-folder of Web Design called Images.
- All links to files and images on website should be relative, not absolute.

Standard page properties:

- Title – specified in Design Brief
- Background colour – #00FFFF (hexadecimal code of the colour Aqua).

Standard text properties:

- Text colour – #000000 (hexadecimal code of the colour Black)
- Link colour – #0000FF (hexadecimal code of the colour Blue)
- Visited link colour – #800080 (hexadecimal code of the colour Purple)
- Active link colour – #FF0000 (hexadecimal code of the colour Red)
- Typeface (font) – sans serif
- Text size:
  - Main heading – HTML size 6 (24 pts)
  - Subheading – HTML size 4 (14 pts)
  - Body text – HTML size 3 (12 pts).

Image properties:

- Image height and width must be accurately specified
- Image borders set to zero
- Alt (alternative) text specified by Design Brief.

Design Brief – Standard:

This is the design brief for the standard layout page on which all the pages will be based.

Meta tags:

Each page should have the following meta tag information:

Name	–	Content
Author	–	Your name and centre number
Keywords	–	guinea, pigs, hotel, holiday
Description	–	see individual page design brief

Navigation table:

Table of navigation icons must be placed at the top of each page:

Width 400, Height 48, columns 5, Rows 1, Centred, Cell spacing 0, Cell padding 0 and Border 0.

The images are all width 80 and height 48.

Image	Alt Text	Link
Home	Home Page	Home.htm
Contact	Contact us	Contact.htm
Advice	Practical Assistance	Advice.htm
E-Mail	Messages	E-mail link to guineaPIGS@Farmhalt.co.uk
About	Background	About.htm

Copyright notice:

Each page should have this notice at the bottom:

Copyright © GuineaPIGS 2006, centred, body text size and linked to guineaPIGS@Farmhalt.co.uk

Creating a standard page

1 Microsoft FrontPage® is opened either by selecting the Start button, highlighting the All Programs option and clicking on the FrontPage® option or by double-clicking on the FrontPage® icon on the Microsoft Windows® desktop.

2 The application will open (figure 7.1) with a new page in the work area. If the window is

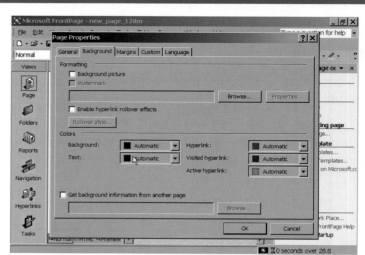

Figure 7.4 **Page Properties window**

not maximised, use the standard buttons in the top right-hand corner of the window to display it filling the screen.

3 The first step is to set the background colour to the one specified in the house style. Select the Format menu and click on the Background option to reveal the Page Properties window (figure 7.4). In the Background tab you will see the Background box with Automatic inserted in it. Click on the down arrow alongside the box and a small palette of colours will appear. Select aqua by clicking on it.

4 This window also allows you to choose the text colour; in this case, the default colour is black, which is also the house style colour, so you do not need to change it.

5 In addition, you can select the colours for hyperlinks. The house style gives the link colour as blue (#0000FF) and visited link as purple (#800080). Set these colours in the same way as you chose the background and body text. Click on the OK button to confirm your choices.

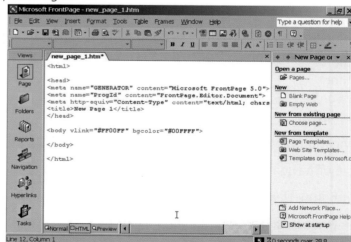

Figure 7.5 **HTML**

6 The web page should now have changed colour to aqua. Click on the HTML tab at the bottom left-hand corner and the corresponding HTML tags for the page will appear (figure 7.5). Microsoft FrontPage® offers default settings which are shown as automatic. If you do not change these settings, they will sometimes not appear in the HTML tags, which may puzzle you. If you do need to see them in the tags, change the colour to a different one, then back to the default, and the tags will appear.

7 Observe that the background colour is shown as <body bgcolor = "#00FFFF">. If you delete the code and insert #008080, then return to the Normal view, you will see that the background colour has changed to teal. This is an alternative way to set the colours. Return to the HTML tags, delete #008080 and replace it with #00FFFF. Your background should now be aqua again.

8 Insert two extra meta tag lines, reading:

<meta name="Author" content= "Your name and centre number">
<meta name="Keywords" content="guinea, pigs, hotel, holiday">

This complies with the Design Brief, but there is an alternative to inserting directly into the HTML. Right-click on the page to reveal a menu, click on the Page Properties option to reveal the Page Properties window. Select the Custom tab and in the User variables, click the Add button. You can now add Name and Value (i.e. content).

The keywords are especially important, since search engines will identify the page based on these words. A search including any of these words is going to locate the page, while other searches will miss it.

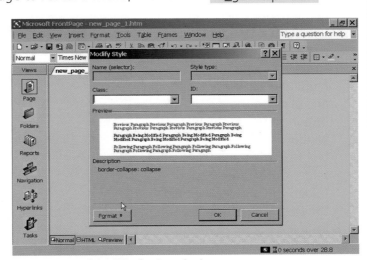

Figure 7.6 **Modify Style window**

9 The next step is to create the navigation table across the top of the page. Select the Table menu and highlight the Insert option to reveal the Table option. Click on Table to open the Insert Table window (figure 7.3).

10 Insert the information about the table from the Design Brief into the window. Click on the Style button to reveal the Modify Style window (figure 7.6) and click on the Format button to open the dropdown menu. Click on

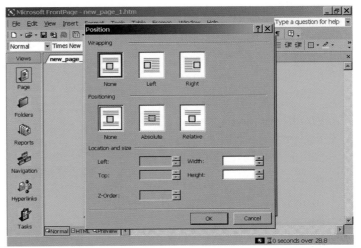

Figure 7.7 **Position window**

Position to reveal the Position window (figure 7.7), which allows you to choose between absolute and relative. Absolute position is one that is fixed in relation to the top left-hand corner of the page, while relative position is one determined in relation to other elements in the text flow. The navigation table is always at the top of the page and is thus a relative position, so click in the Relative box and insert 48 in the Height box. Click on the OK buttons in each window. The table will appear across the top of the page.

11 In each cell of the table you are going to insert a graphic. Click in the left-hand cell to place the cursor and then select the Insert menu, highlight the Picture option and click on the From File option to reveal the Picture window. Change the Look in: box to show the Images sub-folder of the Web Design folder, which is specified in the Design Brief (figure 7.8). Double-click on Home.gif and it will be inserted into the left-hand cell. Repeat the action for Contact.gif, Advice.gif, E-Mail.gif and About.gif. The table may distort during this process, but place the next image in the next cell.

12 When you have inserted all five images, the navigation should look like figure 7.9.

13 Right-click on each image in turn, to reveal a menu and, in some cases, the Pictures toolbar (figure 7.10). Click on the Picture Properties option to open an associated window. In the General tab there is a box called

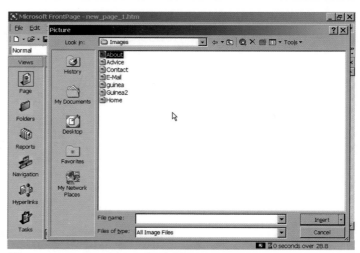

Figure 7.8 Images sub-folder

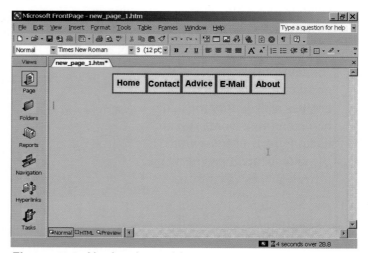

Figure 7.9 Navigation table

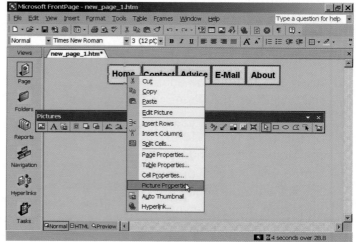

Figure 7.10 Picture Properties

CLAiT Plus 2006 for Office XP

Alternative representations text. Enter the Alt text appropriate to the image (Design Brief standard) e.g. Home image – Home Page, and click on the OK button.

14 Save the standard page by selecting the File menu and clicking on the Save option to reveal the Save As window. Change the Save in: box to read Web Design folder, since the house style requires us to save all files to this folder. Enter the File name: Standard.htm in the box and click on the Save button.

15 At the bottom of each page there should appear a copyright statement. Move the cursor towards the bottom of the page. As the length of pages will vary, the position of the statement is relative to the other contents of the page, so precise positioning is not relevant.

16 Enter in Arial (i.e. a sans serif font), character size 3, centred: Copyright © GuineaPIGS 2006

17 Both the copyright statement and the E-Mail navigation button are linked to an e-mail account. Click on the E-Mail button. It will be highlighted by being enclosed in a frame. Select the Insert menu and click on the Hyperlink option to reveal the Insert Hyperlink window. Select the E-mail Address button to create E-mail Hyperlink (figure 7.11). Enter the e-mail address guineaPIGS@Farmhalt.co.uk and click on the OK button.

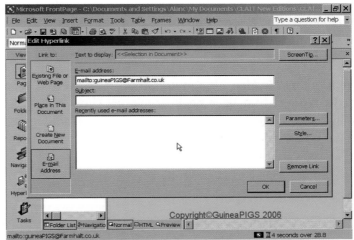

Figure 7.11 Hyperlink

18 Now repeat the operation for the copyright statement. Remember that you must highlight the statement before setting up the link.

19 Save the standard page by selecting the File menu and clicking on the Save option.

20 Close the application by selecting the File menu and the Exit option or click on the application Close button in top right-hand corner.

File names

In creating web pages and sites you will be using a variety of resources in the form of graphic images and files. Microsoft FrontPage® keeps track of these resources. However, if you change a file name or move resources to a new folder, then when the site is operating it will often be unable to locate them, so it is important to retain the original names of files and graphics, as well as the linked resources, and it is good practice to save everything to the same folder. When saving your pages you will often be prompted to save the embedded files. This is a function of Microsoft FrontPage® to help you retain all the data required for the web page.

Downloading files

Often you will seek to download files from websites. On the OCR website (http://www.progress-media.co.uk) are a number of files which are available for users to download. If you would like to practise downloading files, select one of the files with the extension .zip on the OCR website to download. Downloading is initiated by double-clicking the file. A window will appear, to offer you the choice of opening the file or saving it. To open the file requires that you have a compatible application on your computer. In many cases you will want to save the file initially before opening it. If you select the Save option, the Save As window will appear. You need to select the folder in which to save the file in the Save in: box. The file name is normally supplied by the website, but you are free to change it. It is always important to select meaningful names, but do not change the file extension since this allows you to identify the type of file. When you are ready to save the file, click on the Save button. The window will close and a new window becomes visible which shows you the speed at which the file is being downloaded. The speed of downloading depends on the nature of your connection. When the download has been completed, a message will appear in the window. You are then presented with the options to open the file or to end the process by closing the window.

To read a downloaded file requires that you have the type of application used to create it, or specific readers that have been developed simply to read that type of file. Adobe Acrobat® is widely used to produce files for downloading from websites. In order to read an Acrobat file you need the reader software, which is freely available from the the Adobe website (www.adobe.com).

Text formatting

You can precisely control the appearance of the text on your web pages. It can be aligned, emphasised (e.g. emboldened, underlined and in italics) and its size altered. Underline is normally not used on web pages, since to underline a word or phrase is a standard way of showing a hyperlink. Alignment is sometimes known as justification.

The Microsoft FrontPage® formatting toolbar provides the tools to select fonts, character sizes, to emphasise text and align it. Figure 7.12 shows the toolbar.

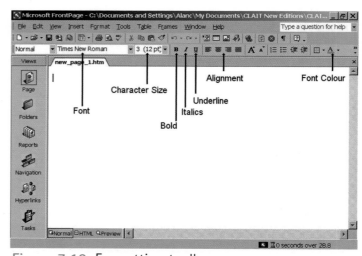

Figure 7.12 Formatting toolbar

Font sizes are shown using HTML as 1, 2, 3, and so on. These are called absolute values, but you can also designate relative sizes. The relativity is to the default value (which is 3), so if you set a value of +2, then the size is two size levels above the default, −1 is one size level less than the default.

In HTML it would read, <FONT=5> </FONT> – set size to absolute size 5, or in relative terms, <FONT=+2></FONT> – set size to two levels above the default value.

There are two types of fonts (typefaces). These are called serif and sans serif. Serif fonts are those with small appendages to the characters, while sans serif are plain. Figure 7.13 shows the difference.

Sans Serif   Serif

Figure 7.13 Serif and sans serif fonts

You can change the colour of the font by highlighting the text and selecting the Font Color icon to reveal a palette of colours. Click on the colour you want for your highlighted text.

Finally, you can insert special symbols into your text by selecting the Insert menu and clicking on the Symbol option to reveal a window of special symbols. They are selected by highlighting them and clicking on the Insert button. The symbol is inserted at the cursor.

Lists

A useful way of displaying information on a web page is a list. Lists are easy and quick to read, often key factors for users of the web. There are two types of lists – ordered and unordered. An unordered list is a simple one, showing all the items equally indented, while an ordered list uses indents to show the relationship between items. For example:

Ordered

- Savings
  - Building Society
  - Bank
  - Coins
- Salary
- Interest

Unordered

- Football
- Politics
- Stamp Collecting
- Driving

In the ordered list, the indentation tells you that building society, bank and coins are all forms of savings. In the unordered list there is no obvious relationship between the items. They may be all equal or unequal. In both types of lists, a wide variety of different bullets are available, including numbers and symbols. Bullets can be inserted from the Formatting toolbar or from the Format menu and Bullets and Numbering option.

Image attributes

Like text, images have characteristics such as size, font and alignment. They are equally as important because you are designing a precise page in which you need to know the exact size of the image. This can be changed by adding a border and altering its alignment (e.g. right, left and centred). If you right-click on an image, a menu appears. Click on the Picture Properties option to reveal the Picture Properties window. The Appearance tab (figure 7.14) opens a window which allows you to change alignment, border thickness and size. If you are changing the size of an image, it is important to specify `Keep aspect ratio` to avoid distorting the picture. Different styles of borders are also available from the `General` tab by selecting the `Style` button, clicking on the `Format` button and `Border` option to open the Borders and Shading window.

All forms of graphical images and pictures can enhance simple text displays. However, for someone who is visually impaired, the pictures are meaningless, and if your page relies on them to convey understanding of the content, you have effectively

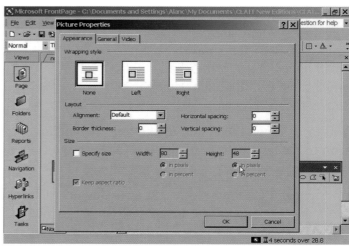

Figure 7.14 Picture Properties window

created a barrier for the user. HTML offers you a way to overcome this barrier using the alt tag. This allows you to add a text description of the image which can be read by a text-only browser, which is typically used by a visually impaired person. Text-only browsers read the text to the user. They are presented with a message rather than a meaningless image. For example:

Before

```
<td><img border="0"
src="Images/Contact.GIF"
width="80" height="48"></td>
```

After

```
<td><img border="0"
src="Images/Contact.GIF"
width="80" height="48"
alt="[navigation link to the contact
page]" ></td>
```

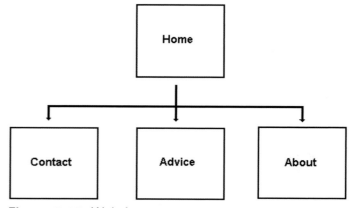

Figure 7.15 Website map

High and low resolution images

The resolution of an image is an important consideration when designing a web page. Resolution is normally measured in terms of pixels per inch with a pixel being a small dot. If you zoom into an image it will appear grainy due to being made up of dots. If we compare two images, the one with the higher resolution will appear sharper and be of a higher quality than the other. Normally we would therefore prefer to use high-resolution images. However, the weakness is that, the higher the resolution, the larger the size of the picture. This means that a web page with a high-resolution image will be slower to load since it is larger.

If you are designing a website then you need to consider the downloading speed of each page. Many web users are browsing and will want a page to load very quickly. If your site is part of an organisational intranet in which each user has a high-speed link then you can probably use high-resolution images. There is no right answer but it is important to realise that a low resolution will improve speed of loading but at the expense of quality, while an equivalent high-resolution image will slow loading but improve quality.

Creating web pages

In exercise 48 you created a standard layout page for a site.
You are now going to create the remaining pages of the site.
The site is being developed for a small business which
provides a guinea pig hotel for families going on holiday who
need their pets cared for while they are away. The pages are:

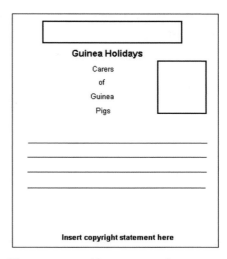

Home page   –   Introduction to the site
Contact page   –   Form to allow users to register
Advice page   –   Advice about keeping guinea pigs
About page   –   Description of the service offered
Guinea Holidays site map

Figure 7.15 shows the map of the Guinea Holidays site.

Figure 7.16 Home page layout

Design brief for home page

1   Design a web page in accordance with the house style guidelines and insert the specified
    content. Save your page as the html document guineahome.htm
2   Page title: Guinea Holidays
3   Additional meta tag: Guinea Holidays provides high quality care of guinea pigs while their
    owners are away
4   Insert the text file Homeguinea.txt and image file guinea.gif, as shown in Figure 7.16.
5   Centre in the headings style: Guinea Holidays
6   Centre in the subheading style: Carers of Guinea Pigs
7   Imported text should be in the body style
8   Format the guinea.gif image as:
    Image: Guinea.gif
    Width: 223
    Height: 169
    Alternative text: Picture of a guinea pig
    Image alignment: Right
    Text alignment: Right
9   Save the page as guineahome.htm

Exercise 49

Home page

1 Microsoft FrontPage® is opened by either selecting the Start button, highlighting the
All Programs option and clicking on the FrontPage® option or by double-clicking on the
FrontPage® icon on the Microsoft Windows® desktop.

2 The application will open with the New Page or Web task pane on the right side of the
display. If you have recently completed the standard page, it will be listed in the Open a
page section of the task pane. It can be opened by clicking on the file. If it is not listed,
click on the More pages option. This will open the Open File window. Change the Look in:

box to read Web Design and your file standard.htm should be listed in the folder. Double-click on it to load it into Microsoft FrontPage®.

3 Select the File menu and click on the Save As option to reveal the Save As window. Change the Save in: box to read Web Design and enter guineahome.htm in the File name: box, then click on the Save button. It is sensible to rename your file (page) early to avoid accidentally overwriting the standard file.

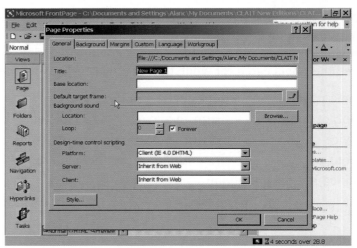

Figure 7.17 Page Properties window

4 Right-click on the page to open a menu. Click on the Page Properties option to reveal the Page Properties window (figure 7.17). Insert the new title Guinea Holidays.

5 Click on the Custom tab to allow you to add another meta tag (figure 7.18). Click on the Add button to reveal the User Meta Variable window. Enter "Description" in the Name box and "Guinea Holidays provides high quality care of guinea pigs while their owners are away" in the Value box. Click on OK button.

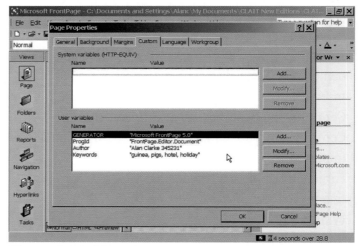

Figure 7.18 Meta data

7 Insert the image guinea.gif into the page by selecting the Insert menu and highlighting the Picture option to reveal the sub-menu. Select the From File option to locate the picture file in the Images sub-folder of the Web Design folder.

8 Right-click on the image to open a menu and select the Picture Properties option, which will reveal its window. In the

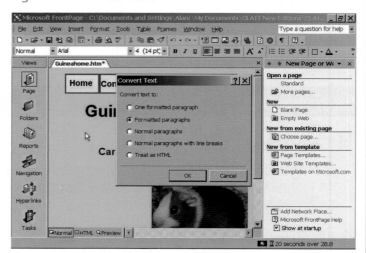

Figure 7.19 Convert Text window

General tab, enter in the Alternative representations text box – Picture of a guinea pig. Select the Appearance tab and change the alignment to right. Click on the OK button.

Figure 7.20 **Home page**

9 Enter the main heading Guinea Holidays on the top line below the navigation table in Arial (sans serif), size 6 text, bold, and centre the text. Leave a blank line and enter the subheading "Carers of Guinea Pigs" in Arial, size 4, bold and centre.

10 You are now going to insert a text file into the page by selecting the Insert menu and clicking on File to reveal the window Select File. Change the Look in: box to show the Web Design Folder in which all your files are stored. Double-click on homeguinea.txt. The Convert Text window will appear (figure 7.19). Select Normal paragraphs and click on the OK button to insert the text.

11 Highlight the new text and change the font to Arial and the size to 3 (house style).

12 Highlight the text again and change the line spacing to double by selecting the Format menu and the Paragraphs option.

13 Select the File menu and click on the Save option. Figure 7.20 shows the page.

14 If you click on the image, it will be highlighted within a frame with handles (small rectangles) at the corners. Microsoft FrontPage® provides a Picture toolbar (View menu, highlight Toolbar and select Pictures). If you explore the toolbar by placing the pointer over each icon, you will discover a series of icons – Rotate Left, Rotate Right, Flip Horizontally and Flip Vertically (figure 7.21). These allow you to rotate and flip your image.

Figure 7.21 **Pictures toolbar**

Try to change the image, but remember not to save the result. Explore the options until you are confident you can make the desired changes.

continued

15 Carefully check your page for mistakes. Microsoft FrontPage® provides a spellchecker, but it is important to read the information and consider the display to eliminate errors. If you find any mistakes, amend the content and save the page again.

16 Close the application by selecting the File menu and the Exit option or click on the application close button in top right-hand corner.

Exercise 49A

Spreadsheet Table

1 In exercise 49 you had the opportunity to insert an image and a text file into a web page. This extra exercise is intended to allow you to practice inserting a spreadsheet table. There is no need to save the results since this task is simply included to allow you to practise.

2 Open Microsoft Excel® and prepare a simple table. Save the file with the name WebTable.

3 FrontPage® is opened by either selecting the Start button, highlighting the All Programs option and clicking on the FrontPage® option or by double clicking on the FrontPage® icon on the Windows® desktop.

4 The application will open with the New Page or Web Task Pane on the right side of the display. If you have recently completed the Home page then it will be listed in the Open a page section of the Task Pane. It can be opened by clicking on the file. If it is not listed then click on the More pages option. This will open the Open File window. Change the Look in: box to read Web Design and your file home.htm should be listed in the folder. Double click on it to load it into FrontPage®.

5 Position the cursor three lines below the text you previously entered in exercise 49 and select the Insert menu and File option. This will open Select File Window. Change the Look in: box to locate WebTable file. Double click on the file and it will appear on the web page.

6 An alternative approach to inserting the table is to copy it using the Copy function in Excel and paste it using the Paste function in FrontPage®.

7 Remove the table using the undo option in the Edit menu and practice copying and pasting WebTable into the page. You can use Undo to repeat the process as many times as you like until you are confident.

8 Do not save the changes since you will need to use the original page later.

9 Close the application by selecting the File menu and the Exit option or click on the application Close button in top right hand corner.

Forms

When designing websites there are many occasions when you want to gain information from your users. You may want users to register themselves on your site. This is often required if your site is a commercial one or you want to know who your users are to help you meet their needs. If you are selling a product or service you will need information from your customers (e.g. credit card details, delivery addresses). Microsoft FrontPage® allows you to create interactive forms so that you can capture information from your users.

To create a form, select the Insert menu and highlight the Form option to reveal a sub-menu. Click on the Form option. A small box will appear with two buttons, Submit and Reset (figure 7.22). Submit is intended to send the information supplied to a designated location, while Reset allows you to clear the information inputted and start again. To create a form you need to enter the different features that make up a form; these are one-line text, scrolling text and check boxes, dropdown menus, push buttons, as well as the Submit and Reset buttons. These are placed at the cursor within the form area by using the sub-menu options. Text can be entered from the keyboard or pasted into the area to explain to users what the purpose of the elements is. Figure 7.23 is an example of a form layout before the interactive elements have been added.

The interactive elements need to have their attributes set (i.e. name and value). To set the attributes you need to double-click on the element and a Text Box Properties window will appear (figure 7.24). This allows you to set the name of the element and its initial value.

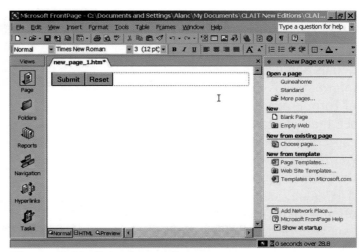
Figure 7.22 Submit and Reset

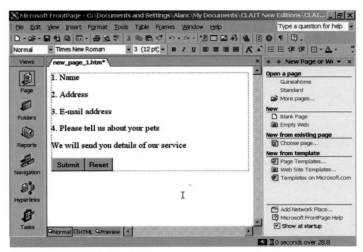
Figure 7.23 Form layout

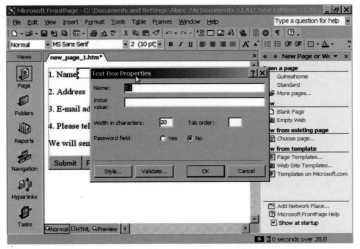
Figure 7.24 Text Box Properties window

The form's properties also need to be established so that the form knows what to do with the user's input. Select the Insert menu, highlight the Form option and click on the Form

Properties option. This opens the Form Properties window (figure 7.25), which will allow you to enter the form details and decide where the information is to be sent. At the top of Form Properties window you will see that you can send the information captured to an e-mail location. When you first open the window, it is likely that some file name is shown in the `File name:` box by default. This is often a folder location on your system (e.g. Web Design), which may be appropriate, but if you need to e-mail the information, it needs to be cleared and an e-mail address entered in the box below.

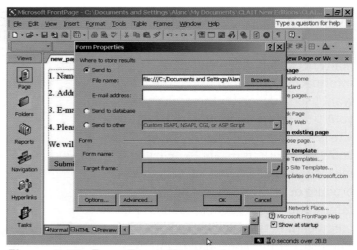

Figure 7.25 Form Properties window

It is important to test the form to ensure that it is operating in the way you need it to, that is, the desired information is being collected and sent to the appropriate location.

Design brief for contact page

Our website Guinea Holidays requires a web page on which customers can register themsleves. This design brief shows how the page should be created.

1 Design a web page in accordance with the house style guidelines and insert the specified content. Save your page as the html document guineacontact.htm
2 Page title: Guinea Holidays Register
3 Additional meta tag: Customer register of interest
4 Insert the text file Contactguinea.txt. Figure 7.26 shows the contact page layout.
5 Centre in the headings style: Guinea Holidays Register
6 Centre in the subheading style: Please enter your details
7 Imported text should be in the body style
8 Turn the imported text into an interactive form (Method = POST, Name = Register action = http://guineaholidays.co.uk/cgi-bin/script).

Figure 7.26 Contact page layout

Name: Name, width 30 characters
Address: Address, width 30 characters and 6 lines
E-mail: Customer, width 40 characters
Please tell us about your pets: Comments, width 30 characters and 10 lines
Submit button: Submit, value = Send your details
Reset button: Reset, value = Clear the entry

Exercise 50

Contact page

1 Microsoft FrontPage® is opened by either selecting the Start button, highlighting the All Programs option and clicking on the FrontPage® option or by double-clicking on the FrontPage® icon on the Microsoft Windows® desktop.

2 The application will open with the New Page or Web task pane on the right side of the display. If you have recently completed the previous exercises, the Standard file will be listed in the Open a page section of the task pane. It can be opened by clicking on the file. If it is not listed, click on the More pages option. This will open the Open File window. Change the Look in: box to read Web Design and your file standard.htm should be listed in the folder. Double-click on it to load it into Microsoft FrontPage®.

3 Select the File menu and click on the Save As option to reveal the Save As window. Change the Save in: box to read Web Design and enter guineacontact.htm in the File name: box, then click on the Save button.

4 Right-click on the page to open a menu. Click on the Page Properties option to reveal the Page Properties window. Insert the new title Guinea Holidays Register.

5 Click on the Custom tab to allow you to add another meta tag. Click on the Add button to reveal the User Meta Variable window. Enter Description in the Name box and Customer register of interest in the Value box. Click on OK buttons.

6 Enter the main heading Guinea Holidays Register on the top line below the navigation table in Arial (sans serif), size 6 text, bold, and centre the text. Leave a blank line and enter the subheading "Please enter your details" in Arial, size 4 and centred.

7 You are now going to create a form on the next line. Select the Insert menu, highlight the Form option and click on the Form item.

This will insert a small box surrounded by a dotted line (figure 7.27). The cursor is flashing alongside the Submit button.

Figure 7.27 Form

8 Insert a text file into the form by selecting the Insert menu and clicking on File to reveal the window Select File. Change the Look in: box to show the Web Design Folder in which all your files are stored. Double-click on contactguinea.txt. The Convert Text window will appear. Select Normal paragraphs and click on the OK button to insert the text. Figure 7.28 shows the inserted file.

9 To turn this layout into a form you need to add the form elements (e.g. single-line boxes). Position your cursor alongside the Name label and select the Insert menu, highlight the Form option and click on the appropriate form item. Click on the Textbox (i.e. a single-line box) and it will be inserted alongside Name. Repeat this action to insert:

Address: Text Area (i.e. a scrolling text box)
E-mail: Textbox (i.e. a one-line text box)
Please tell us about your pets: Text Area (i.e. a scrolling text box)

You need to align the interactive elements to present a professional appearance.

10 Figure 7.29 shows you the completed form

11 You have now created a layout, but you need to define what each element will accept. Double-click on each element and it will reveal a properties box. Enter the name of the element, width and number of lines.

12 Now set the attributes of the two buttons Submit and Reset by double-clicking on them to reveal the Properties window. Change the Name and Value to align with the Design Brief. Notice the label on the button changes.

13 The final stage of designing your form is to decide what you are going to do with the information. Select the Insert menu, highlight the Form option and click on the Form Properties item. This will open the Form Properties window, which allows you to name your form, enter the file name of the form details, an e-mail address to send details to or another action. In this case, if you enter invented information, you may crash when you test the page or receive messages such as the site is unavailable. You may also get error messages when entering invented information. In the assessment you will be provided with the correct details that will work with your form.

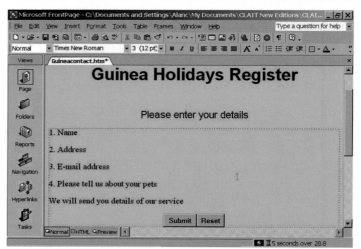

Figure 7.28 Convert Text window

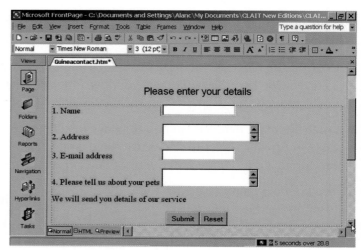

Figure 7.29 Interactive form

14 If you click on the HTML tab, you will see the language associated with the creation of the form. Look for the item – form method="POST" and the lines below.

The HTML tag associated with creating an interactive form is Form. It has an attribute called Method that indicates the way that the form details will be transferred from the browser to the computer server to the script processor. The script processor will handle the information. Method can have two values, which determine how the information is sent. These are POST and GET.

15 Your final design can be viewed using the Preview tab.

16 Select the File menu, click on the Save option and save as the file name guineacontact.

17 It is important to test your form and, in particular, that the information is sent to the chosen location. In this exercise we have provided you with a fictitious website to send data to, so testing is limited, but you can enter information and try out the form. You will probably be presented with error messages when you submit your data. The Reset button should operate successfully.

18 Carefully check your page for mistakes. Microsoft FrontPage® provides a spellchecker, but it is important to read the information and consider the display to eliminate errors. If you find any mistakes, amend the content and save the page again.

19 Close the application by selecting the File menu and the Exit option or click on the application Close button in top right-hand corner.

Design brief for advice page

Our website Guinea Holidays requires a web page that will provide advice to customers. This design brief shows how the page should be created.

1   Design a web page in accordance with the house style guidelines and insert the specified content. Save your page as the html document guineaadvice.htm

2   Page title: Guinea Holidays Advice

3   Additional meta tag: General advice about the care of guinea pigs

4   Insert the text file Adviceguinea.txt and image file guinea2.gif, as shown in figure 7.30.

5   Centre in the headings style Guinea Holidays Advice

6   Imported text should be in the body style

7   Format the guinea2.gif image as:
    Image: Guinea.gif
    Width: 251
    Height: 225

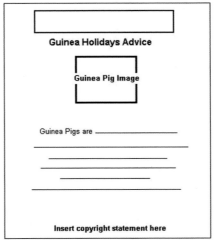

Figure 7.30 Advice page layout

Alternative text: Picture of a guinea pig

Image alignment: Centre

Text alignment: Centre

8 Save your page as guineaadvice.

Exercise 51

Advice page

1 Microsoft FrontPage® is opened by either selecting the Start button, highlighting the All Programs option and clicking on the FrontPage® option or by double-clicking on the FrontPage® icon on the Microsoft Windows® desktop.

2 The application will open with the New Page or Web task pane on the right side of the display. If you have recently completed the previous exercises, the Standard file will be listed in the Open a page section of the task pane. It can be opened by clicking on the file. If it is not listed, click on the More pages option. This will open the Open File window. Change the Look in: box to read Web Design and your file standard.htm should be listed in the folder. Double-click on it to load it into Microsoft FrontPage®.

3 Select the File menu and click on the Save As option to reveal the Save As window. Change the Save in: box to read Web Design and enter guineaadvice.htm in the File name: box, then click on the Save button.

4 Right-click on the page to open a menu. Click on the Page Properties option to reveal the Page Properties window. Insert the new title Guinea Holidays Advice.

5 Click on the Custom tab to allow you to add another meta tag. Click on the Add button to reveal the User Meta Variable window. Enter Description in the Name box and General advice about the care of guinea pigs in the Value box. Click on OK buttons.

6 Enter the main heading Guinea Holidays Advice on the top line below the navigation table in Arial (sans serif), size 6 text, bold, and centre the text.

7 Insert the image guinea2.gif into the page by selecting the Insert menu and highlighting the Picture option to reveal the sub-menu. Select the From File option to locate the picture file in the Images sub-folder of the Web Design folder.

8 Right-click on the image to open a menu and the Picture toolbar. Select the Picture Properties option, which will reveal its window. In the General tab enter in the Alternative representations text box – Picture of a guinea pig. Select the Appearance tab and change the alignment to centre. Click on the OK button.

9 Insert a text file into the page by selecting the Insert menu and clicking on File to reveal the window Select File. Change the Look in: box to show the Web Design Folder in which all your files are stored. Double-click on adviceguinea.txt. The Convert Text window will appear. Select Normal paragraphs and click on the OK button to insert the text.

10 Highlight the imported text and change it to Arial and size 3.

11 Preview your page to check it conforms to the design brief (figure 7.31).

12 Select the File menu and click on the Save option. Save your page using the file name guineaadvice.

13 Carefully check your page for mistakes. Microsoft FrontPage® provides a spellchecker, but it is important to read the information and consider the display to eliminate errors. If you find any mistakes, amend the content and save the page again.

Figure 7.31 **Advice page**

14 Close the application by selecting the File menu and the Exit option or click on the application Close button in the top right-hand corner.

Design brief for about page

1 Design a web page in accordance with the house style guidelines and insert the specified content. Save your page as the html document guineaabout.htm

2 Page title: Guinea Holidays Information

3 Additional meta tag: Background information about Guinea Pig Holidays

4 Insert the table, as shown in figure 7.32

5 Centre in the headings style Guinea Holidays Information

6 Table should be centred in the body style

7 Save your page as guineaabout.

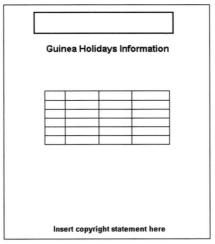

Figure 7.32 **About page layout**

Exercise 52

About page

1 Microsoft FrontPage® is opened by either selecting the Start button, highlighting the All Programs option and clicking on the FrontPage® option or by double-clicking on the FrontPage® icon on the Microsoft Windows® desktop.

2 The application will open with the New Page or Web task pane on the right side of the display. If you have recently completed the previous exercises, the Standard file will be listed in the Open a page section of the task pane. It can be opened by clicking on the file. If it is not listed, click on the More pages option. This will open the Open File window. Change the Look in: box to read Web Design and your file standard.htm should be listed in the folder. Double-click on it to load it into Microsoft FrontPage®.

3 Select the File menu and click on the Save As option to reveal the Save As window. Change the Save in: box to read Web Design and enter guineaabout.htm in the File name: box, then click on the Save button.

4 Right-click on the page to open a menu. Click on the Page Properties option to reveal the Page Properties window. Insert the new title Guinea Holidays Information.

5 Click on the Custom tab to allow you to add another meta tag. Click on the Add button to reveal the User Meta Variable window. Enter Description in the Name box and Information about Guinea Holiday service in the Value box.

6 Enter the main heading Guinea Holidays Information on the top line below the navigation table in Arial (sans serif), size 6 text, bold, and centre the text.

7 Insert a table into the centre of the page with 2 columns and 4 rows and a border size of 1, by selecting the Table menu, highlighting the Insert option and clicking on the Table item. Enter the number of columns, rows, size of border and centre alignment.

Open: 1 April to 31 October

Cost: £25 per week for a single
    guinea pig
    £45 per week for two
    guinea pigs

Extra: Visits to a vet at cost plus £5 for each trip

Special Diets: Cost of diet plus £2 per week

8 To adjust the column widths you place your pointer over the column divide line and it will change shape to a double-arrowed pointer. If you hold down the mouse button, you can drag the line to the position you desire.

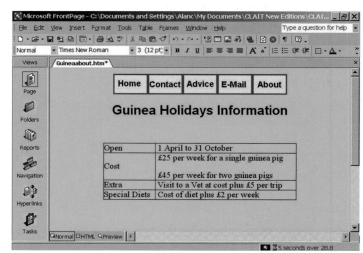

Figure 7.33 About page

9   Preview your page to check it conforms to the design brief (figure 7.33).

10 Select the File menu and click on the Save option.

11 Carefully check your page for mistakes. Microsoft FrontPage® provides a spellchecker, but it is important to read the information and consider the display to eliminate errors. If you find any mistakes, amend the content and save the page again.

12 Close the application by selecting the File menu and the Exit option or click on the application Close button in top right-hand corner.

Hyperlinks

The World Wide Web is a non-linear environment; you navigate around websites and within sites using links. These connect the different pages and provide the routes between the different parts of the site. You can even link within a page. You have considerable freedom when creating links. You can create multiple links from a page to many others or a single connection. The choice is yours. Your links can be to:

■ another page of the same website
■ another page of a different website
■ an e-mail system so that you can send messages
■ a bookmarked/anchored section within a page.

This freedom to create many different types of links can lead to users getting confused when using the site, so you need to consider your reasons for the link carefully. In the exercises you have consistently employed a navigation bar with icons to link to different parts of the site. This provides a consistency that will help users to navigate the site. Each icon serves as a link to another page or to an e-mail system.

Links can be anchored to both text and images, and need to be employed consistently to assist users to understand your approach. Text links are normally underlined to indicate that they are a connection to another page. Image links are normally shown by the mouse pointer changing shape when it moves over the link. Links between pages normally take you to the top of the new page, but you can also link to particular parts of a page. Microsoft FrontPage® calls these areas bookmarks, but they are sometimes called anchors. They are often useful within a long web page, so that you can move quickly between the different sections without scrolling down. Figure 7.34 shows the use of anchors within a long page.

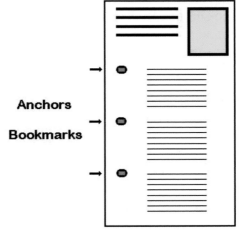

Figure 7.34 Anchors/Bookmarks

Anchors provide a useful means of helping users navigate within a page. Often they offer a link to return to the original location, so users avoid being confused about where they are. To a user it is often difficult to distinguish between a link within a page or to a new page or even to a new site.

You have now created all four pages that make up the website and it remains for you to create the hyperlinks between the pages which will produce the site. Exercise 51 concentrates on creating hyperlinks.

Exercise 53

Linking

1 Microsoft FrontPage® is opened by either selecting the Start button, highlighting the All Programs option and clicking on the FrontPage® option or by double-clicking on the FrontPage® icon on the Microsoft Windows® desktop.

2 The application will open with the New Page or Web task pane on the right side of the display. If you have recently completed the previous exercises, the Guineahome.htm file will be listed in the Open a page section of the task pane. It can be opened by clicking on the file. If it is not listed, click on the More pages option. This will open the Open File window. Change the Look in: box to read Web Design and your file Guineahome.htm should be listed in the folder. Double-click on it to load it into Microsoft FrontPage®.

3 You need to create links between the home page and the contact, advice and about pages. In addition, you will also link the image to an external site.

4 Click on the Contact button and select the Insert menu, then click on the Hyperlink option to reveal the Insert Hyperlink window. Click on the Existing File or Web Page button (figure 7.35). Change the Look in: box to Web Design folder and double-click on guineacontact.htm.

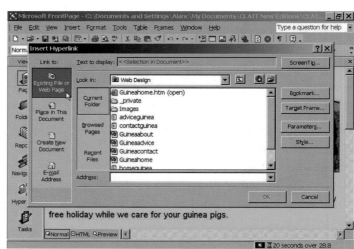

5 Repeat this process for the Advice and About buttons, linking them to the advice and about pages.

Figure 7.35 Contact hyperlink

6 You can check that the links work by using the Preview tab. Sometimes the Preview does not work, so, alternatively, select the File menu and the Preview in Browser option to reveal the Preview in Browser window. Click the Preview button and your pages will appear in your browser display.

7 Hyperlinks are very useful and it is always good practice to create a link so that you can return. Create links from Advice, Contact and About to return to the Home page.

8 If you wish, continue the process so that from any page you can move to all the others using the navigation bar.

9 Check the links work correctly using the Preview tab or Preview in Browser option. You may find that you get error messages when you test the Contact page link, due to using fake information during its creation.

10 To create an external link from the image, click on the guinea pig image to enclose it in a frame, then select the Insert menu and click on the Hyperlink option. Select the Existing File or Web Page button and enter the URL of the site you want to link to (select a site you would like to link to e.g. http://www.hodderclait.co.uk) and click on the OK button. You can also use your browser to locate the site. If you test this link when you are not connected, you may see an error message indicating that you are not connected.

11 Select the File menu and click on the Save option.

12 Select the File menu and click on the Save option for each page.

13 Close the application by selecting the File menu and the Exit option or click on the application Close button in top right-hand corner.

Testing

You have created a small website and tested it using the Preview tab within Microsoft FrontPage®. However, this is not a substitute for testing your site using a browser. So open your browser by clicking on the browser (e.g. Internet Explorer) icon on your desktop or select the Start button, highlight the All Programs option and click on the browser (e.g. Internet Explorer) option.

Enter the path to your file guineahome.htm (e.g. C:\web design\guineahome.htm) and press enter. Alternatively, double-click on the file in the Web Design folder. Your home page should appear in the browser work area (figure 7.36). You can now try each link. This process is essential in that you are testing the pages in the real environment. The pointer should change shape into a hand when it is placed over a link.

There is a simpler approach, which is to select the File menu and the Preview in Browser option. This will open the Preview in Browser window in which you can choose a suitable browser. You need to click on the Preview button to open the page in the browser. You can then check your links and display.

Testing is important to ensure your

Figure 7.36 Testing

users are not fustrated when using the website. However, even when the links operate perfectly, it is easy for a user to become disorientated in a site.

One way of reducing disorientation and users getting lost is to provide a site map to help navigation. It is also useful during the design process in that it provides an overview of the whole site.

Publishing a website

We have concentrated on creating the individual pages and the website. However, once this is completed you need to be able to publish your site by moving it to the server (computer) on which it will be stored. Many Internet service providers and other organisations offer space on which you can store your site and people can access it on the World Wide Web. These providers are often called the host. The initial step to publishing your site is to know the address of the host organisation. In most cases, you will also need the user name and password of the host.

There are several ways of publishing a site. These are:

1   HTTP – you can use the Hypertext Transfer Protocol (HTTP) to publish your site, providing the server on which your site will be based has the Microsoft FrontPage® Server Extensions installed on it. If it does not, error messages will be displayed.

2   FTP – you can use the file transfer protocol if your chosen server does not have the Microsoft FrontPage® Server Extensions installed. However, if you publish on a server without the extensions, it is likely that some of the features of Microsoft FrontPage® will not work.

3   Local system – you can also publish your site on your own system. This is useful when you want to ensure that you have a full copy of all the files you need for the site. In a sense, you are backing up the site, which is always useful to do.

The first step is to select the File menu and Open Web, which will open the Open Web window. You then need to select the correct folder in which your web pages are stored. Once you have located the correct folder, you need to click on the Open button. You may see a warning message telling you that Microsoft FrontPage® needs to add extra information to your files. You can agree by clicking on the OK button. A new area will be displayed in the Microsoft FrontPage® window called Folder List (figure 7.37). This displays your web pages and sub-folder

Images, but you will notice that a new sub-folder called _private has been added. Microsoft Frontpage® creates this folder in which to store the results from your form. A folder or file which begins with an underscore (i.e. _) is a hidden file or folder.

The next step is to select the File menu and the option Publish Web to open the Publish Web window (figure 7.38). This allows you to enter the web address (i.e. URL) of your host in Enter publish destination, and then to click on the OK button. This will open

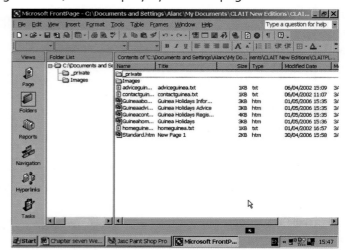

Figure 7.37 Folder List

another window to ask you to enter the user name and password of the host if you are connected to the Internet. Once you have entered the password, click on the OK button. Microsoft FrontPage® will now connect to the host computer (i.e. server) and you will see a window open that shows you the process of uploading your files. Once the process is finished, a message will appear. You will be asked if you want to view the site. If you are not connected or entered a made-up URL (e.g www.guineapig.co.uk), an error message will appear.

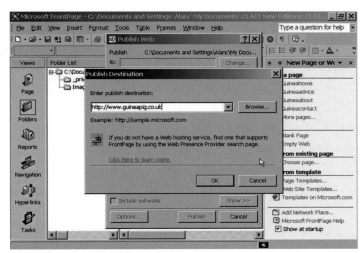

Figure 7.38 Publishing website

You will need to upload files every time you want to update or extend the site. The process is the same, except that you will be asked if you need to overwrite files. This is very similar to copying files between folders on your own computer. Messages appear to ask you if you want to overwrite a file.

More practice

You are going to create a site that is intended to sell organic food. The site will have four pages – home, customer, product information and background about the location. Figure 7.39 shows the Organic site map. It is important to notice that there are links between all the pages.

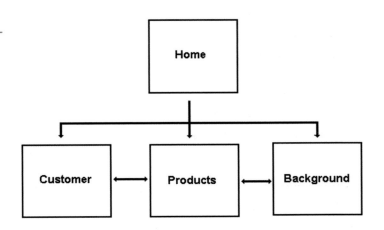

Figure 7.39 Organic site

Activity 1

1   Create a folder to store your website pages and resources called Organic.
2   Within the Organic folder create a sub-folder called Images.
3   On the Hodder Education website (www.hodderclait.co.uk) you will find all the images and files required to create the website. Download the files from the site. All files should be saved to the Organic folder, with all image files stored in the Images sub-folder.
4   The files required to develop the Organic website are:
    ■   Images – background.gif, customer.gif, e-mail.gif, home.gif, products.gif and countryside.gif
    ■   Text – Homenew.txt, registration.txt and information.txt

Activity 2

Standard/master page

1   Load Microsoft FrontPage®.
2   Open a new page and save this page with the file name Organic Standard.
3   All links to files and images on the website should be relative, not absolute.
4   The standard page and text properties are:
    - Title – Standard
    - Background colour – #008080 (hexadecimal code of the colour Teal)
    - Text colour – #000000 (hexadecimal code of the colour Black)
    - Link colour – #0000FF (hexadecimal code of the colour Blue)
    - Visited link colour – #800080 (hexadecimal code of the colour Purple)
    - Active link colour – #0000ff (hexadecimal code of the colour red)
    - Typeface (font) – sans serif
    - Text size:
        - Main heading – HTML size 7 (36 pts)
        - Subheading – HTML size 5 (18 pts)
        - Body text – HTML size 3 (12 pts)

5   The image properties are:
    - Image height and width must be accurately specified
    - Image borders set to zero
    - Alt text specified by Design Brief.

6   The following meta tags need to be created:
    Author: Your name and centre number
    Keywords: rural, organic, food

7   Create a navigation table across the top of the page with the following characteristics:

    Width: 400
    Height: 48
    Columns: 5
    Rows: 1
    Centred
    Cell spacing: 0
    Cell padding: 0
    Border: 0
    The images are all width 106 and height 48.

Image	Alt text	Link
Home	Home Page	Homenew.htm
Customer	Book a holiday	Booking.htm
Products	Information about	Product.htm the organic products
E-Mail	Messages	E-mail link to organic@countryside.co.uk
Background	Background information about the location	Background.htm

8 Create the copyright notice across the bottom of the page. It should read: Copyright © Organic Countryside 2006. Enter the notice in the body text size and centre the text. Link the E-mail navigation bar element and the copyright statement to organic@countryside.co.uk.

9 Save the page as the file Organic Master. Figure 7.40 shows the standard/master page.

10 Close Microsoft FrontPage®.

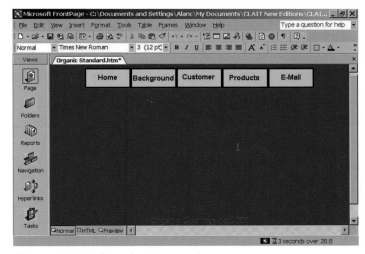

Figure 7.40 Standard page

Activity 3

Home page

1 Load Microsoft FrontPage®.

2 Load Organic Standard file and save this page with the file name homenew.

3 You are going to create a home page for the site, based on the layout shown in figure 7.41.

4 Title of the page: Organic Foods

5 Add the following meta tag: Organic Countryside is a supplier of high quality organic foods

6 Add the text file Homenew.txt and image file countryside.gif, as shown in the layout.

7 Centre in the headings style: Organic Countryside (sans serif, HTML size 7 – 36 pts).

8 Centre in the subheading style: High Quality Organic Food (sans serif, HTML size 5 – 18 pts).

9 Imported text should be in the body style (sans serif, HTML size 3 – 12 pts), with the text double-spaced and left-aligned.

10 Format the countryside.gif image as:

Width: 230

Height: 173

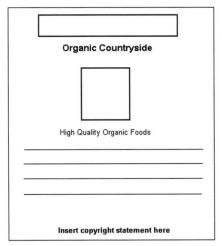

Figure 7.41 Home page layout

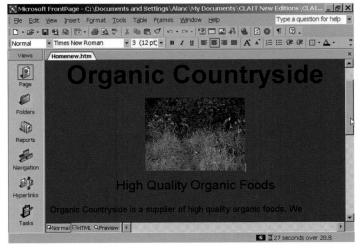

Figure 7.42 Home page

Alternative text: Picture of countryside

Image alignment: Centre

Text alighment: Centre

11 Save the page as homenew.htm. Figure 7.42 shows the page.

12 Carefully check your page for mistakes.

13 Close Microsoft FrontPage®.

Activity 4

Customer page

1 Load Microsoft FrontPage®.

2 Load Organic Standard file and save this page with the file name booking.

3 You are going to create a customer page for the site, based on the layout shown in figure 7.43.

4 Page title: Customer Registration

5 Additional meta tag: Customers can register on the mailing list

6 Insert the main heading: Customer Registration (sans serif, HTML size 7 – 36 pts). Centre the heading.

7 Create an interactive form and insert the text file registration.txt, as shown in the layout.

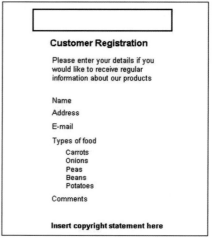

Figure 7.43 Customer page

8 Subheading should be sans serif, HTML size 5 – 18 pts.

9 Imported text should be in the body style (sans serif, HTML size 3 – 12 pts).

10 Turn the imported text into an interactive form (Method = POST, Name = Register action = http://organiccountryside.co.uk/cgi-bin/script):

Name: Textbox (i.e. one-line text box)

Address: Text Area (i.e. scrolling text box)

E-mail: Textbox (i.e. one-line text box)

Types of Food
   Carrots: Option button
   Onions: Option button
   Peas: Option button
   Beans: Option button
   Potatoes: Option button

Comments: Text Area (i.e. scrolling text box)

11 Element Attributes

Name: Name, width 20 characters

Address: Address, width 30 characters and 5 lines

E-mail: Customer, width 50 characters

Radio button: Food, value = Carrots,
Radio button: Food, value = Onions
Radio button: Food, value = Peas
Radio button: Food, value = Beans
Radio button: Food, value = Potatoes

Comments: Comments, width 30 characters and 8 lines

Submit button: Submit, value = Send your details

Reset button: Reset, value = Clear the entry

12 Save the page as booking.htm. Figure 7.44 shows the page.

13 Carefully check your page for mistakes.

14 Close Microsoft FrontPage®.

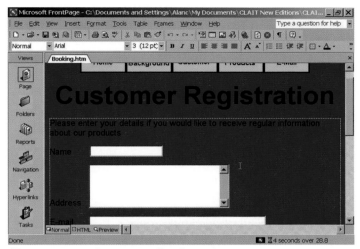

Figure 7.44 Customer Registration

Activity 5

Products page

1 Load Microsoft FrontPage®.

2 Load Organic Standard file and save this page with the file name products.

3 You are going to create a products page for the site, based on the layout shown in figure 7.45.

4 Page title: Products

5 Additional meta tag: Information about the available products

6 Enter the main heading Products. Centre and embolden the headings in the headings style (sans serif, HTML size 7 – 36 pts).

7 Insert the text file information.txt, as shown in figure 7.45.

8 Imported text should be in the body style (sans serif, HTML size 3 – 12 pts).

9 Check the text for mistakes and adjust its presentation to produce the best effect.

Figure 7.45 Products page layout

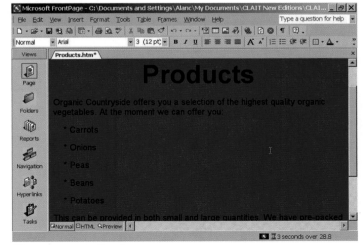

Figure 7.46 Products page

10 Save your page as product.htm. Figure 7.46 shows the page.

11 Carefully check your page for mistakes.

12 Close Microsoft FrontPage®.

Activity 6

Background page

1 Load Microsoft FrontPage®.

2 Load Organic Standard file and save this page with the file name background.

3 You are going to create a background page for the site, based on the layout shown in figure 7.47.

4 Page title: Background

5 Additional meta tag: Background information about the location of Organic Countryside

6 Enter the main heading Food Information (sans serif, HTML size 7 – 36 pts). Centre and embolden the heading.

7 Insert the table, as shown in figure 7.47.

8 Table should be centred in the body style (sans serif, HTML size 3 – 12 pts)

Directions: Take the M1 to junction 24 and follow signs to Newtown
Opening Hours: 9 to 6 pm Monday to Saturday
Refreshments: Green Vegetable Hotel
Car Parking: Spaces 50 cars

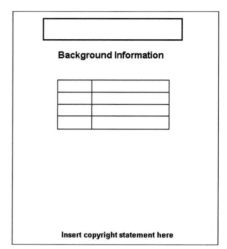

Figure 7.47 Background page layout

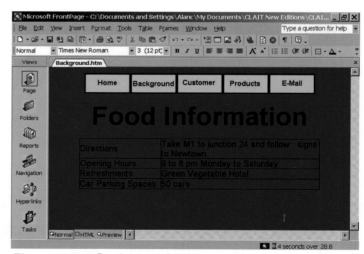

Figure 7.48 Background page

9 Use the borders function in Format menu to enclose the table (width 1).

10 Save your page as Background.htm. Figure 7.48 shows the Background page.

11 Carefully check your page for mistakes.

12 Close Microsoft FrontPage®.

Activity 7

Links

1 Load Microsoft FrontPage®.
2 Load Organic Countryside home page.
3 Create links between the four pages.
4 Test your links using the Preview in Browser option. Correct any mistakes.
5 Save all your pages.
6 Close Microsoft FrontPage®.

SUMMARY

1 Load Microsoft FrontPage®

Select the Start button, highlight the All Programs option and click on the FrontPage® option or double-click on the FrontPage® icon on the Microsoft Windows® desktop.

2 Background colour

Select the Format menu and click on the Background option to reveal the Page Properties window. Select the Background tab. Click on the down arrow alongside the Background box and a small palette of colours will appear. Select the colour of your choice.

3 Text colour

Select the Format menu and click on the Background option to reveal the Page Properties window. Select the Background tab. Click on the down arrow alongside the Text box and a small palette of colours will appear. Select the colour of your choice.

4 Link colour

Select the Format menu and click on the Background option to reveal the Page Properties window. Select the Background tab. Click on the down arrow alongside the Hyperlink box and a small palette of colours will appear. Select the colour of your choice.

5 Visited link colour

Select the Format menu and click on the Background option to reveal the Page Properties window. Select the Background tab. Click on the down arrow alongside the Visited hyperlink box and a small palette of colours will appear. Select the colour of your choice.

6 Active link colour

Select the Format menu and click on the Background option to reveal the Page Properties window. Select the Background tab. Click on the down arrow alongside the Active hyperlink box and a small palette of colours will appear. Select the colour of your choice.

7 Hexadecimal colours

Colours are shown using their hexadecimal code in HTML. For example:

- #00FFFF – aqua
- #008080 – teal.

8 Meta tags

Additional meta information can be inserted directly into the HTML code. For example:

```
<meta name="Author" content= "Your name and centre number">
<meta name="Keywords" content=" guinea, pigs, hotel, holiday ">
```

or you can right-click to reveal a menu, click on the Page Properties option to reveal the Page Properties window. Select the Custom tab and in the User variables click the Add button to reveal the User Meta Variable window. Add Name and Value (i.e. content).

9 Insert table
Select the Table menu, highlight the Insert option to reveal the Table option. Click on Table to open the Insert Table window.

10 Insert graphic
Select the Insert menu, highlight the Picture option to reveal sub-menu of options (e.g. From File).

11 Hyperlinks
Select the Insert menu and click on the Hyperlink option to reveal the Insert Hyperlink window. There are four buttons displayed down the left side of the window. These relate to different types of links.

12 Image attributes
Right-click on an image to reveal a menu. Click on the Picture Properties option to reveal the Picture Properties window. The Appearance tab opens a window which allows you to change alignment, border thickness and size. Different styles of borders are also available from the General tab display by selecting the Style button, clicking on the Format button and selecting a Border from a dropdown list.

13 Page properties – meta tag
Right-click on the page to open a menu. Click on the Page Properties option to reveal the Page Properties window. Click on the Custom tab, which lets you add another meta tag. Click on the Add button to reveal the User Meta Variable window.

14 Image – alt tag
Right-click on the image to open a menu and select the Picture Properties option, which will reveal its window. In the General tab enter your text in the Alternative representations text box. Click on the OK button.

15 Forms
Select the Insert menu, highlight the Form option and click on the Form item.

16 Form elements
Position your cursor where you want to place the element and select the Insert menu, then highlight the Form option. Click on the desired element (e.g. Textbox).

17 Form element – attributes
Double-click on each element to reveal a properties box. Enter the name of the element, width, number of lines, and so on.

18 Testing
Click on the Preview tab within Microsoft FrontPage®, or select the File menu and

Preview in <u>B</u>rowser option, or open your browser, enter the path to your file (e.g. C:\web design\guineahome.htm) and press Enter .

19 Publishing website

Select the <u>F</u>ile menu and Open <u>W</u>eb to open the Open Web window. Identify the location of your web pages. Click on the <u>O</u>pen button. A warning message may appear, telling you that Microsoft FrontPage® needs to add extra information to your files – agree by clicking on the OK button. A new area will be displayed in the Microsoft FrontPage® window called Folder List.

Next select the <u>F</u>ile menu and the option P<u>u</u>blish Web to open the Publish Web window. Enter the web address (i.e. URL) of your host in Enter publish destination and then to click on the OK button. This will open another window to ask you to enter the user name and password of the host if you are connected to the Internet. Microsoft FrontPage® will now upload your files.

Unit 8

8

Electronic Communication

This chapter will help you to:

- use advanced e-mail features to coordinate information
- set up distribution lists and use an address book
- manage mailbox and folders,

This chapter covers unit 8 (Electronic Communication). There are no preconditions for studying this unit. However, its content does assume that you have the skills and understanding that are provided by the OCR Level 1 ICT course CLAiT 2006 (e.g. Unit 8: Online Communication and Unit 1: File Management and e-Document Production).

Assessment

After studying unit 8, your skills and understanding are assessed during a three-hour practical assignment. This is set by OCR and marked locally. However, the marking will be externally moderated by OCR. This ensures that the standard is being applied correctly across the many different providers of OCR CLAiT Plus. If you are unsuccessful, you can be reassessed using a different assignment.

An alternative approach is for you to be assessed by an assignment set by OCR or designed for your centre. These assignments cover all the assessment objectives included in the unit. You will need to complete an OCR evidence checklist, explaining how each assessment objective has been covered.

Microsoft Outlook® XP

Microsoft Outlook® XP (2002) is an application designed to help you organise yourself. It is widely used by employers and other organisations to help their staff. It provides you with a variety of systems, including:

- a comprehensive e-mail system
- a personal and group work scheduler
- a contact and address book
- a desk diary

- a project manager
- a work monitor.

The application is illustrated in figure 8.1. This shows the view of the Microsoft Outlook® XP e-mail inbox. The application is divided into a series of areas. These are, from left to right:

- Shortcuts – there are three sets (i.e. Outlook, My Shortcuts and Other Shortcuts)
- Folder List
- List of e-mails in the inbox – top area
- Preview of the current e-mail – bottom area.

Across the top of the application are the normal menu and toolbars, which are part of many Microsoft Windows® applications.

The Shortcuts area provides a list of icons that link you to the various functions of Microsoft Outlook®. The three sets of shortcuts are accessed by buttons at the bottom of the area. The Outlook® Shortcuts are displayed by default and provide you with connections to:

- Outlook® Today
- Calendar
- Contacts
- Tasks
- Notes
- Deleted items.

The My Shortcuts group provides links to:

- Inbox
- Drafts
- Journal
- Outlook® Update.

The Other Shortcuts group provides links to:

- My Computer
- My Documents
- Favorites.

These allow you to access the files and folders of the other applications on the computer.

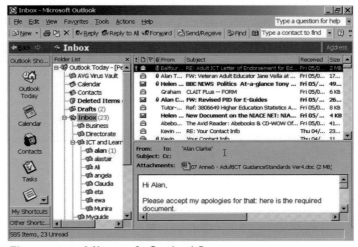

Figure 8.1 Microsoft Outlook®

The Folders List shows you the folders associated with Microsoft Outlook® (e.g. Inbox, Sent items and Outbox). You can add folders to your list to store e-mails (e.g. Ali, Alastair and Angela). The Inbox holds e-mails sent to you, Sent Items stores messages you have sent and Outbox holds those messages before they are sent. You can create additional folders so that you can store your messages in any way that you choose.

Creating an e-mail message

E-mail is an effective communication medium for almost everyone. In business, e-mail has had an enormous effect on communications. It combines a rapid transmission method with useful record-keeping features. The e-mail system automatically records the date and time the message is sent, while the sender's details are attached so that the recipient can easily identify who has sent the communication. The initial message is retained in the reply, making it simple to understand the context of the message without having to look at files or other records. E-mail can be stored in an appropriate folder, enabling complete records of transactions to be maintained.

This is very useful if misunderstandings happen or people disagree about decisions that have been made. Paper communications suffer from often only providing a partial record in that dates, names and details are sometimes missing. It is often not clear what they are responding to or who has been sent copies.

E-mail automatically provides this information and filing is a simple matter. Paper records are more easily lost or misfiled.

E-mails are created by selecting the New button on the standard toolbar to reveal the Message window. This is divided into two main areas:

- the address area in which you place the e-mail address of the person(s) you are e-mailing (i.e. To... box), the address of any other people you want to copy the message to (i.e. Cc) and, finally, the subject of the message. When you address an e-mail it is critical to ensure that you are accurate. A single mistake (eg. reversing letters, misspelling) will ensure that the message is not received. There is also the danger that the message will be sent to the wrong person. Perfection is required with all addresses. If you send a message with an incorrect address you will later receive an e-mail containing an error message, such as Mail delivery failed: Returning message to sender. The sender is the Mail Delivery System.

- the message area where you enter your communication.

There is an extra box called Bcc, which you can add to the message. This enables blind copying in which you copy the message to another person or persons, but their names will be hidden in the recipient's copy of the message. Blind copying is used to maintain confidentiality. The option is added to the message by selecting the down-arrow button next to the Option button on the toolbar, to reveal a list of options, and clicking on the Bcc option. The new message window is shown in figure 8.2.

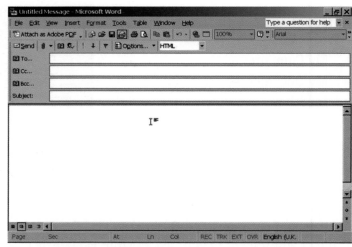

Figure 8.2 Bcc option

Format options

Microsoft Outlook® offers three format options. The ability of e-mail recipients to read the different formats varies. The three choices are:

- Plain text
- Rich text (RTF)
- HTML.

Plain text

These messages do not have any formatting or other features. You cannot use images within plain text messages. Attachments can be included in plain text messages, but there is a risk that they cannot be read by the recipient of the message.

Rich text (RTF)

This is a format designed to be read by most word-processing applications. It allows you a range of formatting opportunities, such as font sizes, alignments and lists. Some recipients may receive attachments that they cannot read.

HTML

Almost everyone can read an HTML e-mail message. It also provides some formatting possibilities for your messages.

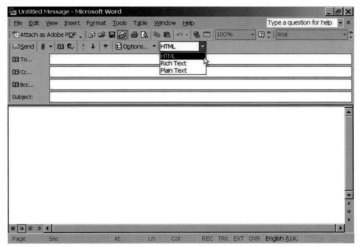

Figure 8.3 Format

The e-mail toolbar provides access to the three choices (figure 8.3). You need to consider who you are sending the message to in order to select the most appropriate format.

Priorities

When you send an e-mail it is possible to indicate whether the message is important by adding a particular symbol. This is achieved by clicking on the icon indicated by an exclamation mark (figure 8.3). Other related options are low importance and the follow-up flag. This provides a means of creating a reminder to follow up a message.

Most e-mail users get a large number of messages. Within a company you will get messages about your work, social matters, car parking, people selling items and many other issues. It is therefore useful to indicate when one is important so that recipients can identify that it needs immediate attention. Figure 8.4 shows the purpose of some of the icons on the standard toolbar.

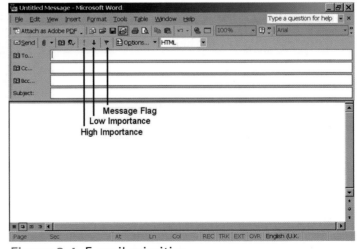

Figure 8.4 E-mail priorities

Exercise 54

Creating an e-mail

1 Microsoft Outlook® is opened either by selecting the Start button, highlighting the All Programs option and clicking on the Outlook® option, or by double-clicking on the Outlook® icon on the Microsoft Windows® desktop.

2 Create a new e-mail by clicking on the New icon to reveal the message window. Add a blind copy option to the message window by selecting the down-arrow button next to the Option button on the toolbar, to reveal a menu of options, and clicking on the Bcc option. You will notice an extra line is added to the message window (figure 8.2).

3 Create the message below:

To: Janet123@yahoo.co.uk
Cc: John456@yahoo.co.uk
Bcc: Sheila789@yahoo.co.uk

Practice

This is a practice e-mail

If you are working with a group of other learners, substitute the three e-mail addresses with those of your peers. Send the e-mail and see how it appears to the recipient (figure 8.5). You can also send e-mails to television or radio programmes if you would like to practise. Many programmes give their e-mail addresses so you can respond to their content.

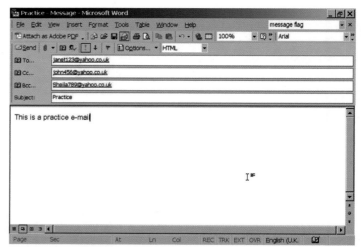

Figure 8.5 Practice message

4 Give the message a high priority by selecting the High Importance icon on the toolbar.

5 If you are interrupted before you can finish your e-mail, you can save it to complete later. Select the File menu and click on the Exit option. A message will appear asking you if you want to save your message. Click on the Yes button. Your message will be saved as a draft in the folder list (i.e. Drafts) and you will see the number of drafts increased by one. To retrieve it, simply click on Drafts and a list of them will appear in the main work area. Click on the Practice message and send the e-mail.

6 To send the message, click on the Send button on the toolbar. If your system is connected to the Internet the message will be sent. If not, it will be stored in the Outbox until the next time you make a connection (figure 8.6). Observe in the folder list that the Outbox item has a number in brackets indicating the number of messages waiting to be sent.

7 Close Microsoft Outlook® by selecting the File menu and clicking on the Exit option or by clicking on the close button in the top right-hand corner of the application. You may be presented with a message informing you that there are unsent messages in your Outbox and asking if you would still like to close the application. Say yes.

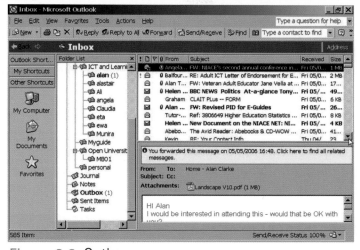

Figure 8.6 Outbox

Receiving e-mails

E-mails may be received every time you connect to the Internet. They will be held in your Inbox until you are ready to open them. Figure 8.1 shows the Inbox, with a series of messages listed in the top box, while the contents of the highlighted e-mail are shown in the preview box. There are several choices of displaying your inbox available to you through the View menu, highlighting Current View and selecting from one of the options that is revealed.

Mail folders

Most people find that the number of messages they receive grows rapidly when they begin to use e-mail. This indicates the value of e-mail, but to benefit from e-mail once the numbers start to grow, you need to be organised. You will often want to refer back to messages in order to take advantage of them, so you need to store them in a way that makes retrieving them a straightforward process. The normal way of storing e-mails is to establish a series of mail folders for the main people who send you messages. By creating a series of folders in which to store mail, you

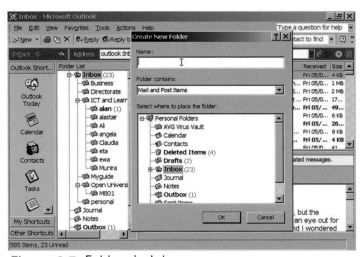

Figure 8.7 Folders in Inbox

make it quicker to locate the ones you need. If they are all stored in a single folder, you will quickly find hundreds if not thousands of messages stored in it, so that finding a particular one is very difficult. A single folder is the equivalent of keeping all your papers in a pile on your desk. You will find it difficult to find the papers you need.

To create a new mail folder in the Inbox, highlight the Inbox folder and select the File menu, highlight the New option and click on the Folder option. This will open the Create New Folder window (figure 8.7).

The folder is created by entering the folder name and then highlighting where to locate the folder in the Select where to place the folder area. In Figure 8.7 the folder will be placed within the Inbox folder. When you are ready, click on the OK button to create the mail folder.

Once you have created a series of mail folders, you may want to move messages between them. This can be achieved by dragging and dropping – open the mail folder in which the messages are stored, click on the selected message and hold down the mouse button. The message can then be dragged over the new folder and the button released. The message will have moved to the new location (folder). Dragging and dropping needs to be practised, but is an efficient and effective way of moving messages between folders.

Move messages

In the last section we created folders in which to store e-mail messages. E-mails were moved between folders manually. The emphasis was on creating archives of old e-mails, but there is another aspect of mail folders, which is to create ones so that incoming messages can be sorted into them. Outlook® provides functions to establish rules that will sort e-mails automatically into different folders. This is the equivalent of manually sorting your mail into different groups, depending on who sent them.

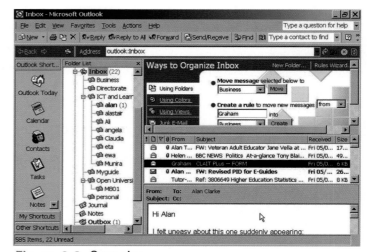

Figure 8.8 Organize

The Organize button in the Inbox area of Microsoft Outlook® provides the function to create rules to automatically move e-mail into different folders. Alternatively, select the Tools menu and Organize option. Either method will open the Ways to Organize Inbox window. Figure 8.8 shows the Ways to Organize Inbox window with a rule displayed. If you highlight an incoming message and then select Organize, you can choose to move future e-mails sent from that address to a specific folder. This requires you use the option Using Folders.

To access the moved e-mails you need to select the folder. The e-mails that the folder contains are then displayed in the working area.

Within Organize are other options, such as:

■ Using Colors
■ Using Views
■ Junk E-mail.

Using Colors allows you to colour-code e-mails sent from particular addresses so that they are easy to identify in a crowded inbox. Using Views changes the way that e-mails in the Inbox or selected folder are displayed. Some of the options include:

CLAiT Plus 2006 for Office XP

- By sender
- Unread messages
- Messages with autopreview.

This again offers you the opportunity to organise your e-mails to meet your needs.

The final option, Junk E-mail, allows you to colour-code junk mail and that with adult content, based on filters within Microsoft Outlook®. You can also automatically move or delete unwanted e-mail using junk mail options.

Signatures

You can add a signature to your e-mail by selecting the Tools menu on the toolbar of the message window, then Options. Next choose the General tab and click on E-mail Options , and finally the E-mail Signature tab. The E-mail Options window will be revealed (figure 8.9).

You can now create a signature for your e-mail. An alternative approach is to select the Tools menu on the

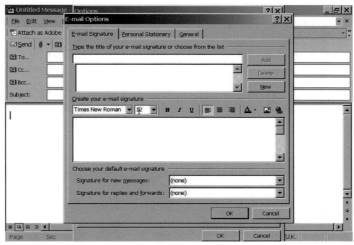

Figure 8.9 E-mail Options window

main application (e.g. Inbox) and click on the Options item, then on the Mail Format tab. This will reveal a Signatures button, which will open a Create Signature window.

Attachments

One of the major advantages of using e-mail is that you can attach files of information to your messages. These can be of any type, but you must always remember that in order to open the attached file, your recipient must have access to the application that created it, or a compatible one, otherwise the file cannot be opened; unfortunately, this is a regular problem with e-mail attachments. You can reduce this problem by considering what applications your recipient is likely to have, or by asking them. If you do not know if a recipient has the particular application, it is sometimes useful to convert files into generic formats. For example:

Microsoft Word® file – convert into a text file or a rich text file, which are opened by most word processors.

You can attach many files to a single e-mail and they can be a mix of different formats. However, it is useful to consider the size of each file and the overall size of the attachments. Some e-mail systems limit the size of e-mails that they will accept, so you may have your messages refused unless you limit their size. Also, if you are sending a message with attachments to a home computer, it is likely to have a low speed connection to the Internet, so large attachments will be downloaded very slowly. Few home recipients will be pleased if your e-mail takes 20, 30 or 60 minutes to download. They are paying the telephone costs.

It is good practice to consider file sizes and, if they are too large, send several e-mails with a single attachment or compress the files so that their size is reduced.

Compress

In order to reduce the size of an attachment you can compress the file using a compression application or utility. There are several available. WinZip® is one of the best known and can significantly reduce the size of a file. You can compress one file or many. The result is called an archive. In order to access the individual files in an archive you need to decompress the files. This requires either the full application or the WinZip Self-Extractor, which will only decompress an archive. The self-extractor is free.

Compressing files is very useful in that you can send large amounts of information as an attachment efficiently, without causing recipients problems of slow downloads or exceeding system limits.

You can download WinZip from its website for a trial period.

E-mail problems

E-mail attachments are often associated with virus infections. It is therefore important to have up-to-date virus protection. Most modern virus protection software can be configured to check all incoming and outgoing messages. Both are critical to prevent the spread of viruses. Whatever virus protection product you choose, it is important to pick one that regular updates the software, since viruses are continuously changing and new versions are being released.

In addition to virus infection, there is also the potential of being infected with spyware, which seeks to monitor your system and could be recording your passwords and other sensitive data. Spyware is also often passed between systems through e-mail, so it is important to have good protection on your system. There is a range of spyware protection applications available. It is important to have a system that is regularly updated.

A final threat is simply to receive advertising e-mails. These are called spam and often advertise offensive products. In some cases, they are associated with attempts to get money from you fraudulently. Microsoft Office® allows you to block spam, using the Organize function to stop junk mail.

Exercise 55

Signatures and attachments

1 Microsoft Outlook® is opened either by selecting the Start button, highlighting the All Programs option and clicking on the Outlook® option, or by double-clicking on the Outlook® icon on the Microsoft Windows® desktop.

2 You are going to create a new signature, so select the Tools menu and click on the Options item to open the Options window. Click on the Mail Format tab and the Signatures button to reveal the Create Signature window. Click on the New button and Create New Signature will open (figure 8.10). Enter your name and click on the Next, then Finish buttons. Close the open windows. You will now be able to select your name as a signature for your messages.

3 Click on New to create a new e-mail message. Click in the message area and select the

<u>I</u>nsert menu and highlight the <u>A</u>utoText option and then the <u>Signature</u> option to reveal a signature list you can choose from. Select your own name and it will be inserted at the cursor in the message area.

4 Now enter the following message

To: Janet123@yahoo.co.uk
Cc: John 456@yahoo.co.uk
Bcc: Sheila789@yahoo.co.uk

More Practice

This is a practice e-mail to demonstrate adding a signature and an attachment

Signature

If you are working in a group, address your e-mail (To: Cc: and Bcc:) to other members of the group. This will allow everyone else to practise receiving e-mail and let you see what your message looks like when it is received. Figure 8.11 shows the finished e-mail.

5 E-mails are not limited to the message you enter at the keyboard. You can attach files of any type. To add an attachment, select the <u>I</u>nsert menu and the <u>F</u>ile option to reveal the Insert File window. Change the folder in the <u>Look in</u>: box to locate the file of your choice. Select it to add to your message (figure 8.12) by double-clicking on the file. You can add many files to the same e-mail by repeating the process. An alternative

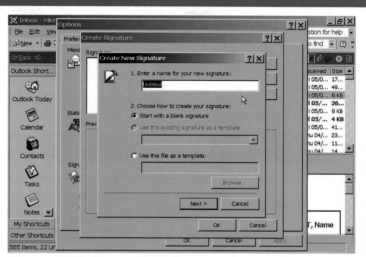

Figure 8.10 **Create New Signature**

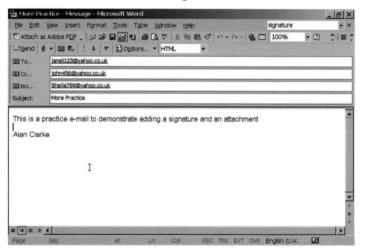

Figure 8.11 **E-mail with signature**

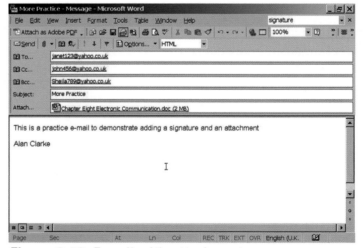

Figure 8.12 **E-mail with attachment**

Electronic Communication

287

approach is to select the paperclip icon on the toolbar, which will open the Insert File window.

6 Send the message by clicking on the Send button on the toolbar.

7 Close Microsoft Outlook® by selecting the File menu and clicking on the Exit option or by clicking on the Close button in the top right-hand corner of the application. You may be presented with a message informing you that there are unsent messages in your Outbox and asking if you would still like to close the application. Say yes.

Address book

In addition to sending and receiving messages, Microsoft Outlook® also provides facilities to store the e-mail addresses and details of your contacts. Without these components you would need to maintain a paper address book. An electronic system not only duplicates the features of a paper address book, but in addition allows you to establish mailing lists or groups, so that you can send a message to a group of users as easily as sending one to an individual. This is very useful in any organisation (e.g. members of a team).

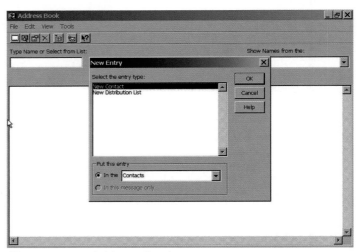

Figure 8.13 Address Book

Microsoft Outlook® provides you with an address book (figure 8.13). You can enter new contacts or create distribution lists. By selecting the New Entry icon on the address book toolbar, you reveal the New Entry window, with two choices – New Contact and New Distribution List. This allows you to add individual contact details or establish a mailing group.

There is a legal aspect to keeping contact details of individuals. The Data Protection Act ensures that you register information kept on individuals. If you intend to create records of individuals as part of your business, then you need to seek advice.

Alternative approach to creating a group/distribution list

There is an alternative method of creating a distribution list. Select the

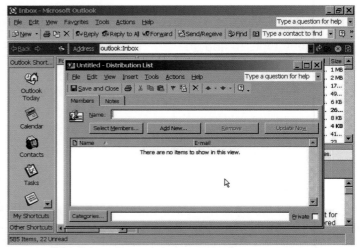

Figure 8.14 Distribution List window

File menu, then highlight the New option to reveal a menu of choices. Click on the Distribution List option to open the Distribution List window (figure 8.14). To select from the existing address book contacts, you need to click on the Select Members button. New contacts are added to the list by clicking on the Add New button.

Exercise 56

Address book

1 Microsoft Outlook® is opened either by selecting the Start button, highlighting the All Programs option and clicking on the Outlook® option, or by double-clicking on the Outlook® icon on the Microsoft Windows® desktop.

2 Select the Tools menu and click on the Address Book option. This will reveal the address book (figure 8.13). To add a new contact or new group (i.e.

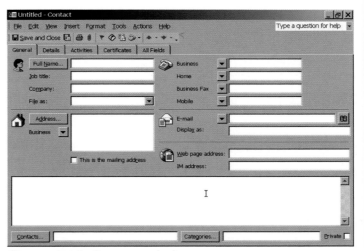

Figure 8.15 **Contact window**

distribution list), click on the New Entry icon to reveal the New Entry window, with two options. Click on the New Contact option to reveal the Contact window (figure 8.15). You will notice a series of tabs across the top of the window that allow you to categorise your information. Explore the different tabs until you are familiar with them.

3 Return to the General tab and enter the following contact in the Full Name and E-mail boxes:

Ms Jane Ann King, JAKing@example.co.uk

Accuracy is important since you will later rely on this entry for your e-mails. Check each entry carefully.

Click on the Save and Close button. The new contact will appear in the work area.

4 Add the following contacts:

Dr William MacDonald, William.Mac@example.co.uk

Miss Belinda Lomas, Belinda@example.co.uk

Mr Albert Woods, awoods@example.co.uk

Figure 8.16 shows the address book after the contacts have been added. You will have noticed that you have not entered any information beyond name and e-mail address. You can extend your entries by double-clicking on the item (e.g. Albert Woods), which will open the Contact window and allow you to add extra information. Obviously you could have entered all the information when you first added the new contact, but there are occasions when you initially have only partial data.

5 The other option available from the New Entry icon is to create a new distribution list. If you click on the New Distribution List option you will reveal the Distribution List window. Enter a group name – Example – and click on the Select Members button to reveal the Select Members window (figure 8.17).

6 You can create a group based on existing contacts, new contacts or a mixture. To add existing contacts to your group, highlight the contacts and click on the Members button. Add the four contacts you created earlier to your group. To add a new contact, click on New Contacts button to reveal the New Entry window and enter a contact (e.g. E Example) in the normal way. As soon as you click on the Save and Close button the entry appears in the list of existing contacts for you to select for your group. When you have completed your selections, click on the OK button to return to the Example Distribution List window. Click on the Save and Close button again and your group will be added to your list of contacts.

7 Close the Address Book by clicking on the close button in the top right-hand corner of the window. To access the address book contacts, open a new e-mail by clicking on the New icon on the toolbar to reveal the message window.

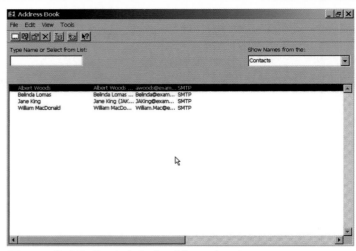

Figure 8.16 Completed address book

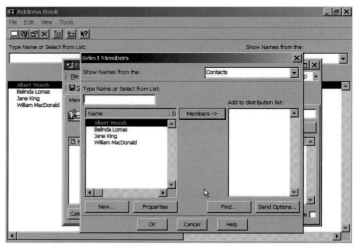

Figure 8.17 Example Distribution List

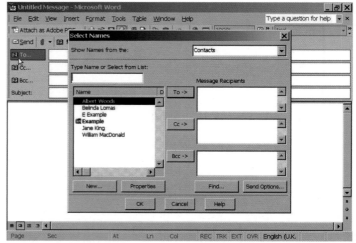

Figure 8.18 Select Names window

Select the To... button to show the Select Names window (figure 8.18). You can place any contact or group into the To, Cc or Bcc fields by highlighting the entry and clicking on the appropriate field button.

8 Practise using the window to select different contacts until you are confident that you can use the address book.

9 Microsoft Outlook® also provides you with the means to print your contacts and groups. Select the Print icon on the Contact or Distribution List window toolbar to print the information.

10 Close all the open windows by clicking on the close button in the top right-hand corner of each window.

11 Close Microsoft Outlook® by selecting the File menu and clicking on the Exit option, or click on the Close button in the top right-hand corner of the application. You may be presented with a message informing you that there are unsent messages in your Outbox and asking if you would still like to close the application. Say yes .

Personal information manager

Microsoft Outlook® provides a number of functions to help you to organise your life. The three main ones are (figure 8.19):

- a calendar
- a to do list
- notes.

The calendar allows you to schedule your work on a daily, weekly or monthly basis, over many months, while the to do list lets you create a list of tasks you need to complete. The notes are essentially the electronic equivalent of post-it notes – brief pieces of information, reminders and useful items of data.

The to do list of tasks can be presented in a variety of ways. Select the View menu, then highlight the Current View item to reveal a list of options (figure 8.20). Figure 8.19 shows the Day/Week/Month View with AutoPreview.

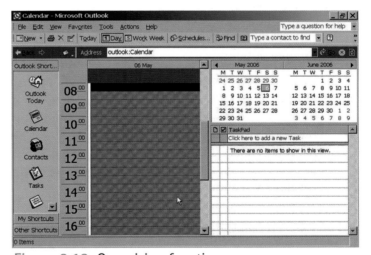

Figure 8.19 **Organising functions**

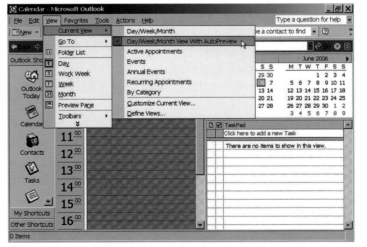

Figure 8.20 **Current views**

Exercise 57

Planning your work

1 Microsoft Outlook® is opened either by selecting the Start button, highlighting the All Programs option and clicking on the Outlook® option, or by double-clicking on the Outlook® icon on the Microsoft Windows® desktop.

2 You are going to create a calendar for a typical business person, complete with a to do list of tasks and notes.

3 Click on the Calendar icon in the Outlook® Shortcuts list on the left-hand side of the display. Close the Folder List pane if it is open. Select the View menu and highlight the Current View option to reveal a list of options. Click on the Day/Week/Month View with AutoPreview. It will change the display to show the calendar and to do list (figure 8.19). The calendar will show the date you are working on and offers you the choice of a complete 24-hour period to book appointments in. If you want to change the date, simply click on the desired one in the monthly calendar in the top right-hand corner. Change the date to your birthday – you can change the month by clicking on the arrow buttons to move backwards and forwards through the year.

4 You can change the view of your calendar to show a single day, a working week (i.e. five days), a seven-day week or a month, by selecting the View menu and clicking on the options (figure 8.19). Explore the different options and return to a single-day view once you are confident.

5 In the calendar you are going to enter the appointments for the first Monday in June (in my case, 5 June 2006), so change the date. The appointments for this day are influenced by the organisation always having a staff meeting on the first Monday of every month. Enter Staff Meeting at 10.00. As you enter Staff Meeting, you will notice it is enclosed in a box. If you place your mouse pointer over the box outline, it will change shape and you can drag the box to cover more time. Your staff meeting will last three hours (e.g. 10 am to 1 pm).

6 The staff meeting is a recurring appointment every month and the calendar allows you to set this up without having to enter the same information 12 times. Select the Actions menu and click on New Recurring Meeting to reveal the Appointment Recurrence window (figure 8.21). Click on the Monthly radio button in the Recurrence pattern area and you will see that the first Monday of each month is offered as an option. Click on

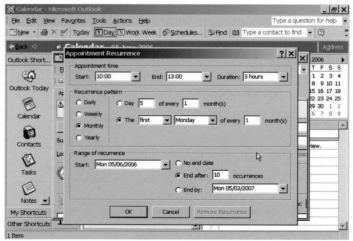

Figure 8.21 Appointment Recurrence window

the radio button alongside the option to set the pattern. You can also set the end date for the recurrence – No end date, End after: a set number of events or End by: a given date. Set it to End after: 10 occurences. Click the OK button to close the window and set the meeting.

7   You will notice that the window under the Appointment Recurrence window is still open. It is called Untitled – Meeting. This lets you name your meeting and also invite other people to participate in the meeting using e-mail. If you are working in an organisation with an electronic network, Microsoft Outlook® can be used to schedule meetings by sending e-mails to everyone who needs to attend. This adds an extra dimension to managing your individual information. Close the window.

8   If you double-click on the appointment in the calendar, the window will reappear. In the middle of the window is a picture of a bell and Reminder item. This enables you to ask Microsoft Outlook® to remind you about your appointments. The down arrow next to the reminder provides you with a range of choices of how long before the meeting or appointment you want to be reminded. Explore the options and choose two hours. Click on Save and Close to exit the window and return to Calendar.

9   Now enter a lunch appointment at 1.00 for one hour with Jim Brown, and a meeting with the Sales Manager at 3.00 for 30 minutes.

10 It is good time management to write lists of the key tasks that need to be done. In this case, we are going to create a new list:
   ■ Reply to the enquiry from Acme Tools
   ■ Begin work on the quarterly business report
   ■ Telephone the production manager
   ■ Write a letter to James Little plc
   ■ Send samples to King Ltd

11 Click in the area Click here to add a new task (TaskPad) and, when you have completed an entry, click elsewhere to see it added to the list. Enter all five tasks. Figure 8.22 shows a completed list and calendar. When you have completed a task, click in the radio button alongside it to insert a tick and see a line placed through it to show the task has been completed.

12 Explore the different ways of presenting the to do list by selecting the View menu, then highlighting the Current View and Task Pad View to show the list of options. Consider each option in turn. If you double-

Figure 8.22 TaskPad

click on any of the to do tasks or on the Click here to add a new task area, the Task window will open (figure 8.23), letting you add more detail to your tasks.

13 Revise each of your to do list entries to show start and finish dates:

Start Date: Monday
Due Date: Wednesday
Reply to enquiry from Acme Tools

Start Date: Monday
Due Date: Tuesday
Begin work on quarterly business report

Start Date: Tuesday
Due Date: Thursday
Telephone production manager

Start Date: Wednesday
Due Date: Thursday
Write letter to James Little plc

Start Date: Thursday
Due Date: Friday
Send samples to King Ltd

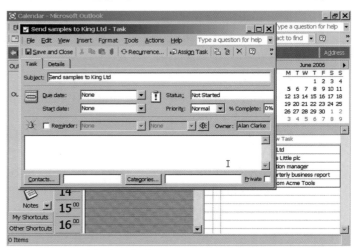

Figure 8.23 **Task window**

14 Most days you will need to make a note of events, pieces of information or simply things to remind you to take action. Microsoft Outlook® allows you to do this by selecting the File menu, highlighting the New option and clicking on Note to reveal a blank note. Enter "Remember to ask Mary about the statistic report". Close the note by clicking on the X button. Enter another note – "Find out if the enquiry from Benn Ltd has been answered" (figure 8.24). Close the note when you have finished.

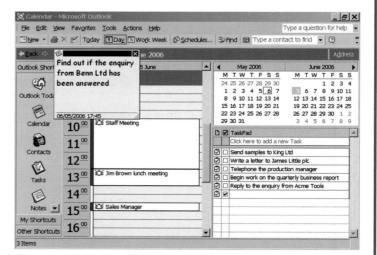

Figure 8.24 **Creating a note**

15 Notes are of little use if you cannot recall them. Click on the Notes icon on the

Outlook® Shortcuts area to the left of the display. Figure 8.25 shows you your notes. If you double-click on the one you want to see, it will expand. To remove the message, highlight the note with a single click and press the delete key.

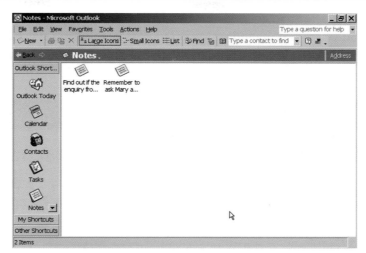

Figure 8.25 **Displaying notes**

16 You can copy and paste into your notes using the menu available when you right-click in the note. This enables you to insert large amounts of information into a note, including the contents of a file.

17 To print the calendar, select the File menu and click on Print Preview. If the preview is satisfactory, click on the Print button.

18 To print a note with it visible on the screen (click on the Note icon), select the File menu, click on the Print option and the OK button.

19 To print a to do list, click on the Tasks icon so the list is visible, then select the File menu, click on the Print option and the OK button.

20 Print your calendar, to do list and notes. Hard copy is useful since there are many occasions when you need to know your schedule, to do lists or notes while away from the computer.

21 Close Microsoft Outlook® by selecting the File menu and clicking on the Exit option, or click on the Close button in the top right-hand corner of the application. You may be presented with a message informing you that there are unsent messages in your Outbox and asking if you would still like to Close the application. Say yes.

Updating your calendar

Establishing a calendar is only a part of the overall task, since it is just as important to be able to change entries or even delete them.

To remove an item you need to single-click on the item to highlight it, then select the Edit menu and click on the Delete option. This will remove the entry, unless it is a recurring item, when it will open the Confirm Delete window where you can delete the single item or all occurring items.

To alter a calendar item, all you have to do is to highlight it. You can then change the text, add extra items or a new entry.

Electronic Communication

If you double-click on the item, the appointment window will open, allowing you to change start and end times, set the alarm reminder and invite attendees.

It is important to keep your calendar up to date, including removing any conflicting appointments. A calendar's effectiveness is seriously reduced by inaccurate information. If it is not maintained, it will lead to mistakes. You will not gain anyone's confidence if you miss an appointment or prepare for one which has actually been cancelled.

Exercise 58

Creating an e-mail with an attachment

1 Microsoft Outlook® is opened either by selecting the Start button, highlighting the All Programs option and clicking on the Outlook® option, or by double-clicking on the Outlook® icon on the Microsoft Windows® desktop.

2 Create a new e-mail by clicking on the New icon to reveal the message window.

3 Create the message below:

To: Frank.Williams@practiceattachment.co.uk

Attachment

This is an e-mail to show you how to add an attachment.

If you are working with a group of other learners, substitute the e-mail address with one of your fellow learners. You can send the e-mail and see how it appears to the recipient.

4 Add an attachment by clicking on the Insert file icon (it looks like a paperclip). This opens the Insert File window. Select the folder in which your attached file is stored in the Look in: box, then highlight the file and click on the Insert button. Your attached file will appear in the Attach... line of your e-mail. You can attach several files by repeating the process. Each attachment can be a different type of file (e.g. word-processing, images).

5 To send the message, click on the Send button on the toolbar. If your system is connected to the Internet, the message will be sent. If not, it will be stored in the Outbox until the next time you make a connection. Observe in the folder list that the Outbox item has a number in brackets, indicating the number of messages waiting to be sent.

6 Practise sending messages with attachments, either to imaginary addresses or, preferably, to other learners on your course. Continue to practise until you are confident that you understand the process.

7 Encourage your colleagues to send you e-mails with attachments, but if you are on your own, you can send yourself a message.

8 When you receive an e-mail with an attachment, you can read the file by double-clicking on it. This will open the file, providing you have the associated application software on your system (e.g. Word files require Microsoft Word®). You can save the file using the application software in the normal way anywhere on the system, and read the attachment later using the application software. Practise with the attachments.

9 If you do not have a suitable application, you will be presented with a warning message.

10 An alternative to opening a file is to select the File menu and the Save Attachments option to reveal the Save Attachments window, which allows you to save your file in any folder. Practise saving your attachment in this way.

11 A third way to save your attachment is to select the File menu and the Move to Folder option. You can save the e-mail and attachment to a folder within the mail system. This is useful should you want to save messages to particular folders.

12 A fourth way of saving an attachment is to simply drag it to your new folder. Highlight the attachment and hold down the mouse button, then drag it to the new folder and release. It will have been copied to the new location. Copy the attachment to the Notes icon and your attached file will now be available from within a note. This is useful when you are dealing with several e-mails and want to refer to the attachment as soon as you have completed dealing with the messages.

13 It is important to spend as much time as you can practising the different approaches to dealing with attachments.

14 Close Microsoft Outlook® by selecting the File menu and clicking on the Exit option, or click on the Close button in the top right-hand corner of the application. You may be presented with a message informing you that there are unsent messages in your Outbox and asking if you would still like to close the application. Say yes.

Page setup

You may want to display or print your calendar in a variety of formats. With the Calendar selected and displayed, you can change its appearance by selecting the File menu, then highlighting the Page Setup option to reveal a menu of choices.

The choices include:

- Daily Style
- Weekly Style
- Monthly Style
- Tri-fold Style
- Calendar Details Style
- Memo Style
- Define Print Styles

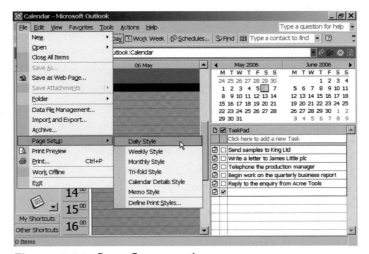

Figure 8.26 **Page Setup options**

When you click on the option, the Page Setup style window opens, providing additional choices. In particular, you can add a header and footer to the printout to identify the calendar (figure 8.27). Simply enter the text into the template provided.

With the calendar, the to do list, notes or contacts displayed, you can choose from a variety of page setups to show and print.

Printing

E-mail, calendars, to do lists and electronic notes are all extremely useful, but they do not eliminate the need for paper. If you are away from your office, unless you have everything stored on a laptop computer, you will need a copy of the key documents and messages. In many locations it is difficult to use a laptop, while paper can normally be studied in almost any location. When travelling, a printout of your calendar is very useful. If you add copies of

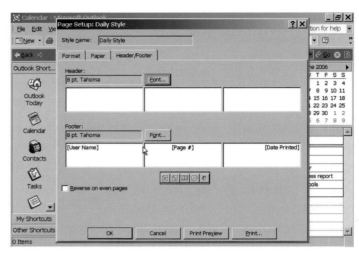

Figure 8.27 Header and Footer

contact details for the people you are meeting and any relevant e-mail messages, then you are well prepared.

Microsoft Outlook® provides extensive facilities for printing messages, calendars and contact details. Printing e-mails, calendars or contact details requires that you select the File menu and click on either the Print or Print Preview options. It is good practice to preview before you print. If you are then satisfied with the appearance of the printout, you can simply click on the Print option within the preview window. If it is not correct, then close the window and select the Page Setup option to change its appearance.

Screen print

If you need to capture what appears on the screen, press the Print Screen key. A copy of your screen display is made and stored on the Microsoft Windows® clipboard. You can then paste the image into an application of your choice, such as Microsoft Windows® Paint, from where you can print the display. If you want to copy only the contents of the active window, press the Alt and Print Screen keys together. This is often required during the assessment to provide evidence that you have undertaken the required tasks.

More practice

Take screen prints to practice providing evidence that you have completed the tasks.

Activity 1

1   Add these new contacts to your address book (figure 8.28):

Name: Mrs Wendy James
Title: Personnel Manager
Address: Queens Ltd
                 23 Long Lane
                 Leicester
                 LE12 9LL
Telephone: 0116 567 4599
E-mail: wendy.james@queensleicester.co.uk

Name:	Ms Lori Davis
Title:	Personal Assistant
Address:	Square Paints Ltd
	Alliance Drive
	Manchester
	M34 9RL
Telephone:	0161 777 9999
E-mail:	ld_Square@squarepaints.co.uk

Name:	Dr Paul Brookes
Title:	Director
Address:	Unicorn Ltd
	West Way
	Nottingham
	NG38 9KK
Telephone:	0115 678 9888
E-mail:	Paul_Brookes@unicorntoday.co.uk

Name:	Ms Jane Raymonds
Title:	Human Resource Manager
Address:	Highways Ltd
	567 South County Road
	Mansfield
	NG45 7JK
Telephone:	0999 567 3400
E-mail:	Jane.Raymonds@highways.co.uk

Name:	Mr Tom Jenkins
Title:	Personnel Officer
Address:	Sunshine Ltd
	Kingsway
	Liverpool
	L89 3DD
Telephone:	0151 768 1111
E-mail:	Tomj@sunshine.co.uk

2   Establish an e-mail distribution list based on the five contacts.

3   Call your distribution list Humanresources.

4   Save your distribution list.

5   Print a copy of the five contacts, showing their full name, telephone and e-mail address. Figure 8.29 shows a copy of the distribution list.

6   Print a copy of the distribution group.

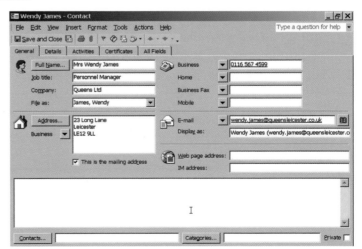

Figure 8.28 New contact

Activity 2

1 Create a sub-folder within the Inbox to store e-mails about human resource matters from the five contacts and any internal messages. Name the folder Human.

2 Save an incoming e-mail message within this folder and also in a folder outside of Outlook® Today.

3 Create three more sub-folders within the Inbox, called First, Second and Third.

4 Move the e-mail message stored in Human to the folder called Second.

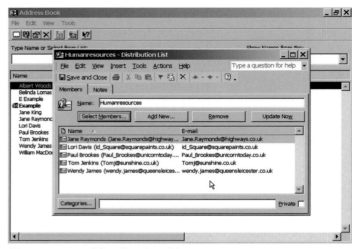

Figure 8.29 Distribution List

Activity 3

1 Decompress a zipped (compressed) archive.

2 Save the files to a folder outside the Outlook® Today folder.

3 Compress the files again, using a suitable application to form a new archive called New.

Activity 4

1 Enter the following appointments and meetings into your calendar:

Day	Start Time	Finish Time	Appointment/Meeting	Notes
Monday	10.00	11.00	Staff Meeting	Recurring every week
Tuesday	9.00	9.30	Conference Update	
	11.00	15.00	Interviews for Receptionist	
	16.00	17.00	Annual Review – David Jones	
Wednesday	10.30	11.45	Telephone Conference	
	14.30	16.00	Meeting with Training Manager	
Thursday	9.00	9.45	Progress Report	
	15.00	16.30	Review of Annual Report	
Friday	10.45	11.45	Meeting with Dr Lord	
	12.30	14.00	Lunch meeting with Production Director	

2 Print a copy of your diary for the week, making sure that all the information is shown in the printout. Add a header to the printout, showing your name.

3 For the same week, prepare a list of tasks to do. Enter the list below:

Subject	Due Date
Prepare for interviews for Receptionist	Tuesday
Make notes for the telephone conference	Wednesday
Read Annual Report	Thursday
Confirm lunch with Production Director	Friday

Figure 8.30 illustrates the calendar and to do list.

4 You need to make some notes. Create the two notes below:
Note 1 (figure 8.31):

   Key points for the telephone conference on Thursday

- costs must be covered by the project
- project completion date is likely to be missed
- we need an extra month to finish our tasks

Note 2:

Annual Report

Check that in the report:

- the department has been accurately described
- details of all the personnel mentioned are correct – job titles, spelling of names, etc.
- costs and sales figures are right

5 Print copies of your to do list and notes:

To Do list – print in Table Style

Notes – print both notes in Memo Style

For all the printouts, add a header containing your name, centre number and date.

Activity 5

1 After you have read the Annual Report, you need to contact the editor of the report to comment on the contents. If you are working within a group, ask a colleague to act the part of the editor and reply to your comments.

2 Create a signature for yourself:

Your Name

With a sentence describing yourself (e.g. I am 54 years old and have grey hair)

3 Create the e-mail below:

To: Janet@madeup.co.uk (substitute the correct address)

Subject: Annual Report

Dear Janet,

I have now had an opportunity to study the Annual Report. I liked the new layout which I thought presented the information better. However, there are one or two small errors in the spelling of people's names which need to be corrected. I have attached a file of staff names.

Best wishes

Alan

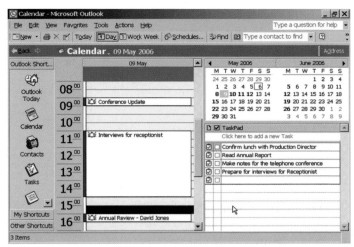

Figure 8.30 Calendar

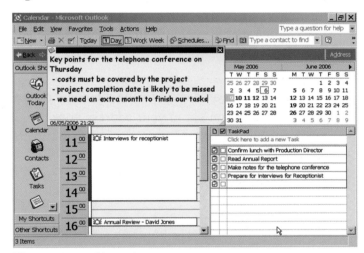

Figure 8.31 Note 1

4   Add the signature you have created to this e-mail.

5   Attach one or more files to this e-mail to practise sending an attachment. Figure 8.32 shows the e-mail.

6   If you are working in a group, ask one of your colleagues to send you a similar e-mail with an attachment.

7   Drag and drop the attachment into the Notes to copy the file.

8   Copy the e-mail that has been sent to you to another member of the group.

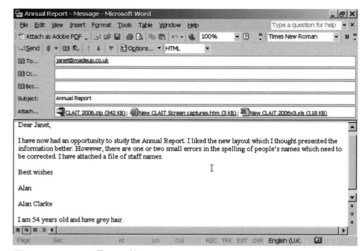

Figure 8.32 E-mail

9   Save the original e-mail into the Human folder you created in activity 2.

Activity 6

1   You need to send an e-mail to the members of the Humanresources distribution group.

2   Use the distribution list in your address book.

3   Create the e-mail below:

Subject: Meeting

Next Thursday at 3pm I would like to hold a meeting to discuss the changes to Human Policy that the board have agreed at their last meeting. Could you please let me know if you are able to attend.

4   Add the signature you created in activity 5.

5   Attach three files of your choice to the e-mail.

6   Indicate that the message is being sent with High Importance.

7   Blind copy the message to another person. Figure 8.33 shows the e-mail.

8   Print a copy of the e-mail.

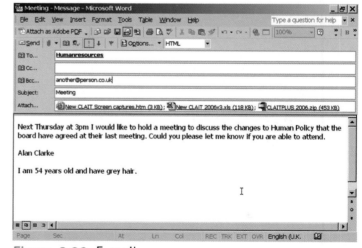

Figure 8.33 E-mail

Activity 7

In order to become a competent user of Microsoft Outlook®, you need to practise a range of tasks. The main ones are:

■   sending and receiving e-mails

■   saving the messages to folders within Outlook® Today

■   creating new folders within the Inbox and Outlook® Today

- decompressing archives and saving the files to appropriate folders outside the Outlook® Today area
- copying and moving files between folders
- creating and applying signatures
- adding new contacts to your address book
- creating distribution lists
- sending e-mails to distribution lists
- adding meetings and appointments to your calendar
- creating to do lists and notes.

SUMMARY

1 Open
Select the Start button, highlight the All Programs option and click on the Outlook® option or double-click on the Outlook® icon on the Microsoft Windows® desktop.

2 Create an e-mail
Select the New button on the standard toolbar to reveal the Message window.

3 Blind copies (Bcc)
Select the down-arrow button next to the Option button on the toolbar to reveal a short list of options and click on the Bcc option.

4 Priorities – High Importance
Click on the icon indicated by an exclamation mark (i.e. High Importance) in the message window.

5 Create a signature
You can add a signature to your e-mail by selecting the Tools menu on the toolbar of the message window, then Options. Next choose the General tab and click on E-mail options and finally the E-mail Signature tab. The E-mail Options window will be revealed. You can now create a signature for your e-mail. An alternative approach is to select the Tools menu on the main application (e.g. Inbox) and click on the Options item, then on the Mail Format tab. This will reveal a Signatures button, which will open a Create Signature window.

6 Address book
Select the Tools menu and click on the Address Book option. This will reveal the address book.

7 Add new contact
Click on the New Entry icon. Click on the New Contact option to reveal the Contact window.

8 New distribution list
Click on the New Entry icon and then on the New Distribution List option, to reveal the Distribution List window; or select the File menu, highlight the New option and click on the Distribution List option to open the Distribution List window.

9 Calendar
Click on the Calendar icon in the Outlook® Shortcuts list on the left-hand side of the display.

10 Change date
Click on the desired date of the monthly calendar.

11 Change calendar view
Select the View menu and click on the option of your choice.

12 Recurring appointments
Select the Actions menu, click on New Recurring Appointment to reveal the Appointment Recurrence window.

13 Notes
Select the File menu, highlight the New option and click on the Note option.

14 Print
Select the File menu. Click on Print Preview and then on the Print button.

15 Page setup
Select the File menu, highlight the Page Setup option, to reveal a menu of choices, and select your option.

16 New folder
Select the File menu, highlight the New item and click on the Folder option to reveal the Create New Folder window; or click on the down arrow next to the New button on the toolbar.

17 Attachment
Click on the Insert file icon (i.e. a paperclip) to open the Insert File window.

18 Save an attachment
Double-click on the attachment to open the file in the associated application software (e.g. spreadsheet files require Microsoft Excel®). Save the file using the application software.

Alternatively, single-click on the file to highlight it and then select the File menu and the Save Attachments option to reveal the Save Attachment window. Or, drag the attachment to a folder, highlight the attachment and hold down the mouse button to drag the attachment to the new folder, then release.

19 Save messages and attachments to folders
Select the File menu and the Move to Folder option to reveal the Move Item window, which lists mail system folders.

20 Enter tasks
Click in the area Click here to add a new task (TaskPad) and enter the item.

21 Change task views
Select the View menu and highlight the Current View and TaskPad items to reveal a list of options.

22 Task details

Double-click on the entry to reveal the Task window.

23 Message formats

Option on the e-mail toolbar provides access to the three choices (i.e. Plain text , <u>RTF</u> and HTML). You need to consider who you are sending the message to in order to select the most appropriate format.

24 Block spam

The Organize button in the Inbox area of Outlook® provides the function to create rules to automatically move e-mail into different folders. Alternatively, select the <u>T</u>ools menu and Organi<u>z</u>e option. Either method will open the Ways to Organize Inbox window.

Glossary

Application - a software program designed to perform a task such as desktop publishing, designing a database or designing a web page.

Bar Chart – a chart which represents numerical information as bars of different lengths.

Bitmap – an image composed of many dots called pixels. The more pixels in a given amount of space (e.g. a square inch) the clearer the image or the higher the resolution of the picture.

Boot – the process that occurs when you switch on the computer. It involves the loading of the operating system (e.g. Windows 98) and checking of the equipment to ensure that everything is ready for you to use.

Browser – an application which allows you to access a World Wide Web page. Each page has a unique address which is called a URL (Uniform or Universal Resource Locator) which, when entered into the browser, allows it to find the site and view its contents.

Byte – the basic measure of memory. A byte is sufficient memory to store one character (e.g. a letter or a number).

Column Chart – a chart which represents numbers and columns of different lengths.

CPU – Central Processing Unit: a silicon chip which controls the operation of the computer.

Database – a way of storing information so that its contents can be extracted in many different combinations and ways.

Desktop – the main display of the operating system and normally the first display you see after the computer has loaded the operating system (e.g. Windows).

Desktop Publishing – an application which allows text and images to be combined in many different ways so that many different forms of printed document can be designed (e.g. newsletters and posters).

Directory – a list of World Wide Web addresses related to a particular topic or subject.

DTP – see Desktop Publishing

E–mail – a message which is sent electronically through the Internet or over a local network.

Field – an individual piece of information stored on a database usually as part of a record.

File – a collection of digital (computer) information. There are many types of file such as word–processing, graphic and spreadsheet files.

Floppy Disk – a small magnetic disk on which you can store a small amount of information in the form of files.

Folder – a location on the computer in which you can store files.

Font – characters can be printed and displayed in many different styles. These styles are known as fonts.

Format – a way of structuring the computer information stored in a file on a disk or drive. There are many different types of file format.

Formula – a method of calculating parts of a spreadsheet automatically.

Greyscale – a way of describing an image which is shown in a range of shades of grey rather than in different colours.

GUI – Graphical User Interface: a Windows 95 type display in which icons, windows and a mouse pointer interact to produce an easy to use environment.

Hard Disk – a large magnetic disk, which is located inside the computer, on which a large amount of information can be stored.

Hardware – the physical components which make up the computer.

HTML – Hypertext Markup Language: a specialist language which is used to design World Wide Web pages so that they can be read using a browser.

HTTP – Hypertext Text Transfer Protocol: specifies how to access documents on the World Wide Web (e.g. http://www.bbc.co.uk)

Hypertext – Pages of a web site are linked together through a number of hypertext connections. These are shown by underlined words, coloured words, icons and graphic pictures. The links allow the user to jump between different parts of the site or even between sites.

Icon – a small picture which represents a computer function or operation.

Internet – a super network of networks which links millions of computers throughout the world.

ISP – Internet Service Provider: a commercial company that provides connections to the Internet for individuals and companies.

Justification – a way of laying out text, e.g. left justification means that text is aligned so that its left edge is parallel with the paper's edge when it is printed.

KB – Kilobyte: a measure of memory (i.e. 1024 bytes).

Laptop – a portable computer with a screen built into its cover.

Line Graph – a graphical way of comparing two or more sets of numerical information.

MB – Megabyte: a measure of computer memory (approximately a million bytes).

Memory – a measure of the computer's capacity to perform tasks and to store information.

Menu – a method of displaying options.

Operating System – software that provides the instructions to make the hardware work.

Password – a series of alphanumeric characters that limits access to a computer system.

Personal Computer – an individual computer which is normally used by one person at a time.

Pie Chart – a graphical representation of information by showing it as slices of a circle so that the size of each slice is proportional to the data.

Pixel – graphic images are made up of many small rectangular areas which are called pixels.

Port – a way of connecting peripheral devices (e.g. printers) to a computer.

Query – a way of asking a database of information a particular question. Normally, this takes the form of identifying particular combinations of information (e.g. all customers who have ordered more than £100,000 during the last three months).

QWERTY – this is the order of the top line of alphabetical keys on the keyboard.

RAM – Random Access Memory: the computer's working memory in which the computer carries out its functions once it is switched on. It only exists while the machine is on. If the power is switched off, so is the memory.

Record – a group of related fields of information which you find in a database.

Resolution – this is a way of describing the quality of an image, monitor or printer. The quality is described in terms of the dots which make up the image. That is, the more dots the higher the quality of the image, monitor display or printer output.

ROM – Read Only Memory: the computer's permanent memory, built into the structure of the silicon chips. It is not lost if the power is switched off.

Search Engine – an application that allows you to search the World Wide Web for a web page containing information on a specific topic or to search within a website for a particular item of information.

Software – computer programs written to allow you or the computer to carry out certain tasks such as constructing databases.

Sort – a way of presenting information in a spreadsheet or database (e.g. alphabetically).

Surfing – the process of wandering around the World Wide Web in search of interesting information.

Table – the part of a database in which information is stored as a series of records and fields.

URL – Uniform Resource Locator: the unique address of a World Wide Web site that allows a browser to locate the site.

Vector – an image that is defined by mathematical formulae rather than pixels. This defines the start and finish of the line and allows it to be easily changed. A vector image can be resized and it will stay in perfect proportion.

Virus – a computer program designed to cause harm to a computer.

Web page – a document which forms part of a website.

Website – a collection of pages on the Internet.

Word Processor – an application which allows you to create and manipulate documents.

WWW – World Wide Web: a collection of millions of websites and documents spread across the world as part of the Internet.

Window – rectangular area of the screen in which computer applications and information is displayed.

Wizard – Many Windows applications include Wizards that are used to perform complex tasks more easily by allowing the user to choose between options.

Index